A Traveler Disguised

Judaic Traditions in Literature, Music, and Art
Ken Frieden and Harold Bloom
Series Editors

A Traveler Disguised

THE RISE OF MODERN YIDDISH FICTION
IN THE NINETEENTH CENTURY

DAN MIRON

With a Foreword by Ken Frieden

SYRACUSE UNIVERSITY PRESS

First Syracuse University Press Edition 1996
96 97 98 99 00   6 5 4 3 2 1

This book was originally published with the assistance of the YIVO Institute for Jewish Research.

Originally published in 1973. Reprinted by arrangement with Schocken Books.

The paper used in this publication meets the minimum requirements of American National Standard for Information Sciences—Permanence of Paper for Printed Library Materials, ANSI Z39.48-1984. ∞™

Library of Congress Cataloging-in-Publication Data
Miron, Dan.
    A traveler disguised : the rise of modern Yiddish fiction in the
nineteenth century / Dan Miron ; with a foreword by Ken Frieden.
        p.   cm.—(Judaic traditions in literature, music, and art)
    Reprint. Originally published: New York : Schocken Books, 1973.
    Includes bibliographical references (p.   ) and index.
    ISBN 0-8156-0330-4 (paper : alk. paper)
    1. Mendele Mokher Sefarim, 1835–1917—Criticism and
interpretation.   2. Yiddish fiction—19th century—History and
criticism.   I. Title.   II. Series.
PJ5129.A2Z742   1995
839'.0933—dc20   95-30450

For David and Uriel

CONTENTS

A section of illustrations follows p. 94

FOREWORD

Ken Frieden

A *Traveler Disguised* was the first major scholarly work in English on Yiddish literature, and since its appearance in 1973 it has remained the seminal study of Yiddish fiction during the nineteenth century. By focusing on the figure of Mendele the Bookpeddler in the works of S. Y. Abramovitsh, Dan Miron brings to light both aesthetic and historical dimensions of Yiddish culture.

Prior to Miron's book, American readers had few reliable sources of information about Yiddish literature. The success of *Fiddler on the Roof*—the 1964 Broadway musical and 1971 Hollywood film based on Sholem Aleichem's stories—inspired several popular paperbacks that surveyed the terrain. New translations of Sholem Aleichem and other authors followed. When I. B. Singer received the Nobel Prize for Literature in 1979, it was evident that Yiddish authors were finally admissible into the pantheon of world writers. But the critical tradition in English was not equal to the task of selecting the canon.

Eastern European Yiddish culture was destroyed a generation before it attained widespread recognition in the West. Starting in 1864, modern Yiddish writers experimented with a broad range of artistic forms. By 1900, classic Yiddish fiction by Abramovitsh, Sholem Aleichem, and I. L. Peretz had established the basis for this emerging literary tradition. In 1908, at the first Yiddish language conference in

Chernovitz, Yiddish was declared to be the national language of the Jewish people. Subsequently, until World War II, innumerable Yiddish authors produced significant works of poetry, fiction, and drama. But the Nazi genocide put an end to every Yiddish cultural center in Europe.

Given this historical context, it required heroic strength on the part of Dan Miron to take up the Yiddish torch. As a student in Jerusalem, Miron received encouragement and training from Dov Sadan and Chone Shmeruk. Even more decisive was his doctoral study at Columbia University in the 1960s, which brought him under the tutelage of a remarkable father-son team. To quote Miron's original preface to *A Traveler Disguised,* the merits of his book "must be attributed to a considerable extent to the scholarship, wisdom, and friendly guidance of my two unforgettable teachers, Max and Uriel Weinreich."

The emergence of a great center for Yiddish studies in New York was a direct consequence of the rise of fascism in Europe. The YIVO Institute for Jewish Research *(Yidishe visnshaftlekhe institut)* was founded in Vilna in 1925 and then transferred to New York in 1940. In cooperation with the Linguistic Circle of New York (and later the Department of Linguistics at Columbia University), the YIVO Institute became the leading force in Yiddish studies. It fostered research on Yiddish language, literature, history, and culture; among its notable serial publications are *YIVO bleter* and the *YIVO Annual of Jewish Social Science.*

Dan Miron's accomplishment was to apply the vast resources of the YIVO Institute toward the literary project that became *A Traveler Disguised.* The opening chapters raise basic questions in the development of modern Yiddish fiction, while the later chapters turn to the work of S. Y. Abramovitsh. Miron begins by asking: How did modern Yiddish literature come into being? What cultural forces shaped it? Why did some Jewish authors decide, at a specific historical moment, to write in Yiddish rather than in Hebrew? Miron first responds to these questions in general terms; he then probes deeper, through astute analyses of Abramovitsh's works. At the center of attention is "a traveler disguised," the enigmatic persona of Mendele the Bookpeddler.

Mendele the Bookpeddler *(Mendele Moykher-Sforim)* was, as Miron shows, Abramovitsh's main literary invention. Like many other Yiddish writers, Abramovitsh initially wrote in Hebrew. When he switched to Yiddish in 1864, he created the old-fashioned character Mendele as his mouthpiece, a kind of mask that conceals the author's identity. This led to a basic opposition between Mendele's apparent traditionalism and Abramovitsh's commitment to reform. Out of this split emerges a trenchant irony that permeates Abramovitsh's fiction.

Miron presents a number of other significant dimensions of Abramovitsh's fiction in its literary and cultural milieus. Moving beyond the Mendele phenomenon, for example, he discusses the role of multiple voices ("polyphony") in the novels. He also considers the uses of Yiddish parody, as when Mendele seems to draw from biblical forms only to subvert them. He contrasts the literary functions of Abramovitsh's Mendele the Bookpeddler and Sholem Aleichem's Tevye the Dairyman. And Miron points to Western European influences (represented by authors such as Laurence Sterne) on Yiddish writing. As the first scholar to reexamine Yiddish prose using the methods of American literary criticism, he provided new direction for future researchers.

A *Traveler Disguised* is, in short, a sustained reflection on the conditions and potentials of Judaic literature. Miron had the vision to see that Abramovitsh, writing in Yiddish and Hebrew, responded to many of the underlying issues that confronted other modern Jewish writers. As such, Miron's book has become a classic study of the first classic author in Yiddish fiction.

PREFACE

A *Traveler Disguised* was written thirty years ago as a dissertation under the supervision of the two great Yiddish linguists of our century, Max and Uriel Weinreich. Max, a historian of the Yiddish language and of the culture of Ashkenazi Jews, was the leader of the YIVO Institute for Jewish Research since it was founded in Vilna in 1925 and functioned as the head of the YIVO in New York. Uriel, his son, undoubtedly the most brilliant scholar ever to enter the field of Yiddish studies, was recognized even in his thirties as one of the most innovative and respected theoreticians of general linguistics, besides being an eminent Yiddishist. If there was ever a man who could fully integrate Yiddish studies as a whole within a comprehensive contemporary concept of cultural studies and devise the scholarly methodology through which such integration could be realized, he was the one. In order to study with these two luminaries, I left Israel and my busy life as a young and upcoming Israeli literary critic and scholar and went to New York, to Columbia University (where Uriel Weinreich then held the Atran chair of Yiddish studies), to the library and archives of the YIVO—all of which have since become a second home to me, a home away from my Israeli-Hebraic one. I "adopted" the Weinreichs, both father and son, as models of the true academic man and educator, almost as father figures.

Both gave me their priceless time (Uriel was already aware of his incurable condition), their attention, and their encouragement. The latter was, of course, needed more than anything else. After all, my field of expertise was that of Hebrew literary studies. My decision to write a dissertation not only away from the Israeli universities in which I had been reared but also out of the pale of that field was regarded as a reckless "adventure." For me this adventure was not only unavoidable but also eagerly sought after. For one thing, I believed (under the influence of my teacher Dov Sadan) that a fully conceptualized understanding of the contradictory/complementary roles played by Hebrew and Yiddish vis à vis each other in the rise of modern Jewish culture and literature was a *conditio sine qua non* for any meaningful comment on Jewish creativity in either language. I also deeply felt that in order to get to the roots of my native Hebrew-Zionist culture, I had to remove myself from it temporarily, to look at it from a distance and from a vantage point which was in some way close but also not friendly to it. What vantage point better than the field of Yiddish studies could I find? Immersing oneself in it would be like looking at oneself through the eyes of a competitive and unidentical twin. Also, under the historical circumstances, it would be like watching oneself through the eyes of a murdered and betrayed ancestor.

These urges sent me away from Israel to New York. However, they did not in any way mitigate my position as an outsider among the Yiddishists I found there. Huddled together in their hermetic, shrinking circles; desperately clinging to hopes and hatreds, beliefs and tensions which had virtually died in the 1940s along with the great Yiddish speaking community of Eastern Europe, and in the 1950s with the remnants of the Yiddish speaking American Jewish community; decimated by the processes of acculturation and Americanization, they observed me with both puzzlement and suspicion. On the one hand they could not but be pleased with this "refugee" from the camp of the victorious Hebraic "enemy," who seemed to be adopting their hopeless cause (or was he?). On the other hand they quickly recoiled from the "foreignness" of someone who was walking all over their own turf but intentionally and quite carefully avoiding the well-worn paths which they, or rather their teachers at the beginning of the twentieth century and during the two interbellum decades, had paved alongside it.

My need to examine, through a study of the conceptual and artistic

roots of modern Yiddish culture, the archeology and genealogy of my
own Hebrew one dictated a constant widening of the scope of my
dissertation in a way which was frowned upon by most academic in-
structors and supervisors. Instead of limiting myself to writing a conventional formalistic-thematic monograph on the work of Sh. Y.
Abramovitsh, the founding father of modern artistic Yiddish (and Hebrew) prose fiction (as I had planned), I felt the need to embark upon
a much more abstract and sweeping generalization concerning the
"aesthetics" of the entire nascent Yiddish literary culture of the nineteenth century, an aesthetics which I conceived of as originating in
the recognition of ugliness rather than in the experience of the beautiful. Uriel Weinreich, a totally unconventional thinker in his own field,
immediately became interested and even excited. Now, he said, he
felt how the chick was vigorously stirring inside the shell of my project, picking against its walls, asserting its own life and energy. It was
Uriel who prodded and helped me in writing a book for which the full
chutzpa and naïveté of a very young scholar were needed.

   Chutzpa and encouragement were vital as I went through my research and pondered its results. In every possible way my thinking
went against the grain of the collective wisdom of the Yiddish literary
critics and scholars of the past. Presumptuously enough, the territory
I was trying to chart was not a distant and untrodden one; the texts I
focused on were by no means neglected or underrated. On the contrary, most of them were "classical" and celebrated. The satires and
novels of Sh. Y. Abramovitsh had been commented on by every important Yiddish and Hebrew critic and literary historian since the end
of the nineteenth century. Dozens of comprehensive essays of interpretation and evaluation and a few book-length monographs had been
dedicated to them. Among these, some were truly brilliant and exhila-
rating; many others were at least edifying and helpful. I found myself
particularly drawn to the writings of the two chief Soviet Yiddish literary historians and critics, Max Erik and the superbly gifted Meyer
Viner (who was also, in the manner of Jurij Tynyanov, the author of
excellent historical fiction). In spite of having written their seminal
studies mostly during the 1930s, in the worst days of Stalinism and
under the vigilant stare of cruel cultural watchdogs, they managed to
be illuminating and insightful.

   However, as much as I admired what the best Yiddish (and Hebrew) critics wrote on Abramovitsh and on the shaping process which

conditioned his art, I knew myself to be outside of their "tradition."
To them Abramovitsh-"Mendele" (the two were not differentiated) ·
was the firm cornerstone of a lofty literary temple. He was the quintessential modern Jewish artist who observed and faithfully recorded
historical Jewish life in the Eastern European *shtetl*. To me Abramovitsh and his Mendele were something quite different. "Grandfather
Mendele" as the supreme sage and artist, I knew, was an invention, a
myth, which had been intentionally and quite hastily patched together
during the 1880s, primarily by that modern Jewish arch-mythologist
and fabulist Sholem Aleichem, and which had no bearing whatsoever
on the real intellectual and artistic endeavor of Abramovitsh before
the 1890s (when the writer himself was pleasurably duped by his
fabricated image). The myth was urgently needed as the center of a
scheme which would function as a working hypothesis for young writers to create a Yiddish national literature; before the 1880s Yiddish
writers had not suspected that their literary productions amounted to
a "literature."

Abramovitsh, a follower of the Jewish Enlightenment, a restless
thinker and an artist who was constantly looking for new ways, in-
vented the character Mendele the Bookpeddler and increasingly made
him shoulder heavy and heavier narrative burdens because he could
not otherwise extricate his art from a narrow and deadening format.
He needed Mendele as a host, a confrancier of sorts, a go-between, an
informant and a spy, who would form the connective link between the
modern westernized Jewish writer and the traditional "benighted"
world he was exploring, rather in the way some introjects can help one
negotiate a rudimentary collaboration between one's alienated ego
and Id. Mendele was close enough to the modern Jewish world; his
obsessive critical bent, his unmitigated sarcasm, and his tendency to
detect greed and stupidity underneath the veneer of spirituality made
him as bitter a critic of traditional Jewish society as any the Enlightenment could wish for. At the same time Mendele was still an integral
part of this society. The emotional undercurrents which sometimes
pierced through his sarcasm flowed from the hidden wells of traditional mentality. In moments of defeat and irrational reaction to calam-
ity he identified with its premodern sensibilities. Thus a Mendele and
only a Mendele could help the Jewish artist partly overcome the drastic limitations of an art based on "the aesthetics of ugliness." If Yiddish
was the quintessential expression of the ugliness and deformity of the

exilic Jewish condition, how could a Yiddish artist penetrate the very core of that condition and still expect to perform or function as an artist, i.e. as one who interprets experience by applying to it aesthetic criteria? Only with the help of a Mendele, or rather, only through a process of splitting which would allow the artist to project a segment of his own personality as a creature which in many ways was part of that condition and could exhibit its deformations but which also would be on speaking terms with the other segments (the "good" and beautiful ones), could this be done.

Thus to me the Mendele phenomenon was a desperate attempt on the part of a modern Jewish artist to break through the walls of his own being. Through Mendele that artist, a rationalist committed to the goals of the Enlightenment, could allow the *Jewish other voice,* that which emerged from the dark recesses of the traditional mentality, to make itself heard. Of course, Mendele distorted that voice and undermined the messages it conveyed by his relentless satirizing. However, he could also listen to it and make us, the readers, follow its inherent inflection, be swept by its congenital rhythm. With him, then, some kind of artistic inner dialogue became possible for the first time in the development of both Yiddish and (eventually) Hebrew fiction. The essential connection, as far as I could see it, was not between the artist's eye and the observed mimetic object (Jewish society) but between the artist's official self and his "other" self. This other self, although still despised and criticized, was allowed to speak. Thus the refusal to differentiate between Abramovitsh and Mendele indicated to me a basic misunderstanding of Abramovitsh's art and of modern Jewish literature as a whole. It was, essentially, a refusal to listen to the *other* within us, the result of a deep need to blur and deface the "otherness" of that other.

This view, I fully knew, would be both alien and annoying to those who had consecrated "Mendele" as the foundation of a modern, humanistic, "constructive" Yiddish culture. The Weinreichs' encouragement was, therefore, needed precisely because both had come from *within* this culture but were also completely free from its inherent provincialism and were scholars of immaculate integrity and of the liveliest intellectual receptivity. If I could not convince them then I could not convince anybody, I thought. But if I *could* convince them, perhaps, I did not need to convince anybody else. The writing of *A Traveler Disguised* was, then, done within the framework of a constructive, friendly struggle—to my mind the most productive and happy framework for the growth of a scholar whose goal is not the duplication or enhancement of preexisting positions. Each point I made had to withstand scrutiny and some resistance. Each allegation had to be supported by a host of illustrations (a mere fraction of which could be incorporated into the written dissertation, let alone the book which was based on it). This was wonderfully bracing and energizing. Uriel, younger than Max and thoroughly modern in his intellectual outlook, was fully and quickly won over. Max, with some lingering reservations, followed through. Both won not only my deepest gratitude but also my veneration for their open-mindedness and their staunch scholarly integrity.

When *A Traveler Disguised* was finally published in 1973 both Uriel and Max were not among the living. The reception of the book by the New York Yiddishists was characterized, as could be expected, by consternation mingled with perplexity. Only the great poet Yankev Glatshteyn, who carefully listened to the gist of my thesis as I expounded it at the annual YIVO banquet in November 1971 (a few weeks before his death), warmly welcomed it as a much needed reversal of perspective. The reviewers of the book dismissed the differentiation between Abramovitsh and Mendele as mere quibbling. They vehemently rejected the notion that modern Yiddish literature was deeply rooted in negation. They sincerely wondered how such a wrong-headed notion could be supported by so many "genuine" illustrations. As for the main thrust of my argument, the presentation of Mendele as the mediator between "us" (modern, westernized Jews) and the "little Jew," the dark Jewish other, they did not even argue with it; they probably did not understand its meaning.

Thus for a certain time *A Traveler Disguised* had no real readers. Those who could have accepted the intellectual perspectives it tried to open did not know the texts and the cultural history which the book analyzed. Those who were familiar with the texts and the history experienced the conceptual world out of which such a book could have emerged as alien, cold and uninhabitable. However, soon enough the real readers of the book started to appear. Even as the book went out of print it became something of a starting point, or at least a central point of reference, for younger scholars who throughout the 1970s and 1980s became interested in Yiddish literature and particularly in the art of Sh. Y. Abramovitsh. The book was constantly mentioned in the new professional literature which was now produced in growing quantities. It was particularly helpful to scholars who were educated and trained in centers where the literary commentator was expected to go beyond both positivist, historical bio-bibliographical erudition and formalistic analysis of separate poems and stories, i.e. he was expected to conceptualize and problematize a general cultural issue. Thus in France it was used in studies exploring the meaning of "Jewish space." In 1984 the French-Jewish scholar Regine Robin systematically referred to it in her *L'amour du Yiddish* and used it as one of her main tools for assessing the cultural significance of the various attitudes towards Yiddish as a language and as a tool for artistic creativity. In America the impact of the book slowly reached beyond the pale of academic Yiddish studies. Thus in 1988 Cynthia Ozick, who used it as a vantage point in her essay "Sholem Aleichem's Revolution," graciously referred to *A Traveler Disguised* as the "enchanting study" in which some of the "marvels" she was discussing had been originally "revealed."

The time perhaps has come for a reissuing of the book: reissuing rather than rewriting. Obviously, thirty years after the inception of the book and more than twenty-five years after its publication, I could not now edit it, expand it here or correct it there, etc. Rather, I could perhaps rewrite it. I could conceivably find new formulations for ideas which have not only expanded but also changed. Among other things, when I wrote *A Traveler Disguised* I was completely ignorant of Lacan's theories of narrative and of his notion of the textual subconscious "other." Perhaps those theories and that notion were then (in the 1960s) not fully crystallized and current even in Lacan's own psychoanalytic center. Whoever is familiar with Lacan's ideas (and many are nowadays) cannot but see how helpful they could have been in the process of my thinking. Would I now have taken upon myself the task of rewriting *A Traveler Disguised,* I should have to "Lacanize" my argument as well as my interpretations of Abramovitsh's texts. This, undoubtedly, is a very worthwhile project, which I might yet be tempted to tackle. However, it would result in an altogether new book or books. So perhaps I might just as well allow *A Traveler Disguised* to remain unchanged.

I need to warn the reader that I refrained even from changing the bibliography at the end of the book. Of course, throughout the past three decades a host of new publications, among them many of my own, have been added to the literature which deal with the topics I touched upon in A *Traveler Disguised*. Among these publications, some are at least as important (if not more important) than those I chose to list in 1973 (the bibliography was selective even then). The interested reader is, therefore, kindly requested to use the existing bibliography only for reference to the sources which I consulted when writing the book, a list of the texts against which the precision of my quotations as well as the cogency and originality of my critique could be checked and assessed. Unfortunately I still cannot recommend any fuller and more recent list. The absence of a comprehensive, up-to-date bibliography of Yiddish literary studies is sorely felt by all concerned in the field.

DAN MIRON

Columbia University
February 1995

PREFACE TO THE
ORIGINAL EDITION

THIS STUDY PURPORTS to examine some historical and artistic aspects of the rise of modern Yiddish fiction in the nineteenth century, mainly through an analysis of the fictional figure of Mendele Moykher-Sforim —Mendele the Bookpeddler. It is not an attempt at a chronological delineation of the history of nineteenth-century Yiddish fiction, although it pays close attention to chronology and to historical considerations. Nor is it a specialized study of the art of Sh. Y. Abramovitsh— the creator of Mendele Moykher-Sforim who has eventually come to be known by this name—although it examines some of the aspects of this art in detail. The line it follows is rather that of a speculative argument; an argument concerning the cultural significance and artistic possibilities of the art of fiction under certain historical circumstances.

At its core, then, this study is meant to present the application of historical and critical hypotheses to a concrete literary situation. It is based on theoretical speculations, although an effort is made to substantiate speculation with sufficient evidence. The figure of Mendele looms large in it because it is regarded as the core of this evidence. Yet it remains an illustration and not the ultimate subject of examination. Readers somewhat acquainted with recent American criticism will have no difficulty in detecting in the analysis of Mendele the influence of the current interest in "the rhetoric of fiction" and in the artistic uses of the ironic mask, or persona,° in satire. This debt to many contemporary critics who have developed the concepts and the speculative instruments of what might perhaps be referred to as the Neorhetorical Criticism is readily acknowledged. However, this study was not intended to fall into the category of rhetorical analysis. The rhetorical position of the figure of Mendele and its functions as an ironic persona are analyzed as indications of a historical-cultural-literary situation, not as mere specimens of the art of ironic storytelling. Oriented as it is toward the examination of literary technique, the study is intended to amount to a general statement concerning the emergence of modern Yiddish fiction in the nineteenth century as a partial reflection of the crisis of modern Jewish culture.

Whether this intention has been realized or not is, of course, for others to judge. If, however, some measure of success has been achieved, it must be attributed to a considerable extent to the scholarship, wisdom, and friendly guidance of my two unforgettable teachers, Max and Uriel Weinreich. This book is based on a study written as a doctoral dissertation under their supervision. I completed the research for my dissertation and started to write it under the supervision of Uriel Weinreich, that great, bright hope of Yiddish scholarship in our generation. It was his teaching of Yiddish and linguistics at Columbia University that attracted me to this country, and I found in him not only the most original, open-minded, and humane scholar I had ever had the privilege to know, but also a dear friend, whose untimely death in 1967 (at the age of forty-one) is still too painful a memory to allow me to elaborate on the meaning my work with him holds for me. Uriel Weinreich saw and corrected considerable parts of my study, but not all of it. His advice, however, informs it throughout, for every concept I have employed was adopted or formed with his help. It was under his influence that I attempted to widen the limits of the subject, which had originally been conceived of along more technical literary lines, toward cultural and historical prospects. It was he who encour-

---

° The term "persona," as used in this study, should always be distinguished from what Wayne Booth, in his *Rhetoric of Fiction*, called "the implied author," even in cases where it is said to stand for "the author." The persona, or mask, Booth explains, is only "one of the elements created by the implied author and . . . may be separated from him by large ironies," while the concept of "the implied author" includes "the moral and emotional content of each bit of action and suffering of all the characters. It includes, in short, the intuitive apprehension of a completed artistic whole" (*The Rhetoric of Fiction* [Chicago, 1961], p. 73).

aged me to investigate the artistic conventions of nineteenth-century Yiddish fiction against the background of the cultural status of the Yiddish language at the time. In every way he helped me to see the complex relationship between the position of the language and the forms of the literature created in it. I must, therefore, emphasize his share in whatever merit may be found in the following pages (without committing his formidable scholarly reputation to any faults of mine).

Upon Uriel Weinreich's death, his father, Max Weinreich, the dean of Yiddish studies for almost fifty years and the leader of the YIVO Institute for Jewish Research throughout its history, took the supervision of my work upon himself. To him it meant primarily the completion of yet another of the projects in which his son had invested thought and energy during the last years of his life. To bring to completion as many of his son's projects as was possible under the circumstances was the task this proud and indomitable scholar set for himself at that, the darkest hour of his life, setting aside his own work, including his *magnum opus, The History of the Yiddish Language*, which is about to appear now, three years after his own death. Constant contact with him during long months of hard labor soon deepened a personal and a scholarly relationship and made the impression he left on this study almost as deep as the one left by his son. His unparalleled expertise in any matter related to the history of the Yiddish language and literature and his well-known scholarly severity were of the greatest help. Although he is not with us to hear it, I cannot but express my deep gratitude to him for taking interest in my work and spending on it time and much effort in his bereaved old age.

I am happy to use the opportunity and acknowledge my longstanding debt and gratitude to my teachers Professors Dov Sadan and Khone Shmeruk of the Hebrew University in Jerusalem, who introduced me to Yiddish and to the study of Yiddish literature.

I would also like to mention here the name of Meyer Viner, the great Marxist critic and historian of nineteenth-century Yiddish literature, whose thinking, although different from mine in so many respects, greatly influenced me, and whose articles and monographs, written forty years ago, so far from having run their course of usefulness, are always a source of new insight.

The writing of this study obviously involves quoting and paraphrasing numerous passages written in Yiddish and, in many cases, in

Hebrew. Since it seemed pointless (as well as impractical) to burden
the published version with a host of passages in languages not understood by a large segment of its intended readership, all quotations are
rendered in translation, leaving but exceptionally few (mainly excerpts
of verse) in transliteration. This decision involved various difficulties.
It prescribed drastic curtailment and, in many cases, total elimination
of purely stylistic analysis of the texts under consideration. It also put
out of the question an attempt at a systematic differentiation between
the Hebrew and the Yiddish faces of Mendele, since, self-evidently, no
real insight into the complex system of nuances and divergences in
Abramovitsch's bilingual presentation of his Mendele could be gained
without direct reference to the original works in both languages.

Another major difficulty arose from the challenge of the translation
itself. Since very few Yiddish and Hebrew texts of the nineteenth century are available in English translations, and not all available translations are usable, I had to do most of the translating myself. This
proved a most difficult and embarrassing task. For one who is not an
artist and whose English is not native to be faced with the challenge of
translating into English long passages from the works of Abramovitsh,
one of the greatest (if not the greatest of all) prose stylists in Yiddish as
well as in Hebrew, is an unenviable position. Nevertheless, the challenge had to be faced. Of all the translations of Abramovitsh's works
available, and they are not many (see the selective bibliography), I
found I could make some use only of G. Stillman's translation of *Dos
kleyne mentshele* (*The Parasite*) and M. Spiegel's translations of
Masoes Binyomin hashlishi (*The Travels and Adventures of Benjamin
the Third*) and *Di klyatshe* (*The Nag*), and I hereby express my thanks
to the publishers of these books (Thomas Yoseloff, Schocken Books,
and Beechhurst, respectively) for permission to quote from them. Most
of the translations, however, are mine. Unable to render in English the
artistic vigor of the originals, I tried at least to follow them with accuracy, but that too proved in many cases all but impossible. While my
Yiddish texts were all highly idiomatic and teeming with figures and
allusions characteristic of Eastern European Jewish *shtetl* culture, my
Hebrew ones were imbued with biblical and postbiblical quotations,
paraphrases, parodic allusions, and reminiscences, word-plays, riddles,
etc. For biblical material the King James Version was often helpful,
but with the Yiddish I had to do the best I could with my own insufficient resources. In both cases to follow the original literally was to

come up with an English rendering both ludicrous and incomprehensible.

The problem of transliteration, although less absorbing, was almost as difficult as that of translation. With no accepted literary idiom or orthography nineteenth-century Yiddish is not given easily to transliteration, as witness the wilderness of chaotic and idiosyncratic transliterations one encounters in most English publications dealing with Jewish culture in general and with Yiddish in particular. There is no way of being certain of one's transliteration, unless one is prepared for the tedium of reconstructing the sound of each word in the dialect supposedly appropriate to the case (e.g., the "Ukrainian" dialect in the case of Sholem Aleichem; the "Polish" in that of Perets, etc.) and rendering it into phonetic symbols. In a nonlinguistic literary study such as this, this was, of course, impracticable. The transliteration system I have used is that of a layman. The rendering of consonants follows the usage of the YIVO in its nonlinguistic publications, with two exceptions: I retained the Slavic softening of the "l" in the title *Di klyatsche* (for no better reason than that Abramovitsh himself persisted in doing so) and bowed to the widely accepted transliteration of Sholem-Aleykhem as "Sholem Aleichem." I did not, however, capitulate to the absurd rendering of "Sholom," which falls between two chairs: the Israeli, "Sphardic" pronunciation—"Shalom"—and the Yiddish one—"Sholem." I have not retained the Germanization of the orthography to which so many of the nineteenth-century Yiddish writers adhered, and in which some of them "religiously" believed ("I warn you most strongly and solemnly not to change even one iota in my orthography in this article. If you intend to disregard this warning, better send me back my article and we shall annul our literary engagement even before it starts," wrote Abramovitsh to one of his editors). Germanisms of morphological nature (e.g., *shprakhe* instead of *shprakh*) have been retained. All Hebrew words and titles have been transliterated according to current Israeli usage (even where it departs from traditional grammar; e.g., *sfarim* instead of *sefarim, akhronim* instead of *akharonim*, etc.). However, Hebrew words used within a Yiddish context have been transliterated according to the Ashkenazic pronunciation and accentuation current in Eastern Europe (e.g., *Masoes Binyomin hashlishi*—the Hebrew title of a Yiddish work). The apostrophe which occurs in transliterated Hebrew words (e.g., *lu'akh*) is intended to emphasize the bisyllabic nature of the vowel sequence.

For reasons which will become obvious to the reader, I have invariably referred to Abramovitsh rather than to the more widely known Mendele Moykher-Sforim. However, I did not apply the same rule to Rabinovitsh–Sholem Aleichem for two reasons: first, while the difference between Abramovitsh the writer and Mendele the character is explained in detail in the second half of this study, the distinctions that should be made between Rabinovitsh and Sholem Aleichem are not discussed. (They are discussed in my monograph *Sholem Aleykhem—Person, Persona, Presence*, New York, 1972). Second, although a distinction between Rabinovitsh and Sholem Aleichem is as necessary as the one that separates Mendele from Abramovitsh, it should be of a different nature. In the case of Abramovitsh the difference between the author and the fictional character is crystal clear. In the case of Rabinovitsh it is not. The literary "being" or "presence" Sholem Aleichem *did* invade the privacy of the author, who even signed his will both as Sholem ben Nokhem Rabinovitsh and as Sholem Aleichem.

Finally, I extend my thanks to my teachers, colleagues, and friends who read different drafts of this study and suggested numerous corrections and improvements: Prof. James L. Clifford of the English Department of Columbia University; Prof. Marvin I. Herzog of the Department of Linguistics of Columbia University and of the Max Weinreich Center for Advanced Jewish Studies at the YIVO; Mrs. Rachel Erlich, also of the Max Weinreich Center; Mrs. Dina Abramovitsh, the librarian of the YIVO in New York, who most courteously put at my disposal the treasures of the YIVO library. The illustrations included in this book were culled from the archives and library of the YIVO. For the permission to use them and for the help in their selection I thank the Institute and its chief archivist, Dr. Isaiah Trunk. I am particularly grateful to my friend John Thornton, who did his best to improve my English.

The executive committee of the YIVO facilitated the publication of this book by a grant for which I am doubly grateful, since I regard it both as an encouragement and an honor. In this connection I cannot but mention, and with deep gratitude and sorrow, the name of Samuel Lapin, the late executive secretary of the YIVO, who had initiated this grant shortly before his untimely death last February. His passing away deprived the YIVO of the man who during recent years had

been its moving spirit and deprived me of yet another dear, unforgettable friend.

My wife, Yael, my best reader and severest critic, shared with me
the years of labor that went into the writing of this study and left her
mark on it, as she does on everything which I manage to get done.
Without her help the present book—written in a foreign language on
foreign soil—would have never been completed and published. It is
dedicated to her with my love.

DAN MIRON

New York
Winter 1973

A Traveler Disguised

CHAPTER ONE

THE COMMITMENT TO YIDDISH

אַחַי הַסּוֹפְרִים,
אַל תִּטְּרוּ לִי אֵיבָה
אִם לִי שְׂפַת בֶּרִיל
וּשְׁמֶרִיל עֲרֵבָה —

וּבְבוּז לֹא אֶקְרָא
„עִלְּגִים" לְלְשׁוֹנָם,
כִּי לְשׁוֹן עַמִּי
אֶשְׁמַע מִגְּרוֹנָם!

(י. ל. פרץ, מַנְגִּינוֹת הַזְּמַן, כ"א)*

THE ONE CONDITION which, more than all others, determined the character of nineteenth-century Yiddish literature is the fact that it was written in Yiddish. Prima facie this statement hardly seems necessary; at best it is a truism bordering on tautology. Applied to Hebrew literature of the nineteenth-century, one might argue, a parallel statement might have made sense: the fact that a host of writers—not one or two eccentrics—dedicated themselves to the writing of poems, novels, plays, and essays in an unspoken language associated in the mind of the people with ritual and the study of the holy texts and thoroughly understood by few may seem a historical oddity that calls for an explanation. To understand it at all, we must begin by investigating the nature of these writers' commitment to Hebrew; we must study the anatomy of that overpowering loyalty which was expressed by Y. L. Gordon, the greatest nineteenth-century Hebrew poet, in his famous lines:

* "My fellow writers, don't hold it against me that I find pleasure in the language of Berl and Shmerl and that I don't deride it as a language of 'stammerers,' for it is my people that I hear speaking through them." (*Manginot hazman*, "The Melodies of Our Age," section XXI, in *Kol kitvey Y. L. Perets*, Vol. IX, second part [Tel Aviv, 1957], p. 40.) Berl and Shmerl—common Eastern European Jewish names. Perets' poem, written in Hebrew, addresses the community of Hebrew writers.

1

Eved la'ivrit anokhi ad netsakh
La kol khushay bi litsmitut makharti.[1]

("I am the slave of Hebrew forever; I put all my senses at her disposal
for good.") But as for the commitment to Yiddish (if a literary employment of this language could be deemed a commitment), why should it
be noticed at all? What other language would have been more natural
for Yiddish-speaking authors to employ in addressing a Yiddish audience?

Moreover, while the literary use of Hebrew for purposes which
were not directly connected with liturgy, learning of the religious law,
and religious edification had been very rare and sporadic among the
Ashkenazic Jewish communities of Germany and Eastern Europe prior
to the last decades of the eighteenth century, there was nothing new
about the writing of belles lettres in Yiddish. A Yiddish literature of a
non-ritualistic (the term "secular" would have been misleading) nature
existed for hundreds of years, during which Hebrew literature of a
comparable function (edifying entertainment; sometimes plain entertainment) had not been produced by Ashkenazic Jews outside of Italy.
True, Yiddish literature never occupied a high position in the cultural
hierarchy of traditional Ashkenazic Jewry. It always addressed itself to
the unlearned, particularly to women. For those who could absorb
themselves in the learning of the Torah to waste their time on it was
considered sinful. Still, it was an accepted (or rather tolerated) institution. Its masterpieces—the great epics, romances, and novelettes, written from the fifteenth to seventeenth centuries (such as the famous
Shmuel-bukh, Bovo-bukh, and *Mayse-bukh*)—did not lose their wide
appeal until very late in the nineteenth century, and to them was
added toward the end of the eighteenth century and at the beginning
of the nineteenth the immensely popular literature of hasidic legend
and hagiography, which was also written (in part) in Yiddish. While
the "naturalness" of a Hebrew literature which had no religious function could, therefore, be questioned, that of a Yiddish one, it seems,
was ensured by precedent as well as by continuous practice.

If Yiddish seems to have been the natural medium to employ in all
branches of Jewish literature, it is much more so with regard to fiction,
with which this study is mainly concerned. While Hebrew of the nineteenth century was lacking in the linguistic facilities indispensable for
narrative, Yiddish seethed with living idiom and abounded with the

warmth and elasticity so congenial to the creation of readable fiction. Faced with the problem of creating dialogue, for instance, Hebrew novelists were at their wits' end. They could not produce the faintest semblance of actual speech without breaking the rules of their own stylistic etiquette,[2] and even when they managed to bring themselves to do that, the results were usually pitiable. At the same time, Yiddish fiction writers had God's plenty to pick and choose from. How could a fiction writer of any artistic sense hesitate between the two languages? In 1862 young Abramovitsh (1836?–1917), who was to become the major Yiddish fiction writer of the century, had to conclude the introduction of his first novel, which he wrote in Hebrew, by entreating the "sympathetic reader" to understand "how bitter a toil it is to write about such matters [i.e., Jewish contemporary life] in our holy tongue . . . and against how many obstacles the Hebrew writer must stumble on such a path! "[3] In the novel itself, whenever he wanted to impart to the narrative the flavor of lively speech, he had to resort to crude, literal translations of Yiddish idioms.[4] Are we to wonder then that his second narrative was written in Yiddish? The wonder is rather that he wrote the first one in Hebrew. Even disregarding artistic considerations, there remained the simple fact that Yiddish was the only language understood by the overwhelming majority of Eastern European Jews. In this connection some of the rare pieces of statistical evidence concerning the market possibilities for Hebrew and Yiddish works of fiction in the nineteenth century may be cited: Abraham Mapu's *Ahavat tsiyon* ("Love of Zion," 1853), the most celebrated Hebrew novel of the century and an immediate "success," had sold 1200 copies by 1857.[5] In 1858 a Hebrew adaptation of Eugène Sue's *Mystères de Paris* caused a sensation and made everybody envious of the adaptor, as 2000 copies of its first part were sold in one year.[6] At the same time the Yiddish fiction writer A. M. Dik (1814–1893), whose novelettes were printed at the same printer's shop as *Ahavat tsiyon* and *Mystères de Paris*, informed his readers: "One hundred thousand copies of my books have already been sold, and new orders from the booksellers arrive daily."[7]

If this leaves room for emphasizing further that Yiddish should have been the "natural" language for nineteenth-century Jewish fiction writers, the following may be added: both Hebrew and Yiddish novelists of the time were fully committed propagandists of the *Haskala* (the Jewish Enlightenment movement). As such, they deeply be-

lieved and constantly asserted that their main intention in writing
fiction was to be "of use to the people," to contribute to the education
of the "unenlightened," "to set a mirror" in front of the Jewish masses
so that they could see how much they were in need of improvement.[8]
That this goal could be pursued in Yiddish far more effectively than in
Hebrew is evident. Indeed, the confidence of Hebrew novelists that
they were useful to the people must seem somewhat preposterous to
anyone not equipped with a well-adjusted historical perspective. For
example, Hebrew fiction writers of the *Haskala* were lashing the *hasidim* and, especially, the institution of the *tsadik* (the sanctified hasidic
leader) for decades without seeming to notice that the masses of the
"duped" adherents of the "sect" knew no Hebrew beyond a few
phrases of the prayer. Yiddish writers were quick to detect this disparity between means and ends. Yisroel Aksenfeld (1787–1866), the first
Yiddish novelist, explained in a letter (written in 1841) to Uvarov, then
Russian minister of education, that it was because of this disparity that
he decided to write his novels and dramas in Yiddish rather than in
Hebrew or German:

> Many Jewish writers have toiled to free their brethren from the error in
> which they live, to make them realize the wildness of their superstitions;
> above all else, they have toiled to rescue them from the harmful effect
> of the influence of the *hasidim*. This is a sect which conceals under its
> mask of piety grave moral defects, corrupts manners, and stands in the
> way of culture. Moved by true patriotism [i.e., Russian patriotism] and
> pure morals, Jewish writers turned their pen against the *hasidim*—but
> with no success. Indeed, the means they employed could not be ex-
> pected to undo an evil which had struck its roots so deep: they wrote
> their works either in Hebrew or in German. How could these works
> have any effect when the common people, for whom they were des-
> tined, knew neither of these languages? Other means had, therefore, to
> be employed: one had to write in a language which the common Jewish
> people would understand. . . .[9]

If we are to measure the impact of the antihasidic campaign in Hebrew literature by quantitative evidence—such as number of editions
—we must pronounce Aksenfeld's judgment correct. Even *Megale-
tmirin* ("Revealer of Hidden Things") by Yosef Perl (1773–1839), undoubtedly the best-known and the most brilliant Hebrew satire written in the course of the antihasidic campaign, had a very limited circulation. It was first published in 1819 and was not republished for more

than forty years. The limitations of the modest revival it enjoyed in the 1860s and 1870s (three editions), when the *Haskala* was at its highest tide, should be gauged by comparison with the enormous success of a Yiddish antihasidic satire written at the time: *Dos poylishe yingl* ("The Polish Boy") by Y. Y. Linetski (1839–1915). Published first in the Yiddish weekly magazine *Kol-mevaser* ("A Heralding Voice") in 1867 and then in book form in 1869, this satire was read by literally everybody. While *Megale-tmirin*, in which the language of the ignorant *hasidim* was exquisitely mimicked in crippled Hebrew, could be fully enjoyed only by those who were able to see its parodic point, i.e., by those who knew Hebrew well enough to feel the comic effect of its methodical disfiguring, the popularity of the vituperative and explosively funny *Poylish yingl* met with no such obstacle. Not even the fierce opposition of the *hasidim*, experts at physical suppression of undesirable literature though they were, could bring it to a halt, for the book was avidly read by the *hasidim* themselves. It is worthwhile to quote at some length a few descriptions of the popularity of this book written by contemporaries as evidence of the immense rapport which nineteenth-century Yiddish fiction achieved with the Jewish masses. Alexander Tsederboym (1816–1893), the editor of *Kol-mevaser*, told (in 1869) about the success of Linetski's story when it was serialized in his magazine:

> The story caught the interest of the public to such an extent that people, waiting impatiently from week to week for the new installment, would read it immediately whenever the most recent issue arrived, even before they read the latest news. That applies not only to the subscribers of *Kol-mevaser*, but also to other people, who would buy or borrow the magazine only in order to read the story. More than that: *hasidim*, who are enemies of *Kol-mevaser* in general—let alone of the author of this story, whom they would gladly see dead—even they would look every week for the new issue and read *Dos poylishe yingl* with pleasure. . . .[10]

If Tsederboym, the editor of *Kol-mevaser* and a *maskil* (exponent of the *Haskala*), cannot be regarded as an objective witness, we can support his evidence with that of a German missionary, one Dr. Ferdinand Weber, who in 1872 visited Russia and a year later described his tour in a book, *Reiseerinnerungen aus Russland*. As a missionary, Weber took a special interest in the orthodox Jewish masses of Russia, and he was so impressed with the success which such a "heretical" book as *Dos poylishe yingl* (by then already available in book form) had achieved with these common folk, that he included in his travelogue a whole chapter of it in transliteration. He wrote:

> At the time of my visit to south Russia, a book titled *Dos poylishe yingl* made an extraordinary impression on the orthodox Jews. It is written with so much wit, that everybody—especially the young—is eager to read it. It is, however, sweetened poison. The author lives in Odessa,° and the *hasidim* have done whatever they could to suppress his book and to deter him from further publications of the same kind.[11]

The most interesting evidence concerning the success of Linetski's satire is supplied in the memoirs of M. Spektor (1858–1925), who at the time was a hasidic youth (in about a decade he was to become one of the most popular Yiddish fiction writers).

> *Hasidim* young and old read the book through. They roundly cursed the author, but read it they did. Linetski's *Poylish yingl* was "looked into" even in the *tsadikim*'s very "courts," and—who knows—perhaps even by the *tsadik* himself. Here too the author was met with dire curses, called by the most humiliating names; still, his book did not go out of circulation. Once you opened it you could not tear yourself from it. You had to read it from cover to cover. Whoever got the book passed it on. Accompanied by curses it went from hand to hand, till in a few weeks it looked like grandmother's tattered, disintegrating prayer book.
>
> Throughout Poland and the Ukraine there was not a single Jew—man or woman, let alone youngsters—who did not read this book. Most people, once they had done reading it, threw the book contemptuously away, but many were influenced by it and secretly shied away from hasidism. In several cases people were turned by it into professed apostates and were not deterred by an open war with their parents and with the *hasidim* in general.[12]

All through the 1870s and the early 1880s *Dos poylishe yingl* was republished by pirate presses. Nobody can tell the exact number of its editions.[13] It certainly sold tens of thousands of copies, perhaps more.

One could go on with similar pieces of evidence, but there is also abundant evidence of a different, contradictory nature, which must be accounted for, evidence that indicates that the "naturalness" of

---

° As an inhabitant of Odessa, the author had to be a "modern," Europeanized Jew, which explains his antihasidic tendency.

Yiddish as the language of Jewish literature in the nineteenth century is doubtful.

ii

Several phenomena in the development of nineteenth-century Yiddish literature make questionable the apparent suitability of Yiddish as a literary medium. The most conspicuous and also the most enigmatic of these is the fact that the great majority of Yiddish writers did not write exclusively in Yiddish. To be exact, of all nineteenth-century writers of consequence, only three wrote Yiddish from the start and never resorted to any other language for literary purposes. Two of these have already been mentioned here—Aksenfeld and Spektor. The third is the poet and playwright S. Etinger (1803?–1856). Even they (with the exception of Spektor) employed other languages for personal correspondence (Etinger, German; Aksenfeld, Russian and Hebrew). All the others were to some extent—often to a considerable extent—bilingual writers. Some even wrote in more than two languages.

The phenomenon of true literary bilingualism or multilingualism—the ability to achieve not only proficiency but also a creative command of two languages or more—has been rare from the emergence of Romanticism at the end of the eighteenth century and had been on the wane since the decline of Latin as the cultural language of Europe. A recent sketch of the development of multilingualism in European literature[14] shows that, while in the Middle Ages and the Renaissance for most authors to employ more than one language in their different works and sometimes even in a single (macaronic) work was as natural as it is for educated people nowadays to communicate on different levels of their language in different situations and for different purposes, modern authors, in order to seriously practice bilingualism, have to challenge the whole structure of our literary culture. Multilingualism in literature goes against our cultural grain. It contradicts our basic modern (i.e., Romantic) notion of good and "true" literary expression. This expression, we have become inclined to assume, cannot survive the loss of utmost directness, which means that it is usually not to be achieved in any but a native tongue. The few writers who mastered a second language to the extent that they could develop an independent, personal style in it are looked upon as prodigies. That is why multilingualism in European literature, once the hallmark of an integrated, internationalist culture, has dwindled during the last two hundred years to the status of a cultural curiosity, and has been practiced in the most idiosyncratic, unsystematic, and sporadic manner by a few individual writers, who cannot be said to represent anything like a continuous phenomenon with a development of its own.

Against this background we must set the inherent multilingualism of modern Jewish literature and particularly its Hebrew-Yiddish "internal bilingualism" (coined by Max Weinreich, this term indicates the coexistence of two languages, both belonging to one ethnic group, but functioning differently within the different contexts of the group's life and culture. "External bilingualism" indicates the coexistence of two languages belonging to different but coterritorial ethnic groups, both being employed by members of one of these groups for communication with the members of the other.)[15] It immediately gives rise to difficult historical and aesthetic problems. Of course, it was inherited from the premaskilic, traditional culture of Ashkenazic Jewry, which allotted to Yiddish a distinct, although culturally subordinate, place beside the holy tongue. In many respects the relationship between the two languages was not substantially different from that of Latin versus the vernaculars in the Middle Ages and the early Renaissance, although unlike the international Latin, Hebrew, as the language of religion and the higher forms of cultural communication, emphasized Jewish particularism rather than counterbalanced it. Within the framework of a premodern cultural hierarchy governed by religion, the coexistence of the two languages was, then, as "natural" as it had been under similar circumstances in all European societies. However, once the Hebrew–Yiddish internal bilingualism entered the modern era in the history of Ashkenazic Jewry, its self-evident raison d'être vanished. It underwent considerable changes, and became a phenomenon both problematic and full of tensions of various kinds. Were it to follow the pattern set by the development of the Latin-versus-vernacular bilingualism, Hebrew should have been eliminated as the cultural (and literary) language of the secularized segment of Ashkenazic Jewry. But this was not the case. On the contrary, what happened was that with secularization, first in Germany and then gradually in the large Jewish concentrations in Eastern Europe, Hebrew, for the first time in the history of Ashkenazic Jewry, became the major language of a nonreligious Jewish literature. The cultural subordination of Yiddish to Hebrew became even more pronounced than it had been earlier, but its contents changed. While in earlier times Ashkenazic Jews had created belles lettres almost solely in Yiddish (deeming the holy tongue to be too good for such a profane occupation), now Yiddish trailed for almost a whole century behind Hebrew in Jewish belles lettres as well as in other areas. During the nineteenth century, as already mentioned, almost all Yiddish writers wrote Hebrew as well. Significantly, this was not the case with most Hebrew writers, who would not "degrade" their pens by writing Yiddish (although it was their major, and sometimes only, spoken language). The community of Yiddish writers, then, formed a part of a more extensive literary community, a small circle submerged in a larger one. During the first quarter of the twentieth century this situation changed. Hebrew–Yiddish bilingualism remained a highly characteristic phenomenon in Jewish literature, but its Yiddish component emancipated itself from its subordination to the Hebrew one. The relationships between the two literary communities at the time can be graphically designated in the form of two converging, equally large, circles, with a very large coextensive center but also with large peripheral segments, covered by a single language. Since the 1920s, the central coextensive segment has been shrinking, and the present relationship between the two circles is merely tangential. This whole development calls for both an aesthetic and a sociolinguistic–historical explanation, of which only some rudiments have been offered until now.[16] For the purposes of our argument, however, the emphasis of the problematic nature of the Hebrew–Yiddish literary bilingualism in its nineteenth-century phase will suffice.

The aesthetic aspect of this bilingualism calls for consideration on two different levels. On the one hand, the very possibility of bilingual stylistic creativity as a "normal" or at least persisting phenomenon must be aesthetically accounted for. On the other hand, we must deal separately with particular cases of bilingual excellence. While the "normality" or commonness of Hebrew-Yiddish bilingualism raises difficult questions concerning the different aesthetic goals generally pursued in each language, those raised by the bilingual excellence of highly creative individuals are of a most baffling nature. Some nineteenth-century writers were able not only to use both languages with complete mastery but often to write the same piece in Yiddish and in Hebrew with equal (though far from identical) stylistic brilliance. Their achievements defy and actually annul all accepted distinctions between the "original" text and its translation, and they thoroughly undermine the normal aesthetic hierarchy, which prefers the former to

the latter. Abramovitsh performed the most dazzling feats in this respect, but some other writers—from Perl at the beginning of the century to Perets toward its end—did not trail far behind him.[17] It has become customary in our criticism to take pride in the bilingual
excellence of our nineteenth-century masters and to extoll their ability
to bridge the gap of translation into which most renderings of literary
masterpieces inevitably sink. From the vantage point of modern, "expressionistic" poetics, however, this ability must seem strange, if not
suspicious. Indeed, there were writers—the Hebrew thinker and
fiction writer M. Y. Berditshevski, for example—who regarded this duality as aesthetically pernicious,[18] and on certain aesthetic grounds
they were clearly right; it is only that these aesthetic grounds somehow do not apply to Jewish literature of the nineteenth century. It
still, however, remains for us to arrive at those aesthetic principles
which do apply to the special phenomena with which this literature
confronts us. Whatever these may be, aesthetic elucidation alone will
not do. It must be remembered that the great stylists were not the only
ones who felt the urge to write in more than one language; that, in
fact, this urge is manifest in the works of those who were said to lack
stylistic sensibilities altogether. "Shomer" (N. M. Shaykevitsh, 1846–
1905) was a novelist who catered to the most primitive class of readers
and who worked more like a producer of literature than like a writer.
In less than three decades he produced literally hundreds of fictional
works which were immensely popular. Yet he too cared to write some
of his "highly interesting novels" of adventure and high romance and
many of his short stories in the exclusive holy tongue as well as in
Yiddish.[19] Historically, his bilingualism is as enigmatic as that of Perl
and Abramovitsh, and perhaps more so. We might not be inclined—although perhaps we should be—to trouble ourselves with the aesthetic
aspect of the bilingual creation of his *Mot yesharim o kayin* ("The
Death of the Righteous or Cain"), a long, intricate, melodramatic, and
"trashy" historical novel. However, the reason that he troubled himself with it is historically, if not aesthetically, as intriguing as the question of why Abramovitsh went to the infinite trouble of revolutionizing
the style of Hebrew fiction so that he could rework in Hebrew the stories which he had already polished and repolished in Yiddish (as well
as write in Hebrew some new stories which were then to be reworked
in Yiddish).

   In whatever way these questions may be answered, they clearly indicate that Yiddish was not an altogether "natural" literary medium. For all its advantages as a spoken language, as the language of a potentially vast reading public, it did not fulfill all the needs of the writers who employed it; it left some part of their literary personalities in need of another linguistic outlet.

In this connection it should also be noted that Yiddish was almost never the first choice of nineteenth-century Jewish writers. Even those Yiddish writers who did not develop as pronounced bilingualists, indeed even those who eventually became "pure," conscientious "Yiddishists" (Linetski, for instance), made their debuts and performed at least a part of their literary apprenticeships in another language. In some cases the linguistic peregrinations which preceded settling down to Yiddish were rather lengthy. Most celebrated of these is the case of Y. L. Perets (1852–1915). This enormously influential writer, who around the turn of the century changed the whole atmosphere of Yiddish literature, and as it is usually put, "modernized" it, had to travel far and wide before he was prepared to publish anything in Yiddish. He began his literary activity in 1875 with poems in Polish; then, for more than ten years, he was known as a writer of Hebrew poems and fables. His first Yiddish publication (the narrative poem *Monish*) was made as late as 1888, and in it he saw fit to devote a section to a versified discourse on the inappropriateness and deficiency of Yiddish as a poetic medium.[20] In most cases such a lengthy preparation was unnecessary; writers reached Yiddish in a roundabout way, but not in such a long one. Abramovitsh, for instance, made his debut as a Hebrew writer in 1857; his already-mentioned first Hebrew novel appeared in 1862; his first Yiddish work of fiction, *Dos kleyne mentshele* ("The Little Man"), was serialized in *Kol-mevaser* in 1864. With others the process was even quicker. Linetski's first publication—a Hebrew one, to be sure—occurred in 1865; by the end of 1867 Linetski was already one of the best-known Yiddish writers (*Dos poylishe yingl* was one of the first things he published after his shift from Hebrew to Yiddish). This, however, is not of great importance. What is important is that Yiddish writers had to grope in the dark, to wander in a linguistic twilight before they found the way to their medium. Short as their wanderings may have been, they are heavy with meaning. They imply that, throughout the nineteenth century, young men with literary aspirations would not resort "naturally" to Yiddish. That they switched to Yiddish may indicate that they found it hard or even impossible to activate their talents, or to pursue their cultural and social goals in other languages; that they did not begin with it, however, indicates that Yiddish was not a part of their notion of literature and that they had to overcome certain inhibitions in order to conceive of it as such.

That the commitment to Yiddish involved the suppression of misgivings and inhibitions cannot be doubted. For almost all Yiddish writers of the nineteenth century the moment of linguistic transition was accompanied by agitation and by a consciousness of crisis that resulted in a pressing need to explain and vindicate themselves. The short Hebrew passage from Perets which I quoted at the opening of this chapter as a motto was published one year before *Monish*. The apologetic tone, the plea not to be hated for a "weakness" for Yiddish are characteristic. Even of those three writers already mentioned who wrote Yiddish from the very start, only Etinger did not feel the need to explain or justify his choice of language.[21] In a prospectus he circulated to solicit subscriptions for the works he intended to publish, he related how, when still a student (Etinger was a physician by profession), he had come across two anonymously published Yiddish books, one an adaptation of *Robinson Crusoe*[22] and the other a comedy,[23] which he erroneously described as an adaptation of *Tartuffe*:

> I saw that the books found favor with a great number of people; that is, they pleased both the connoisseurs and the uneducated. . . . For a number of reasons I would rather not say whether they were well-written or not. In any case, the idea to write in plain Yiddish certainly appealed to me; that everybody can see, for I immediately decided to find out whether I possessed the talent to write in that language and in that style.[24]

In its straightforwardness and, one might say, lightheartedness, this passage is unique among nineteenth-century documents concerning the literary use of Yiddish, which are as a rule apologetic and ponderous. Etinger treats here with equanimity and objectivity his decision to write Yiddish, almost as if it were a historical fact to which one would attribute neither negative nor positive values. Everybody, he says, can see for himself that he liked the idea of writing Yiddish, since he "immediately" proceeded to realize it. Yiddish had an appeal for him, and he saw no need to rationalize this appeal or to expatiate on its nature; indeed, he gives the impression that he had no clear-cut reasons for writing Yiddish or, for that matter, for writing at all. The success of other writers challenged him, and without any soul-searching he tried to imitate them and even to improve upon them. In most literatures, especially those of ages as unsophisticated as Etinger's, such an initiation would be commonplace; not so in nineteenth-century Yiddish literature. Here, Etinger's very "normality" made him exceptional. Even a naive writer such as Dik, who has been often represented as a folksy raconteur, blissfully unaware of the problems and difficulties of literature, explained that he could bring himself to write Yiddish only after realizing that as a Hebrew writer he would never be able to make a living. "I degraded my pen," he confesses, while boasting of the excellent sales of his Yiddish books, "by writing numerous stories in the language which, to our great shame, is the spoken dialect of our people in this country." [25] He would not have done it, he continues, had he not been convinced that Jewish women, who could read no other language, were in dire need of enlightening and edifying reading material. Characteristically, he made this confession in the introduction to a Hebrew publication (1861), for it was to the community of Hebrew writers and readers that he felt he owed an explanation (Perets' poem, too, is addressed to the Hebrew writers). Abramovitsh never thought it necessary to explain to his Yiddish readers why he began his career in Hebrew and why he kept writing his articles on public topics in Hebrew even as he became the most highly regarded Yiddish writer of his generation.[26] However, when in 1889 he was asked to write an autobiographical sketch for a Hebrew literary lexicon, the need for an explanation of his shift from Hebrew to Yiddish was immediately clear to him. Indeed, it is quite obvious that self-vindication on this point was one of his major interests in writing this famous sketch. It is worthwhile to compare Etinger's almost convivial declaration that Yiddish appealed to him with Abramovitsh's laborious explanation of why, after the publication of *Limdu hetev* ("Learn to Do Good"), his first Hebrew novel, he decided to continue his belletristic work in Yiddish:

> Then I communed with my heart, saying, Here I am, observing the ways of our people and striving to write novels for them on Jewish subjects in the holy tongue, which most of them, as they speak only Yiddish, do not understand. What hath the author of all his labor and of the vexation of his heart, if he is of no use to his people? The question For whom do I labor? gave me no rest and greatly embarrassed me. . . .[27]

Written twenty-five years after the transition had been made, these sentences indicate that the agitation it had involved was still strongly felt. They retain the original atmosphere of consternation in their very phrasing, tortuous and heavily reminiscent of the style of Ecclesiastes.[28] In them Abramovitsh is still "communing with his heart," explaining an act which in his eyes did not cease to appear morally and aesthetically ambiguous.

Later on in this explanation, Abramovitsh develops a highly suggestive analogy which deserves closer attention. This analogy presents Yiddish as "a strange woman," and Yiddish compositions as her illegitimate issue. Abramovitsh compares the few respectable writers, "one of a city and two of a family," who sometimes "visited that cursed woman" to clandestine philanderers, and he even goes on to describe his own relations with the language in terms of sinful sexuality. He was afraid, he says, "to profane the honor of his name" by letting himself be seduced by this "strange woman" and by "giving my strength unto that foreigner." Almost all the admonitions of the writer of Proverbs against sexual relations with non-Jewish women are invoked in the discussion of his doubts and consternation before the decisive step was taken.[29] He counterbalances these admonitions with the image of the redeemed harlot, who, in many parts of the Bible, symbolizes Israel reunited with God. Like Hosea, he had mercy "upon her that had not obtained mercy," and he "betrothed her unto him forever," [30] and like King Ahasuerus in Esther he "speedily gave her things for purification with such things as belonged to her," [31] and she became "a well-favored matron" who "bore him many children." [32] In short, Abramovitsh conceived of his resort to Yiddish as a promiscuous affair redeemed by marriage and by orderly procreation. Nothing can be more suggestive of the illegitimacy of Yiddish as a literary medium in the eyes of nineteenth-century Jewish intellectuals.

iii

It is largely because of this air of promiscuity which went with the literary use of Yiddish that until the 1860s a modern Yiddish literature was publicly almost nonexistent. Dik was the only Yiddish writer whose works had been published freely and constantly before 1862 (he started to publish in the late 1840s).[33] Other writers of the first half of the nineteenth century—M. Lefin (1749–1826), Y. Perl (1773–1839),

Y. B. Levinzon (1788–1860), Aksenfeld and Etinger—circulated their works surreptitiously in handwritten copies; they would "conceal them under their coats," as Abramovitsh put it, "lest their nakedness be uncovered and their honor turned into shame." [34] Voluntary suppression was by no means the only reason for lack of circulation. Indeed, in some cases it did not exist at all. We know now (what Abramovitsh and early historians of nineteenth-century literature could not know) that some early Yiddish writers were prevented from publishing their works not by their own inhibitions but by suppression from the outside. After the documents concerning the life and works of Etinger were assembled and analyzed, it became apparent that the author wanted very much to publish his works and was prevented only because he would not consent to cuts and changes demanded by the czarist censor. [35] When the historian Sh. Ginzburg was given access to the archives of the government, he found that Aksenfeld (who wrote about thirty novels and plays, of which only one novel and four plays survived), [36] spent the last third of his life vainly petitioning governors, ministers, and even the czar himself to overrule the refusal of printers intimidated by the *hasidim* to publish his works. [37] The sporadic and surreptitious development of Yiddish literature in the first half of the nineteenth century had much to do with the unfavorable circumstances under which Jewish culture developed in the Russia of Nicholas I (1825–1855), especially with the government's policy with regard to Jewish publications. [38] It had, of course, to do with the reactionary and repressive tendencies of the regime in general. It is not accidental that *Kol-mevaser*, the first Yiddish magazine, was started in 1862; that Aksenfeld's only surviving novel, *Dos shterntikhl* ("The Headband"), the first full-fledged modern Yiddish novel, was published in 1861, though it was written in the 1840s or even earlier. [39] Etinger's major work, the comedy *Serkele*, written in the late 1820s or early 1830s, was published in 1861 and performed for the first time in 1862. This sudden liberation of Yiddish literature is part of the general liberation of cultural life in Russia which took place during the first years of the regime of Alexander II, and it only indirectly or partially involves the internal factors to which Abramovitsh alluded in his comparison of the literary use of Yiddish to extramarital relations. Still, this suggestive comparison contains a significant truth. It not only applies to those writers such as Perl and Levinzon who did voluntarily suppress their Yiddish works [40] but also explains, or at least sets in context, some other phenomena characteristic of the development of Yiddish literature both before and after its external suppression was alleviated.

Abramovitsh's analogy, his allusion to the "promiscuity" of Yiddish literature, may explain, for instance, the unusually large number of the so-called pen names of Yiddish writers in the nineteenth century (and to a large extent also in the twentieth century). This may seem a matter of no great consequence, and indeed it is rarely discussed as a general literary phenomenon by critics and literary historians.[41] Later on I shall try to suggest that the usage of pen names—which was so widespread that the author of the first textbook on the history of nineteenth-century Yiddish literature saw fit to append to his text an index of pseudonyms[42]—is a phenomenon of major literary importance, which bears directly on the aesthetic and stylistic premises upon which the art of modern Yiddish storytelling was based, and which calls for a detailed critical treatment. The nature and artistic function of some of these pseudonyms (or rather masks, for the so-called pen names of most Yiddish writers are names of imaginary personae whose voices the authors assume, but who must be differentiated from the authors as we differentiate Bickerstaff or Gulliver from Swift or Yorick from Sterne) are complicated. Yet, there can be no doubt that one of the main origins of the pen name tradition was the assumption, often unconscious, but more often not, that somehow the literary employment of Yiddish was "illegitimate," and that a Yiddish writer should do everything in his power to keep the largest distance possible between his creative activity and his personality. As a matter of fact, some of the major Yiddish writers, such as Abramovitsh-Mendele and Rabinovitsh-Sholem Aleichem, succeeded, in spite of their wide popularity, in protecting their personal "selves" from the public eye and in living in the popular imagination through their fictitious personae alone.[43]

Late in his life, Abramovitsh was asked by some younger admirers how he came to write Yiddish and why he decided to appear in Yiddish—from the very start—disguised as Mendele Moykher-Sforim ("Mendele the Bookpeddler"). Here are excerpts from his answer as recorded by Sholem Aleichem in his essay "Fir zenen mir gezesn" ("There We Sat, Four of Us"):

> it transpired that writing in Yiddish, that is, speaking to all the Jewish people in their own language, had long attracted him . . . but, as forty

years ago [i.e., in the 1860s] the writing of Yiddish was still considered a disgrace, particularly for the kind of young, enlightened man he was . . . he kept his first Yiddish composition, *Dos kleyne mentshele*, a guarded secret. He took great care that no one should see him at it, and he invoked for it the name of a living person, one Senderl, a bookpeddler who used at that time to make his rounds with his horse and wagon in the vicinity of Barditshev.°. . . He wrote the *Kleyn mentshele* in no more than three days, with fear and trembling, and sent it to Alexander Tsederboym for the *Kol-mevaser*. Seeing the name Senderl the Bookpeddler on the title page, Tsederboym was stricken with the suspicion that this was a sally aimed at himself [Alexander-Sender-Senderl]. After some deliberation—a Jewish editor never feels obliged to stand on ceremony with a Jewish author, let alone in those early times—he changed the name from Senderl to Mendele, and this is how Mendele Moykher Sforim made his first appearance in the world.[44]

The credibility of this story (Abramovitsh's stories about his literary fortunes "in those early times" were often too neatly constructed to be quite accurate) is beside the point. Whatever element of fiction it may contain, it certainly reflects the atmosphere in which Abramovitsh began his career as a Yiddish writer and in which others before him (see Dik's explanation of his reasons for hiding behind a pen name)[45] and after him began theirs. "Forty years ago the writing of Yiddish was still considered a disgrace," wrote Sholem Aleichem, referring to the 1860s ("Fir zenen mir gezesn" was published in 1908) as if they were a remote age of barbarism; but nobody knew better than he that Yiddish literature remained "disgraceful" long after the 1860s; that, in fact, those early primitive times he spoke of continued at least up to the mid-1880s. Did not his acquaintance, the Hebrew scholar M. A. Shatskes (1825–1899), as late as 1879 or 1880, sell the manuscript of his Yiddish narrative masterpiece, *Der yidisher farpeysakh* ("Jewish Spring"), for publication under another person's name,[46] "lest his nakedness be uncovered and his honor turned into shame" (to quote Abramovitsh once again)? And was not the writing of Yiddish considered a disgrace, necessitating the use of a mask, even in the early 1880s, when Sholem Aleichem himself decided to try his hand at it?

As a literary beginner, Sholem Rabinovitsh (1859–1916) wrote in Hebrew, and, to some extent, in Russian. His father, a Hebraist of the

° Abramovitsh lived in this commercial center of Volhynia during the first decade of his literary career (1859–1869).

old, loyal school and a moderate *maskil,* deemed him a great future
Hebrew novelist, "a second Mapu." Sholem Rabinovitsh himself was
quite satisfied with his flimsy Hebrew articles (which his father believed "were read all over the world," since they were published in the
respectable magazine *Hatsfira*)[47] until the appearance of a new
Yiddish weekly made him realize that he could write his stories and
feuilletons in the spoken language. He was at the time (1881–1882) so
ignorant of the previous development of Yiddish literature that he believed the new weekly (*Dos yidishe folksblat*—"The Jewish People's
Magazine"; this magazine, founded and edited by the ubiquitous
Tsederboym, appeared between the years 1881–1890) to be the first
Yiddish magazine, and, as he tells us in one of his autobiographical
sketches he was utterly "surprised . . . by the simplicity of the idea":

> Here you have a newspaper, the author thought, printed in such a sim-
> ple language that every Jew—even women—can actually read it! From
> then on this thought would sneak up on him: Can the Hebrew language
> with its fine figurative style give sustenance to anybody except those se-
> lected few who have mastered it? That's one point, and the other: In
> any case, even when you write Hebrew, you think in Yiddish—wouldn't
> it be better for you to write the way you think?
>
> But how can one bring oneself to write in a language which "every-
> body speaks"; still worse—a language in which they print women's
> prayer books? It was then that the pen name Sholem Aleichem was in-
> vented; a pen name behind which the author hid his identity from rela-
> tives and acquaintances, especially when, due to changing circum-
> stances (he married a rich girl), he found himself in the very thick of a
> plutocratic society . . . which regarded even mere contact with writers
> (let alone with Yiddish ones) as a disgrace. . . .[48]

The experience described here is in some ways so similar to the one
described by Abramovitsh in both his autobiographical sketch and in
his story about the origin of the name Mendele Moykher-Sforim, that,
in spite of the distance between two literary generations, the two experiences may be said to follow one pattern, or to develop the different stages of one "progress": a puerile stage of undisturbed Hebraism; a "discovery" of Yiddish as a possible literary medium; a stage
of "incubation" characterized by soul-searching and a consciousness of
crisis; a shift (not necessarily final) to Yiddish under a pen name. Most
writers of the nineteenth century, and even some of the twentieth, had
to make this "progress" before establishing themselves in Yiddish.

There were, of course, significant variations, depending on the times, environment, and personality of each writer concerned. In spite of their remarkable similarity, there are differences between Abramovitsh's and Sholem Aleichem's description of their initiation to Yiddish. First, there is a significant difference in tone. Both writers wrote down their experiences exactly twenty-five years after the initiation had been accomplished (Abramovitsh, 1864–1889; Sholem Aleichem, 1883–1908), but the passage of time and the gratification of literary success did not equally affect their attitudes toward the crisis which preceded it. For Abramovitsh, as we saw, the edge of the crisis was not completely dulled. As we read his record, we realize that his temporary desertion of the holy tongue (for by 1886 he had already resumed his activity as a Hebrew fiction writer) was for him a source of constant embarrassment. Sholem Aleichem treated the crisis as a reminiscence of his literary apprenticeship, an event distanced and objectified enough to be presented as a little comedy. Abramovitsh repeated the thoughts about which he had "communed with his heart" at the time of the crisis with full belief in their continuing validity; Sholem Aleichem's young man discovering that newspapers could be published in a language actually understood by everyday people was meant to look funny. This is both a temperamental and a historical difference. Abramovitsh was not only the more somber man and immeasurably the more thorough Hebraist, he was also the product of a different age, a representative of a generation whose negative attitude toward Yiddish was rooted much deeper than that of the generation of the 1880s.

Another difference between Abramovitsh's and Sholem Aleichem's transition from Hebrew to Yiddish—a difference endowed with a social significance—may be observed in the direction of the pressures that the two writers had to overcome as they reconciled themselves to their new literary medium. Abramovitsh was vulnerable to pressure from one quarter primarily, that of the conservative, loyal Hebrew *maskilim* (whom he characterized in his autobiographical sketch as "our writers, those grammarians who said: Let us strengthen our language, the holy tongue; what have we in common with the common people?").[49] Sholem Aleichem had to face a double opposition: that of his father (representing the traditional Hebraists) and that of the Russianized Jewish bourgeoisie, who by his time had become a powerful social factor in the development of Jewish culture, and a factor scarcely less hostile to secular Yiddish literature than the *hasidim* had been in the first half of the century.[50] It is obvious, however, that Sholem Aleichem carried this double weight much more easily than Abramovitsh had carried his seemingly lighter one. The reason for this is that Abramovitsh was very much attached to the conservatism he found himself bound to defy; he shared many of its ideals and assumptions, and his conflict with it was actually internal, a conflict within his own consciousness. As for Sholem Aleichem, though he played the part of the Russianized gentleman and though he began his career as a genuine Hebraist, neither the aristocratic mannerisms of the former nor the fierce loyalty of the latter were ingrained in his intellectual make-up. In his case, the conflict was largely external, and therefore he could bear opposition with ease and even with grace.

Whatever their differences, the basic relation between the two experiences is, as I said, one of resemblance. This seems to me nowhere more manifest than in the strange air of complete naiveté which pervades the rationalization of the shift to Yiddish as recorded by the two writers (in both cases in the form of a short interior monologue). Both as a writer and as a person, Abramovitsh was the opposite of naive. Yet his reasoning in this matter is so elementary as to seem primitive. So ponderously does he go about discovering what for us is self-evident (that literature should be written in a language accessible to its intended readers), that we cannot help but find him somewhat comic. Sholem Aleichem, as I suggested, was intentionally comic in the dramatization of the conflict. He exaggerated the elements of simple-mindedness in his self-portrait as a young man, perhaps for no better reason than to make the short piece more entertaining. It should also be taken into account that the piece was written for a Russian newspaper, the readers of which could not know much about the rivalry of Hebrew and Yiddish. The author had to simplify his story as much as he could. Still, with all allowances for the occasion of its writing and with all its comic accessories stripped, the piece seems almost unbelievable in its description of the naive discovery of Yiddish as a possible literary medium. It seems unthinkable that to this most Yiddish of Yiddish writers the idea of writing in his native tongue simply did not occur, that he had to discover it in an encounter with an outside influence, and that, when discovered, it surprised him by its simplicity. We have to remind ourselves that this writer, who could not imagine the possibility of a short-cut between his Yiddish thinking and his Hebrew writing, later wrote what many consider the quintessential Yiddish.[51] This radical innocence of the young Sholem Aleichem is perhaps the most significant piece of evidence proving that Yiddish was not a natural literary language for nineteenth-century writers; that, indeed, according to the natural or the unconscious order of things, this language would have been automatically passed over when a writer first meditated on the proper means for literary expression. Yiddish as a literary language remained throughout the century something to be discovered and painfully digested, an "idea," a possibility, a challenge, not a self-evident certainty.

A dim sense of this "abnormality" of Yiddish as a literary medium persisted for a long time, until World War I and even later. It outlived for many decades the final collapse of its ideological infrastructure. A documentation of the shadowy afterlife of this typical nineteenth-century phenomenon involves a study of the complex artistic, linguistic, and ideological presuppositions of twentieth-century Yiddish literature, and must be attempted in a different place. However, one illustration can indicate what part of Abramovitsh's and Sholem Aleichem's difficulties in accepting their roles as Yiddish writers was carried into the twentieth century. Dovid Bergelson, in many respects the most accomplished and significant writer of Yiddish fiction after the three "classics," started his literary apprenticeship just like them not in the language he was to bring to the pinnacle of its stylistic sophistication, but rather in Hebrew and Russian, particularly in the former. In his semi-autobiographical novel *Bam Dnyeper* ("At the Dnieper") he relates how his protagonist Penek, a budding writer, after experimenting with Hebrew, conceives the idea of writing a story in Yiddish. This occurs as he is being reminded of Yankl, his father's coachman, a great hero of Penek's childhood. Recollecting the scene of Yankl's departure from the family's rich "white house," the center of the *shtetl*, after long years of service, Penek decides to make it the core of a story, which he immediately sets out to write. He realizes even before starting that Hebrew will not do as a linguistic medium in this case, and that Yankl's own "simple language" will have to take its place. This shift from Hebrew to Yiddish in itself does not trouble him in the least, for he is completely free from any preconception concerning the alleged unworthiness of Yiddish as a literary tool. What does trouble him, however, is the discovery that Yankl's "simple language" eludes him; that, in fact, it is extremely difficult for him to satisfy his

artistic needs in writing Yiddish and that with him the use of this language goes against the grain. It is much more natural and easy for him
to write Hebrew, a language with which he has grown familiar
through the reading of so many books. Hebrew is always at the tip of
his pen. Quotations from the Bible, Mishna, Midrash, etc. fill his memory "to the point of bursting and spurting with every sneeze of his."
He feels that it is not so much that he knows how to use the Hebrew
words; he is rather being used by them. The Hebrew language itself
speaks freely through him. As far as Yiddish is concerned, Penek de-
jectedly realizes, such intimacy is not to be hoped for. He may, indeed,
learn how to use Yiddish words, but he will never enjoy the felicitous
feeling of "being used by them." He will have to learn to manipulate
them, to write Yiddish "with difficulty." Indeed, Bergelson intimates,
it is precisely this realization that becomes the starting point for the
development of Penek's (i.e., of Bergelson's own) particular style and
artistic mode as a Yiddish writer. What Penek experiences in the first
decade of the twentieth century is different from Abramovitsh's anguish of the 1860s and Sholem Aleichem's compunctions of the early
1880s in as much as ideological and social factors do not play a role (at
least not consciously) in his recoiling from Yiddish. This, however, only
adds emphasis to the unconscious and seemingly inexplicable lack of
familiarity with the language and the unreadiness for its artistic use.
Again, like in the cases of Abramovitsh and Sholem Aleichem, one
should take into consideration the fact that, coming from the greatest
Yiddish artist of his generation, such a confession cannot but have far-
reaching implications.[52]

iv

Abramovitsh's and Sholem Aleichem's suggestive descriptions of
their initiation to Yiddish literature may explain or set within the correct context another phenomenon related to the general usage of pen
names by nineteenth-century writers but of an even wider significance: the conspicuous lack of a sense of tradition and continuity in
the literary consciousness of these writers. Here Abramovitsh's and
Sholem Aleichem's experiences differ sharply from that of Bergelson's
autobiographical Penek. Trying to recapture the character and the
speech of Yankl the Coachman in Yankl's own "simple language,"
Penek has at his disposal at least one established literary precedent on

which he can draw: Sholem Aleichem's popular sketches of *shtetl* life. True, he rejects the Sholem Aleichem manner after having experimented with it for a while. "It is too easy," he feels, too "simple" to suit his complex vision, and he must find a new and "difficult" way of writing Yiddish.[53] This, however, is no more than a characteristic instance of the dialectics of "convention and revolt" in literary development, and it is through these dialectics that the sense of literary tradition is most concretely realized. Young Penek is certainly not devoid of this sense, when he starts his difficult apprenticeship as a Yiddish writer. Most of his nineteenth-century predecessors were.

As for the older Yiddish literature of the Renaissance, nineteenth-century Yiddish writers could not derive from it any sense of tradition or continuity. On the contrary, they vehemently denied any connection with it and referred to it with utter contempt. Some of them condescendingly tolerated the Yiddish "women's prayer books" and the *Tsene urene* (the popular adaptation of the narrative sections of the Torah designed for women who could not read the Hebrew original);[54] but the literature of legendary epic and romance, the *Bovo-bukh*, *Tsenture-venture*, etc., strongly offended their maskilic sensibilities with its heady blend of "superstitions," supernatural occurrences, and "impossible" plots. So did the popular genre of prose and partly rhymed novelettes (*Mayse-bikhlekh*), which still flourished at the time. Even A. M. Dik, who himself wrote very much in the tradition of the *Mayse-bikhlekh*, and is regarded by many as a writer standing on the border between the old and the new Yiddish literatures,[55] branded the older popular fiction not only nonsensical but also immoral.[56] Abramovitsh let his Mendele carry this fiction in his wagon and make numerous sarcastic comments on its superstitious, nonsensical plots, as well as on its popularity.[57] Sholem Aleichem did not have one good word for it either. He associated it with whatever he regarded as worthless in contemporary Yiddish literature. (For example, he accused the popular Shaykevitsh of undermining the efforts of Abramovitsh, Linetski, Goldfaden, and Dik, who had renovated Yiddish literature by carrying it away from the old genres, replacing the *Tsene urene* by "a living literature," the *Bovo-bukh* by the novel, the hasidic hagiography by real poetry, the liturgy by satire. With Shaykevitsh Yiddish literature allegedly relapsed into its old, worthless manner.)[58] Perets was the first important writer who tried both to associate himself with the tradition of the older literature of romance and legend and to rehabilitate it, but in that, as in so many other matters, he broke away from the ideology and thematics of nineteenth-century Yiddish literature.

If the old literature, written in the so-called middle-Yiddish, could not provide nineteenth-century writers with any feeling of historical depth, hasidic writing was for most of them (as we shall see in the following chapter) nothing but a target for explosion, a potent vehicle used by their cultural enemies for their anti-Enlightenment purposes. However, even their own maskilic literature did not strike nineteenth-century writers as a continuous, historical phenomenon. Starting in the last decade of the eighteenth century (with two antitraditional comedies), the so-called modern Yiddish literature was developed with some regularity throughout the nineteenth century. Both personal and literary contacts between earlier and later writers can everywhere be discerned.[59] In fact, the historian would find it a relatively easy task to draw fairly straight lines of development along the history of literature throughout the century and would even have enough evidence to establish some traditions: for example, a tradition of comedies, beginning with the two bourgeois comedies written in Germany toward the end of the eighteenth century (and usually regarded as opening the canon of modern Yiddish literature) and leading up to the comedies of A. Goldfaden and Sholem Aleichem, written over a hundred years later. Yet, until the mid-1880s it is with difficulty that we trace any consciousness of the existence of a Yiddish "literature." There seems to have been no sense of accumulation of literary experience. On the rare occasions when Yiddish writers of the 1830s and the 1840s were mentioned during the second half of the century (for example, in the magazine *Kol-mevaser*, which appeared between 1862 and 1871), they were paid tributes of personal friendship rather than acknowledged as literary ancestors,[60] and their works, which were never referred to in terms of historical development and relationship, were occasionally cited as proof of the respectability of Yiddish.[61] No real interest in these works can be detected before 1888. Debts to the efforts and achievements of predecessors were almost never acknowledged. In 1841 Aksenfeld stated that he was the first who saw the need to combat the influence of the *hasidim* by propagandist Yiddish fiction, ignoring the fact that this need had been noted, and to some extent even met before him by some writers of the Galician *Haskala*.[62] In 1861 Dik presented as his own innovation the idea that some sort of enlightened literature should be written in Yiddish for those who knew no other language.[63]

Abramovitsh explained the difficulties involved in his decision to write Yiddish thus:

> the Yiddish language was in my time [i.e., the early 1860s] an empty vessel; nothing was written in it but babbling, nonsensical and misguided compositions, the products of stammering simpletons, people without a name; and these were read by the women and the lower classes, while the rest of the people, though they could read no other language, were ashamed to read them lest their foolishness be revealed in public.[64]

Consequently, he described his own *Kleyn mentshele* as "the cornerstone of the new Yiddish literature," [65] ignoring Dik's numerous novelettes. (It is perhaps at Dik that he aimed his venomous remark concerning the "stammering simpletons, people without a name." Dik published many of his works either anonymously or only under his initials.) Abramovitsh did not see fit to mention as an exception even Aksenfeld's *Shterntikhl*, a novel which is supposed to resemble his own writing.[66]

In 1876 Y. M. Lifshits (1828–1878), the first modern Yiddish lexicographer and the most ardent propagator of the literary use of Yiddish among the *maskilim*, complained that Yiddish literature was "worth nothing" and that its writers, whom he characterized as "either coarse, ignorant fellows or jesters," wanted "not to earn their pay but to cheat it out of you";[67] and this in spite of the fact that by 1876 Abramovitsh, an acquaintance of Lifshits', had already published such works of fiction as *Fishke der krumer* ("Fishke the Lame," 1869) and *Di klyatshe* ("The Nag," 1873); A. Goldfaden (1840–1908) had published *Dos yidele* ("The Little Jew," 1866), his best collection of poems, and *Di mume Sosye* ("Aunt Sosye," 1869), his first full-fledged comedy, and Linetski had scored enormous success with *Dos poylishe yingl* (1867–1869). As late as 1881–1882, young Sholem Aleichem was unaware that Yiddish was not only "a language in which they print women's prayer books," [68] but also a language of some seventy years of modern literary use. Sheer ignorance was only in part the reason for this. Even when it existed (and in some cases, such as Abramovitsh's or Lifshits', there could have been no ignorance at all), it was a mere symptom of something much more significant. The crucial point was

that Yiddish writers did not feel their activity to have any historical
relevance, in the sense that they did not regard it as an activity with a
"past" and a "future." They saw no continuity between their predecessors and themselves and, in many cases, acknowledged no connection between themselves and their contemporaries. As late as 1888,
when this attitude was already undergoing a sweeping change,
Abramovitsh was much displeased with Sholem Aleichem for mentioning him (with Linetski and Goldfaden) as one (the first) of "the
three giants" of Yiddish letters and asked him "not to group me with
such writers with whom I do not care to mix." [69] This reflected not
only his formidable arrogance but also a traditional streak of separa-
tism characteristic of many of the older Yiddish writers, who were not
accustomed to think of themselves as members of a literary community. In the same year the novelist Y. Dinezon (1856–1919), in whose
character there was no trace of haughtiness, confessed to the sin of a
habitual disrespect for an ignorance of his contemporaries' achievements. In an article which was actually the first historical survey of
nineteenth-century Yiddish literature, he admitted his insufficient
knowledge of his subject matter, adding the following explanation:

> The fate of our Yiddish is the exact opposite of the fate of the Hebrew
> language. Those who write in the holy tongue intend their articles and
> books to be read solely by Hebraists, i.e., by people who are writers and
> *maskilim* in their own right. With Yiddish it is the other way round. No
> Yiddish writer expects his book to be criticized in another's book; no
> one expects to be either honored or ridiculed by a fellow writer. The
> truth is that Yiddish writers read Yiddish less than all other people do,
> and till now I myself did not behave better in this respect than anyone
> else. Therefore, I simply lack the information necessary for selecting
> from those books which have appeared in Yiddish during the last several
> years those better ones which are worth criticism.[70]

The fact that until the late 1880s the very existence of a modern
Yiddish literature (or, for that matter, of any Yiddish literature) was
generally ignored, and that the continuity and development of the
literary use of Yiddish did not surface into consciousness even in the
minds of the best Yiddish writers, must be remembered in our discussion. We cannot afford to overlook it if we want to achieve a historical
understanding of an age which seemed remote and half legendary
even when its foremost representatives were still alive. By ignoring it

we may be led to an all too easy imposition of our own social, aesthetic, and linguistic premises on a literary situation to which they are foreign. Many modern readers of nineteenth-century Yiddish literature, including critics and historians, were so thoroughly conditioned by the ideology as well as by the reality of the normalization of Yiddish language and literature, that they were all but incapable of pursuing the far-reaching implications of a situation in which both language and literature lacked cultural status and accepted norms: yet this was the state of Yiddish literature up to the mid- or late 1880s. Most readers and critics of the works of "Mendele" (Abramovitsh), for instance, were so intimately acquainted with the "tradition" of Mendele, with the notion that "Mendele," the "grandfather" of both modern Yiddish and modern Hebrew literatures, had founded the modern Jewish art of prose fiction, prescribed its norms, and ensured its artistic standard, that they could not imagine a historical reality where no consciousness of norms and standards existed and where the very idea of a "tradition" was an impossibility. The anachronistic approach to nineteenth-century Yiddish literature, especially to its "classics" (the works of Abramovitsh, Sholem Aleichem, etc.), is so prevalent, that it is worthwhile to stop for a short examination of the way in which the consciousness of the Yiddish literary tradition was intentionally created in the 1880s. Of course, this stupendous task of endowing Yiddish literature with a past as well as with an air of normalcy would not have been carried out, if the times were not ripe for the reconsideration of the status of Yiddish.[71] Still, it should be realized how conscious and artificial (in a sense bordering on the "artistic") were the pseudo-historical constructions, forged in the 1880s and accepted in a very short time—a decade or two—as historically unquestionable.

The "tradition" was created in the 1880s by a few writers and journalists (such as M. Spektor, the historian S. Dubnov, who was at the time publishing literary reviews under the pen name "Criticus," the formerly Hebrew *maskil* E. Shulman, and others) who wrote mainly for *Dos yidishe folksblat*, for the two literary almanacs, which began to appear toward the end of the decade (Spektor's *Hoyz-fraynt* and Sholem Aleichem's *Folks-biblyotek*) and for some Jewish-Russian newspapers. However, its artistic semblance of truth and its wide and immediate acceptance owe so much to the methodical zeal and the unique talent for suggestiveness and mythmaking of one writer, that one may almost say that it was created singlehandedly by Sholem Alei-chem.

Sholem Aleichem was the first Yiddish writer who felt a strong need to regard his literary activity as a part of a historical entity. We saw that in 1881–1882, just before he began to write Yiddish, he knew next to nothing of the existence of a Yiddish literature. It was only after he became a Yiddish writer that he discovered in his father-in-law's library the slim volumes of Dik, Etinger, Abramovitsh, Linetski, Shatskes, et al. However, his thirst for literary status, for precedent, tradition, and good order was extremely pressing, and so he set out quite consciously to create them. Take, for instance, this comparison made in a review he wrote in 1884:

> In Russian literature the names of Gogol and Turgenyev will live for-ever, for the former was a satirist and the latter a humorist, and both were great poets. Our poor Yiddish literature, too, has its humorist (Abramovitsh) and its satirist (Linetski)—of course, on a smaller scale.[72]

Here Sholem Aleichem was taking a revolutionary step. The "poverty" and modest scale of Yiddish literature notwithstanding, it was pro-nounced a literature comparable to great literatures and susceptible to aesthetic and literary categorizations. Above all else, Abramovitsh and Linetski emerged in this comparison of Yiddish with Russian literature as well-known historical figures. Sholem Aleichem made them seem so just by referring to them as if their literary presence were self-evident. This he continued to do in the many articles and critical *feuilletons* he wrote during the following four years. The air of a well-established literary tradition and of a lively literary milieu is conveyed in every one of these articles. Writers are treated in them not only as if they were known and accepted as grand public figures but also as if their places in a literary hierarchy had been long recognized and agreed upon. Phrases like "our greatest Yiddish writer" (i.e., Abramovitsh), "our foremost Yiddish satirist" (i.e., Linetski),[73] "the three giants" (Abramovitsh, Linetski, Goldfaden),[74] or the recognizably lower-graded "our pleasant Yiddish writer" (i.e., Dik)[75] were employed here abundantly and promiscuously, almost as epithets. Even historical terms such as "the age of Linetski"[76] were produced on the spur of the moment and with great ease.

In 1888 Sholem Aleichem published two critical articles of great historical interest. One, "Shomer's mishpet" ("Shomer's Trial"), a pamphlet in the form of a dramatized trial, denounced with sharp acerbity the popularity of the prolific N. M. Shaykevitsh. The other, "Der yidisher dales in di beste verke fun unzere folks-shriftshteler" ("Jewish Poverty in the Best Works of Our Popular Writers"),[77] discussed and highly praised works by Abramovitsh, Goldfaden, Dik, Linetski, Spektor, and Shatskes. In both articles, literary judgment was passed according to the criteria of a primitive "realism." Sholem Aleichem branded Shaykevitsh a *romanmakher* ("fabricator of novels") and a writer of *shund* ("trash") because instead of the reality of Jewish life, his novels were filled with facile daydreams, improbable fabulae, and sentimental happy endings. He praised Abramovitsh, Linetski, et al. for remaining loyal to reality, which in the case of Eastern European Jews meant poverty. The two articles were interrelated by yet another critical idea, which, to our discussion, surpasses that of social realism in importance: the idea of literary legitimacy. Sholem Aleichem found it insufficient to accuse Shaykevitsh of bad writing; he had to pronounce him a literary usurper. In his eyes, Shaykevitsh's sin consisted not only in deluding his readers with cheap romanticization of life but also in drawing their attention and their financial support away from writers who deserved it. Consequently, what Shaykevitsh produced was not only poor but also illegitimate literature. The disparagement of Shaykevitsh went hand in hand with the establishment of "the great tradition" in Yiddish fiction. Thus, Sholem Aleichem introduced the idea of an "establishment" to Yiddish literature and for the first time forced readers and writers alike to make value judgments in terms of hierarchical groupings. These terms were so readily absorbed, that in a short time the groupings he created and the values he recommended seemed to be part of the reality of nineteenth-century Yiddish literature, whereas, as we have seen, almost nothing of the sort had really existed before him. It should therefore be emphasized that Abramovitsh did not at all approve of Sholem Aleichem's groupings, and he even dissociated himself from the attack on Shaykevitsh.[78] Linetski vehemently refused to regard himself as a member of a group, second in rank to Abramovitsh. The older Yiddish writers, whom Sholem Aleichem organized into a hierarchical tradition, clung to their individualism, but they could not undo what had already been done. Like old frontier farmers who found themselves in the midst of a growing town they either readjusted themselves to the new reality (Abramovitsh) or wasted the rest of their lives in grumbling (Linetski).

Sholem Aleichem created the historical consciousness of Yiddish literature by different methods. The publication of the *Folks-biblyotek* is often cited as his major contribution in this direction, but this is not wholly true. The aim of the *Biblyotek* was to present Yiddish literature as possessing all the accessories of a normal world of letters. Considerable editorial efforts were made also to present it as having a tradition, to evoke a sense of its past. Sholem Aleichem urged older writers to contribute their literary reminiscences;[79] he made it his policy to publish the "underground" Yiddish works of the earlier part of the century;[80] he commissioned for the *Biblyotek* the first "History" of Yiddish literature, etc.[81] As an editor he was certainly exploring the unknown past of Yiddish literature, but he was not alone in doing so. In 1888, even before the appearance of the *Biblyotek*, Spektor made inroads in the same direction in his *Hoyz-fraynt*, a literary almanac, which although less ambitious and comprehensive, did not differ fundamentally from that of Sholem Aleichem.[82] The *Biblyotek* itself, a great innovation though it was, does not represent the unique contribution of Sholem Aleichem to what may be described as the "institutionalization" of Yiddish letters. That contribution he made not as an editor and a publisher but as a myth maker. Sholem Aleichem dramatized the existence of Yiddish literature by providing it with "good" and "evil" characters, a villain (Shaykevitsh) and a hero (Abramovitsh). The legend of Abramovitsh as the "grandfather" of Yiddish letters, which Sholem Aleichem launched when Abramovitsh was fifty-two years old (he himself was then twenty-nine years old) can be considered the basis of our conception of modern Yiddish literature as a historical institution. He was generally inclined to refer to his favorite writers as old men. Only twenty years Linetski's junior, he described him, on the eve of the latter's fiftieth birthday, as "our old veteran" and expressed his admiration for the energy manifested by "our old Yiddish writers." [83] People scarcely in their fifties he described as if they were tottering octogenarians. In this he camouflaged even from himself the shortness and scantiness of the tradition he was fabricating.

By the adoption of Abramovitsh as a "grandfather," however, he gained for Yiddish literature much more than the dignity of old age; he supplied it with a living symbol of authority and legitimacy. The grandfather myth obviously involved myths of a grandson and of an inheritance, in short, a dynasty. Once Abramovitsh was accepted as a reigning sire, it went without saying that only his legitimate progeny were to inherit the kingdom; moreover, it also became evident that a kingdom did exist; a kingdom which had a past and was looking toward a future.

Sholem Aleichem chose to bring the grandfather myth to public attention after working on it privately for quite some time[84] in the dedication of his novel *Stempenyu* "to his dearly beloved grandfather, Reb Mendele Moykher-Sforim" (1888; *Stempenyu* was published as a supplement to the first volume of the *Folks-biblyotek*). In this long dedication—one of the most important documents in the history of modern Yiddish literature—he made every effort to convey the idea that he was Abramovitsh's recognized disciple; moreover, he created the image of Abramovitsh not as the propagator of natural science, as he has been known at the beginning of his literary career, or as the biting satirist he eventually came to be considered, but as the supreme artist, the austere and patient craftsman, and above all else, the old, wise wizard, the Olympian of Yiddish literature. This image of Abramovitsh fixed itself in the consciousness of readers and critics as no other image was ever to do. Many of the old writers (particularly the once-successful Linetski) could not regard this enthronement with equanimity, but their objections, which sometimes reached the point of frenzy, were of no avail. The myth of the grandfather was too pleasant, too flattering, too vital to be given up. It met a spiritual need. By supplying it Sholem Aleichem made readers and writers suddenly conscious of the sovereignty, the expanse, and the potentialities of their culture. The consciousness of history, real or imagined, often makes history.

Sholem Aleichem's ingenious fabrications (Grandfather Mendele is as much a creation as his fictional Tevye the Dairyman and Menakhem-Mendl) took root immediately. What was unimaginable in 1885 was taken for granted in 1895. In 1880 Yiddish writers did not suspect that they had a history; by the early 1890s they already had produced one "classic" writer; before the century ended *The History of Yiddish Literature in the Nineteenth Century* was written in English for American readers by a Harvard instructor.[85] This sudden emergence of self-consciousness is perhaps the most important factor in the change that took place in modern Yiddish literature during the 1890s; a change which brought its first, formative epoch to an end. Usually, the launching of the new epoch is connected with the name of Y. L. Perets, who is supposed to have introduced the "modern" element to Yiddish let-

ters. Perets' modern revolution was real enough, as we shall have opportunity to realize, but it was not the only revolution which took
place at the time. Sholem Aleichem revolutionized Yiddish literature
as much as Perets did. His, however, was a "conservative" revolution,
i.e., his revolutionary idea was that there existed in Yiddish something
worth conserving, prolonging, developing. In many respects Sholem
Aleichem's revolution went much deeper and further than Perets'.
What it initiated—the grandfather myth, the semblance of tradition,
the sense of the past—still exerts an overwhelming influence on
Yiddish criticism (with results not entirely beneficial, as I shall suggest
later on). Perets' innovations have long been outgrown.

For the purposes of our discussion Sholem Aleichem's historiciza-
tion of Yiddish literature is of utmost importance. If we study it as a
reaction to the state of Yiddish literature as Sholem Aleichem found it,
it can be highly edifying, but we must learn to beware of it, of the false
order and normalcy it attributed to what had been both disorderly and
abnormal. As a piece of historical evidence, the legend of the grandfather is invaluable; as a historical interpretation it is a distorting
reflection. It would be perfectly legitimate to make a historical distinction between readers and writers who still remembered the reality of
Yiddish literature before 1888 and those who grew up after 1888 and
accepted the legend of Abramovitsh the grandfather as a reality. The
"pre-grandfather" people retained a sense of the historical flatness of
modern Yiddish literature; the "post-grandfather" ones often treated
this literature as a grand historical institution. Consequently, they
could not in many cases be expected to understand the abnormality of
nineteenth-century Yiddish writing. Perets, a pre-grandfather man and
himself a newly made "classic" writer, opened a lecture on Yiddish literature thus:

> It is perhaps ridiculous to lecture on a literature as young and poor as
> the Yiddish one. For one hundred rubles, perhaps for less, you can pur-
> chase all the books which this literature has produced, and they will all
> find a place in one bookcase, and not a very large one at that. It is a lit-
> erature which has only one tombstone in the graveyard (A. M. Dik). The
> oldest writer after Dik [Mendele] has recently taken part, together with
> the youngest among his great-grandchildren, in a literary soirée in
> Odessa. . . .[86]

This lecture was given in 1910. In 1908, however, Perets had to exert all his influence on the younger littérateurs, scholars, and dilettantes who had convened in the town of Tshernovits for the first Yiddish *shprakh-konferents* (language convention) to deter them from proclaiming Yiddish the national language of the Jewish people and its literature the national Jewish literature.[87] These younger people saw nothing ridiculous in treating Yiddish literature as an authoritative cultural establishment. How could they? Wasn't Perets himself, their leader, a symbol of paternal authority? And the "grandfather," who could not or would not come to the convention, wasn't he a venerable symbol of a great literary past? (They cabled him a telegram phrased like a message addressed by the House of Lords to an old, bed-ridden king.) It is hard to conceive of a "classic" writer employing a language that was not associated with the idea of art; it is almost impossible to sense the reality of an inferiority or a disgrace experienced by a regal "grandfather." That is why the very commitment to Yiddish of the writers we are about to discuss must be emphasized, and why the unnaturalness of the language as a literary medium in the nineteenth century must be firmly grasped as a background for our argument.

CHAPTER TWO

A LANGUAGE AS CALIBAN

PROSPERO: . . . Come on,
We'll visit Caliban my slave, who never
Yields us kind answer.
MIRANDA: 'Tis a villain, sir,
I do not love to look on.
PROSPERO: But, as 'tis,
We cannot miss him: he does make our fire,
Fetch in our wood; and serve in offices
That profit us. What ho! slave! Caliban!
Thou earth, thou! speak!

(*The Tempest*, Act I, Scene II, 307–14)

DESPITE ITS BEING the native tongue of Eastern European Jewry, Yiddish was not—until the 1890s—a "natural" medium for conscious artistic use. If we have to employ terms such as "natural" or "unnatural" in this connection at all, then we must pronounce Yiddish as "unnatural" a literary medium as Hebrew was at the time—though in a completely different, perhaps in a diametrically opposed and complementary way. For a writer, the decision to choose Yiddish as his medium was much harder than the decision to employ the stiffened and often unresponsive holy tongue. While the latter decision would at least secure for him a membership in an intellectual community of sorts and connect him with a great and hallowed literary tradition, the former would isolate him, place him outside any recognized literary framework, sever him from all national poetic traditions he cared to associate himself with, and drive him into what seemed to be an intellectual wasteland. Hebrew writers could not expect the response of a wide audience, but they were keenly aware of their historical role as the founders of a "new" Hebrew literature, which they regarded as revolutionary and at the same time restorative. They were rebeling against the immediate literary past in order to restore the greatness of a tradition which began with the Bible itself and which included the glorious "Golden Age" of the Hebrew medieval poetry written in Spain and in Provence.[1] Yiddish writers, we saw, had no use either for the immediate or for the remote past of their own literature, which they seldom bothered to read and learn. Nor did they have much respect for their contemporaries or, indeed, for their own literary efforts. Thus the decision to write literature in Yiddish was a conscious and painful act of self-commitment, which determined to a considerable extent not only the social status and affiliations of the writer concerned but also his literary and artistic identity.

Such a phenomenon must have had its roots deep in the social and cultural history of European Jews, and to extricate them from their subterranean past is not an easy task. Nor is it the proper goal of this study, since it calls for the analytical methods and scholarly equipment of sociolinguistics and of the history of ideas, while the aims and methods of this study are those of literary history and criticism. Nevertheless, I intend to discuss that aspect of the negative attitude toward Yiddish, characteristic of nineteenth-century Jewish intellectuals, which has a direct bearing on the literary character and quality of nineteenth-century Yiddish fiction. I do not believe that a relevant critical analysis of this fiction can be attempted without venturing some answer to the question of why and how these authors felt constrained, isolated, even degraded, when they came to write in the language they and their readers understood best.

An answer to these questions should, I think, be sought in the conception of literature and in the linguistic-aesthetic assumptions which these authors shared with all the adherents of Jewish Enlightenment. I do not propose here to take sides in the controversy between those historians who regard modern Yiddish literature as originating exclusively from the Enlightenment movement (M. Viner, Max Erik, et al.) and those who find some of its origins in the writings of the *hasidim* as well as in a literary "twilight zone" between the orthodoxy and the *Haskala* (Sh. Niger, Z. Reyzen, et al.).[2] The contention that only through the ideology of the *Haskala* did modern Yiddish literature come to regard itself in literary terms as a separate entity would, it seems to me, be commonly agreed upon.

The fact mentioned first in this connection by most historians is the fierce opposition to Yiddish of the eighteenth-century fathers of the Jewish Enlightenment in Germany. This opposition carried the full authority of the venerated Moses Mendelssohn (1729–1786), the fountainhead of the *Haskala* and its undisputed hero at least until the 1870s.[3] This opposition was propagated and spread by the members of the Mendelssohnian circle, who vilified Yiddish as a linguistic hodgepodge, a jargon that barred Jews from contact with their neighbors and doomed them to isolation from civilization. Being nothing more than disfigured German blended with disfigured Hebrew, it made them the laughingstock of Europe. Animosity continued to gain momentum throughout the nineteenth century, even as the language was driven from all but the most backward and rustic circles of the German-Jewish population. While Yiddish was losing its last hold in Germany, German-Jewish intellectuals developed their antipathy to it to a high pitch. The great historian H. Graetz, in his *History of the Jews*,[4] assigned to Yiddish the part of a minor but obnoxious villain in the historical drama of Judaism and would not hear of translating his *magnum opus* into this hateful dialect, which he labeled "a half-bestial language."[5]

Such attitudes put enormous pressure on any *maskil* who was considering the possibility of employing Yiddish for literary purposes. In fact, it drove the nineteenth-century Yiddish adherents of the Mendelssohnian Enlightenment to an absurd position: they were striving to humanize and Europeanize the Jewish people through a linguistic medium that was itself the very symbol of medieval Jewish segregation and isolation; they were struggling to spread the "light" of the *Haskala* through a language branded as one of the powers of darkness and, as such, marked for extinction.

The Yiddish writers of the nineteenth century regarded themselves primarily as teachers of the people and referred to their literary activity in educational terms, but it was precisely on educational grounds that the members of the Mendelssohnian school found Yiddish most objectionable. The objection to Yiddish as an educational tool was one of the main incentives for Mendelssohn to undertake a German translation of the Bible, an enterprise which, as he says in a letter, had not been a part of his original "life's plan."[6] He began it when he realized that without such a German Bible, his own children would have to be taught the Torah (i.e., the Pentateuch; Jewish education traditionally began with the study of some parts of the Pentateuch) either with the help of the old Yiddish translations, which he found intolerable, or of Christian translations, which did not conform to the *masora* (the Jewish tradition of the biblical text). Later on, when the translation was already well under way, he was persuaded that by presenting the Jewish people with "a better translation and with a better commentary than those they already possessed," he might be of use at least to "a considerable part" of the nation; with the help of such a work they would be able to make "a first step toward civilization [*Kultur*]; that civilization from which unfortunately they were so far removed that one might almost give up any hope for their improvement." [7] The "first step toward civilization" was obviously equated by Mendelssohn with the elimination of Yiddish from Jewish education.

If in his public utterances Mendelssohn, always a soft-spoken man, was not explicit enough in this matter, his disciples certainly made up for his reticence. In their contributions to the raging controversy that soon developed around the biblical translation and commentary, they made education in Yiddish a target for their fiercest attacks. One of them stated that such an education must result in intellectual as well as moral corruption. Since Yiddish lacked rules and grammar and was under no formal discipline, no one educated in it "could have a true concept of anything whatever." Yiddish education left its victims barred not only from true methods of cognition but from all virtues and "true" religion as well: "all rational understanding, true piety, and genuine morality rest on clear and precise concepts," and those could not be attained without a "methodical study" of a disciplined and regulated language.[8] No wonder that writers whose professed aspiration was to spread "true methods of cognition," "true religion" (as opposed to the mystical religiosity of the *hasidim*), and "genuine morality" (in which European manners were understood to be subsumed) would turn to this allegedly degenerate, or even pernicious, language with much doubt and uneasiness.

Of course, in Eastern Europe maskilic tactics had to undergo a change. For many *maskilim* the very fact that they lived among Yiddish-speaking people, had themselves been raised as Yiddish speakers, and were forced to use the language for purposes of daily communication, was an additional reason for despising it and resenting its constant presence. Nonetheless, the more realistic among them as well as the so-called more democratic (i.e., those concerned with the enlightenment of the "masses" and not only with that of the middle class) had to concede that here Yiddish could not be immediately done away with, as in Germany. The sentence Mendelssohn and his disciples had passed on it would have to be at least temporarily suspended. This does not mean that they changed their basic attitude toward Yiddish. There is little evidence to support the contention of the historian R. Mahler that the attitude toward Yiddish grew more positive the further the *Haskala* movement spread from its original German centers into Poland and Russia, so that one can clearly distinguish between the attitude of the Ukrainian and Polish *maskilim* (who lived where German was neither an official language nor one widely known), on the one hand, and that of the German and Galician *maskilim* on the other.[9] On the contrary, it is quite easy to document a contradictory hypothesis and prove that, as the *Haskala* moved into the great concentrations of the Eastern European Jewish population, where it became more militant, the resentment against Yiddish gained in acerbity, for the "mixed language" was felt to be an obstacle much more real and resistant than it had been in Germany twenty or thirty years earlier. Eastern European *maskilim*, however, simply understood that the circumstances of the Jewish masses in the backward, more than half-feudal countries of Poland and Russia were completely different from those of the German Jews. Self-concentrated in the midst of Slavic peasant people and unexposed (as Mendelssohn's German-Jewish bourgeoisie had already been) to contacts with the non-Jewish middle class, these masses remained unapproachable in any language but Yiddish. Although Mendelssohn's German Bible (with its supplementary Hebrew *be'ur*, or commentary) was everywhere to some extent effective in helping people make "the first step toward civilization," it was so only in individual cases (in spite of the fact that during the "liberal" era of Alexander II the Russian government, under the influence of the assimilated Jewish intelligentsia, made an effort to force Mendelssohn's translation on the *melamdim*, the traditional Jewish teachers, with the purpose of replacing the Yiddish translations of the Bible).[10] The masses knew it only as *treyf-posl* (forbidden, unholy books), read by scoffers and apostates, and, on occasion, the object of a semi-ritual burial (along with the holy text, it could not be burnt). German, therefore, remained a foreign, unknown language as far as the majority of Eastern European Jews was concerned. Hebrew, especially in southern Russia and in Galicia (where knowledge of it was much rarer than in the north), was accessible only to a very small part of the Jewish population. For a more extensive audience, Yiddish had to be resorted to—and that fact had to be faced. Realizing this, however, did not make the actual employment of the despised language any easier. A German-Jewish physician of the Mendelssohnian era who settled among Eastern European Jews and adapted in Yiddish a popular book on household medicine (*ca.* 1790) frankly acknowledged the painful-

ness of the situation. In order to write the book, he says in the introduction, he had to wait for his language to get sufficiently corrupted;
he had "to teach himself bad German." Enlightened German Jews, he
anticipated, would ridicule his book; of the Hebraists he asked patience and forgiveness. He was ashamed of himself, but what was he to
do? He wanted to save his ignorant coreligionists in Poland "from an
untimely death." [11]

Other *maskilim* treated the situation in a more cool-headed and
less apologetic manner, and the possibility exists that a few of them
(such as the playwright Etinger), while they did not challenge the
Mendelssohnian anathema, were not *in fact* as hostile toward Yiddish
as their ideology demanded. This possibility exists, for instance, in the
case of M. Lefin-Satanover (1749–1826), the central figure of the *Haskala* movement and literature in Galicia and the western parts of the
Ukraine at the end of the eighteenth century and the beginning of the
nineteenth. Lefin, who was born in Podolia, spent four years in Berlin
(in the 1780s), where he saw the light under the auspices of the great
Mendelssohn himself and mixed with the members of the circle as
they were translating the Bible and writing the *be'ur*. He was not the
only "Polish" (i.e., Eastern European) Jew thus privileged, but it was
he who went back to the east with the conscious intention of bringing into its thick darkness the light of Berlin. This he faithfully and diligently did all his life, producing numerous popular books (most of
them translations and adaptations) and attracting to himself all the
young *maskilim* of Galicia, where he spent most of his creative years.[12]
Almost all of Lefin's books were written in Hebrew, in which language
he proved a great stylist and an innovator of far-reaching influence.
However, from the very start, he was himself convinced and also convinced some of his disciples that in order to combat the spreading influence of the *hasidim* and their mystical doctrine, which he abhorred
and regarded as a great danger to the mental stability and moral fiber
of the Jewish people, something like a maskilic Yiddish literature
would have to be created. Since most hasidic authors used Yiddish
without compunction, thus attracting to their lore and legend the attention of an ever-growing audience, the *maskilim* too had to resort to
Yiddish. Lefin arrived at this conclusion as early as 1792, when he recommended, among other measures intended to "enlighten the Jewish
people of Poland and correct their mores," [13] the publication of a
Yiddish maskilic magazine and the development of a satirical literature

in Yiddish, which would undo the pernicious influence of the hasidic hagiographical literature. This did not necessarily indicate any significant deviation from Mendelssohn's attitude toward Yiddish. Lefin insisted that the use of Yiddish by the *maskilim* was to be temporary, as the language would in time be superseded by Polish, the study of which, he advised, should be made obligatory by the Polish state. (His recommendations, it should be remembered, were made a few years before the dissolution of this state by its final partition. They were, in fact, submitted to the members of the Polish *seym*, who throughout the early 1790s were discussing ways and means for enhancing the cohesion of the Polish population and were ready to consider methods for "improving" and "enlightening," i.e., polonizing, the Jews.)[14] It would seem that Lefin recommended nothing more than a temporary change of tactics. However, the claim has been made, and with growing persistence and polemic acrimony, that he went far beyond that; that in fact his attitude toward Yiddish was thoroughly "positive."

Lefin conceived of a grand project, which was both a continuation and, in a way, a negation of Mendelssohn's translation: he wanted to supply the Jewish masses of Poland and the Ukraine with a new Yiddish translation of the Bible, or at least of some parts of it, a venture which greatly scandalized the more conservative Mendelssohnians and caused such a furor, that he dared publish no more than the Book of Proverbs (1814), although he had completed in manuscript the translation of Psalms, Job, and Ecclesiastes as well.[15] Moreover, Lefin developed quite consciously a new approach to the problems which the translation of the Scripture involved. He shied away not only from the style of the old Yiddish translations (the ones Mendelssohn and his disciples had hated so much) but also from the influence of modern literary German, contending that the idiom suitable for the translation was the modern, thoroughly slavicized Eastern European one (or as he significantly phrased it, "our Jewish tongue as it is spoken among us today").[16] The surviving portions of his translations prove that he was also able to put this "theory" into practice with brilliant success, for he undoubtedly possessed that rare talent and stylistic sensitivity which are indispensable for a successful rendering of a "classical," celebrated text into a lively, contemporary idiom. For these feats Lefin was canonized by twentieth-century Yiddishist scholars and critics as the founder of modern Yiddish literature and the initiator—in theory and practice—of the literary use of "authentic" (i.e., non-Germanized, Eastern European, idiomatic) Yiddish. This was why the assertion that Lefin did not differ significantly from other *maskilim* in his evaluation of Yiddish and its place in Jewish culture, when recently made by a well-known scholar,[17] caused something like a shock and triggered heated polemics.[18] The details of these polemics need not concern us here. The overall impression, however, is that the pedestal some scholars are trying to erect for Lefin as the forerunner of modern Yiddishism seems to consist of insufficient, flimsy bits of evidence cemented with much historical wishful thinking.[19] There can be no doubt that *post factum* Lefin was one of the great pioneers of the literary use of modern Yiddish and that to minimize his achievement in this particular area of modern Jewish culture, as some ultra-Zionist historians do,[20] is absurd. However, to consider him as the conscious proponent of the cultivation and literalization of Yiddish is to attribute to him intentions he probably could not have had, intentions quite alien to the whole context of the *Haskala* movement at the time. Those who point at the high quality of his biblical translations as proof of his "positive" intention confuse ideological intention with aesthetic results and illustrate a characteristic misunderstanding of many great achievements in nineteenth-century Yiddish literature, which far from resulting from their underlying ideological intentions, were reached in an aesthetic process which involved the overcoming of these intentions. The biblical translations, brilliant as they are, were not conceived of as artistic or linguistic demonstrations, but rather as tools for the raging battle against hasidism. We should remember that the Bible as a whole was understood by the *maskilim* to present not only divine revelation but also the human rational capacity at its highest. Moreover, Lefin wanted to bring to the common people those parts of the Holy Book through which elements of religious rationalism and philosophical, "pure," and universal devotion could be absorbed. It was not by accident that he chose to launch the publication of his translation with the Book of Proverbs, the cornerstone of the biblical "literature of wisdom," in which the element of human rationalism is stronger than in any other part of the Bible. (The incentive to do the translation was similar to that which made him prepare a popular Hebrew edition of Maimonides' *Moreh nevukhim*, "A Guide to the Perplexed").[21] Though it was very much owing to Lefin's influence that the necessity for some sort of a Yiddish literature gained its initial recognition

among the *maskilim*, we do not know that either he or most of his followers had any conscious respect for the language or any belief in its
future as a literary and cultural medium. Many of his followers, while
writing Yiddish, would publicly express their contempt for it and call
for its speedy extinction.[22] Y. Sh. Bik (1772–1831), his only disciple
who manifested real respect for the historical role played by Yiddish in
the life of Eastern European Jews, alienated himself from his closest
fellow *maskilim* and was regarded by them as a reactionary.[23] Reminding the detractors of Yiddish, who regarded it as mere animal
noises, that this was "the language our fathers and forefathers in Poland used for the last four hundred years," [24] he lost intellectual contact with most *maskilim*. Within the framework of their ideology and
cultural predilections an attitude like his toward the native language
could not be suffered.

The *maskilim* who wrote Yiddish could not help but have a bad
conscience about it. This is the reason they had to rationalize their
very act of writing. Almost every one of them had to make again and
again the naive discovery that the majority of the Jewish population in
Russia and Galicia were, after all, approachable only through Yiddish.
They chopped the elementary logic of their standard apologetics with
ponderous deliberation from the beginning of the century until the
time of Sholem Aleichem, not because they were intellectually inane,
but because on this particular point they were debilitated by an ex-
hausting internal strife. They went so gracelessly and so obsessively
about the business of self-vindication because they themselves were
hardly satisfied with their arguments. Indeed, they frequently found
themselves enmeshed in frustrating contradictions.[25] Whatever they
said publicly in self-justification, the Yiddish-writing *maskilim* knew
the language was stigmatized and through it they were stigmatizing
themselves.

ii

The inhibitory effect which the Mendelssohnian heritage of contempt generally had on the development of modern Yiddish literature
has been noted and, to some extent, documented by many historians;
what has not been clearly perceived or sufficiently emphasized is the
particular effect it had on the aesthetic sensibilities of Yiddish writers
and thus on the development of belles lettres in Yiddish.

The Jewish "enlightened" intellectuals of eighteenth-century Germany objected to Yiddish on many grounds: educational, cultural, social (it "contributed not a little to the 'impropriety' of the common Jew," as Mendelssohn put it),[26] even economic. Their antipathy, however, was primarily an aesthetic revulsion. As much as they rationalized it in educational and social argumentation, what really gave edge and venom to their objection was their feeling that Yiddish was ugly, "deformed." It goes without saying that this reaction was conditioned by social and cultural factors, but that does not change the fact that Mendelssohn, for example, though he spoke Yiddish in his youth and even wrote letters in Yiddish when he had to,[27] recoiled from the language with that spontaneity which reflects a genuine revolt of the aesthetic sensibilities. In his introduction to the translated Pentateuch he mentioned the ugliness and crudity of the available Yiddish translations as the primary justification for the new publication, and he did it with a vehemence which for him was quite rare, and which can be fully conveyed only in his own Hebrew words: The Yiddish translations, he said, were written *"bilshon ilgim mekulkal umoshkhat me'od; tig'al ba nefesh hakore hayode'a ledaber tsakhot"*[28] ("in a language of stammerers, corrupt and deformed, repulsive to those who are able to speak in a correct and elegant manner").° It is clear that Mendelssohn did not make a distinction between the biblical translations he found so repulsive and the Yiddish language itself. What he referred to as "a language of stammerers, corrupt and deformed" included both the allegedly bad style of the individual translators and of the Jewish-German "dialect" in general. To Mendelssohn it was clear that ugliness was an inherent trait of this "dialect" and was a direct result of the fact that Yiddish was not a language at all; it was only "a mixture" of Hebrew and German, and as such it lacked the unity and harmony without which the use of a language could not be conducted according to aesthetic norms. As "a mixture," it could not strive for any linguistic stability and was doomed to remain chimerical, barbarous, and repulsive. In a letter concerning the formulation of a special Jewish oath for the courts of Prussia, a matter upon which he was consulted, Mendelssohn warned against the employment of Yiddish, "that mixture of

° The expression *daber tsakhot*, which describes the linguistic-aesthetic ideal of the *maskilim*, is untranslatable. It means many things: to speak in a lucid and orderly manner, to have good style, to possess stylistic elegance and poise, to speak a grammatically correct language, etc.

Hebrew and German," with arguments characteristically of an aesthetic (and not a pragmatic or juridical) order. It would give him much pain, he said, to see the Jewish-German dialect recognized by the laws of the country. He would prefer the oath to be written and recited "either in pure German or in pure Hebrew or in both . . . only no mixing of languages!" [29]

This was hardly a logical argument. Mendelssohn and his disciples knew very well that some of the most highly developed European languages consisted of "mixtures" (for example, like most German intellectuals of his day, Mendelssohn had a high regard for English and for English literature), but this was not brought to bear on their attitude toward Yiddish. This discrepancy on the part of men trained in logic proves how deep and emotional their antipathy to the language was. It is probably this emotional antipathy that made more than four generations of *maskilim* repeat the argument that Yiddish was a disgraceful "mixture" of languages, even after they had been explicitly reminded (by Bik) that "the languages of France and England were mixtures of German, Gaulish, Latin, and Greek . . . and being thus mixed they became capable of producing sublime poetry as well as a high and excellent style." [30] The disgrace of being a mixture followed Yiddish everywhere. N. H. Vayzl, the major Hebrew poet of the *Haskala* in Germany (1725–1805), indicted the Yiddish language in verse:

> Kisfat goyey erets malel lamadnu,
> Akh lo kahem daber tsakhot khamadnu,
> Nakhnu ilgim, siftey amim balalnu.[31]

("We learned to speak the language of the people of the country, but unlike them we did not care to speak it correctly;° we are stammerers, we have confounded the languages of the nations.") I. Y. Aykhl (1756–1804), another Hebrew writer who, like Vayzl, was a member of the maskilic Berlin circle, wrote a comedy (*Reb Henokh oder vas tut me damit*—"Reb Henokh, Or What Can You Do About It?"; written in the 1790s) in which Yiddish took a major part in a grotesque world of linguistic chimeras. Although this comedy, certainly the most interesting artistic product of the German *Haskala*, can by no means be regarded as a mere satire on Yiddish, as some of the early historians maintained, its tendency to subject the language to ridicule is unmis-

° Again the expression *daber tsakhot* is used.

takable. Spoken by the old-fashioned Jewish burghers of Königsberg, Yiddish is exposed in the play as a barbarous dialect, through comparison with legitimate, "pure" German. It is equated with the stammering, tourist-like German of a French émigré (the comedy takes place in the first years following the French Revolution) and of an expatriated English physician. It is even compared with the unintelligible jargon of a pretentious philosophy student who insists on employing Kantian terminology in a casual, coffee-house conversation. In short, Yiddish is exhibited among other linguistic monstrosities as "mixed," "comic," "deformed," a deviation from the norm (which, of course, is elegant, literary German), and a symbol of thick provincial darkness. Considered by many the first opus in modern Yiddish literature, Aykhl's comedy illustrates what, as we shall presently see, was to be the major aesthetic use of Yiddish until Abramovitsh and Sholem Aleichem: the use of the antinorm, of Caliban.[32]

As the focus of the *Haskala* shifted, in the first decades of the nineteenth century, from Germany to the east, the reputation of Yiddish as the incarnation of linguistic ugliness was kept alive not only by the sworn Hebraists but also by many of the *maskilim*, who compromised themselves by writing in it. In whatever way they explained their Yiddish writing, they always conceded that they could not claim any aesthetic status for it, since the language itself was inherently ugly. Their awareness of the antiaesthetic nature of the medium they were using must be emphasized if the linguistic-historic context of nineteenth-century Yiddish fiction is to be truthfully reconstructed. It is worth remembering, for instance, how conscious of the deformities of "the mixed language" Y. B. Levinzon, the so-called "Russian Mendelssohn," was. In addition to numerous Hebrew compositions, he wrote two pamphlets of considerable social significance in Yiddish and was promoted for this by some historians to the rank of forefather of Yiddish literature. Here is what he had to say about Yiddish:

> You know how Nehemiah complained of the mixture of languages the Jews had brought from the Babylonian Exile: "and their children speak half in the speech of Ashdod and could not speak in the Jews' language nor in the languages of other peoples." [33] It was not only that they were ignorant of the holy tongue, but that they had no one language which they could speak perfectly without mixing it with other languages. Had they had such a language, he would not have complained, for what he complained of was the mixture of languages. . . .

. . . and this is also what happened to us, Polish and Russian Jews. We cannot speak Hebrew, and we do not know the languages of the peoples in whose countries we live. . . . The language we do speak in this country, the language which we borrowed from the Germans and which is called Judeo-German, is completely corrupt, for it is mixed with crippled words adopted from Hebrew, Russian, French, Polish, etc., and even its original German words are "scattered and peeled" and "there is no soundness in them."

. . . From all this you conclude that we must know at least one language perfectly and that, needless to say, the language of the country in which we live; this undoubtedly must be mastered. We know that the greatest *tanaim* exhorted their contemporaries to master the language of the state and use it invariably, especially if it was a pure* and a rich language.

Rabbi Yehuda said: "Why speak Syrian in Erets Israel [Palestine]? Speak either the holy tongue or Greek," for Greek was a very pure and rich language, and it was then also the official language in Palestine; and Rabbi Yosef said: "Why speak Aramaic in Mesopotamia? Speak either the holy tongue or Persian" . . . and thus we can say: Why speak Yiddish in this country? speak either correct German or Russian, for Russian is the language of the state, and it is also a very pure and rich language, which does not lack in beauty and pleasantness, and it possesses all those high qualities which make a language perfect.[34]

Levinzon's aims were social and cultural, and he objected to Yiddish primarily as an obstacle in the way of closer relations between Jews and Russians. However, his argumentation, for all its biblical and talmudic quotations, was typically aesthetic, like Mendelssohn's argumentation in his letter concerning the Jewish oath. Although he himself wrote Yiddish with an unerring stylistic sense (his two Yiddish pamphlets are today immensely more readable than his copious Hebrew productions), he assumed that it was corrupt and ugly. To him this was so self-evident, that he believed it the easiest point to get across to his audience. To convince Russian Jewry that contact with Russian culture would be beneficial to them was a difficult matter, but to convince them of the aesthetic deficiencies of Yiddish was, he thought, quite easy. This was a point on which allegedly no serious differences of opinion could exist. Wasn't the notion of Yiddish as an intrinsically ugly language inherent in the very names by which it was

* Levinzon uses the adjective *tsakha* which we have met already in the verb combination *daber tsakhot*. It means not only "pure" but also "correct," "elegant," etc.

referred to throughout the century? For it was only at the end of the nineteenth century and in the twentieth century that the language had become universally known as Yiddish—the language of the Jews (*Yidn*). In the previous century it had first been called *Yidish-daytsh* (Judeo-German) and, later (until the time of Sholem Aleichem and Perets), *Zhargon* ("jargon")—the former name designating the language as a corrupt German spoken by Jews and the latter degrading it further to the class of sublanguages, incoherent mechanisms of linguistic communication, gibberish.[35]

This conception of Yiddish as "jargon" presented enormous difficulties to writers who, like Abramovitsh, were strongly inclined to stylistic perfectionism. To appreciate the full weight of these difficulties, one must also comprehend the *maskilim*'s opposing notion of Hebrew as an intrinsically beautiful language. If to them Yiddish was all earth and dross, Hebrew was "heavenly" and "divine." A *maskil* who chose to write Yiddish had not only to reconcile himself to the deformities of Caliban, but also to prefer them to the perfections of Ariel. Indeed, he had to prefer the woodsticks, crabs, pig-nuts, and morasses of the "ridiculous monster" to the coral-bones, pearl-eyes, and all the "rich and strange" treasures of the sprite. The *maskilim*'s adoration of Hebrew was semitheological. Mendelssohn, their teacher, subscribed to the traditional axiom that Hebrew was the language spoken by God himself. In his introduction to the translated Pentateuch he not only stated that God addressed Adam, Moses, and the prophets in Hebrew, but also went into lengthy arguments in order to prove that he pronounced it exactly the way it was preserved by the *masora*.[36] The *maskilim* believed that Hebrew was, as they put it, "the daughter of God," or "the Heavenly," and their attitude toward it often assumed the character of a semireligious cult.[37] However, this linguistic cult, like most expressions of religiosity on their part, was essentially secular. Their concept of the godliness of Hebrew was necessarily vague; what it amounted to in most cases was an aesthetic evaluation in religious phraseology. The divine nature of the language was regarded as manifest, not in any superhuman potential but in aesthetic perfection, in supreme beauty. The *maskilim* firmly believed that Hebrew as preserved in the Bible was the most "beautiful" language in existence. They conceded that its beauty was tarnished in postbiblical times by disuse and even corrupted by abuse (the "mixture" of late elements with the language of the Bible; again, the notion of linguistic "mixture" is associated with aesthetic corruption) and that lately it had been in a very bad way. This, however, only added to their elation as writers of "pure" Hebrew, for were they not, like the great Renaissance dilettantes, restoring a long-lost, an almost forgotten perfection?

Thus, while the writing of Yiddish forced the *maskilim* to renounce a priori aesthetic values for the sake of an immediate response to an educational emergency, the writing of Hebrew was for them an act of aesthetic faith. Of course, the Hebrew writers of the *Haskala*, just as their Yiddish colleagues, regarded literature as an educational tool, but by the very nature of their linguistic medium, they were not faced with the necessity of choosing between the pleasing and the instructive. Indeed, from the very beginning of *Haskala* literature, Hebrew writers speculated on the methods of unifying the pleasing and the instructive in poetry, their assumption being that this unification could be fully realized through "pure" Hebrew and through an aesthetic investigation of the Bible. Were not the pathos of the prophets, the lyricism of the psalmist, and the philosophical grandeur of the writer of Job the best proofs that a union of sublime poetry and profound moral instruction was not only possible but, perhaps, inevitable? [38] This notion of aesthetic didacticism, of moral instruction through the beauty of poetic diction (*melitsa*), was dominant in the literary thinking of the Hebrew *maskilim* at least until the 1860s, when it was challenged by writers and critics influenced by the antiaestheticism of the Russian "radical" critics, such as Tshernishevski, Dobrolyubov, and Pisarev. The changes which this challenge brought about in Hebrew literature were considerable (among others, the turning of a thorough Hebraist like Abramovitsh to "the mixed language" and the fact that *Hamelits*, the major Hebrew magazine of the day, suffered publication with a Yiddish supplement). These changes, however, did not suffice to undermine the basic assumption that the writing of Hebrew was in itself an aesthetic activity. Those who really questioned this assumption (the critics Kovner and Lerner, for instance; among the nineteenth-century Hebraists they were, perhaps, the only ones who drew far-reaching consequences from their alignment with the Russian antiaestheticians) could not remain Hebrew writers for long. Sooner or later they had to denounce their own Hebraism as a sentimental waste of energy. Those who continued to write Hebrew remained loyal to the notion that a piece of good Hebrew writing was not only a means of education but also an aesthetic achievement of enduring value. Even many of those who, like Abramovitsh, decided at a certain point to shift from Hebrew to Yiddish remained under the aesthetic spell of the holy tongue and were haunted by its power, so that they either craved a return to it (Abramovitsh) or fulminated against it (Linetski).

Despite isolated protests,[39] the idea that Hebrew was "beautiful" per se was generally accepted throughout the nineteenth century, even by Yiddish writers. The much despised Shaykevitsh probably expressed the general feeling of his Yiddish colleagues in this matter, when he made Yiddish concede to Hebrew (in a versified dialogue between the two languages that strangely interrupts the story of one of his "highly interesting" novels) complete aesthetic superiority.[40] Indeed, Yiddish literature at the time could not be associated with the idea of beauty. How could one write aesthetically in a language that was considered the quintessence of deformity? Yiddish belletristic composition could not and did not then claim artistic self-sufficiency. It was regarded as a means, not an end, and as such it was intended to perform its educational duty and sink into oblivion. Until the 1880s, no Yiddish writer dreamed of literary longevity, let alone literary immortality. Even Abramovitsh, when already well into his Yiddish phase, referred to the language as worthy of literary use only for the time being, as long as the Jewish masses could understand no other language. He therefore recommended that it should *not* be improved and developed.[41] Two decades before him Aksenfeld had written, taking it for granted that artistic literature and the writing of Yiddish were mutually exclusive: "My goal was not to set myself up as a writer (for I could have written in a European language) but only to be of use to my brethren who suffer under the yoke of superstition. . . ." [42] As late as 1889, the following statement was made in refutation of the argument that Yiddish literature might endanger the development of Hebrew literature:

Had we the slightest ground to believe that this could happen, we would certainly prefer our hand to dry up rather than let it take up the pen to write Yiddish. Who does not know that the majority of contemporary Yiddish writers are themselves Hebrew writers and cherish the holy tongue no less than those fanatics who wage war for its sake? . . . We regard Yiddish only as a means of educating the people, not as an end in itself. Therefore, it cannot harm our Hebrew literature at all . . . whenever the happy time arrives in which there will be no need for Yiddish, all of us will, of course, rejoice with all our hearts. This, however, is still far, far away, and who knows who among us will live to see it? In the meantime, Yiddish is still indispensable for the people.[43]

It should be noted that this reference to Yiddish as a means, the elimination of which in some happy future would make everyone rejoice,
was made not only at the time when Sholem Aleichem's rehabilitation
of Yiddish was well under way, but actually in Sholem Aleichem's own
Folks-biblyotek and by a Yiddish-writing scholar who was introducing
the first Yiddish work on the history of Yiddish literature!

The dissociation of the Yiddish language from aesthetic values and
of Yiddish literature from a possibility of artistic self-sufficiency was so
influential and universal throughout the nineteenth century, that it left
deep marks even on those few pioneers who, from the 1860s onward,
were groping for a new concept of Yiddish and of its function. Y. M.
Lifshits, who developed a defense of Yiddish with endless patience,
was—after Bik—the first *maskil* to suggest that no language is inherently beautiful or ugly and that Yiddish cannot be regarded as corrupt
since, as a language in its own right (he was among the first, if not *the*
first, to refer to it systematically as Yiddish),[44] it had not gone through
any process of change from perfection to imperfection. He conceded
that Yiddish was still a fluctuating, unstabilized, and in many ways, un-
developed language, but that seemed to him all the more reason for
diligent work on the part of writers and linguists, whose task it would
be to channel its development. He did not for a moment doubt that
this "mother tongue" of the Jewish people (Lifshits made a distinction
between "mother tongue" and "national language": Hebrew is the national language of all Jews, Yiddish the mother tongue of the Eastern
European Jews)[45] deserved to be treated with as much respect as any
other language.

Even Lifshits, however, for all his sobriety and perspicacity, did
not escape the frustration arising from the supposed aesthetic
offensiveness of Yiddish. In his case the frustration was revealed in
self-defeating polemic ardor. In refuting the indictment of Yiddish as a
corrupt and ugly language, Lifshits was driven to take the position that
a language does not and cannot possess inherent aesthetic and logical
norms, i.e., a language is a mere system of signs, in itself neither beautiful nor correct. Only the concepts it symbolizes, he argued, have to
do with beauty or truth. In an article published in *Kol-mevaser* in
1863, he said:

> The truth is that one cannot refer to a language as corrupt at all, for lan-
> guage is only a sign which stands for thought; therefore, every nation

may devise whatever signs it wishes, as long as its people understand each other. Now, a corrupt concept is truly corrupt.[46]

In an article published in the same magazine a few years later, Lifshits insisted upon this notion of linguistic symbolism in an even more simplified version:

> The Jews must be humanized, and the means for that can be found not in language but in concepts. A million corrupt words cannot do as much harm as the least corrupt concept, and a million correct words are not as useful as the least concept, provided it is clear and distinct.[47]

Lifshits never answered, in fact he never raised, the question of how a concept can be conveyed clearly and distinctly in corrupt words. In his reaction to the powerful anti-Yiddish sentiment, he was clearly overreaching himself. The Mendelssohnian *maskilim* doomed Yiddish to extinction because they believed that only through a well-regulated language could one achieve true methods of cognition, genuine morality, etc. Lifshits, in his aggressive apologetics, had to resort to the other extreme and deny any intrinsic connection between language and thought. It goes without saying that such a conception of language is utterly uncongenial to the development of imaginative literature. Thus, Lifshits had nothing to contribute toward an aesthetic rationale of Yiddish literature; at least he had nothing positive to contribute to it, for he may have raised the morale of Yiddish writers in a negative way by undermining the cult of Hebrew, a language to which he referred as "moldy." [48] But this notion did not express Lifshits' own sense of language. This is proven by his Yiddish dictionaries, in which he demonstrated a keen sensibility for the historical particularity of Yiddish. It was a sensibility utterly at odds with his theoretical denial of the importance of all those aspects of language which could not be related to its function as an arbitrary symbolical mechanism in the service of an abstract system of concepts. In this self-contradiction, Lifshits resembles artists like Abramovitsh, who, while committed to a theory incapable of recognizing Yiddish as suitable for artistic use, were in practice dedicating their lives to the exploration and to the amplification of the artistic possibilities of "the mixed language."

iii

This gap between theory and practice accounts for many of the crippling influences present throughout the development of nineteenth-century Yiddish belles lettres. When it is stated that the artistic use of Yiddish was not then considered feasible, it is not meant that until the 1880s or even the 1890s, works of considerable artistic achievement were not actually written by the Yiddish *maskilim*. Etinger's comedies, fables, and epigrams contain many instances of artistic felicity. The stylistic feats of the all but anonymous author of the parody *Gdules reb Volf* ("The Greatness of Reb Volf")[49] are carried to the point of acrobatic virtuosity. The Yiddish version of Perl's *Megale-tmirin* bears witness to its author's inimitable sense of artistic play as much as the Hebrew version does, although in a substantially different way. The surviving portions of Lefin's translation of the Bible undoubtedly testify to the sensitivity of a master stylist; even the much cruder stylistic techniques of Aksenfeld in his plays and in *Dos shtern-tikhl* demonstrate the artist's firm grasp of the relationship between the dynamics of language and those of social development. The artistic excellence of Abramovitsh's works, even of the early ones, is self-evident. What is implied by my argument is that Yiddish belles lettres were not supported by positive aesthetics (in fact, they were developed in the face of aesthetic negation): when Yiddish-writing *maskilim* attained stylistic excellence, they were not realizing their professed "poetics," but, so to speak, were double crossing their own literary ideology. This, among other reasons, is why the artistic achievements of the Yiddish *maskilim*, brilliant as they sometimes were, remained of a limited nature for such a long time.

   This can be illustrated by what may be described as the theoretical basis some *maskilim* devised for writing fiction in Yiddish. Their "theory of Yiddish fiction," if such a grand name may be assigned to such a limited entity, can almost be summed up in one sentence: The main form of fiction which can legitimately exist in Yiddish is satirical parody. This idea was hinted at for the first time in Lefin's French pamphlet. Lefin pointed out that the influence of hasidism, so inimical to "the enlightenment of the Jewish people in Poland," was to a large extent spread and strengthened by the rapidly expanding hasidic literature of legend and hagiography. In order to combat the influence of this literature, which Lefin believed endangered the rational powers of the Jewish mind, he proposed, in addition to physically suppressing it through state censorship, to strengthen the rationalistic tendency in the Jewish reading public by several kinds of publications: popular editions of the philosophical works of the great Jewish medieval rationalists, books on natural science, etc. in Hebrew. This, however, he knew would not suffice; besides positive rational education, the *maskilim* had to use methods of rationalistic destruction, and that is what Lefin assigned to Yiddish fiction. It had to make the *tsadikim* ridiculous through their own style and manner. It had to bring out the inanity of their allegedly bizarre and incoherent writings. In short, Lefin called for a Yiddish literature of parody as a destructive weapon in the literary war with the *hasidim*. We know that he tried himself to create a model for such literature by writing a parodic biography of the founder of hasidism, Israel Ba'al-Shem-Tov, who had by then been canonized in numerous legend cycles and thus offered excellent material for the parodist. This early maskilic parody on the hagiographical literature of the *hasidim* has not survived. It is possible that Lefin himself suppressed it when he found it superseded by the brilliant *Megale-tmirin* of his disciple Perl, which is indeed the best example of the fiction Lefin recommended.[50]

This *raison d'être* of Yiddish fiction was redefined and somewhat extended by Aksenfeld in his letters to S. S. Uvarov as well as in the literary, or quasiliterary discussions among his heroes in *Dos shterntikhl*. While Lefin assigned to Yiddish fiction the task of parodying a certain type of literature, Aksenfeld implied that parody of life itself would prove a more potent weapon in the campaign against the *hasidim*. In *Dos shterntikhl*, he contended that the task of uprooting hasidism must be carried out, or at least begin, by parodic exposure of the *tsadikim*'s imposture. His mouthpiece in the novel, Oksman, relates how he cured an entire town of its hasidism by assuming for one day the guise of a *tsadik*. Within a few hours he managed, with the proper grimaces and jargon, to make the whole population believe in his sainthood, whereupon he revealed his identity and made the people realize how easily they let themselves be taken in. He concludes the story thus:

> We must find instruments for ridiculing them [the *tsadikim*]; we must, indeed, ridicule them with their own instruments; with their ever-flowing, incoherent sermonizing, with their smirks, with their insinuating grimaces—we must ridicule them so that the common people will jeer at them in the streets. Then they will go out of circulation. In addition to that we must request the czar to order that a ukase be issued to the effect that every Jew should at least be able to read and write [i.e., read and write Russian]. Jews will read the remarkable compositions of

the excellent young Russian writers we have nowadays, and our whole life will be changed. The *hasidim* and their *tsadikim* will be chased away with stick and brick.[51]

Aksenfeld developed here as in many other places, a theory which can be associated with the "aesthetics of ugliness."[52] Its basic assumption is that ugliness may be used aesthetically if it is made by artistic manipulation to pronounce itself as ugliness, i.e., to imply the aesthetic norm in a negative way. This makes Yiddish artistically useful, since by its deformity it is endowed with characteristics of an aesthetic antinorm. "We must find instruments for ridiculing them; we must, indeed, ridicule them with their own instruments," Aksenfeld said and he certainly included the Yiddish language among "their" instruments which had to be employed to ensure its self-defeat, i.e., parodically. Since Yiddish was an integral part of a deformed reality, it could be useful for making the deformity aware of itself. "Mixed," "corrupt," and "disorderly," the language contained all those traits in Jewish life which the *maskilim* thought must be exposed, ridiculed, and corrected or eliminated, and one had only to bring out, to heighten its inherent linguistic monstrosities in order to expose the nonlinguistic ugliness of Jewish life to ridicule. In short, what the artist must do with Yiddish was not stabilize and refine it but, on the contrary, methodically apply to it techniques of stylistic exaggeration. From this position the following conclusions emerged as to the possible nature, function, and future of Yiddish fiction.

First, it was bound to be given largely to mimicry, that is, to the exposure of deformities through an exaggerated imitation. That made it by nature theatrical and farcical. Aksenfeld envisaged Yiddish fiction and drama as scenes from a staged farce or an elaborate practical joke (with an educational purpose)[53] in which irregularities, both physical (grimaces, smirks, ridiculous gestures) and linguistic (incoherence, stylistic idiosyncrasies, accents, speech defects) are constantly mimicked.

Second, the educational function of Yiddish fiction was to be mainly destructive, for Yiddish, by its very nature distorted, could not impart wholesomeness; it could only imply it negatively. Characteristically, Aksenfeld divided the process of the literary education of Russian Jews into two parts: the first, performed by Yiddish writers, would be to discredit hasidism, to explode the prestige of the *tsadikim*. That would leave the Jews neatly prepared for the second part, which would be performed by the "excellent young Russian writers," whose "remarkable compositions" would be the source of the positive education of the Jews, since Russian, "a pure and a rich language which does not lack in beauty and pleasantness," as Levinzon put it, was capable of imparting wholesome concepts in wholesome words.

Yiddish fiction was also to be destructive in another sense, a more literary one: it was to be antilegendary; it had to check the imagination, an ally of the *hasidim;* it had to bring its readers back to reality and rational causality. Therefore, Aksenfeld insisted in his letters to Uvarov that Yiddish fiction must portray "life itself," and even be based on true stories. He wrote that the Yiddish writer must "discover in real life both comic and instructive events, attract the reader with a plot which would retain the fine form of an interesting story and yet point throughout to the truth." [54] We know that in at least some of his compositions Aksenfeld portrayed "real" people and dramatized "true" events. It is worth remembering, by way of comparison, that while this first Yiddish novelist recommended a nonfictional veracity, A. Mapu, the first Hebrew novelist and Aksenfeld's contemporary, contended that the "false imagination" of the *hasidim* could be cured not by a nonliterary veracity, but by "truthful imagination"; that fiction must be not only true but also colorful, elevating, and above all else, beautiful.[55] The difference between the aesthetic positions of the two languages is significantly reflected in this difference between the two writers' thoughts on fiction.

Third, Yiddish fiction, like Yiddish literature in general, had to prepare for its own extinction. Since its function was to clear the ground for positive influences which were to come from foreign sources, it would (with the help of the czar's ukase) eventually eliminate itself. Aksenfeld's Oksman prophesies that the whole process will take no more than fifty years.[56] This suicidal principle was the final and inevitable consequence of the "aesthetics of ugliness." If the ugliness of Yiddish had to be manipulated in order to expose and eliminate the deformities of Jewish life, then the language would at some point correct itself out of existence.

These were the basic theoretical assumptions which informed the writing of the main part of Yiddish fiction up to a very late stage. In practice, of course, many other, sometimes contradictory trends influenced Yiddish fiction writers. These, however, were rarely recognized in literary generalizations. The ideology of Yiddish fiction remained close to that of Aksenfeld until the time of the young Sholem Aleichem. Not all the *maskilim* derived these far-reaching conclusions from it and pursued its suicidal logic to the bitter end. Many of them, especially those less given to ardent ideological considerations (like Etinger) wrote Yiddish without a pronounced awareness of the destructive self-contradiction inherent in their activity. Most of them, however, were either directly influenced or subtly permeated by the attitudes it involved. Many accepted the idea that the function of Yiddish fiction was that of destructive exposure. Even Dik, who had adopted the ideology of the *Haskala* in its mildest form and in many of whose stories parody and satire are nonexistent, when asked why he had chosen to write in crude "jargon" rather than in the beautiful Hebrew tongue, replied, "An old building is not to be wrecked with the prick of a needle, but with the pounding of sledgehammers." [57] The analogy expresses in a figurative manner Lefin's and Aksenfeld's assumption that it is the task of Yiddish writers to perform the heavy work of wrecking and that they should leave the more refined and rewarding tasks of literature to those equipped with better tools.

As for the idea of the self-extinction of Yiddish and its literature, although it was not often distinctly and straightforwardly elaborated, it too is constantly echoed in the Yiddish *maskilim*'s observations about their literary practice. It lurks even in the thinking of the most ardent "Yiddishists" among them, such as Linetski. Linetski's case is of special interest because it is quite clear that with him the dead weight of the traditional negation of Yiddish was often alleviated—even in theory—by contradictory notions, so that from time to time (especially in his writings of the 1870s) he would refer to the language in surprisingly positive and "modern" terms. Linetski, however, was no theoretician, but rather a passionate polemicist, who never tried to harmonize his own conflicting attitudes. His thinking on "the problem of language" was flagrantly inconsistent, and therefore very revealing— from the historian's point of view. In one article in 1876, for instance, he supplied Yiddish literature with three different *raisons d'être*. In one passage he said, "We shall make a literature out of Yiddish, for only in Yiddish can the spirit and character of the unhappy Jewish people be reflected, and it is of those books in which the people's character is reflected that true literature consists." [58] Here we have the typical romantic conception of language and literature as the expression of national character or "genius" applied for the first time to

Yiddish. Given the background of *Haskala* thinking this was undoubtedly a radical, even a revolutionary innovation. Thanks to passages like
this Linetski was presented in some modern histories of Yiddish literature (mainly those written in the USSR) as the great "democratic" vin-
dicator of the Jewish masses and their language. This was not wholly
unjustified, for in the 1870s, when the *Haskala* ideology reached its
final and perhaps also its fullest bloom, Linetski was giving expression
to a belief, which even in the twentieth century was adopted only by
some of the Yiddish Communists and the most radical of non-Commu-
nist Yiddishists, i.e., the belief that Yiddish was not only capable of
producing respectable literature but that it was the only language in
which a genuine, "true" Jewish literature could be created. One
should, however, pay attention to the other two reasons for the existence of a Yiddish literature, which Linetski mentions in the same article. One of these takes us back to the trite apologetics of the earlier
maskilim ("Since the common people know no European language, let
us rescue them through their own language").[59] The other one goes
much further and actually approaches the idea of self-elimination. According to it, Yiddish is to be preferred to Hebrew as the language of
Jewish literature, because it "is much closer to Russian than Hebrew"
and would render the transition to this language smoother.[60] This third
argument was by no means a passing "aberration" with Linetski. It
was fully and patiently developed by him in another article, published
almost at the same time as the first editorial of *Yisrolik*, the short-lived
weekly which he and Goldfaden began in 1875. This editorial, as
might have been expected, poses and attempts to answer the question,
how can a Yiddish magazine enhance the progress of the Jewish Enlightenment? Its answer is wholly imbued with the self-negation which
is so characteristic of the Yiddish literature of the *Haskala*. The gist of
it is that Yiddish newspapers and magazines and, for that matter,
formal Yiddish literature as well are meant to neutralize the opposition
of the older Jewish generation to the maskilic tendencies of the young,
particularly their study of foreign languages (Russian, first and foremost). Linetski argues here with the opponents of Yiddish, those propagandists who protest its use for cultural purposes and demand its immediate replacement by Russian. It is not, however, their basic
assumptions that he disagrees with, but rather their tactics. They are
impractical hotheads: "Should we get hold of Anshl the *shames*
["beadle"] and shove Russian down his throat?" he asks. "No, my

brothers. You will achieve nothing by force." It is impossible and also
unnecessary to make the older generation "thoroughly enlightened."
What is necessary is to expose it little by little and unobtrusively to
modern ideas in order to make it "look with equanimity at the new
generation as it goes its own way"; that can be achieved by the
Yiddish media alone, since on them the Yiddish-speaking public depends for news and entertainment. "Once a Jew reads a newspaper,
and let it be a Yiddish one, he pretends to be unaware of the fact that
his son studies foreign languages, for he has already been convinced
that the study of foreign languages as well as of other disciplines is not
necessarily harmful to Judaism." Linetski closed his editorial with a
plea for patience addressed to the "hotheads" and with a general appeal to the Jewish public: "Throw away your obduracy and let your
children have their way . . . indeed, there is no reason why you too
should not make every effort to become acquainted with the language
of the country. . . ." [61]

Yiddish and Yiddish literature are treated in this article (which, by
the way, has never been, to my knowledge, discussed or even mentioned in Yiddish criticism and literary history) only in terms of the
Haskala's tactics. The language is that of "Anshl the *shames*"; the literature is not the "true" Jewish literature, the only literature which
may contain "the spirit and character of the unhappy Jewish people,"
but an entertainment—educational in a deceptive way—for Anshl and
his contemporaries, who are not and who will never be "thoroughly
enlightened." It is addressed to an old and passing generation, while
the young generation, who so diligently pursues the study of foreign
languages, will have no use for it—that goes without saying. Thus, the
literature itself is necessarily ephemeral, a temporary enterprise
formed to bring about its own extinction.

iv

To our taste there is something particularly unsavory about this article. It cannot be pleasant to contemplate an artist such as Linetski,
whose works owe a considerable part of the appeal they may hold
even for the modern reader to the vividness and wealth of the Yiddish
in which they were written, treating his own artistic medium with
utter disrespect and announcing its eventual elimination in a tone of
patient optimism ("step by step we shall reach the summit; little by lit-

tle we shall achieve perfection," he assured the "hotheads"). However, dealing with such articles, the historian had better be on his guard lest his analysis, which should be aimed at historical understanding, lead to nothing more than unhistorical disrespect. We must observe and study Linetski's self-contradictions and even self-degradation with historical sympathy if we are to gain an understanding of his artistic and cultural achievements and limitations and, indeed, of the achievements and limitations of the whole of nineteenth-century Yiddish literature.

It should also be remembered that inconsistencies, discrepancies between theory and practice, etc., indicate, at least in this instance, not mental weakness or sloth; on the contrary, they indicate restlessness, tension, readiness for intellectual adventure. It is in the writings of the duller, the more sentimental, and the less daring Yiddish writers that contradictions are undetectable, or are only noticeable in an unemphatic manner. With these writers the official ideology in which they were initiated as apprentice *maskilim* rested unchallenged and intact. The sturdier Abramovitsh, Lifshits, and Linetski could not maintain this docility. Because of their spiritual vigor, their commitment to the official ideology was often all the more thorough and exacting; yet they could not altogether stifle the ever-growing need to assert the status of Yiddish as a literary language and to proclaim themselves as legitimate writers and artists. Hence, the tension between their theory and their practice or among the different "theories" to which they gave utterance. This tension results from a conflict between a well-entrenched system of cultural attitudes and those contradictory trends which may have originated from within the system, but to which the system could not allow free development if it were to retain its integrity. The *Haskala* initiated the renewed literary use of Yiddish for its own limited purposes of cultural warfare, but the new Yiddish literature, having once been set on its course, could not confine itself to the limitations initially imposed on it.

Discord, even confusion, were inevitable under these circumstances, and they characterized Yiddish literature throughout the century, even when it was supposed to have liberated itself from its confining maskilic matrix. Y. L. Perets, for example, was one of the first to rebel openly against the assumptions that only a purely utilitarian literature could be written in Yiddish and that a Yiddish writer should not aspire to any literary "beauty." He was perhaps the first to propagate in Yiddish what might be described as a full-fledged aesthetic heresy; at least, he was the first who consciously preached aestheticism as a heresy. In a letter to Sholem Aleichem (in whose *Folks-biblyotek* his *Monish* had recently been published), he remarked:

> After the publication of *Monish*, I received letters of the highest praise, yet all those who praised the poem and who hailed its appearance remarked that *Monish* would not be understood by the common people and so why write it [in Yiddish]? I call all our common people to witness: true, they *understand* according to their limited capacity, but they *feel* beauty, they sense the atmosphere of the poem; and this is the aim of poetry—not to clothe with poetic figures something known already, but to open new heavens, to create new concepts, to penetrate their [the common people's] minds with ideas of an exploratory nature, not to tell them what has long been known.[62]

This, indeed, was a revolution. Here Perets was actually turning the tables on the ideology of nineteenth-century Yiddish literature. It is not only that he questioned the validity of its attitude toward "the common people," but also—and this is of greater importance in our discussion—that he discarded its conception of the literary methods of imparting instruction. While most Yiddish writers of the century regarded themselves as disseminators of "true concepts," or rather as wreckers of "false concepts," and conceded that achieving literary beauty was, by the very nature of their medium, beyond their ken, Perets decided that literary beauty was both attainable in Yiddish and necessary if "new concepts" (the difference here between "true" and "new" is a significant one) were to "penetrate" the minds of the people. They regarded Yiddish literature as capable only of instructing, not of yielding aesthetic pleasure. He asserted, however, that it was capable of yielding such pleasure even to those who were still uninstructed, implying that aesthetic perception was antecedent to reasoning and moral judgment, at least within the boundaries of the literary experience. This implication, that literature is primarily beautiful and only secondarily instructive or, rather, that literature must be beautiful if it is to be instructive, undermined the whole ideological structure which the Yiddish *maskilim* had erected with so much pain and misgiving.

    With this revolt against the negative aesthetic ideology of his predecessors under way, however, Perets continued at the same time to disregard Yiddish itself as a medium conducive to poetry. His avowed

aim was to aestheticize Yiddish literature, and yet his persistent feeling
was that the language as such could not be associated with the beautiful; as an artistic medium he thought it unresponsive, unreliable, and
indeed, frustrating. "There is a great difference between you and me,"
he once wrote to the Hebrew poet Byalik. "You work in steel, I—in
sandstone." [63] To him the failure of the language was primarily its
physical unattractiveness. In his very first Yiddish publication he expressed himself on this point in a most revealing manner. Digressing
from the narrative of *Monish*, he explained why he could not develop
the theme of love in the poem:

> Mayn lid volt andersh gor geklingen
> Ikh zol far goyim goyish zingen,
> Nor nisht far yidn, nisht zhargon.
> Keyn rekhtn klang, keyn rekhtn ton,
> Keyn eyntsik vort nit un keyn stil
> Hob ikh far "libe," far "gefil". . . .

> Zhargon far libe—iz toyt un mat,
> Keyn eyntsik vort nisht tsart, nisht glat,
> Un khotsh do lopne oyfn ort,—
> Es hot keyn leblekh, varm vort!

> Oyf yidish makh a komplement,—
> Es kumt aroys on fis on hent:
> "Mayn lebn, zele, oy, mayn shetsl!"
> Es hot a taam vi lakrets pletsl.
> Es hot keyn gayst, es hot keyn zalts—
> Un shmekt nokh tsu mit genzn-shmalts! . . .[64]

("My song would have sounded completely different,/ Had I sung it
for gentiles and in their tongue,/ Not for Jews, not in Yiddish./ No
proper sound, no proper tone,/ Not one single word and no style/
Have I for love, for feeling. . . . / Yiddish for love—it falls flat;/ Not a
single smooth or delicate word,/ And go wrack your brain—/ You find
no warm expression./ In Yiddish pay a compliment—/ It will come
out a hopeless cripple./ 'My life! my soul! Oh, my treasure!'/ —It
tastes like licorice pastry,/ It has no spirit, it lacks salt,/ And what's
more, it smacks of goose fat! . . .")

Yiddish cannot properly express love, as this passage clearly indicates, because it offends the aesthetic sensibilities. It has no proper
tone; it lacks style; its very sound is grating. As Perets doggedly elabo-

rates on this, it becomes more and more apparent that he is judging
the language by sensual criteria and that he finds it physically unattractive. It has no "smooth" and "delicate" words, he insists, as if he
were touching the coarse, scarred skin of the language's body; then,
shifting from touch to taste, he reaches a climax of disgust with metaphors of licorice pastry and goose fat. However, even before uttering
this aesthetic condemnation of Yiddish, Perets had qualified it. Its alleged unattractiveness, its coarse, prickly texture, he said, were a direct reflection of the tragic Jewish fate. Even before the publication of
Monish, Perets contended (in Hebrew, *Manginot hazman*, XXII), that
the exilic Yiddish rather than biblical Hebrew offered the proper expression for the communal-historical Jewish experience of persecution.
Here he elaborates on this:

> Undzer yidish hot nor vitsn,
> Hot nor dunern un blitsn;
> Zi hot nor verter vi di shpizn.
> In 'im lakhn veynen rizn.
> Zi dresht dos layb vi mit riter;
> Zi iz vi gal, vi pyolun biter.
> Iz in gantsn blut un trern:
> Yedn oysdrik kenstu hern
> Vi der yam di tsores zidn,
> Vi es krenkt dos harts dem yidn.[65]

("Our Yiddish knows only witticisms,/ Has only thunder and light-
ning,/ Only words like lances./ In it giants laugh and weep./ It
threshes the flesh as if with flails;/ It is bitter as gall and wormwood./
It is all blood and tears;/ In every expression you can hear/ How the
sea of troubles boils,/ How the heart of the Jew pines.") This endows
Yiddish, uncouth and devoid of softness and sweetness as it allegedly
is, with a certain grandeur. As the language of the persecuted and deprived it is full of power, of expressive intensity, if not of beauty. However, it is precisely this particular intensity of Yiddish which makes it,
according to Perets in *Monish*, unsuitable for individualistic poetic expression, for it is the intensity of a communal experience, not of an individual one. The language can adequately express the common de-
nominators of the existence of the Jewish people (as opposed to the
uniqueness of the individual Jew). Only "giants," that is, multitudes,
can weep or laugh in it. It cannot afford the proper expression for
Monish's emerging individuality. But this emerging of the hero's indi-

viduality, his surfacing—through erotic love—from the depths of the communal life, his deviation from "the path of the righteous" and shying away from the traditional ideals of learning and saintliness, this is what Perets was actually concerned with in his poem. He was not trying to give voice in it to the communal "giants," but rather to the new individual Jew, torn from the community, attracted by perfections which it did not respect, and craving for a beauty alien to community traditions. *Monish*, he said in his memoirs, was a poetic self-portrait.[66] The alleged unsuitability of Yiddish as an expression of Monish's love is highly significant. (The passage dealing with the deficiencies of Yiddish occurs in the poem as its protagonist outgrows his innocent childhood and early adolescence and falls in love with a "strange," unorthodox and perhaps non-Jewish girl. As long as he had to describe Monish's innocent conventional childhood and his life as a dedicated talmudic scholar Perets found no fault with the language.) It indicates an alleged unsuitability for self-expression as such, i.e., for poetry—as Perets understood and defined it.[67] This, as we shall see in the next chapter, was the most persistent and far-reaching consequence of the self-negating "logic" which nineteenth-century Yiddish writers developed out of their maskilic ideology, the result of which I referred to as their aesthetics of ugliness.

v

The Yiddish writers of the *Haskala* found themselves in an ideologically insoluble quandary. They were supposed to enrich the world of their readers with those values which their medium, as they conceived of it, could not express. Whatever they regarded as elevated, spiritually and culturally absorbing, was out of their reach. Yiddish was suited for rendering "common" life and everyday conversation but became a "mute" language when it came to "loftier matters." This impasse was reached again and again throughout the century by the best writers. The specific nature of the "loftier matters" from which Yiddish was allegedly barred varied from writer to writer and from generation to generation. Levinzon, still somewhat a Mendelssohnian, argued in 1828 that besides being ugly and mixed, "this our language could suffice only for vulgar subjects or common conversation," but was completely invalid when philosophical, moral, and religious concepts had to be used. "When we want to name a concept of a loftier nature," he asked rhetorically, "we run out of words, don't we?" [68] Writing in the 1860s, Gotlober, a well-known Hebrew poet whose belletristic works still worth reading are almost only those he clandestinely wrote in Yiddish, characteristically emphasized the deficiencies of Yiddish in another area. The language, he insisted, did not possess "enough words for expressing one correct idea, especially in the field of the sciences, where it is completely impotent, so that a person who speaks no other language can be regarded as no better than a mute." [69] Perets, in the 1880s, was disturbed by his inability to express psychological nuances in Yiddish and was compelled to use foreign expressions in his poems, which he offered to explain to "the uneducated reader" in special notes. "I could not constrict my ideas," he wrote to Sholem Aleichem, "to fit the common people's means of expression. Disregarding the people's idiom, I strove toward a language which would best describe sensations and emotions." [70] Thus he asserted that "new expressions must constantly be added" to Yiddish.[71] Even Sholem Aleichem, who was critical of the all-too-eager adoption of foreign expressions conceded that without such words as *kritik, poezye,* or *komizm* literature could not function.[72] Obviously, as far as he was concerned, the "loftier" matters were of a literary nature. These differences do not, however, obscure the fact that the inadequacy of Yiddish as a literary language was commonly agreed upon.

What the Yiddish writers complained of had, of course, no direct connection with their preconceived ideas about the alleged ugliness of their medium. They were dealing with concrete obstacles, originating in the objective historical-linguistic situation, rather than with ideological difficulties. In the time of Abramovitsh and Linetski, and even of Sholem Aleichem and Perets, Yiddish had yet to become a fully equipped literary language. It still would not admit the discipline of a normative grammar. "Like a city that is broken down and without walls, it has no grammar and no rules or restrictions concerning parsing and spelling," the Hebrew poet Y. L. Gordon wrote to Sholem Aleichem (upon being invited to contribute to the latter's *Folks-biblyotek*), suggesting that the efforts to "revive" Yiddish as a language for literature were barren as well as dangerous.[73] Sholem Aleichem himself, although he could not agree with the poet, stated that "as long as we have no Yiddish grammar, we shall wander in the dark, and there will be tumult and confusion in our language." [74] Moreover, Yiddish had yet to emerge from the welter of various dialects and form itself as a unified literary language. Its dialectological differentiation was at the time so extreme as to present real hindrances not only to full appreciation of the musical flow of rhythm and rhyme (Perets mentioned the difference between the so-called Polish and Ukrainian dialects as one of the reasons why he thought Sholem Aleichem would not be able to enjoy his poems),[75] but also to sheer comprehension. A publication meant to cater to the whole Eastern European Jewish population, or even to a considerable part of it, faced in these respects a grave problem, as we learn from A. Tsederboym's complaint: "The differences between one part of the country and the other are very pronounced. One man laughs at another and hardly understands him . . . but even in towns a few miles apart Yiddish is spoken differently and different words are used." [76] Above all else, we saw, Yiddish had an intellectually deficient vocabulary and lacked words for "loftier matters."

All these were real difficulties, which obstructed the development of Yiddish literature even after the ideological preconceptions discussed in this chapter had been dispelled. The vicissitudes of grammar and vocabulary continued to challenge Yiddish writers even as the cultural and aesthetic attitudes toward the language were undergoing a sweeping change. However, in the consciousness of nineteenth-century writers the objective linguistic situation and the ideological negation of Yiddish were fused into one indivisible feeling of dissatisfaction, and the "aesthetics of ugliness" formed the spiritual matrix of this feeling. All other factors were poured into it and subsequently took its shape, and that is why the understanding of the artistic development of nineteenth-century Yiddish literature in general and of nineteenth-century fiction in particular depends primarily on the reader's grasp of the far-reaching implications of a subjective (i.e., ideological) state of mind rather than of the objective state of the language. Linguistic matters, we must understand, were "aesthetically" treated by nineteenth-century writers. For instance, it was the *maskilim*'s accepted notion that grammatical "confusion" and dialectical divergency in Yiddish stemmed from the original aesthetic sin of "mixture" or "corruption" of Hebrew and German. They believed in a linguistic myth which attributed to Yiddish an aesthetically "pure" past as well as a "fall." The currently spoken language, according to this, was a spoiled, debased, and deformed idiom, which once, in its primeval purity, had not deviated from "correct" German.[77] If it could, therefore, regain a certain measure of comeliness, it had to reidentify itself with the mother-tongue. (In one of his stories, A. M. Dik recommended that the Jewish community of a town which he described as "the capital of the province Utopy" be a model for all Jewish communities to emulate. One of the primary elements of the utopian nature of this community is the linguistic proficiency of its members. All the town's citizens can "speak and read Russian fluently, and among themselves they speak a highly refined Yiddish, which is almost pure German.")[78] It is against this background of a mythological linguistic fall that one should understand the *maskilim*'s attitude even as it manifested itself in the technical minutiae of their practice of writing and printing in Yiddish. For instance, their decision to establish in Yiddish the current German spelling as much as the Hebrew alphabetical system would allow; a decision which resulted in an orthography that made neither phonetic nor grammatical sense. They also decided to use the German gender system as judge in many cases of difference between the dialects.[79]

What is most pertinent to our argument is, therefore, the basic aesthetic rejection of Yiddish, its condemnation in terms such as "corruption," "mixture," and "deformity." Even when referring to the language as merely "ungrammatical," the writers under discussion were expressing their aesthetic revulsion. Here lies the basic paradox, the inherent self-contradiction that bedeviled Yiddish literature throughout the century and tore it from within, so that despite great energy and much talent it rarely achieved artistic self-sufficiency.

The literary use of Yiddish was grafted onto the body of the *Haskala* literature, and took—despite much resistance—because one could logically and irrefutably prove that it filled a vacuum. It, and it alone, could talk directly to the Jewish masses of Eastern Europe, whom this literature was supposed to enlighten. This was the unique advantage of Yiddish literature over all other branches of Jewish literature at the time. Paradoxically, this advantage also disadvantaged it artistically. As the language of the un-Europeanized masses, Yiddish could not possess all the attributes of what the Europeanized writers regarded as a *Kultur-sprache*, and yet through it they were supposed to express their developed sensibilities and enlarged intellectual interests. It symbolized the cultural poverty of the Jewish people, and yet it was supposed to make them culturally richer. Yiddish, in short, was to be used for purposes for which, a priori, it was considered inadequate.

CHAPTER THREE

THE MIMIC WRITER
AND HIS "LITTLE JEW"

> *"Yidele,* little Jew, what do you have to say?" he
> [Abramovitsh] used to ask whenever he had difficulties in
> finding the proper Yiddish expression.
> "When I must have a certain Yiddish word and cannot
> find it," he would tell me, "then I call on my little Jew,
> place him in front of me, and order him to talk, until he
> discloses the word I am looking for. . . ."
>
> (D. Eynhorn, "Mendele bay der arbet" ["Mendele at
> Work"], in *Ale verk fun Mendele,* Vol. XX, p. 59)

OF ALL THE implications of the "aesthetics of ugliness," the one that
had the longest circulation in the consciousness of nineteenth-century
Yiddish literature and left the deepest impression was the notion that
Yiddish was a language most fit for parody, indeed, a language fit for
artistic use mainly as a vehicle for comic mimesis. Although this notion
was challenged before the end of the century, it accompanied Yiddish
long after and, in some cases, persists even today. It has been, for instance, the basis for employing the language by many popular Yiddish
playwrights who, even in the grandest melodrama, were careful to include malapropisms, parody of accent, speech defects, and incoherent
talk and to employ that trademark of Yiddish comic stage-language,
the irrelevant phrase, which like a grotesque leitmotiv is endlessly repeated by the character it identifies. It had a profound influence on
Yiddish acting style, which retained the tradition of exaggerated intonation and gesticulation until a very late stage. Outside the theater
this notion, though by no means extinct, had long been fading, but in
nineteenth-century fiction it was very powerful. It survived the expira-
tion of the *Haskala,* and it is fully present in the works of Sholem Aleichem. In the course of time the notion may have outwardly changed:
its emphasis may have shifted from a negative to a seemingly positive
evaluation of the possibilities of Yiddish, as if the association of the

language with parody indicated not a deficiency or an inferiority, but rather a "specialty," a pleasing idiosyncrasy. This, of course, did not change the real implication: that Yiddish, an entity inherently deformed, lends itself most readily to caricature. This is what Sholem Aleichem had in mind when in 1884, at the very beginning of his career, he commented on the character of the language:

> Our Yiddish provides more material for satire° than other languages. That is due to the technique of the language: a sideways wink, a parenthetical remark, a nickname, a hyphen—and the sentence is already satirical and forces a smile from the reader. In addition, the language can imitate everybody's manner of speaking (and almost every Jew has his own manner of speaking), and it can also imitate everybody's gesticulations (hand-waving, shrugging and leg-shifting in talk; and where can you find a Jew who talks without throwing about his arm and twisting his whole body?).[1]

In whatever positive way this evaluation of Yiddish may be construed, it is deeply rooted in the aesthetics of ugliness. What Sholem Aleichem says is that the language is by its nature inclined to yield comic effects, i.e., to demonstrate irregularities, to digress from the norms of the true, the reasonable, and the beautiful. As a description of Yiddish this is meaningless. Yiddish is no more satirical or comic or parodic than any other language; as for its "technique," whatever Sholem Aleichem may have meant by the term, there is nothing comic about it either. There is no reason to believe that Yiddish is more apt for the literary reconstruction of peculiarities of speech and style than any other spoken language, and there is certainly nothing in its linguistic mechanism that makes it capable of mimicking intonation and physical gestures without specifically naming and describing them (as Sholem Aleichem himself so often did). Sholem Aleichem's characterization of the language of which he was to become such a master includes no single statement that can sustain the slightest objective analysis. However, for this very reason it is all important as an expression of his attitude toward Yiddish, at least at this early stage of his development. His comments bring to light a basic confusion: in them, a literary technique (parody) is confused with grammar and syntax. The idea of the

---

° At the time Sholem Aleichem applied the term indiscriminately to all specimens of robust comedy. He translated it here parenthetically, for the benefit of those of his readers who might not have been familiar with it, by the word *leytsones*—jesting, joking, mockery. As one can see he aimed mainly at mimetic ridicule.

language is unconsciously identified with that of a certain style, which is not only literary but, one might say, histrionic as well. From this significant confusion some further implications can be abstracted.

First, Yiddish is the way people speak; it is exclusively oral, conversational. Moreover, it is the way "the people," the abstract, collective "common people" speak. As such, it is alienated from the individual writer even as he writes it.

Second, it is a public or communal language, and its existence is primarily social. It is not a language through which the individual consciousness achieves self-awareness. It is almost always the voice of a group, of a community. True, "every Jew has his own manner of speaking," but the peculiarities of "every Jew's" speech are not evidence of his total individuality; they are rather the peculiarities of a comic "character," i.e., they represent not a separate consciousness but a mere digression from a norm. As such, they are themselves a social creation.

Third, the norm cannot be found within Yiddish itself. It is not an individual digression from the usage of the community that makes Yiddish comic. The whole community sounds comic to the writer. "Almost every Jew"—not merely the miser, the pedant, the braggart, the infatuated lover, the jealous husband, or other individuals divorced from a communal normality—has his own comic manner of speaking. The norm from which this comicality digresses must be found outside the world of Yiddish-speaking "people," for the language in itself is comic, i.e., it digresses from a norm which must be set by another language—Hebrew, German, or Russian.

Fourth, it follows, then, that in literature Yiddish must be treated as a given, external reality rather than as a presence within the writer to be activated for purposes of self-expression. A Yiddish writer, especially a writer of fiction and drama, listens primarily to the outside world, to "life," to "society." He catches the rhythms of speech as actually articulated and finished rather than listening to his still unarticulated self, to inner rhythms still half-formed. In short, Yiddish is a language at most fit for artistic imitation, not for artistic expression.

Last, it is a language in which books are written "for the readers," especially for those who know no other language, not for the writer himself or, as Dinezon confessed and many others confirmed, for his fellow writers. Thus, in certain ways, Yiddish literature resembles children's literature, in the sense that it is written not only with an overt educational purpose but also within limits which are not those of the writer's literary consciousness or talent but those of a certain reading public. Writing in Yiddish, much more than writing in other languages, is an act of departure from the self toward an external and communal audience.

I present these conclusions not as actually drawn by nineteenth-century Yiddish writers but as logical speculations on what lay dormant in their attitude toward the language they used. I do not pretend to believe that these writers thought about Yiddish in exactly the terms and logical sequence I have employed, let alone that they expressed their thoughts in so many words. The ambiguous position in which they found themselves because of their employment of Yiddish was not conducive to such thoughts. As much as it made the development of apologetic argumentation necessary, indeed, with some writers, indispensable, it also made the pursuit of the far-reaching implications of this argumentation very uncomfortable, if not impossible. We have seen that self-contradictions in their attitude toward the literary use of Yiddish were characteristic not only of writers of mercurial temper like Linetski, but also of sober and clear-headed ones like Y. M. Lifshits. We also have seen that even writers like Abramovitsh, whose intellectual acuity and perceptiveness rarely failed them, were reduced in this matter to a naive, elementary reasoning, within whose narrow limits they kept for many years, following the circle of their own footsteps. This, however, does not mean that the far-reaching consequences of their attitude toward Yiddish did not take form in one way or another in their consciousness and did not add pressure to the mental atmosphere in which they had to maintain themselves as writers. If this pressure was rarely fully and openly recognized, it did find expression indirectly in numerous ways, such as the many signs of uneasiness about writing in Yiddish that I have already mentioned. Above all else, it was reflected, as I shall suggest later, in the actual texture of Yiddish writing, especially in fiction. It led to the development of certain narrative techniques and structures and the exclusion of others, to the employment of certain stylistic devices, to certain literary achievements as well as to many demonstrable limitations. It pervaded the whole matrix of artistic consciousness in which Yiddish fiction was formed. Therefore, to understand historically the forms this fiction took, we must try to reconstruct them, even if in a speculative manner. Fortunately, we do not have to rely solely on speculation.

Many points in the hypothetical argument suggested above are fully borne out by historical evidence. Contemporary writers, especially those whose artistic temperament foreshadowed and, in fact, brought about great changes in the aesthetics of Yiddish literature, pointed out some of the implications of the alleged ugliness of Yiddish with considerable perspicacity.

In 1888 Sholem Aleichem, who was then preparing the first *Folksbiblyotek* for publication, received from Y. L. Perets, then known only as a Hebrew poet, a bundle of Yiddish poems accompanied by a rather disturbing letter. In it Perets explained why he thought Sholem Aleichem would not like his poetic experiments. It is perhaps significant that the reasons he cited were expressed in rather vague language, some of it open to different interpretations (the letter, incidentally, was written in Hebrew).[2] Perets was either groping for words to express a thought only half formed in his own mind, or taking care not to insult and antagonize Sholem Aleichem, or both. Only two of his reasons have a direct bearing on our present discussion. The first of them is put in a relatively simple way, though it, too, is not free of obscurities (e.g., in this passage, Perets excluded Yiddish from the category of "living languages," a term which he probably assigned only to the highly developed European languages):

> I am familar with your honor's work. Your aim (as far as I comprehend it) is to write for a reading public that reads Yiddish and Yiddish alone, while I write for myself, for my own pleasure, and if at times I think of a reader, he is a man of the upper class, who is well versed in the literature of a living language.

The second reason is so obscurely worded, that its translation will have to be deliberately interpretative (readers with knowledge of Hebrew are referred to the original quoted in the notes):

> Then there is a great difference between our very subject matter. Your honor clothes [in writing] naked [abstract?], different ideas [absorbed], from a different world, mainly from the everyday world of society, while I, writing for my own pleasure and according to my mood at the moment I take up my pen, fetch [my subjects] from all the worlds together [i.e., from the real and the nonreal worlds, from the external world of society and the inner world of the individual consciousness].[3]

If this translation is correct, then with this letter Perets began his campaign for what was called "the modernization of Yiddish literature," [4] and it can be said to mark the boundary between two kinds of historical consciousness in the development of Yiddish literature: that which was informed by the notion of the language as a medium through which a Jewish writer could not achieve direct self-expression, and that which recognizes, or at least strives to develop Yiddish as the intimate expression of the writer's personality. Perets compared here the idea of a literature which combines abstract ideas (of a maskilic nature, no doubt; ideas concerning education, emancipation, etc.) and a realistic social milieu—ideational intentions and a mimesis of external reality—with an idea of an "esemplastic" literature (to use Coleridge's well-known adjective), which blends all the "worlds," lets all its elements interpenetrate each other, and subordinates them to the writer's urge for self-expression at the moment of writing. Many elements in the distinction he draws can be categorized in terms such as "classic" versus "romantic" or "mimetic" versus "expressionistic." It is clear, however, that under the historical circumstances, Perets was primarily breaking away from a literature based on the aesthetics of ugliness, thus dissociating himself from an externalistic, mimetic, comic perception of reality. Although in the letter Perets referred only to Sholem Aleichem, he was actually dissociating himself from nineteenth-century Yiddish literature as a whole or, to be exact, from the literary ideology of nineteenth-century Yiddish writers, which he rejected on several grounds:

In the first place, it assigned to Yiddish literature the task of dealing only with externals, with naked ideas (abstractions) and with the objectively real texture of social life. It ignored the reality of the individual consciousness in general (Perets was concerned at the time about the absence of any book on psychology in Yiddish and suggested that Sholem Aleichem commission him to write one)[5] and the individuality of the writer in particular.

Second, it was chained to rational causality and limited to the everyday world, estranged from the worlds of fantasy, legend, dreams, etc.

Moreover, it caused Yiddish literature to be written without the possibility of realizing the writer's full imaginative powers; it shrunk them to fit a limited capacity. By this it not only balked the writer but also underestimated the capacities of his audience. As we have seen, it was Perets' contention that even the uninstructed "people" could "feel," if not comprehend, the beauty of full-fledged poetry.

Last, it could not support a truly poetic literature, since it would not allow the writer to let the full range of his consciousness be reflected in what he wrote. Perets' rather defiant assertion that he wrote according to his mood at the moment he took up his pen should be understood as a declaration of poetic freedom. It corresponds to his description of "the poet" as a universally receptive consciousness which is necessarily unstable, wayward.[6] Assuming in his letter that one of the reasons for Sholem Aleichem's anticipated dislike of his poetry would be its impressionistic freedom, Perets implicitly charged him with indifference to the legitimate poetic experience and expression.

The validity of Perets' poetic ideology does not concern us here, for we are interested in it only as a comment on the preceding ideology of Yiddish writers, from which it consciously differed; nor does it make much of a difference in this connection whether the judgment Perets implicitly passed on his contemporaries and predecessors and especially on the addressee of his letter was well-informed and critically sound. As a matter of fact, his knowledge of their writings was, at the time, slight at best (it turned out, for example, that he confused Sholem Aleichem—Rabinovitsh—with Abramovitsh, and while claiming to know the former's "work" and "aim," he was reacting to the latter's *Travels of Benjamin The Third* and *The Nag*, which he had read in Polish translation.[7] This is another illustration of the indifference of Yiddish writers to their colleagues and to Yiddish literature in general until the 1890s). Perets' remarkable intuition, which was often to stand him in good stead when more solid support was absent, sufficed here to enable him to put his finger on the weak points of a literary ideology which, he keenly felt, would be incompatible with the bent of his own talent. Not only did he correctly detect the general tenor of this ideology, but he also unknowingly hit upon Sholem Aleichem's real direction and aim at the time.

Defending his idea of "a Jewish novel" and commenting on the reactions to his *Stempenyu* (in which he had tried to realize this idea), Sholem Aleichem brought up the argument that Yiddish literature must, at least for the time being, limit its aesthetic and intellectual scope to fit the capacities of "the people":

> I write my novels mainly for the common people, that is, for a reading public to which lofty thoughts, "ideas," as they are called, are still for-

eign. Therefore, when one introduces the people through a story to these lofty ideas, one must make them familiar—little by little—with all the rungs of the ladder which leads up to that world referred to as "poetry."

And again in the same article:

> With the common reader . . . we should not soar high all at once. . . . The people will not understand us, and our writing will be wasted. With the people one must proceed gradually, not hurriedly, step by step. . . .

And with the emphasis somewhat shifted:

> Writing for the common people and talking to them in their language, one must present them with images and introduce them to characters with which they are familiar; that is, the heroes must come from their [the people's] own world and of their own class; indeed, they must be found among themselves.[8]

These passages, often quoted by critics with socialist and Marxist tendencies as indicative of Sholem Aleichem's essential "progressiveness," "democratism," and affiliation with "the masses," actually indicate how far, at least in his literary theory, he was from identifying his own literary personality with the masses and with their language. As much as his arguments were meant to present a method of elevating "the people" to the world of poetry, and as much as they implied that such elevation could be attained in Yiddish—though slowly and gradually—they bear the unmistakable stamp of the traditional concept of Yiddish as "their" language (notice the double emphasis: "writing for the common people and talking to them in their language"). It was a medium fit for the description of the familiar ("their own world"), of immediate, well-known social reality ("their own class"), and not of the intellectually or emotionally new ("lofty ideas"). Above all else, it was, for the present, a language adapted to "low" literature, written with constant reference to the limitations of its readers and thus not a literature meant to absorb the full individuality of the writer. It is when we read statements like these that we realize how really revolutionary Perets was in his argument that the writer's main obligation was to himself, to his individuality. He was suggesting that the materials of Yiddish literature should be sought not only in the external, social world but also in the inner world of the individual consciousness or, as he put it, in "all the worlds together."

ii

If until the 1890s, or even until the very end of the century, Yiddish was regarded as unaesthetic, incapable of expressing the individual consciousness, a communal language to be employed only in direct reference to the immediate reality of Jewish life, what then could have been the criteria by which artists such as Abramovitsh and Sholem Aleichem directed their stylistic efforts? This question has particular relevance in the case of Abramovitsh, since it is quite clear that he was searching for some kind of stylistic perfection; but what kind of stylistic perfection could be pursued in the vulgar idiom of a community allegedly devoid of any sense of formal beauty? In the introduction (in the form of a dedication) to *Stempenyu*, Sholem Aleichem quoted Abramovitsh as having addressed to him in a letter this admonitory advice: "On a work of art, dear grandson, one must work, sweat, polish every word. Remember what I tell you—polish! Polish!" [9] It is possible that Abramovitsh never wrote these neatly phrased and quotable sentences (for they are not to be found in the carefully preserved collection of his letters to Sholem Aleichem). It is also possible that the "grandson," in his impetuous myth making, thought he was merely rendering in a more memorable form, statements the "grandfather" had really made; statements that actually differed in tenor and emphasis from the artistic credo into which they might have been refashioned. Even so, the plea for conscientious artistic labor certainly corresponded to a principle inherent in Abramovitsh's literary practice. By 1888, it should be remembered, Abramovitsh had already twice rewritten his *Fishke the Lame* (originally published in 1869, this story was rewritten, but not republished, in 1876 and then completely reworked for publication in 1888). He rewrote once, and perhaps more than once, his *Little Man* (1864, 1879). He was at the time hard at work on a new version of his early *Magic Ring* (1865). Surely all this indefatigable revision must have been informed by some ideal of literary and stylistic perfection. Surely Abramovitsh and many other writers were motivated by a positive aesthetic principle of sorts. They could not conceive of this principle in clearly defined terms. The very nature of the ideological situation made this impossible. No Yiddish writer before Perets had been able to conceptualize his aesthetic impulses into a positive aesthetic rationale, and even Perets, as we have seen, was hampered by grave theoretical difficulties in his efforts to assert himself as a Yiddish artist. Yet, if the way to a positive aesthetic theory was blocked, other outlets could have been found for a strong sense of artistic mission. Abstract concepts were most vulnerable to the negation of the prevailing aesthetics of ugliness, but concrete images, for instance, were much less so. It was all but impossible for a Yiddish writer to announce himself as a creator of beauty, but it was quite possible for him to project himself in an image implying the creation of beauty, such as a nightingale, a musician, a violin (a symbol much in use). Sholem Aleichem, we must realize, revolutionized, perhaps even created, the historical consciousness of modern Yiddish literature not by his critical concepts but by the image of the grandfather–artist.

It is necessary for our argument that we investigate some of the possibilities which may emerge once we begin to reconstruct the conceptual implications of such images, and add them to something like a subterranean artistic self-awareness. At this point, an observation made by the Hebrew writer M. Y. Berditshevski (1865–1921) may offer some help. As a Hebraist who wrote Yiddish ably and quite extensively, Berditshevski enjoyed in his observations on Yiddish and its literature the double advantage of a practitioner's firsthand knowledge and of an outsider's distance, a perspective which the more deeply committed could not have. This may explain in part the extraordinary lucidity and straightforwardness of the following comment on the difficulties which the literary use of Yiddish involved. It is taken from a Yiddish article titled "Far dem tararam" ("Before the Tumult Began"):

> If you want to know the whole truth, then I must own that it is not at all simple to publish a newspaper in Yiddish. Indeed, it is a task difficult enough to intimidate any man. You must understand: Newspapers are published in Yiddish for the benefit of the common people, to serve them as guides; however, as of now we still are not in possession of a language adequate for this task. By no means can we get along with what we have. In Yiddish one can easily talk about the Jew or discuss him, but one cannot tell the Jew about ourselves or discuss with him our thoughts. The language is still so indivisible from the Jew, so thickly rooted in his soul, that all we can say about it is, this is how a Jew talks; this is the means by which he portrays to himself the world and explains to himself the problems of the Jewish people. However, to make the Jew understand through his own language a foreign idea: to cope with

this task one must be a master; one must absorb oneself in it, lose one-self and whatever one possesses in it. One must know how to put every idea in the Jew's own mouth; how to let him understand it as if he him-self said it and in the way he himself would have explained it. Very few people are up to such a feat; one in a thousand; perhaps only one in a generation. You see, anyone can learn Hebrew, provided that he con-fines himself to his desk for a few years, stuffs himself with the Bible and grammar, and reads some *melitse* books [belles lettres, poetry]. The mastering of Yiddish, however, is a gift; a faculty one must be born with. I am speaking, of course, of the real thing, of radical, authentic Yiddish.[10]

I have quoted this passage at length for its wide aura of suggestion and implication and not as direct historical evidence. It cannot be re-garded as the latter for our purposes primarily because it was written at a relatively late stage (*ca.* 1906), and thus it reflects a literary milieu considerably different from that of the earlier period with which our discussion is concerned. Moreover, its subject being the difficulties of the Yiddish press, it bears only indirectly on the problems of imagina-tive literature. All these facts notwithstanding, the passage can have a provocative, catalytic influence on our thinking. In discussing the plight of Yiddish newspapers, Berditshevski touched upon a range of subjects much wider than that to which he was directly referring. By suggesting that what hampered the functioning of these newspapers was the inadequacy of the language and not external (financial, politi-cal) impediments, he hit upon the crucial problem in the development of the literary use of modern Yiddish in all its stages and forms and made a point which is obviously relevant to our argument.

What immediately emerges as a helpful suggestion is the distinc-tion Berditshevski draws in the opening sentences of the passage, be-tween "the Jew"—an abstract, collective, monolithic entity—and "us"—journalists and writers—i.e., between the Jewish masses and the Jewish intelligentsia. This distinction between the Europeanized writ-ers and their non-Europeanized readers is most thorough and far-reaching. It is not only that the writers differ from their readers in taste or range of intellectual interests; the writers and the readers ac-tually inhabit different worlds and make sense of these worlds through different mental mechanisms. They hardly have a common frame of reference. If the literary intelligentsia is able to a certain extent to en-visage the world of "the Jew" ("tell about the Jew") because most of its members had at one stage of their development a firsthand experience of it, it is rarely able to share its own world with the uninitiated "Jew" ("tell about ourselves"). It cannot convey its "ideas," which are admittedly "foreign," outside a limited intellectual territory; at least it cannot be done through Yiddish, for the language, which is still an integral part of the world of "the Jew," cannot correspond to anything beyond its own barriers. Thus, the intelligentsia is gravely hampered in the playing of its official role, that of "guiding" the people. It is a frustrated intelligentsia, since the special historical circumstances under which it has developed have made it largely unfit to carry out the duty which similar intellectual elites naturally assume.

This complete polarization of masses versus intelligentsia cannot, of course, be expected to reflect historical reality. Like most extreme positions that achieve clarity through absolute dichotomies, it oversimplifies certain aspects of the historical situation it pretends to explain while ignoring others. Nevertheless, it has some usefulness. Like similar positions it can, if it carries the weight of serious meditation, throw light on a general and relatively simple principle operating beneath the complexities of the surface. To regard the Yiddish literary intelligentsia and "the people" as inhabiting fundamentally different worlds, or as constituting "two camps" (to use the title Berditshevski gave to one of his best Hebrew novelettes), is to get quite close to the core of the historical truth, as all the evidence offered in these chapters suggests. It was because he differentiated "the Jew" and his world (which includes the Yiddish language) from "us" and "our ideas" in an extreme and, no doubt, simplified manner, that Berditshevski was able to point unequivocally to the historical paradox we have been discussing. Other writers and commentators had certainly sensed this paradox but could not formulate it as simply and as straightforwardly as he did. Against the background of endlessly vague talk about Yiddish literature as "the expression of the people," his position in this matter is extraordinarily perspicacious and edifying.

We realize how edifying it can be when we reach the point Berditshevski makes once his initial distinction is amply clear, that is, when he reaches his conclusion: that because the Yiddish writer and the Yiddish language belong to different worlds, the successful literary use of Yiddish is extremely rare, and involves an attempt on the part of the writer to express his thoughts through the simulated voice of "the Jew" rather than through his own, "natural" voice, To become the good Yiddish writer (perhaps one should say the "ideal" Yiddish writer), Berditshevski insists, "One must know how to put every idea in the Jew's own mouth; how to let him understand it as if he himself said it and in the way he himself would have explained it." Certainly this is one of the more pregnant remarks ever made on nineteenth-century Yiddish literature in general and on its beginnings in particular. What it amounts to is the suggestion that, for his work to achieve the status of art, a Yiddish writer has to conceal his direct identity and to master a technique of self-alienation or even of self-elimination in his writing. For that, the writer has to be endowed with a gift for histrionic disguise and with a sure sense of the proper limitations of feigned innocence. Making "the Jew" talk naturally and fluently and yet express at the same time "ideas" that might be quite remote from his own, the Yiddish writer is required to be a master of dramatic irony. Irony, indeed, must be the very element in which he functions. Though he is by no means always obliged to be ironic in the strict or rhetorical sense of the term (the sense in which irony is "a figure of speech in which the intended meaning is the opposite from that expressed in the word used"),[11] he is always ironic in the sense that with him the very act of speech, the very application of words to thought is a reconciliation of opposites and a deliberate gesture of simulation. By prescribing this difficult remedy for the difficult ailments of the Yiddish *Wortkunst*, Berditshevski put his finger with unprecedented accuracy on the pulse of the artistic vein running throughout the body of nineteenth-century Yiddish fiction. One does not wonder that he was the first, and for some time the only, critic to acknowledge the genial greatness of Sholem Aleichem and to refer to his best works as poetry of universal relevance.[12] If he could persist in this evaluation at a time when it was the fashion among the Yiddish establishment to tolerate the enviable popularity of Sholem Aleichem with the condescending superiority which "pure" art sometimes assumes toward successful entertainment,[13] it was not only because he had sound literary intuition but also because his thinking was directed by sound principles and because he had a true notion of the scope and limitations of contemporary Yiddish literature as a whole.

To be sure, these notions and principles were not expressed in critical abstractions but in an image: the poet assuming a mask, playing the role of "the Jew." A mere metaphor, this is highly suggestive, and it has a concrete bearing on the reality of the artistic employment of

Yiddish by such writers as Linetski, Abramovitsh, Sholem Aleichem, and to a certain extent, even Perets. In order to realize how concrete and direct this bearing is, one has only to recall the numerous historical and biographical examples such as the one offered as the motto of this chapter. Abramovitsh's imaginary calling on his "little Jew" (as described by the poet D. Eynhorn, who was for a time Abramovitsh's secretary) is in every way symbolic. It is the symbol of the nineteenth-century Jewish writer, definitely one of "us," the Europeanized Jewish intelligentsia, immersing himself in "their" world, the world of "the little Jews," in order to function as an artist. He is an actor, impersonating "them," speaking in a voice not his own, and he depends on an imaginary "prompter" who puts the right words in his mouth. Thus he performs the difficult task, which Berditshevski described as putting "every idea in the Jew's own mouth . . . as if he himself said it and in the way he himself would have explained it."

iii

It is worthwhile, I think, to dwell on some of the associations that Berditshevski's conception of the ideal Yiddish writer give rise to. First, he is a dedicated artist. To achieve his goal, he must absorb himself in his work, "lose whatever he possesses in it." Second, he is a mimetic genius. He evokes comparisons from one distinct area, that of the theater or even the circus. One may compare him to a tightrope dancer who skillfully keeps his perilous balance between the historical bias of the language toward the exclusive mentality of "the Jew" and his own intellectual bias toward "foreign" ideas and concepts. One may even compare him to a ventriloquist who is able to assume a voice or voices distinctly different from his own and master them with such mimetic subtlety, with such accuracy of nuance, as to make them express his own "ideas" without letting his audience become aware of his trick. Above all else, this conception of a writer reminds one of the comic actor; the skilled, self-disciplined, highly effective comedian.

These are by no means idle comparisons. They certainly have a bearing on the way many Yiddish artists regarded themselves and were regarded by their readers. Linetski, for instance, established himself in the imagination of his contemporaries as *a beyzer marshelik* ("a sharp-tongued wedding-jester," the title of his first and best-known collection of poems), who was permitted to tell his audience the bitter truth about themselves because he conveyed it by theatrical means. He also liked to compare himself to a wandering minstrel, to a beggar with a lyre, etc.[14] At a certain stage in his career, he wrote satirical *chansons* for the entertainers in the Jewish wine cellars of Odessa, and sometimes he himself would perform.[15] To the end he remained a superb performer of his own works,[16] and a hilarious mimic with a repertoire of celebrated "numbers" (he would stage, for instance, a hasidic *Melave-malke°* and would himself improvise the role of the *tsadik*).[17] The very act of writing was with him a theatrical gesture. Not only did he write a considerable part of his *feuilletons* in a dramatic form, but he conceived of all his works as of theatrical *tours de force*. Each of his collections of *feuilletons* opens with a noisy introduction, which more than anything else resembles the appearance of a vaudeville entertainer on the stage amid applause, laughter, whistles, and provocative interjections. Having bowed to the readers, his persona, Eli Kotsin Hatskhakueli, immediately establishes "contact" with the audience present, exchanges jokes, answers questions, and welcomes old acquaintants with sarcastic congratulations.[18] A similar "act" is performed by Mendele the Bookpeddler in his prefatory addresses, which open most of Abramovitsh's works.

Abramovitsh, as we learn from the numerous reminiscences of those who knew him, was the supreme actor in whatever he did. Many of his letters to his fellow writers can be described only as private epistolary theatricals, and his famous table talk was an elaborate scenic performance.[19] To him writing itself was an essentially histrionic gesture. In the aforementioned article of D. Eynhorn we find this description:

> I remember my first day as his secretary. He was then translating the new chapters of *The Nag*, which had originally been written in Hebrew. Having finished his coffee and rested somewhat, he beckoned to me to be ready with my pen and ordered: Write! From that moment the show started. He was not dictating; he impersonated, acted like a performer on the stage. In front of my eyes living characters began to hover. They gesticulated, talked, and eventually evaporated. From time to time he would remain paralyzed, a fixed grimace on his face, searching for a word. . . .
> When you translate something, he used to say, forget your original,

---

° *Melave-malke* (literally, "ushering out of the queen"; in this case, the holy Sabbath)—the meal eaten at the conclusion of the Sabbath, with singing.

close your book, quarrel with it. Each language has its own grimaces. And so he would stand without a rest for four hours, sob, laugh, get angry, quarrel, talk like a merchant, like an old Jewish woman, like a *rov*, like a *maskil*, mimicking each in his turn.[20]

Perhaps the most revealing part of this vignette is the statement "Each language has its own grimaces," which portrays not only the writer but even language itself as an actor or a clown with his own mimetic manner.

Sholem Aleichem recorded in his autobiography the first manifestation of his artistic nature as an irresistible urge to mimicry and impromptu theatricals. He also attributed this urge to many of his artistically gifted child heroes, such as Motl, the son of the cantor Peyse.[21] All his life he was fascinated by the theater (for which he wrote copiously) as well as by the other performing arts. Three of his major novels deal with performing artists and describe what may perhaps be called Jewish *vie de bohème* (*Stempenyu* describes the world of the *klezmers*, the popular musicians of the traditional Jewish wedding; *Yosele solovey*, "Yosele the Nightingale," is a brilliant cantor; and in *Blondzhnde shtern*, "Wandering Stars," a traveling theatrical troupe is followed from a small town in Bessarabia to the Lower East Side of New York). From quite an early stage of his career he identified himself with the romantic concept of the circus-clown with a fixed expression of hilarity concealing a broken heart. So intensely did he identify himself with this image, that he made it the subject of the little poem he prepared as early as 1905 to have engraved on his tombstone:

Do ligt a yid, a posheter,
Geshribn yidish-taytsh far vayber,
Un farn prostn folk hot er—
Geven a humorist a shrayber.

Dos gantse lebn oysgelakht,
Geshlogn mit der velt kapores.
Di gantse velt hot gut gemakht,
Un er—oy vey—geven af tsores!

Un dafke demlt, ven der oylem hot
Gelakht, geklatsht un fleg zikh freyen,
Hot er gekrenkt—dos veyst nor got—
Besod, az keyner zol nit zen.[22]

("Here lies a simple Jew,/ Who wrote Yiddish for women,/ And for the common people;/ He was a humorist, a writer./ He ridiculed life itself;/ He laughed at the whole world./ The whole world prospered,/ While he—alas—was hard up./ And at that time, when his audience/ Laughed, clapped and had fun—/ Precisely then he pined away—God is his witness—/ Secretly, lest anybody notice.")

In a first version of this epitaph the penultimate line read: "Hot er geveynt" ("he sobbed" instead of "he pined away"), which further emphasizes the connection between the self-portrait of the author and the idea of the actor, since it so obviously smacks of the operatic gesture (Leoncavallo's *Pagliacci* had a strong appeal for Sholem Aleichem).[23] Incidentally, during his later years Sholem Aleichem virtually acted the role of the pining comedian as, not unlike Dickens, he read his stories throughout Europe and the United States with immense success, thereby ruining his deteriorating health.

The idea of the stage and the image of the actor were bound to loom large in nineteenth-century Yiddish literature. Their prominence was postulated by the logic of the linguistic situation. As a communal idiom, external to the consciousness of the writer, Yiddish had to be used mimetically simply because there could be no other way of using it effectively. A language of public communication and not of meditation, it functioned only in actual speech, that is, dramatically. A Yiddish work, whether it was meant to be read aloud or not (and more often than not it was), had a distinct vocal quality; it was written for recitation—if only in the imagination—with the proper intonation and gesticulation. When the writer or his persona spoke it, they addressed an audience, explicitly or implicitly; when a person talked to himself in it, he treated his consciousness as a stage. Abramovitsh's and Sholem Aleichem's works are full of theatrical inner dialogues ("dialogues," because in them the consciousness is dramatized as two separate beings engaged in a discussion; "theatrical," because in spite of being avowedly internal, they are reported as if actually staged, with gesticulations, descriptions of tone of speech, etc.). Whatever artistic use was being made of Yiddish, the presence of the language had to be distanced from one's self, moved into the limelight of a stage, made spectacular and, in a way, impersonal. Staginess was the linguistic reality of Yiddish literature at the time, and there was no way to avoid it. On the one hand, this staginess indicates the basic limitations of the artistic use of Yiddish by nineteenth-century writers. This use was confined to dramatic imitation, to monologues and dialogues of a comic (i.e., "low") nature. Levinzon, with the negative attitude of a *maskil*, defined it quite correctly when he insisted that the language was "sufficient only for vulgar subjects and for common conversations." We have only to drop the pejorative adjectives, or perhaps to replace the words "common conversations" and "vulgar subjects" by words such as "idiomatic dialogues and materials" or "subjects fit for comedy or satire" in order to see how close to the truth he was.

On the other hand, however, this quality of the literary use of the language constituted an outlet for positive artistic effort. Levinzon pointed out the insufficiencies of Yiddish, but unconsciously he was also defining areas where it could achieve artistic excellence—the areas of comedy and dramatized speech. Here was certainly an opening for a notion of artistic pleasure within the boundaries of the aesthetics of ugliness. (Had not Aristotle prescribed that even the ugly could yield a pleasing effect in a work of art, because "the pleasure felt in things imitated" is "universal," and thus, even "objects, which in themselves we view with pain, we delight to contemplate when reproduced with minute fidelity. . . .") [24]

The idea of the theater and the image of the comic actor are suggestive of what might be described as a positive principle in the aesthetics of nineteenth-century Yiddish literature. They are associated not only with the pleasures of artistic imitation, but also with the idea of artistic skill and self-discipline. What is more important, they imply the separateness of art and life, or the autonomy of art. The mimetic writer must shed his private personality and develop another one: independent, objective. In a literature so deeply committed to immediate utilitarian ends, this suggestion could have a considerable liberating influence. It could, and it did, fashion the identity of writers as artists. It is not accidental that the novelist Y. Dinezon found fault with some of Abramovitsh's best works (*Benjamin the Third*, for instance) because, as he put it, "when I read them I have a feeling that the author performs a dance on a tightrope for the benefit of his friends and of other writers, and cares little whether he is being useful to the people or not." [25] This is not accidental, because Dinezon, perhaps more than any other writer, represents the homiletic-sentimental streak in Yiddish fiction; a streak which in his works as well as in those of other minor novelists proved definitely antiartistic, inimical to irony, to conscious structural artistry, to the idea of literary technique, to

stylistic perfection, and favorable to moralistic sermonizing, to un-
bridled emotionalism, and to stylistic sloppiness. Above all else, the
tradition which Dinezon represents objected to the separation of art
from life. But for those Yiddish writers who aspired to artistic self-control such a separation was absolutely necessary. In a sense, they really
were tightrope dancers, and in order to maintain their balance they
had to detach their personal self from their skill. Sholem Aleichem's
epitaph implies that without the disciplined simulation of the clown he
would not have been able to function as the great comedian of the
Jewish people. The theatrical gesture enabled him (as it enabled Mark
Twain) to isolate his bruised self from his comic art. In the introductory chapter to his autobiography, *Funem yarid* ("Back from the
Fair"), Sholem Aleichem developed the same idea from a somewhat
different direction. Here it emerges from an explanation of the difficulties he faced in this book:

> Writing an autobiography, a true, unfabricated life story. Why, that
> amounts to accounting for one's whole life in public, to saying one's last
> confession before the whole world. Indeed, writing one's biography and
> writing one's will are almost the same thing. . . . Besides, it is so hard
> for a person speaking of himself to rise to the moral height required for
> resisting the temptation of showing oneself to the best advantage,
> playing the good fellow whose cheek calls for your pinch. This is why I
> decided to write my biography in a special form, the form of a novel, a
> biographical novel. I shall therefore talk of myself in the third person,
> which is to say, I, *Sholem Aleichem the writer,* shall tell you the true life
> story of *Sholem Aleichem the person* . . . as if it were told by an outside
> observer, a complete stranger, but a stranger who has always been with
> my hero and who has seen him through the seven circles of hell. . . .[26]

For many of Sholem Aleichem's dedicated readers this must have
seemed strangely coy. For decades they had been used to regarding
him as their most familiar friend, a veritable member of the household.
He had talked endlessly with them in the first person, treated them to
his jokes, trusted them with his innermost secrets. With him they had
always been *entre nous,* so to speak, and finally, after thirty years of
public familiarity, to exhibit this maidenly shame, this stage fear, this
need for the technical aid of the third person and of the "special form"
of the biographical novel! In the same way the few remaining readers
of Linetski must have been baffled by the old writer's confession that,
do what he would, he could not bring himself to publish an autobiog-

raphy because "he could not let his naked I," his "deep-hidden I," appear in public, as if literature were a bathhouse (this confession was made in Linetski's last printed work, a slim brochure titled, like Sholem Aleichem's autobiography, *Funem yarid*).[27] After all, hadn't he told the story of his childhood in all its terrible ugliness fifty years before in his *Dos poylishe yingl* (this satire was generally treated as an autobiography), then reiterated it in his *Vorem in khreyn* ("The Worm in the Horseradish"), and again elaborated on it in his *Khsidish yingl* ("The Hasidic Boy")? Didn't his entire literary output amount to one long exhibitionistic autobiography? Both Sholem Aleichem and Linetski tried to use the compositions they regarded as summing up their literary activity for telling the public the long-blurred truth, namely, that they had never revealed to their readers the "naked, deep-hidden I"; that the first person, always assumed with such an air of naturalness, did not represent their personal selves; that with all their familiar garrulity they had concealed as much as they had revealed; that their whole literary achievement was based on a deliberately deceptive duality. Emphasizing and antagonizing the concepts of writer versus person, Sholem Aleichem was plainly out to make even his most naive readers understand this crucial matter: the writer and the man were two different entities. The writer had always accompanied the man, and yet he had remained a stranger to him, an impartial observer. He had seen him through the seven circles of hell, like Dante's Virgil, but he did not share his pains. He understood, sympathized, but never lost his objectivity.

iv

We can now complete this cycle of observations by linking Sholem Aleichem's differentiation between the writer and the person with Berditshevski's distinction between "the Jew" and "us." There can be no doubt that they are significantly related to each other. Of course, the difference between the artist's persona and his individual personality did not necessarily originate from the historical situation that separated the Jewish intellectuals from the Jewish masses; it is, indeed, a difference of a universal character, for it has to do with the nature of art itself. Still, it was absorbed and refashioned by this situation and thus given its specific historical and literary direction. A few illustrations will help make this clear.

The introductory chapter to Sholem Aleichem's *Funem yarid,* written two or three years before the author's death, reflects the enlarged self-knowledge of the aging artist who had had a brush with death and who, already on his way back from the fair, could find time for a leisurely study of himself and his world. But the awareness of the duality of writer and person did not require all this leisure and introspection. It existed even when the writer was impatient to get to the fair. In 1888, that *annus mirabilis* of his career (the publication of two novels, *Sender Blank* and *Stempenyu,* the appearance of the first *Folks-biblyotek,* the long articles on Shomer and on Jewish poverty in Yiddish literature, the establishing of the grandson–grandfather relationship with Abramovitsh, etc.), he wrote a *feuilleton,* in which the narrator, Sholem Aleichem, finds himself in his own home town but in an unfamiliar, modern-looking street. "Be good enough to tell me who lives here in this big brick house?" he asks a Jew who happens to hurry by. A characteristic staccato conversation (quoted here in a somewhat abriged version) develops:

> "Oh yes, here lives. . . . Wait. Wait, I'll remember presently. Oh yes. It seems that no less a person than Monastiryov, Yakov Borisovitsh Monastiryov, lives here."
> "A Jew?"
> "A Jew!"
> "Yakov Borisovitsh?"
> "The same!"
> "Wait a moment, isn't this Yankl Bereles?"
> "I cannot tell."
> "Isn't he the son of Berele Monastrishtsher?"
> "Ask him."
> "No, don't be angry with me. Do understand. There is something. That Yakov Borisovitsh was my schoolmate. We studied together in the same *kheyder,*° and he was. . . ."
> "But where do I come into all this?"
> ". . . But you must understand how important this is for me. After all, a friend of mine—I mean Yankl, Yankl Bereles was my friend . . . and suddenly Yakov Borisovitsh Monastiryov!"

The impatient interlocutor flees, and Sholem Aleichem resumes his

---

° *Kheyder* (literally, "room")—the traditional small private school where most Eastern European Jewish children got their *khumesh* (Pentateuch) and *gemore* (Talmud) education.

walk in the modern street. He discovers—by the brass plaques on the brick and stone walls of the spacious houses—other *kheyder* classmates concealed under crudely Russified and even Christianized (Monastiryov, "of the monastery") names. Among others, he encounters one who gives him an especially disagreeable surprise:

> Solomon Naumovitsh—who could this creature be? A-a-ah? Oh, it's you Sholemke, isn't it? Sholem Reb Nokhem Vevek's son. . . . Fine, fine, very fine indeed. I believe I still remember you when you walked in your little shoes and stockings° and had quite a head for the *gemore*. I thought then that you would certainly end up as a *rov* of a small town, or at least as a *shoykhet*, a *moyel*, a *bal metsise*,°° and what do you know? Here you turn up a Solomon Naumovitsh of all things. What does your uncle Pinye say to this? And Itsik—does he let it be? How come? [28]

This is a private joke, which only a part of the reading public could sense, let alone fully understand, in 1888, although even then, it was quite clear that Solomon Naumovitsh was the author himself. We need, however, the information Sholem Aleichem supplied in *Funem yarid* to know, for instance, that Pinye was his fanatically hasidic uncle. Always suspicious of his brother Nokhem, who in his secret heart was a moderate *maskil*, Pinye took upon himself to guard his nephews from sinning; he was especially circumspect with the high-spirited Sholemke, about whose *yidishkeyt* ("Jewish faith," or "Jewish way of life") he had always had the worst misgivings. It was therefore quite natural for the narrator of the *feuilleton*, obviously acquainted with the family situation of Sholemke, to wonder what Pinye's reaction to the Russification of his nephew's name (as well as to the other changes it implied) could have been. A joke though it is, this little scene is nevertheless also a manifestation of critical self-awareness on the part of Sholem Aleichem; critical self-awareness on two parallel levels, aesthetic and sociological. From the aesthetic point of view, the early *feuilleton* clearly foretells what was to be said twenty-five years later in *Funem yarid*, about the difference between Sholem Aleichem the public figure, the well-known comedian, and the private Sholem

---

° The Jewish shoes and socks are contrasted here to the more Russian boots. Low shoes and white cotton stockings were items of traditional, especially hasidic, attire.

°° *Rov*, rabbi; *shoykhet*, ritual slaughterer; *moyel*, circumciser; *bal metsise*, one who sucks the blood at circumcision. All are *kley koydesh* (literally, "holy vessels")—the clerical elite of the Jewish congregation.

Rabinovitsh. The notion of this difference is employed here for the purposes of comedy, but that does not mean that it was not taken seriously. On the contrary, realized in a comic situation, it is all the more concrete and immediate. The writer–comedian here is literally the outsider, the stranger referred to in the opening chapter of the autobiography. He is perhaps an even more remote personality than this. In *Funem yarid* the writer has accompanied his hero throughout his life; here the narrator seems to have lost touch with Sholemke immediately after the *kheyder* days. If the difference between writer and man has schizoid overtones, here they can be heard much louder.[29] The second level upon which our comic scene is staged is sociological and cultural. The narrator Sholem Aleichem differs from Solomon Naumovitsh in his cultural allegiances. Though he does not directly refer to his position on the problem of tradition and Europeanization in Jewish life, it is clear on which side of the fence he stands, and by what criteria he judges the metamorphosis which has taken place in his old friends' names and, no doubt, in all the other marks of their cultural identity. Though he is not necessarily to be identified with people like Uncle Pinye, he is, at least for the purposes of this specific scene, certainly antagonistic to Solomon Naumovitsh and to what he represents. In any case, there can be no doubt that he still belongs to the world of "the Jew"; he speaks its language and thinks its thoughts. In this respect the opening conversation is of importance. Whatever Sholem Aleichem the writer may be, he is always *on speaking terms* with the common Jewish people. This, indeed, is his central characteristic as a literary persona. He addresses Jewish people, and he listens to them. The ease, the casualness with which the narrator opens the conversation with the unwilling passer-by, his almost tiresome insistence on sharing with him his feelings (a then-current comic device in Sholem Aleichem's *feuilletons*) are indications of his unquestionable "belonging." His familiarity with his occasional interlocutor is that basic familiarity of a monolithic society, where one does not have to know people personally in order to address them freely and even intimately. Besides, the narrator clearly addresses his Jew as a potential ally against Yakov Borisovitsh Monastiryov or, for that matter, against Solomon Naumovitsh. Incidentally, the *feuilleton* not only opens with a conversation in which one party is unwilling to take part but it also ends with such a conversation. The narrator recognizes a childhood friend in a foreign-looking gentleman who is eyeing him rather suspiciously. "Why do you gape at me so, Yoylik? Don't you know me? I am your friend, Sholem Aleichem," he pleads, but in vain. The gentleman, who answers in Russian (the foreignness is conveyed in the Yiddish text by heavy Germanisms), insists that his name is Yevlik Petrovitsh and not Yoylik, that he does not know any Sholem Aleichem, and that he is too busy to be bothered. If this Yevlik Petrovitsh is to be taken as representative of Sholem Aleichem's Russified acquaintances, then we may have here some further comment on the possible relationship between the narrator and Solomon Naumovitsh. Would Solomon, too, have denied his *kheyder* friend his recognition and conversation?

The *feuilleton* we are discussing should perhaps not be overly pressed for "meanings." It is too slight a piece to stand much pressure; but surely it proves Sholem Aleichem's awareness of the ambiguity of his position as a Europeanized intellectual who is also a popular Yiddish humorist. Likewise, it surely indicates the existence of a connection between this awareness and the author's insistence on the separateness of Sholem Aleichem and Solomon, the persona and the person. Moreover, this *feuilleton* is by no means an accident, an isolated case. However slight, it is characteristic. The situation it creates recurs in nineteenth-century Yiddish fiction. It is developed more than once in the works of Abramovitsh. For instance, Abramovitsh has his Fishke the Lame, the itinerant beggar, find his way in the course of his wanderings to Odessa and there have a glimpse of the principal of the local *Talmud-toyre,*° who is also a well-known satirist. This momentary encounter occurs as Fishke is strolling along the boulevards of the southern city with another beggar, with whom he is engaged in a heated argument. Yontl, the other beggar, like Fishke, is a native of the Jewish town Glupsk ("Silly-town," one of the three symbolic Jewish towns that figure in Abramovitsh's works), but he has already stayed in Odessa long enough to refer to it as "our Odessa"; he is already "assimilated," so to speak. Fishke, a newcomer and a person of a much stronger character, constantly compares Odessa with Glupsk and finds

---

° A *Talmud-toyre* (literally, "the study of the Torah," the divine law) was the name given to the charity school usually found in every Jewish community. It was maintained by the community and meant to give the children of the poor the rudiments of a Jewish education. The Odessa *Talmud-toyre* greatly differed from its traditional namesakes, as the fact that in 1881 Abramovitsh was made its principal indicates. It was one of these typical semimodern Jewish educational institutions which aspired to strike a compromise between traditional Jewish values and modern ones. Abramovitsh remained the principal of the institute, at least nominally, until his death in 1917.

the new place absurd as well as obscene. Dress and manners along the boulevards infuriate him. The females, he says, are scandalously half-naked, while the "Frenchified" men are ridiculously overdressed. It is at this point that the *Talmud-toyre* teacher with another Odessa gentleman appear before Fishke's eyes:

> On our way we see two of those fine Frenchies walking toward us. Yontl stretches out his hand; one of the two stops, exchanges a few words with him, and gives him a coin.
>
> "Fishke, do you know who these are?" asks Yontl, proud as a cock, his eyes glistening with pleasure. "The one who gave me the coin is the chief teacher in our *Talmud-toyre*, an acquaintance of mine, mind you! What would you say to that, Fishke? Surely *he* must be good enough for you . . . ?"
>
> "Let all my enemies have such a good year as he is good for me or for anything!" I answer and spit. "Seeing your fine chief teacher, one imagines what sort of a *Talmud-toyre*, God forbid, you must have here. Let me ask you just one question, Yontl: How can you say without a blush that this is how things should be! No, you have already been corrupted, Yontl! You have already become like these people here. . . . A *Talmud-toyre* teacher, you say! Just like our Reb Hertsele Daredevil, not to confuse the holy with the profane! Isn't he? Reb Hertsele Daredevil—this is a real Jew, a Jew with a vengeance! Wherever you don't look for him—there he crops up, and he performs his duties with all his heart. A funeral—he is there; a match is to be clinched—by whom if not by him? Chanting psalms in the graveyard, reading a chapter of *Mishne* to the memory of the deceased—everything is done by him. Once a week he makes his rounds of the town, as the custom is, and do you know what? People come out to meet him with a coin ready in their hand. On *Simkhes-toyre°* he flocks with his *Talmud-toyre* scholars to all the rich people of the town to say the 'He that blessed' benediction, and he is given his blessing-wine in generous quantities! He shouts 'Holy flock!' and the children shout back 'B-a-a! B-a-a!' This is how things should be! and your Frenchy, what about him, eh? What taste can his psalms and 'He that blessed' have! How can his Sabbath benediction or his participation in a funeral, God forbid, be proper?" [30]

Here again is a private joke, but a much richer one than Sholem

---

° "The rejoicing of the law"; the last day of Tabernacles, on which the public reading of the Torah is annually concluded and reopened. It is celebrated with great festivity. In Eastern Europe the scholars of the *Talmud-toyre* and their teachers played in this festivity the part Fishke describes here.

Aleichem's. Here the irony, as almost everywhere in Abramovitsh's
works, is double-edged. Of course, the author makes use of Fishke's
naiveté and satirizes Glupsk through him. The praises Fishke has for
the educational capacities of Reb Hertsele Daredevil turn, in his
mouth, into an exposure of the whole Glupsk-style educational system.
It is important, however, to notice that Abramovitsh is also satirizing
himself through Fishke, for the latter's objections to him as a *Talmud-
toyre* educator are by no means irrelevant. It is not only to the
"Frenchified" appearance that the objections apply, as it is not only to
the Russified name that the narrator in Sholem Aleichem's *feuilleton*
objects. The question posed by Fishke—which remains, significantly,
unanswered—is what kind of education can such a "Frenchified"
Odessa gentleman give to his scholars. Certainly not the authentic
Jewish one, and yet he pretends to run a *Talmud-toyre!* Thus, through
his naive protagonist, Abramovitsh questions his own commitment to
the so-called modern Jewish education, that dubious, eclectic, self-
contradictory amalgam which to this day has not achieved a real integrity either as a system for the inculcating of cultural values or as a
framework for the imparting of unified, meaningful information. This
obviously may also have a bearing on Abramovitsh's commitment to a
modern Jewish literature, a literature, one should not forget, which
from its start considered itself primarily an educational instrument. Indeed, Fishke's encounter with Abramovitsh, light and momentary as it
is, poses by implication the grave problem of whether there exists the
possibility of a real relationship between the Yiddish artist and the
world he portrays. This was a problem which Abramovitsh kept pon-
dering with ever-growing misgivings. To put the matter in its simplest
form: Fishke does not, and never will, comprehend the world of his
"Frenchified" creator. Nothing, as far as he is concerned, could be
more remote and meaningless than the language, concepts, and values
of this world. Doesn't that make the possibility of a complete understanding in the reversed direction somewhat problematical? Such a
possibility, we must conclude, depends completely on the ability of
Abramovitsh to separate himself into two independent entities: one,
the Abramovitsh of Odessa, the well-dressed gentleman, the member
of the educational profession, etc.; the other, an old-fashioned Jewish
bookpeddler, Mendele Moykher-Sforim. It is to Mendele Moykher-
Sforim that Fishke talks about the queer Odessa *Talmud-toyre* teacher,
and it is Mendele who understands his story not only because he talks

the language of Fishke's world but also because he literally understands the words he uses. As Fishke tells his tales of wanderings and
woes, Mendele reminds us several times that, although the story is
being told in the first person, it is not a verbatim rendering of Fishke's
speech, for this speech (of which he gives several examples) would be
incomprehensible to us, the readers, were it not improved upon and
elucidated by himself.[31] Abramovitsh's Odessa, the teachers of its *Talmud-toyre* presumably included, is completely dependent in this respect on the services of a mediator. It needs a Mendele, differentiated
from Abramovitsh, just as much as Glupsk needs a Mendele if it is to
understand the "ideas" of an Abramovitsh.

The separation of Mendele from Abramovitsh had always been regarded by the author as an indispensable condition for his artistic creativity. Answering Sholem Aleichem, who had invited him to partici-
pate in his projected *Folks-biblyotek*, Abramovitsh wrote, "Let it be,
that I have reached an agreement with one party; now it is necessary,
after all, to have a word with the other party as well; I mean with Reb
Mendele himself. My Reb Mendele, poor thing, is indisposed. He is always so occupied by his business, that I am afraid I shall have to work
long and hard before I talk him into confining himself to his desk,
plying his pen, and absorbing himself in writing." [32] From Abramovitsh's next letter we learn that he has already had a word with his Reb
Mendele, that the latter is favorably disposed, and that he will accommodate the young editor, provided that the financial arrangements are
satisfactory. This he has instructed Abramovitsh to convey to Sholem
Aleichem, and he has probably also advised him how and in what language to do it, for his message, indirectly quoted, bears the characteristic marks of his commercial shrewdness. Forcing Sholem Aleichem to
an immediate monetary advance, the arrangement commits him to
nothing in particular. "Mendele thanks you for your willingness to
send him money in advance," Abramovitsh writes, adding, "According
to his calculation, you should send for the meantime *at least* three
hundred roubles. With God's help, everything will turn out well. Mendele will grease the wheels of his wagon, harness his horse, and off will
he drive." [33]

This is an elaborate game of hide-and-seek, played with all the co-
quetry of Abramovitsh's prima-donna manner, an overflow of *esprit*.
Nevertheless, it contains a weighty truth. The author's reference to
himself as a go-between whose task is to make "parties" external to

himself see eye to eye is, as jocular analogies often are, highly revealing. It was quite habitual with Abramovitsh in his fiction to dramatize
the consciousness of his characters, especially that of Mendele, by
splitting it into two different persons engaged in a dispute or a discussion. In fact, what I have referred to as a theatrical internal dialogue
often seems to be connected with his very conception of consciousness, or at least of an aroused or troubled consciousness.[34] Thus, the
distinction he makes in his letters to Sholem Aleichem between the
Abramovitsh who writes in Odessa and Reb Mendele, who at the time
is supposed to be somewhere in the small towns of the Volhynian Jewish pale, completely absorbed in his business of bookselling—this distinction may well be taken as reflecting his conception of his own
literary consciousness. Just as he used a theatrical internal duality to
dramatize psychological divergencies within his heroes, so he used this
duality to identify divergencies in the substratum of his creative activity. It is therefore worth noting that between the two aspects of his literary personality, Abramovitsh and Mendele, it is to the latter that the
actual power of creation is assigned. The former is a mere dilettante.
No doubt, from many aspects he is "superior" to Mendele. He is Europeanized; he is well read; he can, for instance, express informed opinions on literary matters in terms which the poor bookpeddler would
probably find incomprehensible. But he is completely dependent on
him as far as the delivery of the story which Sholem Aleichem has
commissioned him to write is concerned. Whenever that Mendele is
for one reason or another "indisposed," he must wait for him with
endless patience, coax him, dance to his tune, and never take a step
forward without him. Only when he sees that Mendele has greased the
wheels of his wagon and harnessed his horse can he be sure that "off
will he drive" and that "everything will turn out well."

Yoysef Perl (1773–1839), one of the leaders of the *Haskala* movement in Galicia in the first half of the nineteenth century and a vigorous enemy of Hasidism. The most brilliant Hebrew parodist of the age, he wrote some of his works in Yiddish as well. The Yiddish version of his parodic masterpiece *Megale-tmirin,* discovered in our century in his archive in Tarnopol (first Hebrew edition 1819), is the first significant artistic achievement of Yiddish *Haskala* fiction. The medals awarded by the imperial Habsburg regime indicate Perl's close relationship with the Austrian authorities.

A page from the manuscript of *Gdules reb Volf,* an accomplished parodic monologue of a hasid, written in the Perl manner by the almost unknown Podolian *maskil* Khayim Malage (probably in the 1820s). Discovered in the Perl archive and published with Perl's *Megale-tmirin,* it is a remnant of the largely extinct body of Yiddish maskilic literature written during the first half of the nineteenth century.

A *shterntikhl*, the decorated and often very expensive headgear, which was part of a Jewish woman's traditional clothing on festive occasions. Varying in size, amount of golden and silver embroidery and pearls, it was obviously a status symbol. Aksenfeld used it as a connective motif in his novel, rendering it a symbol of the medieval irrationalism of the old social and economic order which governed pre-Enlightenment, traditional Jewish life in Eastern Europe.

The rhyming prologue to Yisroel Aksenfeld's *Dos shterntikhl,* the first modern Yiddish novel to achieve publication (1861). One of the thirty-odd dramas and novels written by the indefatigable author from the 1820s to the 1860s, it is his only surviving novel. It was published (decades after its composition) on the eve of the emergence of Yiddish maskilic literature from its underground existence. Copies of the first edition are rare and often in bad condition.

Ayzik Meyer Dik (1807–1893), who because of the mildness of his anti-traditionalism was the only Yiddish *maskil* allowed to publish his works on a regular basis before the 1860s (he started to publish in the late 1840s). Tolerated by the orthodoxy and catering to the simple tastes of an uneducated public, his numerous novelettes enjoyed a very wide circulation and were often republished. Dik was the first popular success in modern Yiddish literature.

The title page of *Di kremerkes*, one of Dik's longer and more novelistic stories (first edition 1865). In their form and the long homiletic and often rhyming subtitles, the title pages of Dik's penny brochures were strongly reminiscent of the title pages of the traditional Yiddish *mayse-bikhl*, as were some of the narrative and stylistic aspects of the stories themselves. Incidentally, the author's name is not mentioned on this title page.

The front page of the first issue of *Kol-mevaser,* the Yiddish maskilic weekly magazine, which for six years (1862–1868) was published as a supplement to *Hamelits,* the major Hebrew magazine of the second half of the nineteenth century, and for another three years (1869–1872) as an independent publication. More than any other event, its appearance in October 1862 indicated the emergence of Yiddish maskilic literature into regular, public existence. Edited mostly by Alexander Tsederboym (1816–1893), it was the center of literary activity in Yiddish throughout the 1860s. The two major Yiddish works of fiction written in that decade, Abramovitsh's *Dos kleyne mentshele* and Linetski's *Dos poylishe yingl* were first serialized in its pages.

The title page of one of the many pirated editions of *Dos poylishe yingl*, the devastating antihasidic satire written by Yitskhok Yoyel Linetski (1839–1915). Its first part was serialized in 1867, and the entire work was published in book form in 1869. It proved a tremendous hit and was read even by ardent *hasidim*. Pirated editions appeared throughout the 1870s and 1880s. However, when the present one was published (1885) the author's popularity had already been dwindling. *Dos poylishe yingl* was Linetski's only major achievement.

Sholem Yankev Abramovitsh (1836?–1917) in 1862. At the time the author, who was destined to become the great innovator of both Yiddish and Hebrew modern artistic fiction, was known mainly as a controversial literary critic and as the adaptor of popular Hebrew articles on the natural sciences. However, in 1862 Abramovitsh published his first novel (in Hebrew), *Limdu-hetev*. In two years he was to turn to Yiddish and, hidden behind the fictional character of Mendele the Bookpeddler, publish his first Yiddish work, *Dos kleyne mentshele*.

The title page of the first volume (*Fishke der krumer*) of an edition of Abramovitsh's collected works started in 1888 (only two volumes appeared). The title (barely perceptible even in the original) reads: "The Complete Works of Mendele the Bookpeddler, published in separate volumes one after the other. Book the First: Fishke the Lame." Abramovitsh's name is never mentioned on this title page (it is mentioned on the Russian title page which follows). The vignette of the old traditional Jew with his wagon and horse against a Ukrainian country background (designed by S. Kishinevski), was also intended to shift attention from the Europeanized Odessa author to his bookpeddler persona.

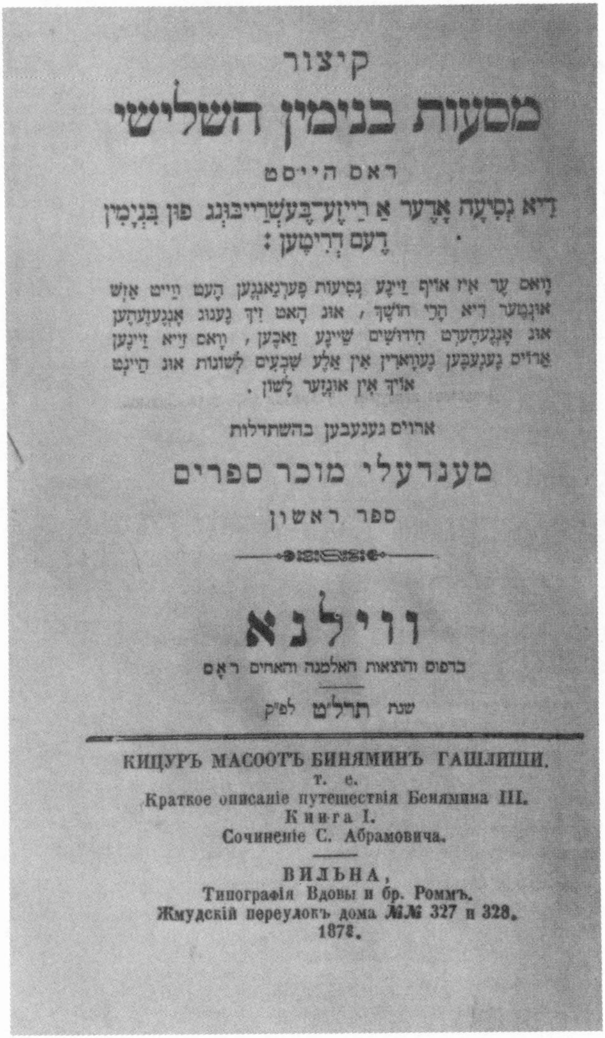

קיצור

מסעות בנימין השלישי

ד א ם ה י י ס ט

די א נסיעה אדער א רייזעבעשרייבונג פון בנימין
דעם דריטען :

וואס ער איז אויף זיינע נסיעות פערנאנגען האט חיים אזש
אונטער די א הרי חושך , אונ האט זיך נעטוג אנגעזעהען
אונ אנגעהערט חידושים שינע זאכען , וואס די א זיינען
ארויס נענעבען נעווארין אין אלע שבעים לשונות אונ היינט
אויך אין אונזער לשון .

ארויס נענעבען בהשתדלות

מענדעלי מוכר ספרים

ספר ראשון

וו י ל נ א
ברפוס והוצאות האלמנה והאחים ראם
שנת תרלי"ט לפ"ק

КИЦУРЪ МАСООТЬ БИНЯМИНЪ ГАШЛИЩИ,
т. е.
Краткое описаніе путешествія Бенямина III.
Книга I.
Сочиненіе С. Абрамовича.

ВИЛЬНА,
Типографія Вдовы и бр. Роммъ.
Жмудскій переулокъ дома №№ 327 и 328.
1878.

The title page of the first edition of Abramovitsh's *Masoes Binyomin hashlishi* (1878). While its Yiddish part refers to the work as "published through the mediation of Mendele the Bookpeddler," its Russian one says simply: "A work by S. Abramovitsh."

Sholem Aleichem (1859–1916) with his father Nokhem Rabinovitsh in 1885. By then, Sholem Aleichem had been publishing Yiddish satires and humoresques for two years. In 1884 his first novel, *Natasha* (later retitled *Taybele*), appeared. As far as Nokhem Rabinovitsh, an old-fashioned admirer of the holy tongue, was concerned, his son's growing popularity as a Yiddish writer was somewhat of a disappointment. He had expected him to become a celebrated Hebrew novelist.

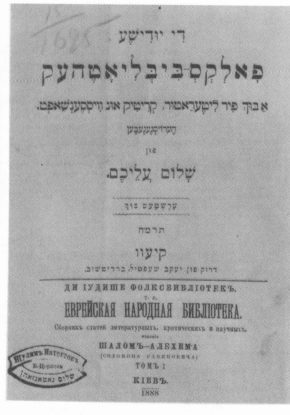

The title page of the first volume of Sholem Aleichem's *Yidishe folks-biblyotek* (1888), the well-known literary almanac, the appearance of which symbolized as well as reinforced the new status gained by Yiddish and Yiddish literature in the nationalistic atmosphere of the 1880s. This volume includes the first book of Abramovitsh's enlarged *Vintshfingerl*, Perets' *Monish*, and the editor's entire "Jewish novel," *Stempenyu*, including the celebrated dedication of the work "to my dear grandfather, Mendele the Bookpeddler," which initiated the "grandfather Mendele" myth.

Yitskhok Leybush Perets (1852–1915) started his career as a Hebrew writer in 1875. Not before 1888 did he publish anything in Yiddish. However, four years later, when this picture was taken, he was already established as the leader of a generation of younger Yiddish writers, who under his leadership completely changed the literary ideology and practice of typical nineteenth-century Yiddish fiction and poetry.

A classic portrait of "grandfather Mendele." The picture was taken during the first decade of the twentieth century, at the height of Abramovitsh's glory as the grand old man of Jewish letters.

Usually Abramovitsh held his literary court in Odessa. However, his loyal adherents were also received and entertained out of Russia, particularly in Geneva, where the "grandfather's" family intermittently spent a few years. In this picture, taken in 1907, Abramovitsh (first from the left) was joined by Sholem Aleichem (standing), Ben Ami (M. Y. Rabinovitsh) and the Hebrew poet Kh. N. Byalik (first from the right). The boat, the diminutive oar (held by Sholem Aleichem), and the conventional photographer's "landscape" backdrop were meant to represent not only the beauties of the Swiss countryside, but also the authors' present occupation (vacationing) as well as their habitual, professional love for nature. The florid signature in the upper left corner is Sholem Aleichem's. Above it Sholem Aleichem inscribed "Fir zenen mir gezesn" ("There We Sat, Four of Us"), the title of his memoiristic essay, in which he described the meeting of the four writers in Switzerland and retold the ·autobiographical anecdotes they had exchanged (including the one on the creation of the "Mendele pseudonym" in 1864).

Abramovitsh and his grandson, a picture taken for a special album published with the "Jubilee edition" of Abramovitsh's Yiddish works. The posture was intentionally "symbolic": Abramovitsh the grandfather teaching his grandson how to read, i.e., "grandfather Mendele" teaches his literary grandsons how to create a Yiddish literature.

An Abramovitsh postcard, one of a series of literary postcards portraying famous Hebrew writers within an elaborate *Jugendstil* frame. Obviously, the lyre, books, inkpot, and feather are the professional insignia. The Hebrew text on the scroll-like area supplies basic biographical and bibliographical details plus the conventional superlatives. Lovers of Hebrew literature used such cards for greeting their literary-minded acquaintances as well as for decorating their own desks.

Another Abramovitsh postcard. The posture of deep and somewhat melancholic meditation is conventional. The photographer took care to include in the portrait the author's inkstand (symbol of his profession) as well as an open piano (representing his muse?). The short text is a quotation from Hershele's proclamation in the prologue (and subsequently the epilogue) to the enlarged *Vintshfingerl:* "I am a thread interwoven in that large piece of fabric which from ancient days is known to the world as the Jew."

A primitive Mendele postcard illustrating the stormy encounter of those two Jewish bookpeddlers, Mendele and Alter, from the opening chapter of *Fishke der krumer*. As in the story, the two curse and lash at each other while wearing their phylacteries and prayer shawls (they dozed off while praying and their wagons collided and got entangled). Soon they will recognize each other, and hostility will give place to cordial familiarity. This particular copy of this rather pathetic postcard was used for the purpose of a "robust" friendly greeting. The writer humorously promised his friend an encounter and a well-deserved "thrashing" in due course. The fact that he chose the Mendele–Alter encounter as the proper illustration for his card indicates the extent to which Abramovitsh's art became part of the popular imagination.

CHAPTER FOUR

ON NATIVE GROUND

> Spare us, oh Almighty God, spare us the loneliness which
> Shloymele felt upon his return to his home town. Loneli-
> ness is bitter in every form; still, there are differences of
> degree and of kind. The unlucky fellow . . . who is a
> stranger wherever he goes, who lonely as a stone in the
> field . . . surely he is miserable enough; but there is a
> great difference between being a stranger and being
> estranged.
>
> (Sh. Y. Abramovitsh, *Shloyme reb Khayims*, part II,
> Chapter 2)

THE DIRECT RESULT of Mendele's willingness to accommodate Sholem
Aleichem and "ply his pen" were the first six chapters of the enlarged
version of *Dos vintshfingerl* ("The Magic Ring"), Abramovitsh's major
novel. In 1865 a short, meager novelette, the author's second composition in Yiddish, had appeared under this name. Now (in 1888),
Abramovitsh promised his editor, he had developed it into "a completely new book, in which I shall throw light on Jewish life and discuss the most important problems we face nowadays." [1] The six opening chapters included a long prologue, "a story about the story," in the
form of a monologue addressed to the readers by Mendele the
Bookpeddler. Sholem Aleichem expected this; not only had Abramovitsh promised him in a previous letter to open his projected new composition with a monologue by Mendele "that will create quite a sensation among our Jewish brethren," [2] but also, by his constant resort to
prefatory monologues, he had made them something taken for
granted. Heralded by the solemn announcement in Hebrew "Omar
Mendele Moykher-Sforim" ("Quoth Mendele the Bookpeddler," or
"Thus spake Mendele the Bookpeddler"), these monologues had become Abramovitsh's trademark, so to speak, and were considered his
unique and inimitable literary characteristic. In the dedication of
Stempenyu to his "dearly beloved grandfather," Sholem Aleichem
wrote, "Under your hand, *Stempenyu* would have turned out completely differently; with you it would have had, besides the 'story it-

self,' a 'story within the story,' as well as a 'story about the story. . . .'
We, young scribblers, give thanks to God when we can deliver the
story itself without a hitch, an uncrippled literary being with all its
limbs in place." [3] Indeed, Abramovitsh seldom allowed his fictions to
begin at the beginning. In most of them, the "story itself" was set
within a monologistic "frame," and this, always brilliantly ironic and
often the spiciest portion in the whole composition, was relished by
the readers as a special treat and regarded as a proof of the author's intricate mastery.

The prologue to *Dos vintshfingerl* is particularly brilliant. Every
passage and sentence in it is heavy with meaning. Indeed, it is one of
the most compact and significant pieces of fiction in nineteenth-century Yiddish literature. Strangely enough, it did not create "a sensation," as the author had predicted. In fact, very little attention has
ever been paid to it. The reason for this could be the fact that it has
rarely been republished in its original form.[4] The writing of *Dos
vintshfingerl* was extremely slow and painful. It dragged on endlessly,
and the novel remained virtually a fragment. When, more than twenty
years after he had begun it, Abramovitsh was pressed to bring the
novel to some formal conclusion so that it could be included in the
Yiddish and Hebrew "Jubilee editions" of his collected works, he had
no choice but to sacrifice the prologue and carve an epilogue out of it.
Diminished in size and importance, its brilliance totally dimmed, it is
now printed as an epilogue in the different collected editions of
Abramovitsh, a mechanical means for tying together the novel's loose
ends rather than the triumphant exposition it was when it headed the
opening opus of the first *Folks-biblyotek*.

It is to an examination of this prologue in its original form that this
chapter is exclusively dedicated. Bearing on our subject in the widest
and most meaningful way, this prologue seems to me an ideal point of
reference around which the discussion may dwell for a while, thereby
shifting from the method of the general survey to a more concrete and
detailed analysis of a single example, as well as from ideas and abstract
attitudes to a living situation and to dramatic relationships.

i

Considering the place and the function which the prologue was
meant to assume in Abramovitsh's *oeuvre*, its extraordinary richness is

not surprising; it is certainly not accidental. The enlarged *Dos vintshfingerl* was conceived from the start as a *magnum opus* of epic dimensions (Abramovitsh referred to it as "an epic"),[5] in a sense, as a "historical" novel. Indeed, it was its historical quality which, according to the author, set it apart from most Yiddish novels written at the time. Whereas most novels (not only those written by the Shomer school) in their plots, intrigues, sets of heroes and antiheroes, etc., obeyed the conventions of romance (love, separation, struggle, triumphant reunification, or tragic fall), this novel was to obey historical reality. It was not to be operated by the machinery of entertainment but rather motivated by the dynamics of history. "The *Vintshfingerl*," Abramovitsh wrote to Sholem Aleichem, "is not just another story such as they write nowadays; it is a *history* of Jewish life. It is not a doll to play with, but a living person with its own lifeblood, soul, human emotions, and human face." [6]

Like many other Russian-Jewish writers and intellectuals, Abramovitsh was conscious that with the pogroms of 1881 an epoch in the history of Russian Jews had come to an end. In *Dos vintshfingerl*, the second long narrative he wrote after the pogroms, he intended to apply the new perspectives concomitant with this consciousness to a broad historical and social vista. The novel was to survey methodically the typical units of Jewish society inside Russia (the *shtetl*, the new commercial center within the Jewish pale, and probably also the typical modern community of the big city) and perhaps even outside it. Chronologically it was to cover a lengthy historical sequence. Beginning in the late 1830s or the early 1840s, it was to reach beyond the early 1880s. Thus, it was to reflect the whole gamut of dread, despair, hope, and disillusionment of the Jewish ordeal in nineteenth-century Russia, from the darkest phase of the regime of Nicholas I,[7] through the hopes which ensued with the accession of his son Alexander II, to the new darkness of the pogroms and the political antisemitism which followed the murder of Alexander. In order to allow the novel to cover such distances of time and place, the form of a biographical progress was chosen. Its hero, Hershele,[8] is born into a destitute family in a tiny Ukrainian Jewish *shtetl*, emigrates as a child to a bigger, commercial town, and eventually reaches Germany, where he becomes a well-to-do, respectable scholar. With the help of a *maskil* benefactor as well as through his own exertion, he rises from the poverty and ignorance of his home town, *Kabtsansk* ("Town of Beggars"; another of Abramo-

vitsh's three archetypal Jewish towns), to enlightenment and comparative affluence as a man of the liberal professions in Leipzig. Then, a
mature man, he visits the scene of his miserable childhood, full of good
intentions toward his less fortunate brethren, conceiving plans to improve their lot, and inspecting the bleak, half-ruined *shtetlekh* (the
time is the aftermath of the 1881 pogroms) in order to come up with
specific recommendations for their rehabilitation. It is here, in one of
these small towns, that we meet him in the prologue. Thus, the prologue (as the fact that it was easily turned into an epilogue indicates)
opens the story not at its beginning but at the point where it was supposed to terminate or to lead to an imminent termination.

Such an opening *in extremas res* is a highly conventionalized procedure in biographical novels of the sentimental type. *Dos vintshfingerl*, in spite of Abramovitsh's professed historical and realistic intentions, in fact retains many features of the sentimental, romantic novel.
This beginning with the return of the wandering hero to his home
town could have been counted among them, were it not used for purposes which transcend the aims and effects of the sentimental homecoming. These purposes have to do with the historical lesson Abramovitsh wanted his novel to convey. It was to embody the wisdom of
retrospection; to emphasize this, it struck the note of retrospection
from the very start. Beginning the story at its end, the prologue was
meant to fix in advance that historical point of view from which every
object and movement in the unfolding panorama to come would be
seen in its true location and dimensions. This opening was also to set in
advance a movement contradictory to that developed by the narrative
itself. The novel as we have it is dominated by one principle of structural development: the principle of desertion, of constant outward
movement. Hershele leaves his home town, his family, his friends, the
girl he loves. As the main narrative reaches its present abrupt ending,
he has just left Russia. What is suggested by this series of desertions
and leave-takings is that the center of things, of goodness, affluence,
knowledge, life itself, lies somewhere outside the limits of the Jewish
world the novel describes and that in order to get to it, one must
ceaselessly move outward. This suggestion was, however, to be modified in the course of the novel; the principle of the outward movement was to be checked at some point, and the prologue foretells this
development by making the hero's homecoming precede (structurally,
not chronologically, of course) his leaving home. True, the prologue

also makes it clear that the hero has no place to go back to, for the world of the *shtetl*, weak and disintegrating even in his childhood, had been badly shaken and was now believed to be facing liquidation. Furthermore, the prologue ironically suggests that it is exactly because of this disintegration of the *shtetl* that the hero, Hershele, returns to it. Still, it is with a homecoming of sorts that the novel opens; with what might perhaps be called "the return of the native."

This is not accidental. The archetypal fable of the native's return, the homecoming of the wandering son and lover, was constantly made use of in nineteenth-century Jewish literature—both Yiddish and Hebrew. Of course, it was conditioned by the ideological bias of the *Haskala* movement and reworked to suit its purposes. The wandering son was usually the young, idealized *maskil*, whose rupture with his family and with the whole community, owing to his maskilic tendencies, drove him out of his home town into the wide world. Once out of the Jewish-Russian pale with its close, autonomous culture and sluggish, half-feudal economy, the wanderer could find "enlightenment" and affluence. He became the hero of the modern Jewish success story, one of those young enterprising *shtetl*-born emigrants—doctors, lawyers, scientists, and scholars—who figure so highly in what may be described as the nineteenth-century "Jewish dream"; almost as highly as those mythical giants, the *shtetl*-born grand "Rothschilds," the Brodskis, the Polyakovs, etc. The eventual homecoming of this hero—a triumphant homecoming, of course—signified therefore the ascendency of the *Haskala* and proved an excellent means of dissolving dramatic conflicts and bringing the plots to a happy ending. This pattern can be found in most dramas written by the *maskilim* from the late eighteenth century onward. It was transplanted to the novel as soon as the *maskilim* began to write novels. It dominates, for instance, the first Yiddish novel, Aksenfeld's *Dos shterntikhl* ("The Headband"), and it significantly influences the structure of the first Hebrew novel to deal with contemporary Jewish life, Mapu's *Ayit tsavua* ("The Hypocrite"). Even Abramovitsh's early Hebrew novel *Ha'avot vehabanim* ("Fathers and Sons") follows it loyally throughout.

In the prologue to *Dos vintshfingerl* this maskilic tradition is clearly echoed, but it is a strange and discordant echo. Repeating in it the homecoming scene, which traditionally resounded with the bright chords of a grand finale, Abramovitsh everywhere darkens it with unexpected, incongruous tones. In short, he summons up the tradition

only to explode it from within, to expose it in its incongruity and inva-
lidity. This is very characteristic of him. However great an artistic innovator he was, he was also a conservative by nature. He was never
willing to break the links with the past, and when he had to question
the relevance of accepted conventions, he preferred to do it indirectly
through the ironic employment of these conventions themselves. Instead of eliminating long-standing patterns, he would follow them, but
with a difference. He would apply the conventional formula, but to an
unconventional situation. Thus, he would subtly discredit it without
openly breaking with it. There is one particular point in the prologue
which beautifully illustrates this subversive technique. Hershele arrives in his home town incognito and drives its inhabitants to a frenzy
of curiosity. The whole town seems to be performing a grotesque
dance of hit-and-run around him. Thus Mendele reminds them of the
great event:

> Kabtsansk! You remember the visitor you entertained last summer, do
> you? You racked your brains; you were at your wit's end: God Al-
> mighty! Where does he come from? Who can he be? What can be his
> purpose here? You could not understand what business he had visiting
> your graveyard, investigating every single detail of your conduct, going
> through all your secret places: your *hekdesh, Talmud-toyre, khadorim,
> shtiblekh.*° Your matchmakers were meditating a match for him; your
> charity beneficiaries, synagogue wardens, beggars, and beggarly non-
> beggars, young and old, descended upon him from every direction like
> locusts and touched him for money. At the same time your dignitaries,
> venerable sages though they are, troubled themselves to welcome him
> in person with a handshake and a "Sholem aleykhem," °° their purpose
> thereby being to put their feelers on him and see through the mystery of
> his visit. . . .⁹

Every reader who is acquainted to some extent with the literature
of the *Haskala* must be aware of a traditional pattern which is being
evoked here. In fact, the pattern goes far beyond the traditions of the

---

° *Hekdesh* (literally, something consecrated, dedicated for ritual or for public use),
the name of the traditional congregational charity hospitals in Eastern European Jewish
communities. The homeless aged and sick as well as wandering beggars stayed there.
These hospitals were usually in such a miserable condition that the word *hekdesh* became synonymous with filth, disorder, tumult. *Shtiblekh* (literally, "small houses" or
"small rooms"), small, hasidic prayer houses.
    °° Literally, "peace upon you (plural)"; the common greeting to a stranger or to a
person from afar, usually accompanied by a handshake.

Haskala and even beyond its foreign influences back to the very beginnings of European literature. What Abramovitsh uses here is the conventional comic sequence of errors and misunderstandings following the appearance of an unknown traveler (who is no less than the long-missing son, relative, lover, husband) and which leads to a comic "recognition"; a procedure begun by the Middle and New comedy writers of Greece and Rome and revived during the Renaissance in numerous "comedies of errors." In the *Haskala* literature—both Hebrew and Yiddish—it was worked over again and again: in Lutsato's allegorical dramas; in Mapu's biblical romances and his contemporary *Ayit tsavua*; in Aksenfeld's comedies both of error (e.g., *Man un vayb, bruder un shvester*, "Man and Wife, Brother and Sister") and of hoax (e.g., *Di genarte velt*, "The Duped World") and in his *Shterntikhl*; in Gotlober's *Dektukh* ("The Bridal Veil"); in Etinger's *Serkele* and the dramatic fragment called (by the editor of Etinger's works) *Der feter fun Amerike* ("The American Uncle"). In dozens of stories, romances, and plays a disguised person, usually a disguised traveler, brings the plot to its denouement in a scene replete with misunderstanding, often as hilarious as the scene of Hershele's arrival in Kabtsansk, followed by a noisy, emotional recognition. In *Dos vintshfingerl*, however, the comedy of errors is not followed by a recognition, and therefore it remains suspended, meaningless, like a piece of music waiting for the resolution of a final chord. Instead of this chord, a strange, wistful pianissimo tone is heard. "The visitor," Mendele informs Kabtsansk, "left without taking his leave," [10] and the town lapsed back to its daily routine. There was simply nobody in Kabtsansk to recognize Hershele. The comedy has become a tragicomedy.

This metamorphosis was given even more emphasis as the prologue was reworked into an epilogue. In the epilogue the confrontation between Hershele and the community of Kabtsansk takes place in the congregational graveyard, which is paradoxically the only lively place in the whole desolate town. The community is mourning the victims of the recent pogrom when the intimacy of their grief is suddenly intruded upon by a foreign-looking, well-dressed gentleman who descends from a carriage. Their first reaction is fear and obsequious deference. The men, forgetting their prayers, gape at the stranger, touch their hats, step back respectfully. The women are hushed in the midst of their shrill lamentations. "The people's faces looked very strange at that moment," Abramovitsh comments. "They betrayed suppressed fear, degradation, and self-abasement before the haughty and the powerful." [11] But then the paralysis is suddenly transformed into a lively, too lively, commotion, and the oppressive scene becomes unmistakably though darkly comic. Against the background of general silence the stranger is heard to inquire in Yiddish after the *shames* (beadle), and everybody is immediately astir; the stranger "is a Jew after all"; raised hats descend, bowing backs come up with a jerk; those who stepped back now crowd around the stranger, indecently eyeing his fine dress; others familiarly shake hands with him. "He speaks Yiddish, he does, the women shout at the top of their voices, pointing with their fingers at the man and staring at him, their faces half smiling half grieving, like a child's after crying." [12] The people of Kabtsansk are swept by an intoxicating feeling of relief. The scene suddenly resembles comic scenes of recognition. Hershele, the disguised traveler, is recognized by his birthmark, which is not a heart-shaped mole or an old scar but his Yiddish speech. We have only to remind ourselves of a scene in the last act of Etinger's *Serkele* to realize how closely Abramovitsh followed here the maskilic convention. Etinger's comedy is brought to its denouement by the arrival in town of a stranger. Dressed in European style and speaking German he is taken, like Hershele, for a gentile dignitary and is obsequiously welcomed by the local innkeeper, until he utters a Yiddish sentence, whereupon he is treated in a completely different manner. Before the Yiddish sentence was uttered, he was "mein Herr" and "eure Gnade," eagerly received and promised the best of everything. Once uttered, it becomes clear that the stranger is "a Jew after all," the innkeeper immediately relaxes his strained rhetoric and switches to the most unceremonial familiarity. Now he would not have the stranger as a guest but rather serve him as a broker, for being a Jew the stranger must either be carrying something for sale or looking for something to buy. As the scene unfolds, the stranger is recognized as the long-missing Dovid Gutherts ("goodheart"), the brother of the shrewish Serkele. Despaired of and mourned for, he arrives on the very anniversary of his supposed death, just in time to save his daughter and her sweetheart from the vile machinations of his sister, and by resolving the tension he brings the play to its end. [13] Abramovitsh may have counted on such literary reminiscences to bring home the full meaning of his graveyard scene, for the initial resemblance only heightens the great difference. Whereas Dovid Gutherts is being really and fully recognized, the rec-

ognition of Hershele through his Yiddish speech is momentary and de-
lusive. Gutherts is reunited with his daughter, whom he sees married
with great festivity; he condones his sister's criminal behavior and re-
creates a world of happiness and justice. All this cannot happen in the
case of Hershele. His parents have long been dead and forgotten.
Their tombstones are barely visible, so deeply sunk are they in their
grassy mounds. No other relative of his survives. His beloved Beyle,
the girl he left when he emigrated to Germany, was given to another
man many years ago, and even as a married woman and a mother she
is not present to welcome him, for she and her daughters have been recently raped and murdered by the raiding mob. The very town is more
dead than alive. The fact that the supposed recognition takes place in
a graveyard is, of course, symbolic. The triumph of the returning hero
demands the presence of an impressed, won-over community. Who
are the witnesses of Hershele's homecoming? Broken, disfigured shad-
ows whose moment of mirth is even more grotesquely pathetic than
their former inability to ignore the stranger in the midst of their bitterest grief. The traditional recognition scene with its geniality and
festivity is here turned into a tragic farce.

ii

The ambiguous relationship between Hershele's homecoming and
the concluding scenes of *Serkele* (or, for that matter, with the concluding sections of *Dos shterntikhl* or *Ayit tsavua*) illustrates the way many
of the best dramatic passages in Abramovitsh "mean." They mean
through the way they relate—overtly and latently—to a wide historical and literary frame of reference. The relationships do not necessarily indicate adherence to the principles informing this frame of reference; on the contrary, they are usually ironic. However, the passages
have the advantage of contextuality. They "sit" right in the midst of a
tangled net of traditions, conventions, motifs, and allusions. One has
only to be acquainted with this literary background to see the connective lines streaming from them in every direction, and to feel the vi-
brating charge of meaning and countermeaning spreading all over.

It is by virtue of this rich contextuality that the prologue to *Dos
vintshfingerl* is an illustration so markedly relevant to our whole argument. Not only does it stand at the very heart of the literary development with which this argument is concerned, it also seems to stand

above it, to be appended to it as an afterthought, a comment, a summing up, even a parody. It marks the central point of intersection in
the development of nineteenth-century Jewish literature: the point at
which the ideology and the artistic traditions of the *Haskala* gave way
to other ideologies and to what has eventually become a new tradition.
Still echoing very distinctly the motifs of the *Haskala*, it nevertheless
closes the breach opened between it and the new, nationalistic literature; and evoking the tone of the maskilic scenes of homecoming and
recognition, it opens a new series of scenes in which both the concept
of home and the meaning of coming back to it are completely different.

The Hebrew words for return (*shiva*) and repentance (*tshuva*) are
closely connected, and Hershele's return to his ruined home town undoubtedly has to do with a mood of repentance. Hershele craves for a
renewed identification with the Jewish people, for a renewed sense of
integration within the continuity of Jewish history. "I am a thread interwoven in that large piece of fabric which from ancient days is
known to the world as the Jew," he solemnly declares.[14] In the epilogue version this declaration is brought to an even higher pitch with
"I am a son of the people, a Jew like all my ancestors, fathers and forefathers." [15] These words, rather than recording reality, are expressions
of a fervent wish, a wish involving an implicit self-criticism. Hershele's
desire to belong to the world of "the Jew" implies a bitter disillusionment with the influences which separated him from it in the first
place, i.e., with the *Haskala* and its literature. This is made explicit
when Hershele, upon his first meeting with Mendele the Bookpeddler,
delivers a fierce attack on literature in general and on the *Haskala* literature in particular. Hershele inquires "what kinds of books" Mendele carries, and as he learns that besides traditional books of prayer
and learning some "other," i.e., secular books can be found in the
bookpeddler's covered wagon, he bursts into a veritable invective. The
details of the occasion are of some interest. Mendele informs the inquisitive foreigner that "It does not pay to bother" with these "other"
books; "they are no good. The Jews in these places would not touch
them." [16] ("These places" are the *shtetl* Tuneyadevke—"Town of
Idlers," another of Abramovitsh's archetypal Jewish towns—and other
small and distant towns like it, for it is in Tuneyadevke that Mendele
and Hershele happen to come across each other.) Now, this seemingly
naive remark, the remark of a merchant who would not pretend to as-

sess his merchandise in any but mercantile terms, is, in fact, a comment as ambiguous as only Mendele could make it. It contains some latent criticism, but exactly of what? Is it a criticism of the "other," the secular, books which are commercially, and perhaps not only commercially, "no good," or of the people "who would not touch them"? Is Mendele pronouncing here a judgment against a certain school of literature or does he just reiterate the old maskilic complaint of the "darkness" and "ignorance" of the Jewish masses? The question is hard to answer. Hershele, however, understands the remark as a criticism aimed at the Jewish people (this, as we shall see, is only one of many indications of his insensibility to ambiguities) and hastens to their defense. "What the Jews of these places need is bread, not books," he retorts, but immediately he qualifies his words. His objection does not apply to the prayer and learning books which are Mendele's chief stock in trade. Only the "others" draw his fire, those "others" which "do nothing but reprove, volunteer advice, and raise an uproar: Fie upon superstition! Fie upon neglect and idleness! Long live Enlightenment!" There can be no mistake: it is the whole Jewish literature of the nineteenth century which he attacks, including Abramovitsh's own maskilic works, for Abramovitsh certainly cried "Fie upon neglect and idleness" and was, at least through the early phases of his literary development, as committed to the ideas of the Enlightenment as anybody could be. As he keeps asserting the right of the Jewish people to ignore the "other" books Hershele's invective almost develops into a dithyramb:

> Bread, they need bread; reproof and advice do not fill an empty belly. No, when it comes to this, even a poem is of no avail. It is ridiculous to accuse abandoned, forgotten machines of standing idle and rusting somewhere in a corner. Better take them up, stand them on their feet, let them work, and be sure they will not rust any more; they would look completely different. . . .[17]

Echoing the slogans of some of the Russian "realist" or "progressive" critics of the 1860s ("What's preferable, Shakespeare or a pair of boots?"), these sentences actually reflect the mood prevailing in the 1880s and the early 1890s among Russian-Jewish intellectuals. Shocked into disillusion with the once-believed-in liberalism of the czarist regime, these intellectuals went into a fit of nationalistic enthusiasm. Many *maskilim* of long standing gave up their ideological com-

mitments in the two or three years immediately following the pogroms. A chauvinistic, highly sentimental literature began to appear,
in which the mistakes of the *Haskala* were endlessly harped upon.
Literary criticism in the spirit of Hershele's invective was quite common and was often written by people who, like Hershele, had formerly
been loyal *maskilim*; people, in fact, whose former loyalties had been
so fierce, that only the most vehement denigration of themselves and
their fellow writers could now regain for them a minimal sense of balance. (M. L. Lilyenblum, a one-time fiery *maskil* now turned no less
fiery a Zionist, attacked his lifelong ally, the poet Y. L. Gordon, with
accusations very much like Hershele's.)[18] Declarations of loyalty to the
common people and to the long-abused fathers and forefathers, such
as Hershele makes, as well as sentimental expressions of longing for
one's childhood *shtetl* were also not lacking. In short, the prologue to
Dos vintshfingerl can be said to contain the quintessence of that ideological turbulence that gave birth to Zionism and eventually to other
Jewish nationalistic and socialistic movements, and which set the
background for a nationalistically oriented Jewish literature.

This does not necessarily mean, as was sometimes assumed,[19] that
Abramovitsh completely identified himself with the new nationalistic
trends. Hershele, in his nationalistic fervor, does not automatically
speak for the author. It is of utmost importance to the understanding
of any of Abramovitsh's mature works of fiction to remain constantly
aware that they are, indeed, fiction, a dramatic representation in
which imaginary characters, including that of Mendele the Bookpeddler, speak for themselves and not, at least not directly, for the author.
Allowing such an awareness to fade amounts to becoming insensible to
the very principle of Abramovitsh's artistic method, which is ironic
juxtaposition. No statement made within the narrative context of one
of Abramovitsh's mature works should be wrenched out of this context
and represented as reflecting the author's "real" position, for on closer
inspection, the work as a whole will be found to supply that statement
with a host of direct or indirect counterstatements. A dialectic of assertion and doubting, of saying and unsaying, is constantly developed
in Abramovitsh's writing, and one must attune one's ears to it, for it is
the soul of what might be described as a polyphonic art. It is, indeed,
the impatient unwillingness or the sheer inability to cope with the
complexities of an intricate polyphony that vitiates much of the criticism written about Abramovitsh by writers who expect him "to speak

out his mind," not in terms of the whole work, the total fictional arrangement of his story, but rather in the terms Hershele uses, that is, the terms of the newspaper or of the political pamphlet. Were we to accept Hershele's terms at their face value and attribute them to the author, the prologue to *Dos vintshfingerl* could not hold for us the significance which, in fact, it does. It would be no more than a piece of literary evidence, symptomatic, but of rather limited importance and easily replaced by hundreds of pieces of evidence having the same validity. But the prologue is much more than a document illustrating the nationalistic intellectual milieu of the 1880s and 1890s. It transcends the status of an argument and rises to that of a symbolic situation, which through the play of statement and counterstatement, through changing tones and developing motifs, amounts in its totality to a comprehensive comment on the Jewish cultural situation in modern times in general and on the paradoxical nature of modern Yiddish literature in particular.

iii

Abramovitsh, as his more accurate biographers tell us,[20] and, indeed, as anyone can see for himself by a careful reading of his works and letters, was never swept away by the nationalistic trends of the 1880s and was never completely turned away from the ideals of the Enlightenment. True, under the first impression of the pogroms he once wrote to Binshtok, his old friend, "I completely agree with Rousseau, who urged man to throw his stupid civilization to the devil and turn back to the forests";[21] but in this no informed reader can see more than a momentary reaction. It is a cry of anguish, not a considered judgment. Abramovitsh never accepted the complete discrediting of the *Haskala* and of its writers; and as it became more and more the fashion to abuse these writers and hold them responsible for every aberration in Jewish life and letters, he went to their defense on several occasions.[22] Not that he was unable or unwilling to examine them critically. In fact, he criticized several aspects of the *Haskala* movement, not only in the later parts of *Dos vintshfingerl*[23] but also in the allegorical *Klyatshe (The Nag)*, written almost a decade before the pogroms and even in such early maskilic works as *Ha'avot vehabanim*.[24] As for the *Haskala* literature, his literary debut, the first book he published, contained a devastating attack on some of its prevalent prac-

tices. His commitment to this literature was based from the start on
the assumption that it needed a drastic, a revolutionary revitaliza-
tion.[25] The *Haskala*, nevertheless, remained the matrix of his art and of
his thought to the end. If he could be critical of it, he could be only
more so of Zionism, which always remained alien to his nature and beliefs. He had respect for a clear-headed Zionist such as L. Pinsker
(which does not mean that he saw eye to eye with him),[26] but he was
full of contempt for the more common type of nationalistic enthusiast
and made this amply clear on numerous private and public occasions.[27] The noisy, bustling, and self-satisfied manner of the Zionists ir-
ritated him to the point of exasperation. Only through his art was he
able to sublimate his furious mood into comedy and caricature.[28] His
weapon against the sentimentality, lachrymosity, and bathos of the
Zionist literature of the day was parody.[29] And there was certainly
much about this literature to appeal to his sense of the ridiculous.

In fact, are not Hershele's enthusiastic speeches meant to sound a
little ridiculous? Or does not the style he uses smack here and there of
parodic intentions? It is impossible, of course, to answer such questions convincingly in a discussion confined to translated illustrations.
Nevertheless, even in such a discussion it must be suggested that the
quality of Hershele's prose indicates Abramovitsh's intention to distance himself from his hero and even to question the validity of the
hero's statements. Hershele's is a poor, broken-winded prose. It is ever
fluctuating between dullness and bombast, and very often it draws itself to the verge of the bathetic abyss. This is made all the more conspicuous by the delicious flow of Mendele's prose which surrounds
Hershele's and intensifies its inferiority. While Mendele's metaphors
(Mendele's style is highly metaphorical) are almost without exception
superbly vivid and masterfully arranged, Hershele, as soon as he as-
pires to be metaphorical, evokes the worst figurative style of nineteenth-century journalism and gets himself hopelessly entangled in his
own overreaching figures. The comparison of the Jewish people to
rusting machines is a case in point. This metaphor is developed with
extraordinary clumsiness and, confusing its tenor (Jews) and its vehicle
(machines), ends with lending the rusty machines not only feet but
also faces.[30] Moreover, it obviously defeats the purposes of Hershele's
own rhetoric. Employed in the defense of the Jewish people against
what is regarded as an unjust criticism, the metaphor, unfortunately,
degrades and humiliates them much more than the criticism it fends

off ever has. The most bullying and condescending *maskil* writer never regarded the Jewish people as mechanical objects. On the contrary, the writers of the *Haskala* always assumed their audience to possess that basic reasonableness without which it could not be deemed capable of correction and improvement, and thus worth even the effort of bullying. Is not Hershele's metaphor, which lowers the Jewish people to the status of automatons devoid of soul, mind, and will, meant to indicate how narrow is his conception of the people he defends and of their capacities and needs? And what about the metaphor comparing Hershele himself to a thread interwoven in that large piece of fabric "which from ancient days is known to the world as the Jew?" It certainly obeys what Alexander Pope in his *Peri bathous* classified as "the first rule" of the bathetic metaphor, i.e., "to draw it from the lowest things, which is a certain way to sink the highest," [31] for it compares an allegedly elevated entity (Jewish history) to a "low" object (a piece of cloth; the connotations imply either fabric trade or even rag-dealing). Straining himself in his enthusiasm to heighten his expression of national loyalty, Hershele sinks it into bathos, and again he unwittingly calls our attention to the mechanical nature of his concept of Jewish nationality. His metaphor envisages the continuity of the Jewish history not as a fact due to the immanence of intrinsic unifying principles but to the mechanical intervention of an external agency, just as the metaphors of the rusty machines envisaged the Jews not as people to be inwardly motivated but as things to be operated from without. What is more, the anonymity of a thread interwoven in a piece of fabric may suggest that Hershele's wish to regain a national identity is, at least in part, a wish for relief from the burden of a personal identity. People regarded as threads or as machines, both duplicable objects, cannot be expected to have much of a personality.

Self-defeating rhetoric represents only one of the many orders of ironic juxtaposition which undermine the pathos of Hershele's penitential homecoming. For Hershele, his actions, opinions, and gestures are measured throughout the prologue against an incongruous background, and thus quietly exposed as irrelevant, or at least as insufficiently relevant to the predicament of the Jews after the pogroms. These ironic juxtapositions are interconnected, or rather, they are centered around some ironic leitmotivs, as for instance, a "sartorial" leitmotiv having to do with fabrics, tailoring, and dress. This motif is developed from the very start of Mendele's encounter with Hershele.

Here is Mendele's record of his first impression of the novel's hero at
their first meeting in the synagogue courtyard of the town of Tuneyadevke:

> I look and see somebody walking about the synagogue courtyard, a mid-
> dle-aged person dressed in a dapper European style, and he looks from
> afar very respectable indeed, God save us, a simpleton if there ever was
> one. He looks—How should I tell you?—like one who enters a bath-
> house fully dressed, where people are naked. For what purpose, I ask
> you, and for whom should a person get all dressed up, if as far as the
> people of Tuneyadevke are concerned, worn-out heels, quite visible
> shoulder blades, bare chests, and threadbare elbows are not a crime,
> heaven forbid! On the contrary, as long as one shows some remnants of
> socks, underwear, and a gabardine coat, one is quite all right. . . . In
> the streets of Tuneyadevke you may, on my recommendation, walk in
> your undershirt, leave your heart bare, let your socks droop, and leave
> unbuttoned those openings which should be buttoned, if you pardon my
> expression, and it will be my fault if you hear one disrespectful word
> . . . but this is beside the point.[32]

The ironic incongruity exposed here is admittedly external. Although
here, as everywhere, Mendele's simplicity is to be suspected (who is
ridiculed here, the too well-dressed Hershele, the slovenly people of
Tuneyadevke, or both?), what the passage points out is the comic contrast between the immaculate European attire of Hershele and the tattered rags of the people he comes to inspect. The comic effect of such
a contrast can be intense, but it is usually quickly spent. It needs not
only distance (it is "from afar" that Hershele looks a complete simpleton because of his dress) but also the element of surprise. It can rarely
outlive the first moment of complete strangeness. Yet in this case it
does. The more we know about Hershele, his sentiments and pretensions, the more ridiculous the contrast between his well-dressed figure
and those of the half-naked *Tuneyadevker* becomes. After Hershele
delivers his invective against the "other" books and stumbles into the
comparison of Jews with machines, Mendele resorts to sartorial im-
agery in order to find expression for his amazement. Hershele's speech,
he says, reduced him for a while to utter confusion:

> Have you ever in your life met with one of those German-looking gen-
> tlemen who talks as if he were one of the common people? . . . Really,
> this is a new fashion, a new cut. How shall I call it? A Berlin-style coat

with a hasidic lining; a *tales-kotn°* tuxedo. Indeed, it is a brand-new commodity of which one must say "shekheyonu." ° ° [33]

This passage begins as a eulogistic comment, but the sartorial metaphors soon give it a satirical turn. They are obviously grotesque. A "Berlin-style coat with a hasidic lining," no matter how highly it is praised, must be a ridiculous object, and a "*tales-kotn* tuxedo" can only be conceived of as an accessory for a "Jewish" vaudeville number. These metaphors could not but be meant to emphasize the basic unsoundness of Hershele's position. A German-looking gentleman who talks as if he were one of the common Jewish people is really a chimera, "a human head combined with a neck of a horse," to use Horace's famous illustration of the ridiculous.[34] And that is not all; the sharpest edge of Mendele's irony is less obvious than the "*tales-kotn* tuxedo" sally. It is concealed behind the overly less damaging descriptions of Hershele's national enthusiasm as "epes take a nayer shnit" ("really, a new fashion," or, in this connection, "a new cut"),[35] a metaphor which slyly suggests that it is nothing more than a fashion, something which comes and goes and may change from one year to the other like the cut of a gentleman's suit. Hershele's fervor may be the "rage" of one season or two, but not a lifelong loyalty.

Later in the prologue the sartorial motif is further emphasized by diverse references, direct and indirect, to the incongruity of Hershele's dress (I shall presently discuss one of these in a somewhat different connection). It reaches its high point with Hershele's wish to become part of "that large piece of fabric," the continuity of Jewish history. The full effect of this pathetic metaphor can now be fully sensed. Hershele's wish is expressed against a carefully prepared background, in which his fine clothes and the tattered gabardines of the people of Tuneyadevke are grotesquely contrasted and combined. The ancient piece of fabric to which Hershele expresses his loyalty, one guesses, must resemble the tattered gabardines and look quite old-fashioned beside the fresh fabric of his Leipzig-made surtout.[36]

° *Tales-kotn* (literally, "a small shawl"), the four-cornered garment which orthodox Jews wear under their shirts; also referred to as *arba-kanfes* and *tsitses*. To the four corners the ritual tassels are sewn.

° ° "Shekheyonu," "who kept us in life"; the thanksgiving "Blessed are you, O Lord our God, King of the Universe, who kept us in life, and preserved us, and enabled us to reach this time!" It is repeated whenever one enjoys something new, such as a new fruit or a new dress.

iv

Another motif around which Abramovitsh centered his ironic tactics throughout the prologue was that of books and their importance. That this is a central motif running through all Abramovitsh's works is indicated by the fact that the writing, editing, publishing, and selling of books constitute the occupation of Mendele, Abramovitsh's chief character. The prominence of the motif is, in fact, one of the links which connects Abramovitsh to the literature of the *Haskala*. The *maskilim* had an overwhelming respect for, and confidence in, the power of the printed word. Consequently, "the book" became an object of veneration, an object of an almost talismanic influence, in the literature of the *Haskala*. The intricate plot of *Megale-tmirin*, the first elaborate attempt at a maskilic work of fiction based on contemporary Jewish life, is dominated by a book, which the *hasidim* desperately try to get their hands on, since it is supposed to insure the downfall of their sect if not eliminated in time. In most of the maskilic novels (including Abramovitsh's *Ha'avot vehabanim*), books are sought after, concealed, found, fought over. They always figure as highly explosive objects which, more than anything else, can change reality. Abramovitsh's first Yiddish fictional work, *Dos kleyne mentshele*, which is written in the form of a confession and will of a repentant sinner, concludes with the writer's instruction to publish his life story in book form and see to it that it will be as widely distributed and read as possible. Through it, the sinner believes, a great moral improvement will get under way. The world will realize that "riches do not secure happiness; that only good will and good deeds make a man happy; that it is better to suffer any privation as an upright, honest man. . . ."[37]

Indeed, this belief in the power of books is the main target of Hershele's invective against them. It is not the ideological principles propagated by the nineteenth-century writers, or even their insolent manner, that enrages him most, but rather the tremendous importance they assigned to themselves and to literature in general, their fascinated, almost superstitious reliance on books. Human misery in some of its basic forms makes literature irrelevant, he vehemently argues ("reproof and advice do not fill an empty belly," etc.), and here he certainly scores a point. His criticism, no matter how poorly phrased, is at least partially valid, and there can be no doubt that in this matter Abramovitsh criticized through Hershele not only Jewish literature in

general but also his own youthful activity. It was certainly not without
a note of grim self-irony that he chose to elaborate on this subject in a
novel based upon and titled after his early, puerile *Vintshfingerl*. Written in the mid-1860s, when the *maskilim*'s attack on the Jewish people's reluctance to allow foreign cultural influences to penetrate their
close world was daily gaining in momentum, the early *Vintshfingerl*
was a typical maskilic enterprise. The brief, rudimentary story was
meant to serve as an introduction to a non-narrative composition.
Abramovitsh, along with other "enlightened" writers believed at the
time that the best way to drive "the cloud of ignorance and superstition" out of the minds of the Jewish people was "to go before them
with the pillar of fire of the sciences." [38] He was then devoting much
time and energy to the popularization of the natural sciences in Hebrew (he wrote many articles on biology, chemistry, etc., his main
achievement in this direction being a comprehensive zoology textbook). In *Dos vintshfingerl* he intended to pursue the same course in
Yiddish. A narrative, he thought, would be a good way to impress the
less sophisticated Yiddish reading public with the importance of scientific knowledge, and so he decided to introduce his compilation with
the autobiography of an imaginary *shtetl*-born author, a poor Russian-
Jewish boy who made good in the west, who could be trusted with the
fictional authorship of the forthcoming publication. Such a success
story would draw attention to the compilation and would also illustrate the argument that the Jews' deliverance from poverty would
come not through supernatural means (the "false" magic ring) but
through knowledge and science ("the true, natural magic ring").[39] The
full title of the book was *The Magic Ring, with Which Everyone Can
Achieve Whatever His Heart Desires and Through Which He Can Become Useful to Himself and to Society*. Never was the confidence of
the *Haskala* in its educational powers more blatantly expressed, and
rarely was a claim to influence on life more crudely insisted upon by a
secular book. It is true that even at that early stage of Abramovitsh's
development the rudiments of an ironic interplay of statement and
counterstatement were already present in his narrative compositions.
The figure of Mendele was already at its work of counterbalancing,
qualifying, and neutralizing pathetic exaggerations, and it is possible
that even the title of the earlier *Dos vintshfingerl* should be understood half in irony. Nevertheless, in this early composition, more than
in others, Abramovitsh was caught at one of the less guarded and per-

ceptive moments of his youth. The fact that he chose this early failure
as the basis for the major novel of his mature years is proof of his unusual ability both to unify the different phases of his long and varied
career into a process of uninterrupted growth and to achieve a measure of self-distance and self-criticism. The sheer retention of the title
Dos vintshfingerl, which mirrored the quintessence of the maskilic
crudity of the first version, indicates both continuity and self-irony;
perhaps it also indicates that with Abramovitsh continuity was
achieved *through* self-irony. On the one hand, he made use of his old,
discarded story as much as he could (in spite of his contention that the
enlarged *Vintshfingerl* was "a completely new book," many of the elements developed in its opening sections were already present in the
first version.)[40] On the other hand, the enlarged version is, in many respects, artistically as well as ideologically, in diametric opposition to
the earlier one. Abramovitsh's ironic combinations are, however,
Janus-faced. He knows how to make double use of his self-irony and
aim it simultaneously at himself and at his hero. He lets Hershele bring
up valid arguments against the self-confidence of literature, but he
makes him do it in a prologue to a new literary enterprise. Hershele is
denouncing books in general and secular ones in particular but he is
doing it in what is, after all, the opening chapter of a new secular Jewish book; and what's more, the new book is allegedly written by himself. This, indeed, is the crowning irony of the prologue. With his
"bread and not books" invective still ringing in the air, Hershele
comes up with the suggestion that Mendele publish not one but two of
his own books. Insisting on the right of the Jewish people to remain indifferent to literature of reproof and advice, he can offer them at the
moment nothing better than literature which will certainly contain
both reproof and advice. Moreover, he seems to do it without the
slightest awareness of the self-contradiction. Indeed, he goes so far as
to claim for his projected books that magical potency, that ascendency
over reality, which he has formerly derided with such animus. The first
of the two books he intends to publish through Mendele is his autobiography. This, he says, will serve the Jewish people "as a mirror" and
thus exert a tremendous corrective influence. "Looking at me, they
[the Jewish people] will really see themselves, and what they will like
or dislike in me they will find in themselves, and thus having through
me a mirror set in front of them, they will be able to see how they
look, poor things. . . ."[41] Such high regard has Hershele for his life

story, that he subtitles it "a present for the beloved children of Israel from their sincere friend," [42] as if to present people who need "bread and not books" with one's autobiography is not grotesque enough without such coy additions as "the beloved children of Israel" and "sincere friend," reminiscent of an album inscription or a birthday card. As for the second book, to which the autobiography is supposed to serve as an introduction, what can it contain save instructions concerning "how to direct one's conduct so as to achieve one's desires and wishes and become useful to oneself and society"? It is not only in this formula that the projected book resembles the old pseudo-scientific compilation (which, by the way, Abramovitsh never brought himself to write). Like the latter, it is supposed to have been originally written "in the German tongue" (the 1888 prologue adds "in a very simple German") and published in Leipzig by Brockhaus.[43] The ironic circle is closed. Abramovitsh lets his hero denounce literature only to overreach himself once again. Doesn't the later Hershele resemble his earlier namesake in every way? In some respects the earlier Hershele (or Hirsch Rathmann) was even more mature than the later one. For all his naive belief in the social value of scientific education, for all his provincial exultation in the technical wonders of Western civilization,[44] he was at least consistent. Hershele of the 1888 prologue constantly stumbles against his own bravura. Assuming the brisk manner of the man of action who could not waste time on mere words ("My friend, Reb Mendele," his letter to Mendele reads, "that I write to you now at all is an indication that all is well. My plan is already on the right path! If it were not so, I would not have written. I have no time for mere friendship letters," etc.),[45] he is, after all, unable to offer anything but words. His plans for the actual improvement of the conditions of the Jews, we are told, are grandiose; but Abramovitsh takes great care never to drop so much as a hint about what they consist of. The only plans of Hershele that we definitely know of are literary, and even these, as it transpires, he is hardly able to carry out by himself. So far from being the man of action, he is not even a professional writer.

The formal function of Mendele's introduction to *Dos vintshfingerl*, like that of most of his prefatory monologues, is that of a publisher's note. As a publisher of the old school (somewhat resembling the eighteenth-century English bookseller), he thinks he owes the public an explanation of how and why the book being offered came to be published under his auspices. Since *Dos vintshfingerl* is supposedly based on an authentic autobiography, its prologue consists largely of Mendele's reminiscences about the circumstances through which he came to know its author, Hershele, and of his explanations of the technical–literary changes the original manuscript underwent before becoming the book now before the reader. This technical part of the prologue is highly interesting. The original manuscript, we are given to understand, was not written in a form accessible to those readers for whom the autobiography is meant, i.e., the common Jewish people. It is not even clear whether it was written in Yiddish. Quite possibly it was written, like the non-narrative composition which it is supposed to introduce, "in easy German." Even if it had been written in Yiddish, it was not written with the specific needs and habits of the Yiddish reading public in mind. Hershele could not find the right tone for his intended readers; how could he, when he had spent most of his life, from his early teens on, in Germany? This is why he considers his chance meeting with Mendele a happy occasion. As a veteran Jewish bookseller and publisher who is perfectly acquainted with the taste of his public, Mendele is the ideal man for him. "I am going to use you for something which you and you only are capable of dealing with," he tells him.[46] Later on, as he sends him from Germany (in the meantime Hershele has returned to Leipzig) the supposed original version of the novel, he gives him a free hand to deal with it as he sees fit: "If you would like to make abridgments, to retain only the core of the manuscript, you may do so. Act according to the best of your understanding. In these matters I fully trust your judgment." [47] Mendele takes full advantage of his permission, perhaps more than the author has bargained for. Not only does he make drastic changes in the manuscript, but he actually decides to rewrite it completely. By the few examples of Hershele's prose that remain, we must judge him perfectly justified in this. Here is how Mendele explains, in his characteristically metaphorical style, the reasons for his decision:

> The story, I realized, is a very good story. . . . The trouble with it is that it is much too long, and the children of Israel, for whom a hint is enough, would be at their wits' end were they to read such a long one. One should not bend the bow too much or it might snap. So I made up my mind to alter it. . . . I cut out only those parts for which I had use, turned them inside out, where necessary applied a patch, and, piecing everything together in the Jewish style, I charmed my stitches and patches out of sight by a spell of mine. The story turns out, it seems, not

badly; it doesn't look like a story at all; and it is told by myself, as if it were mine. Only here and there, when I found it pertinent, I let the author speak for himself.[48]

These remarks are worthy of some attention. First, they show how conscious Abramovitsh was of the technical and structural aspects of literature. In this case he makes his Mendele explain to his readers the nature of the transition from the technique of narration in the first person (which he had invariably employed in his earlier Yiddish fictional works, all except *The Travels of Benjamin the Third*) to that of the third person, or "the omniscient author," with which he was now experimenting; a transition of much importance for the artistic development of modern Yiddish fiction. It was because of lack of attention to such remarks that critics created the legend that Abramovitsh, as "the Jewish artist" par excellence, had nothing to do with such un-Jewish matters as form and composition. These critics were obviously duped by Mendele's feigned innocence.[49] Mendele can express his comments on artistic problems in sartorial analogies; with him the question of composition may assume the form of a question of the correct tailoring of a piece of fabric, but there can be no doubt that he is not only aware of the need for composition, structure, and style but also proud of his abilities as a professional man of letters ("The story turns out, it seems, not badly"). He translates his awareness of literary technicalities into the language of artisans because, as Berditshevski said, Abramovitsh put his ideas through Mendele in the Jew's own mouth and made him understand them as if he himself had expressed them and in such a way as he himself would have done. Besides, the language of Jewish artisans enables him to express his conception of himself as an artificer, a man of technical skill and discipline, who is half tailor and half circus conjurer (he charms his stitches and patches out of the reader's sight with hocus-pocus).

Second, Mendele's remark puts in a nutshell the whole problem of East and West in Jewish literature. The seemingly technical, matter-of-fact information he gives on the measures of adaptation he has applied to Hershele's composition contains a rich comment on what was described by Berditshevski as the gulf between "the Jew" and the Europeanized Jewish writers. It is sustained throughout by an exquisite, if unobtrusive irony. It begins with a compliment to Hershele's performance ("a very good story"); then, with quick gradation, it undermines any claim on Hershele's part to literary competence. With each sentence it becomes clearer that he regards Hershele's manuscript as the work of an amateur and that he does not say so outright only out of a publisher's delicacy toward his author. At first, still cautious, he makes the Jewish reading public the scapegoat. It is, as it were, their inherent Jewish impatience and not the author's incompetence in dealing with his materials that made editing necessary. But Mendele does not pretend that the editing consisted only of abridgments, as one would have expected if the length of the story were the only fault of Hershele's composition. By comparing his work as an editor to that of a tailor, Mendele triumphantly asserts that he is a professional and degrades Hershele's manuscript to the status of "a piece of fabric." The way in which this degradation forms a part of the sartorial leitmotiv is, I believe, obvious. The manuscript has served Mendele as raw material, implying that Hershele's narrative lacked direction, design, and form, or at least that, if it had any of these, it did not conform to "the Jewish style." So the narrative has had to be cut to pieces and readjusted according to a completely new master plan. After this, it is only with difficulty that Mendele restrains himself from proclaiming the story (with which he is obviously pleased) his own creation. He gets very near to this as he advises his readers to read it "as if it were mine." The last shreds of his professed respect for the original manuscript are swept aside, as he informs the public that only those small fractions of it which he, Mendele, found "pertinent" have been allowed to penetrate the finished version. Had the prologue supplied us with no other indications of Abramovitsh's ironic attitude toward his protagonist, these remarks of Mendele alone would have sufficed. Presenting *Dos vintshfingerl* as based on the autobiography of its hero, which had been discarded for literary reasons, the author went out of his way to make us aware of the distance at which this hero was being kept.

v

By now, I am afraid, the impression had been created that Abramovitsh's intentions in the prologue to *Dos vintshfingerl* were to satirize Hershele and through him to discredit the new Jewish nationalism. This would not be correct. Abramovitsh's intentions were too complex to be thus summarized. He did want to emphasize the defects of the nationalistic enthusiasm, and he probably enjoyed the opportunity to deflate its overblown pathos; but these were not his only or even his major interests in the prologue. He certainly did not intend to present Hershele, who was going to figure as the hero of a long novel, as a hopeless dunce. Hershele, as we have already seen, is not always wrong. His arguments, fuzzy as they are, contain some grains of unwitting truth. His attack on nineteenth-century Jewish literature is by no means wholly irrelevant, and his wish for reunification with the common Jewish people is something Abramovitsh certainly sympathized with, although his confidence that such a reunification could be effected by a mere proclamation of loyalty is pitifully naive. In spite of Mendele's reference to his enthusiasm or to "a new fashion," Hershele's integrity is never really brought into question. His sin, if a sin it is, is one of indiscretion rather than of insincerity. His comic defect, the flaw which makes him deserve the punishment of being laughable, may be described as a naive immodesty. Mendele detected it when he compared him to a fully dressed person in a bathhouse. Surely, there is something immodest, perhaps even indecent, about such a person, and the immodesty is made all the more glaring as this person persuades himself that he does "belong" in the bathhouse and is one with the naked people he finds there. It is this lack of propriety, this failure of the senses of time and place which find stylistic correlatives in Hershele's bathos. His prose falls flat because it reaches beyond the limits proper under the circumstances. Hershele lets himself forget that, for better or worse, he is not, and he never will be, one of the people of Kabtsansk and Tuneyadevke. This marks him as fair game for satire, but it also lends him an air of humanity. He is undoubtedly ridiculous, but he is much more than that. While his intentional pathos is constantly sinking into bathos, unintentionally he is often truly pathetic. It is this combination of absurdity and genuine pathos which makes him the significant figure he is, for this combination is always characteristic of Abramovitsh's vision at its purest.

With some changes Hershele could have been worked into a figure of high seriousness. This is what Abramovitsh tried to do as he rewrote the prologue into an epilogue. Through certain cuts and discreet changes in the descriptive details, he refashioned his hero into a subdued, reflective, doubtful observer, painfully aware of his own ambiguous position among the Jews of the Russian pale. Whereas Hershele of the prologue is brisk, cocksure, stumbling, pretentious, his sobered, dulled, double is dejected, almost tearful. This change did not make

Hershele a more appealing or meaningful figure. On the contrary, I believe that it is the main reason for the relative unimportance of the epilogue. Abramovitsh was at his best when he seemed gay and sportive. Casual, jocular, and carefree, he was most tellingly serious. To convey his most profound insights, he had to resort to scenes of frolicsome, zany occurrences, and farce often proved his most happy element. The situation into which Hershele is thrown in the prologue is unmistakably farcical. Take, for instance, his visit to Tuneyadevke. Even before we get our first glimpse of him here, loitering like a "simpleton" in the synagogue courtyard in his conspicuous European dress, we are told that unknowingly he has inspired a terrible awe in the hearts of the townspeople, who suspect him of being a secret agent of the government. So, while he is inspecting the town for his own harmless purposes, stores are being emptied, contraband merchandise is smuggled into secret places, trembling Jews in *yarmulkes* (skull caps) avoid the streets, and the local *melamdim* (teachers) are in mortal fear.° Even Mendele, who has "seen the world" and is not a man easily given to fright, gives Hershele the "evil eye" and does everything he can to avoid coming in contact with him.[50] The impression of Hershele's appearance in Kabtsansk, as we have already seen, is completely different but no less grotesque. In both towns he raises false alarms and communal furor that call to mind the farcical developments which the appearance of a mysterious Khlyestakov or Tshitshikov triggers in the works of Gogol. And all this, we must remember, is happening while Hershele believes himself one with the people, "flesh of their flesh and bone of their bone." [51] Paralyzing Tuneyadevke with fright and sending Kabtsansk into a frenzy, he strolls benevolently in their miserable streets, full of good intentions and ever ready to defend his poor brethren against criticism.

It is by this enormous discrepancy between Hershele's intentions and their results that we can realize the full scope of Abramovitsh's intentions in the prologue. Of course, this discrepancy is comic; it is hilarious; but it is also heart-rending. Abramovitsh has created here a great tragicomic scene of misunderstanding with a wide range of im-

---

° Teaching by unlicensed Jewish teachers (and all traditional Jewish teachers were unlicensed) was officially forbidden, as was the wearing of particularly Jewish clothes (this by an old ukase, dating from the 1840s. See note 36 in the present chapter). Both bans were universally ignored. However, in situations of uncertainty and vague fears, such as the situation Hershele created in Tuneyadevke, people were reminded of them.

plications. It has already been suggested that he was following a long tradition of comic scenes of error and misunderstanding; that Hershele, in a sense, is the disguised traveler of comedy and romance. It has also been submitted that he differs from the traditional comic or romantic traveler, as he is never granted the full and the real recognition that leads to the reunification of son and parents, husband and wife, lover and beloved, lawful prince and loyal subjects, etc. There is nobody to recognize Hershele; but that is not all. It is only one reason why Abramovitsh diverts the classical formula of happy ending into the not-so-happy ending. Another reason, perhaps a much more ominous one, is that Hershele's disguise, unlike that of the hero of traditional comedy, cannot be cast aside. Unlike the Plautian hero who returns to make his peace with his family or the Shakespearean Rosalinde, Hershele cannot take off his foreign dress and resume a state of naturalness, innocence, and grace. His foreign dress, so to speak, has stuck to his body and become one with it. His mask is his face. He only pretends to tear it off, and even that he can do only because he does not begin to grasp how terribly painful, how virtually insufferable, a real tearing-off would be.

"The dress is the man" is the maxim around which every sartorial "philosophy" is developed. In the prologue to *Dos vintshfingerl* this maxim sounds with a bitterly ironical, almost a tragic note. Abramovitsh has employed so many sartorial images here and so emphasized his sartorial comparisons again and again because Hershele's dress symbolizes his historical failure. That he fails we cannot doubt. He comes all the way from Germany to the towns of his childhood to see his brethren in their misery and to feel one with them, but he does neither; his pilgrimage ends in a void. While he is investigating his brethren's poverty, they conceal their clandestine merchandise and touch him for money; while he is under the illusion that his eyes penetrate their secrets, they do everything they can to shut him out. All in all, it is a colossal failure of communication. Even in Kabtsansk, his birthplace, where he was not avoided, where, in fact, people tried to approach him from every direction they knew, even the slightest relationship between the town and its visitor is not established. In that regard, Hershele himself was much to blame, for he did not trouble to make his relationship with the people and the place known. It may well be that to do this was beyond his power. In any case, arriving in the town incognito he proceeded to inspect it without ever conceiving of the idea that the people he was investigating had the right to be told of his purpose or that his inquisitive interest might cause some inconvenience. We have here, indeed, another manifestation of the naive immodesty which is Hershele's comic flaw. His behavior goes only too well with his metaphorical reference to the Jewish people as machines. Whoever requires a machine's permission in order to inspect it? The only point at which some sort of communication is mentioned as taking place between Hershele and Kabtsansk occurs when he suddenly demands "that the floor of the synagogue and the *Talmud-toyre* be washed" and the community is scandalized: "How come! To do such a thing! To wash away the dirt produced by our ancestors!" [52] This, ironically, echoes recurring encounters in the literature of the *Haskala*. Joseph, the son of Shimon, the hero–reformer from one of Gordon's narrative poems, calls among other things, for a great cleanup of the Jewish synagogues. Hershele's demand is actually a verbatim reproduction of a demand made by the *maskil* Gutman in the first version of the *Vintshfingerl*.[53] The maskilic reformers, however, related physical cleanliness to spiritual renovation. The cleaning of the synagogue and the charity school was to them a symbolic gesture, a declaration that the Jewish ritual law and education were being revised and purified, as the rather crabbed couplet of Gordon announces:

> Beyt-hakneset teher me'aremot zevel
> Va'avodat ha'elohim miminhagey hevel.[54]

("He purified the synagogue from heaps of filth;/ The ritual he purged from empty forms.") It is only in this context that the reaction of the community to Hershele's demand makes sense (this reaction, incidentally, is also an exact reproduction of the reaction to Gutman's demand).[55] But Abramovitsh's point in the 1888 prologue is that nothing about the encounters of Hershele and Kabtsansk (or Tuneyadevke) makes sense. Every action and reaction which takes place in the course of the encounter is grotesquely meaningless. The community reacts to the demand as if it constituted a cultural challenge; with Hershele it probably was no more than a momentary physical revulsion. If it were more than that, he failed to explain himself. We do not hear of any dialogue or argument which follows the incident. No further communication; no effort at understanding. We only hear that "the visitor has left without taking his leave."

Hershele in Kabtsansk and Tuneyadevke is a man from whom the power of speech has been taken. The reality of the Jewish *shtetl* paralyzes him into silence. It is against this background that the flowers of rhetoric in his conversation with Mendele should be understood. Mendele revives in him his power of speech. In him he obviously believes he has found a man to whom he can speak, who will understand or at least partially understand him. What makes him attribute these capacities to Mendele? Here is another manifestation of the brilliance and intricacy of Abramovitsh's irony: it is because Mendele deals with books, and not only with prayer books but also with the "other" books, the secular ones, that Hershele trusts him with his confidence. When in the courtyard of the Tuneyadevke synagogue Hershele so insistently asks the bookpeddler whether he carries these other books or not, he does so not only in order to inveigh against them but also to find a man with whom he can have a common language. As one who deals with secular literature, Mendele can be assumed to have an acquaintance with it. Hence, he would understand what Hershele wants to say, for it is with this derided literature, with the world it represents, that Hershele is really on a par. Had he addressed his speeches directly to the people of Kabtsansk and Tuneyadevke, he would have been taken for a raving madman. To find a language which will make his thoughts accessible to them is beyond his powers, and that is why he has use for Mendele, not only as an interlocutor but also as an editor and a publisher. He has written his autobiography, as he explains, wishing it to do for him what he himself was unable to do, i.e., talk to the heart of the common people, prove his belonging to them, make them treat him as an intimate: "For I am a part of that group of people for whom I wrote here my life story. . . . I have shared with them the same predicament, felt the same pains. I want the Jewish people to read it and to know it. . . ." [56] But this, as we know, ends in another frustration, a literary one. Writing his autobiography to prove his Jewish identity, Hershele makes this identity all the more questionable. It is not only that the autobiography cannot prove that a living association between Hershele and the people does, in fact, exist; by its stylistic shortcomings, by the very fact that it needs the mediation of Mendele, the autobiography proves that such a living association does, in fact, not exist.

vi

Far from being a mere satire on the new Jewish nationalism, the prologue to *Dos vintshfingerl* is a comment on the crisis of Jewish culture in modern times and it is a very personal and self-searching comment. I want to suggest that the prologue should also be read as Abramovitsh's personal assessment of his position as a Jewish writer. By this I do not imply that the figure of Hershele is a portrait of the artist himself, though this has often been taken for granted by many readers. The prologue, like the novel it introduces, is a wholly fictional structure, and as such it contains its own frame of reference. Even if Abramovitsh were attempting a self-portrait in it (which is not likely), it would not serve any useful purpose here to dwell upon points of personal resemblance between him and his hero. What I want to point out is not a possible relationship between Hershele and Abramovitsh the man, but a possible correspondence between the tragicomic situation developed in the prologue around Hershele's visit to Kabtsansk and Tuneyadevke and the author's consciousness of the state of Yiddish literature at the time and of his own place in it. That such a correspondence, if it exists, is neither simple nor unequivocal is clear. Nevertheless, it is too important for our purposes to be left unexplored, and its importance is, in a way, connected with its intricacy. It is because such a correspondence must be richly ambiguous that it is so significant.

As a mature artist, Abramovitsh seldom, if ever, posed questions of primary importance to himself in a straightforward, discursive manner. He promised Sholem Aleichem that in *Dos vintshfingerl* he would "sharply analyze the conditions of the Jews, and show what is to be done in order to improve them";[57] but he never did this. For a long time he felt that the novel should include such an analysis (possibly as a separate, concluding section),[58] and this probably was one of the main reasons why he never finished it. It was his way of expressing his deepest and freest thoughts through fictional devices, through fables, through the dramatized consciousness of Mendele, and not through abstract deliberation. Even in his letters one looks in vain for direct comments of considerable conceptual depth. In them, as much as in his fictional works, it is always through objectified situations, through little imaginary dramas, that he can ask the most far-reaching questions and answer them honestly, even ruthlessly. In the preceding chapter I pointed out the significance of the hide-and-seek game he played with Sholem Aleichem, pretending to be a mere mediator between the latter and Mendele Moykher-Sforim. Isn't the same game going on in the 1888 prologue, only in a much more elaborate and meaningful form? Doesn't Abramovitsh, in fact, dramatize in the prologue the relationship between himself and his Mendele by making his Hershele come across the bookpeddler in the synagogue courtyard of Tuneyadevke? Isn't the prologue, among other things, a comment on the tragicomedy of modern Jewish literature?

We can begin to examine these possibilities by simplifying them into this hypothetical question: How would Abramovitsh's own imaginary characters, the people of Kabtsansk, Tuneyadevke, and Glupsk, have reacted were they to encounter their creator not in his guise as Mendele, but as Abramovitsh himself? This is neither an idle nor an illegitimate question to pose, since Abramovitsh posed it to himself and answered it in several comic scenes (one of which—Fishke's encounter with the "Frenchified" principal of the Odessa *Talmud-toyre*—has already been mentioned). He would, from time to time, let his heroes have glimpses of his undisguised self and report their impressions—usually unflattering ones. Couldn't it be that in the prologue to *Dos vintshfingerl* he is playing a similar trick in a somewhat subdued manner? This self-concealment behind the figure of Hershele is, of course, not accidental. It enabled Abramovitsh to broaden the scope and to enrich the meaning of what would otherwise have been another private joke of the type we find in his *Fishke the Lame* or in Sholem Aleichem's *feuilleton* "The Street." A more complete dramatic objectification, a more pronounced self-distancing were exactly what he needed in order to ask the question relentlessly and to answer it with complete freedom: What can be the position of a writer who had long ago cut himself off socially and culturally from the people who not only served him as subject matter but also as an ideal audience? In the prologue to *Dos vintshfingerl* this question is asked against a wide historical background: Kabtsansk and Tuneyadevke are in shambles; their very survival as Jewish habitations is doubtful; their inhabitants are being uprooted from their historical soil, and their future is shrouded in darkness. The Europeanized intelligentsia are not in much better shape. Their maskilic confidences shattered, the Hershele-like intellectuals are indulging themselves in an emotionalism both vague and self-contradictory. They allow themselves bathetic excesses and pretensions to businesslike practicality; they develop both an "orientation to the people" and a conception of the people as mechanical resources to be activated; they denounce the literature of the *Haskala* and are unable to offer anything better. With this background Abramovitsh tries his utmost to achieve not only historical knowledge (*Dos vintshfingerl* was meant to be "a history of Jewish life") but also self-knowledge. For this he must mobilize all his artistic powers; to invent a lively, complex dramatic situation; to suffuse it with his subtlest irony; to give complete freedom to his sense of artistic play and then to play his game in dead earnest. Abramovitsh accomplished all this in the prologue to *Dos vintshfingerl*, and what he came up with is something like the following: he, the Jewish writer par excellence, like his Hershele, is a traveler in disguise—ridiculous, pathetic, blundering, hilariously misguided. Removed from his Odessa headquarters to one of the old *shtetlekh* he so vividly created or, perhaps to his own distant home town, the small northern Kapulye, Abramovitsh would find himself in the midst of the same farce into which he threw his hero. Wouldn't he be either avoided as a dangerous intruder or gaped at and followed in the streets as a freak? Wouldn't he look quite the simpleton in his "Frenchified" Odessa jacket, with his shorn sidelocks and his trimmed literary beard? Above all else, were he to write books for the Jewish people, as he actually does, wouldn't he, like Hershele, have to depend on Mendele the Bookpeddler to cut his manuscripts to pieces and rewrite them "in the Jewish style"? Wouldn't he have to wait for him to grease the wheels of his wagon and to harness his old horse before making any progress?

Were we to look for the one personal experience more than any other we are aware of in the author's life that seems to be reflected in Hershele's visit to his home town, we would have to go back to that bitter boyhood return to Kapulye described in one of the most moving chapters in Abramovitsh's autobiographical novel, *Shloyme reb Khayims* ("Shloyme the Son of Reb Khayim"). Driven from his home town by the poverty into which his family has sunk after his father's death, Shloymele (a slight variation on Abramovitsh's real name, Sholem, Sholemke), a thirteen-year-old boy, goes to another town, where he studies the Talmud, lodges in the synagogue, and boards with charitable members of the community (he "eats days," according to the Jewish expression). In his dejection and solitude he lets his imagination revel in the sights of his Kapulye, which he idealizes into a world of felicitous familiarity and dazzling vividness. Coming home on a visit, however, he suffers the bitterest disillusionment. Outwardly unchanged, the town is a completely foreign place. Even the most familiar objects in his father's house (which is now up for sale) are ominously alien. "Loneliness is bitter in every form . . . but there is a great difference between being strange and being estranged," Abramovitsh comments.[59] Shloymele finds the bitterness of estrangement almost unbearable.

The experience was so mortifying, it left such a deep impression, that Abramovitsh was compelled to incorporate it in the very first work of fiction he wrote, the fragmentary novel *Limdu hetev* ("Learn to Do Good," 1862). Here a similar mortification is inflicted upon the hero, David the son of Elkana, who returns home after long years of study to find no family and no place to go back to. Here Abramovitsh obviously made the most of his painful reminiscences as he aggrandized the woes of his protagonist. *Limdu hetev* teems with the sentimentality and sensationalism which at the time dominated Hebrew fiction, and David's sorrows are given vent in the effusive epistolary manner characteristic of the novels of the old, true sentimental stock. Full of enthusiasm and impatience, David writes in a letter, he flew to his home town:

> But oh, my friend, my hopes were cruelly dashed. . . . There, in the house which formerly, in the good days, delighted my soul, and where I hoped to be happy again—the house for which I pined for many a year —there, when I entered, I found people I did not know, who gathered around and eyed me with great wonder. Upon hearing my incoherent, disconnected questions, they told me that my mother had been dead for these ten years, that my father had left the town never to be heard of again, and that this, his house, had been seized by his creditors. Overwhelmed, I fled the house and rushed to my inn, there to give vent to my tears, for the Almighty hath dealt very bitterly with me. On the morrow, as I stepped out, I found the whole town buzzing: "This is David, the son of Elkana!" Boys saw me and gaped, and the aged arose and stood up. . . . Nobody welcomed me or asked how I was. They only whispered together against me! One pointed at my short jacket, another at my beard and sidelocks, shorn contrary to the Jewish custom; still another spit in my face and growled like a bear. In their eyes—even in my own eyes—I was no better than a criminal. Then my soul was flooded with grief, and I decided to leave the town, which not long before had been my joy, to which I had flown like the doves to their windows. . . .[60]

The reader can use this example of Abramovitsh's very early writing, even as presented here in a makeshift translation, to form some idea of the distance the author covered from this starting point to the maturity which he eventually achieved. For our purposes, however, the important thing to notice is the historical and cultural meaning Abramovitsh added here to the personal experience recorded in *Shloyme reb Khayims*. David the hero is not a Talmud scholar who has been staying in a Jewish town nearby; he is the westernized *maskil* who has been studying for long years in Berlin. The confrontation between him and his home-town community is painful not only because of the fate of his family and the change in his social status (as is also the case of the autobiographical Shloymele) but also because of the cultural allegiances represented by his European jacket and shorn sidelocks. Technically, we already have here most of the elements which were to reappear in the 1888 prologue to *Dos vintshfingerl*. Hershele, like David, returns to his home town from a German city, where he has been engaged in academic activities; like him he comes filled with good intentions to help his brethren and educate them; like him he is singled out by his foreign appearance; like him he completely fails to communicate with the people of his native town; and like him, he leaves the town "without taking his leave." Of course, there are great differences between the two visits, David's and Hershele's, to their childhood *shtetlekh*. The historical circumstances under which the two homebound trips took place are completely different: David faces a Jewish congregation from the time of Nicholas, still almost monolithic and dangerously uninhibited in its hostility to the harbingers of change. What Hershele faces is the weakened, disintegrating Jewish community of the 1880s. David and Hershele, then, in spite of their common weakness for the luxuries of bathos, differ from each other in many ways. Yet we have here a single development from the intensity of personal injury to wisdom gained by self-distancing. In *Limdu hetev* we see this line of development at its very beginning. The author barely distinguishes his hero from himself. He fully shares his agony and frustration. But there is already a difference. By dramatizing his experience of estrangement as a historical confrontation between the *Haskala* and the traditional Jewish community, Abramovitsh made it more than a personal occurrence. Of course, he is wholly on the side of the *Haskala*. The objection of the community to David's ideological alignment makes its attitude toward him all the more despicable. But even in the very midst of his emotional turbulence David is able to make an observation, which is the beginning of a wider understanding of the meaning of his encounter with his home-town community: "In their eyes—even in my own eyes—I was no better than a criminal." The ability to see himself through the eyes of the other side is momentary, but it is already there. In the prologue to *Dos vintshfingerl* we have the line of the development at its other end. In Hershele's visit to Kabtsansk, Abramovitsh's boyhood experience of unsurpassed bitterness and of a crushing sense of alienation is relived. But now, at the peak of his maturity, and after he has constructed the most elaborate machinery of ironic self-alienation, the author is able to see the confrontation in the widest perspective, to divine its comic as well as tragic implications, and thus to state its significance in the most comprehensive terms.

CHAPTER FIVE

THE MENDELE MAZE
1. The Pseudonym Fallacy

"I would but find what's there to find,
Love or deceit."

"It was the mask engaged your mind,
And after set your heart to beat,
Not what's behind."

(W. B. Yeats, "The Mask")

THE CRISIS OF Jewish culture in the nineteenth century is enacted in the 1888 prologue to *Dos vintshfingerl* as a tragicomedy with three symbolic figures: the collective image of Kabtsansk and Tuneyadevke, Hershele, and Mendele the Bookpeddler. The inhabitants of the two *shtetlekh*—tattered, scared, innocent, greedy, and curious—represent "the Jew," to use Berditshevski's distinction once again. Hershele—a prodigal son come home too late—represents "us," the Europeanized intelligentsia. By his conspicuous dress, his good intentions, and his unhappy metaphors he looks ridiculously and pathetically out of place on his native ground; he is simultaneously a "superior" observer, a dupe, and a man in search of his identity. Between these two figures hovers enigmatic Mendele. Of the three, he is clearly the key figure. But for him the whole symbolic structure could not have existed. If the confrontation between Hershele and the *shtetlekh* has been organized into a significant drama—comic, tragic, ironic—it has happened only through the agency of his lucid, comprehensive understanding. Eliminate his mediatory services—his commentary, comparisons, and juxtapositions—and everything either dissolves into sheer absurdity or shrinks into a much narrower vision, where "our" perception and experience, those of Europeanized modern Jews, exclude everything which lies outside their own boundaries.[1]

Mendele is the key figure of the piece, but he is also its mysterious figure. For all his lucidity as an observer, he himself cannot be easily penetrated. Unlike Hershele and "the Jew," he represents more than historical or social reality. He is also an idea, an intellectual potentiality, a spiritual quest, and therefore—a riddle. Who is he? Outwardly, an ordinary Jewish bookpeddler of the old school. The familiarity implied in the diminutive form of his name as well as in its commonness (Mendl) suggest the ordinary Eastern European Jew in his most workaday, unceremonious aspects. In dress and manner he cannot be distinguished from any other representative of "the Jew." Tuneyadevke and Kabtsansk do not suspect him of any deviation from their norms. They regard him as one of their own; not that they are sentimental about him, but they have complete confidence in him. In a certain sense, they even look up to him and ask for his advice. "It so happened," he tells us, "that exactly at the time" of Hershele's mysterious visit to Tuneyadevke he, Mendele, "driving with his wagon on one of his rounds," arrived in town:

> Before I had time to unharness my horse, the whole community was telling me in one breath of the great wonder: "Reb Mendele, we have news for you! A person, some person, a man of sorts has descended upon us! For some reason he looks everywhere; keeps his ears pricked up too. What's more, he makes inquiries; he investigates. The whole thing smells fishy. He may be a spy, eh, what do you say, Reb Mendele? Everything not strictly 'kosher' has, for the time being, been removed from the stores; that goes without saying. . . ." [2]

As a man who has "seen the world," Mendele may possess knowledge which Tuneyadevke, in its utter isolation, cannot be expected to have. The wide experience he has acquired through his itinerant profession —the experience of roads, inns, fairs, strange towns and hamlets, strange people—may perhaps enable him to decipher the secret meaning of the stranger's visit. This possibility, however, makes him neither a superior nor a stranger. Although he has experienced the vicissitudes of the "great" world outside, he is not an outsider. As far as Kabtsansk and Tuneyadevke are concerned, Mendele is like an extension of the communal body.

Yet the intruder, Hershele, as we have seen, is quick to detect the difference that sets Mendele apart from the communal body of Tuneyadevke. Almost from the first moment of their encounter he does not regard him as one of the "local Jews" he has mortified with his philanthropical investigations. These "rusting machines," which he means to benefit by proper lubrication, may be the object of his professions of loyalty; they may even be the unsuspecting beneficiaries of his rhetorical protection. But it is Mendele whom he treats as a fellow human being; to him he talks; in him he senses the possibility of understanding, of an escape from the frustrating seclusion he has experienced in the midst of his "brethren."

Obviously, Mendele has something about him that encourages familiarity. He is not only on speaking terms with all parties, he is virtually their confidant. This situation applies, of course, not only to Hershele and Tuneyadevke but also to the many "parties" Mendele encounters throughout his career in the works of Abramovitsh. He does not have to solicit people's confidence or to repay them with his own. Everywhere he goes, he is incessantly approached, talked to, confided in. He certainly possesses the secret of making himself an immediately and unobtrusively attractive listener. The question that we, the readers who benefit from this special attraction of his, are inclined to ask, however, is whether he uses his powers with the proper restraint and delicacy. Aren't all those who confide in him somewhat misguided? Are Hershele and Tuneyadevke on firm ground with him? Isn't he quite capable of making improper use of the faith they evidently have in him? Hershele, who confided in him so unreservedly, who regarded him as a good friend, and who trusted him with his manuscripts and secret plans, is in fact subjected by him to a subtle, coy, but actually very damaging form of ridicule. His brittle dignity and pathos are quickly reduced by Mendele's light but shattering ironic blows. Hershele's talent as a writer is all but openly discredited by him. His very dress is made fun of. Kabtsansk and Tuneyadevke hardly fare better. Not only does he reserve some of his most treacherous thrusts exclusively for them, but he undermines them, even as he seems to undermine Hershele, by contrasting him with them. A past master of double irony, he often pits one party against another only to see them discredit each other. When Mendele draws an ironic contrast, he usually does not mean to present one of the contrasted sides or positions as a positive or a true norm and denounce the other as an antinorm; he prefers to let two false positions mutually destroy themselves. The contrast between Hershele's ridiculous clothing and Tuneyadevke's complacent slovenliness illustrates this trick of Mendele's. The tattered residents of Tuneyadevke expose Hershele's insensibility to the proprieties of time and place, while his own elegance heightens

Tuneyadevke's sloth and indecent physical familiarity. Hershele is ridiculed as the fully dressed person who intrudes upon naked people in a bath, while the people of Tuneyadevke are ridiculed as permanent bath-dwellers who enjoy the stuffy, dreamlike humidity of their world and cannot stand the slightest exposure to the open air.

Hershele's visit to Kabtsansk, too, is constructed so as to discredit both him and his home town by way of a double-edged contrast. While he turns his homecoming into a farce by his self-mystification and his pose as an impersonal investigator, the town makes itself absurd by racking its brains to find out who he is. He will not divulge so much as his name; the town is already meditating a match for him. He goes about looking into the lives of the people, much against their will, as if they were so many animals; they "descend upon him from every direction like locusts." Which of the two parties, we wonder, inflicts and suffers more damage in this encounter? Both, it seems, emerge from it badly hurt.

Mendele's address, or rather his mock apostrophe, to the people of Kabtsansk (the ironic pathos and the formal rhetoric of the passage justify such designation) merits more attention. It manifests Mendele's fundamentally extrinsic, alien position with regard to Kabtsansk not only by its satiric contents but also, perhaps primarily, through the subtleties of its descriptive style. What reveals his "outsider" attitude perhaps more than anything else, is his constant reference to the community of Kabtsansk, to the *Kabtsansker*, as though they constituted one body, of which they are "members" in the literal sense of the word. This is what makes the Jewish communities Mendele describes on the one hand so definitely and obviously autonomous—each a tiny world in its own right physically separable from all other worlds (if a Mendele-*shtetl* may be described as a grotesque version of a tiny Jewish *polis*, then its unity and autonomy can be said to be that of a literal "body politic")—and on the other hand, so outlandish and grotesque. In the passage under discussion here as well as in numerous other descriptions of Jewish towns in Abramovitsh's works, the bizzare or grotesque nature of the community—the presence of which is experienced in terms of physical contiguity—is expressed primarily through references to the modes of its movement. The *Kabtsansker* in our passage are said to have completely lost their wits because of Hershele's unannounced and unexplained visit. They are going out of their minds. This, however, is illustrated by Mendele with a description of agitation, which somehow does not indicate disorder but rather an innate sense of coordination. The *Kabtsansker* surround the visitor in formation. The charity beneficiaries, the synagogue wardens, the beggars, and the nonbegging paupers, in short, all the categories of inhabitants who want to touch him for money, come first with a sweeping, acrobatic agility (they seem to descend from the air, "like locusts"). Then come the dignitaries and sages of the town with the slower and more deliberate movements of "feeling" and reconnoitering. In the meantime the matchmakers of Kabtsansk are closely observing the visitor, supposedly from some distance, as fair game for their matchmaking forays. While Mendele purports to present a scene of utter disorder, a pandemonium, he actually produces a well-organized dance, or rather a well-staged ballet-like version of disorder. This disorder is rigidly regularized and aestheticized, i.e., it is a disorder viewed from the outside without any reference to the experience of bewilderment and agitation from which it is said to have originated. Thus, completely distanced, it is conceived as an order in itself.

This constantly happens in Mendele's descriptions. The very first paragraphs in Abramovitsh's first Mendele story (*Dos kleyne mentshele*, first version) introduce us to a fictional community that moves in what reminds one of a market scene in an opera with all the supporting cast as well as the chorus on stage, performing a highly stylized version of a "natural" street conversation:

> I saw people in circles: standing, wrangling, talking, laughing, worrying. The circles were in constant flux. In a moment three circles merged into one; another moment—and the one split in three. . . .[3]

In the very first sentences Mendele is made to utter we can sense, then, his "aesthetic" detachment from the community, his attitude toward it as an "object." Already in his debut, in 1864, we must conclude, he has been conceived of as far removed from the inner experience of the Jewish town.

This must be joined to the fact that Mendele is from his earliest appearances a traveler, a man constantly on the move and therefore deprived of (or relieved from) a communal framework. It is not accidental that the description just quoted occurs in a passage that relates what eventually became an archetypal situation in Abramovitsh's works: Mendele has just arrived in a Jewish town or hamlet. He drives straight to the synagogue courtyard, which is the communal center of the town, where he immediately sets about his business, unpacks his merchandise—books, ritual accessories, etc.—unharnesses his weary horse, feeds him, and generally behaves with the purposefulness and equanimity of the practical and experienced man he is. Meanwhile, however, he closely watches the people around him, scrutinizes their behavior and eavesdrops on their conversation. The reasons for this curiosity are partly practical (in the opening section of the first version of *Dos kleyne mentshele*, Mendele justifies or explains his eavesdropping on the conversation of the people of Glupsk with a generalization: "In this world one must know everything, hear everything; it may turn out to be useful"),[4] but generally they transcend mere commercial interest. Mendele is genuinely attracted by Jewish community existence; that is, he is both disgusted and fascinated by it (as he says, he never misses the opportunity to visit, upon his arrival in a Jewish town, the local bathhouse, the ideal place, according to him, for getting a quick and extensive "coverage" of the community's life in its raw "nakedness," of actually getting a "sniff" of its heavy atmosphere).[5] As much as he may be interested, tickled, and entertained by what he sees or hears, however, he always remains a very conscious outsider. His attitude toward the crowded, steamy, closed world of the Jewish community is that of a man used to the solitude, openness, exigencies, and freedom of the road. Their existence, for him, is symbolized by the naked togetherness of the bathhouse, with its stuffy atmosphere and bad smells, because his existence is characterized by direct contacts with wind, sun, rain, dust, and the fragrance of blooming fields. For him they exist as a group, because he is basically a loner, a man on his own. As he himself testifies when he presents himself at the beginning of *Dos kleyne mentshele*, he is far from home and family "almost all the year round," roaming with his merchandise throughout the southern parts of the Russian Jewish pale, staying "at one time here, at another there, and known everywhere"[6] (from the conclusion of the same story we learn that he has not visited his home town and family for almost two years.[7] In another early work we hear of a letter written by Mendele's wife, who complains bitterly of her husband's long absence from home—two years—and indifference to his family).[8] He does not even have an address, and he asks his customers to send their bills in his name to Glupsk, which he often visits, *poste restante*.[9] With such a vagrant mode of existence Mendele must possess at least some streaks of the vagabond's mentality, a touch of his contempt for

the immobility of people who have almost never left the close neighborhood of their little villages. For there can be no doubt that Mendele is not only used to the life of the open road (which he has been
following for many years; according to one source he bought his horse
and set about the business of itinerant bookpeddling as soon as his
bed-and-board years with his in-laws had terminated, i.e., from his
early twenties;[10] according to another, later one, he had had a taste of
several other trades before he finally switched to bookpeddling),[11] he
loves it, and for all his complaints of its hardships, as well as of his aching back, he would not change it for anything. Nothing worse can be-
fall him than to get stranded in one of the little *shtetlekh*, be it even
his own home town. This actually happens only once, in one of
Abramovitsh's Hebrew stories, written after the pogroms of the early
1880s. Mendele's horse, we learn from this story, was "captured" (i.e.,
stolen) by hooligans, who attacked his small home town, Kabtsansk
(Kabtsiel in Hebrew), just before the Jewish high holidays, when he
happened to be there on one of his rare visits. Thus: "Kabtsiel was to
me like quicksand to shipwrecked seafarers. Since my horse, who like
a freighter, used to ship my merchandise far and wide, was captured
and I could not afford to purchase another one, I have had to settle
down—much against my will—in my home-town and sit idle." [12] Mendele makes it abundantly clear that he hated every minute of this
unexpected and interminable vacation because he could not endure
the cloying, provincial atmosphere of the town with its ridiculous
"politics" and inane polemics. In a later Hebrew story, written in the
1890s, where Mendele at long last complies with the spirit of modern
times and changes his horse and wagon for a train, we find a long, lyrical passage in which the charms of the old life of the open road are ex-
patiated on in an exquisite ironic–elegiac manner. The new mode of
traveling is attacked because, unlike the old wagon, the train does not
expose people to the sky, the sun, and the winds, nor does it distract
them, at least for a few days, from their daily routine. The train is "a
traveling town, with all its noise and agitation, with all its inhabitants,
divided according to party and social status and burdened by all their
hatred and envy, their business, competition, and quarreling." [13] It is,
then, the exact opposite, the negation of the idea of freedom from
communal ties, from the tedium and pettiness of a gregarious existence, which for Mendele has become the essence of his own walk of
life.

The freedom of the open road is undoubtedly one of the positive norms upon which Mendele's satire is based. His attachment to it makes him inevitably a satirical observer of communal manners and mores and explains his poignant sense of the difference between himself—a man who must shift for himself, who lives by his wits, and who always asserts his individuality—and "them," who seem to live only by the communal instinct, and are therefore fit for description as members of one body, as ants, mice, or locusts. It also explains why it is particularly "their" constant, agitated movement which appeals so strongly to his sense of the ridiculous. Since "real" movement is the very principle of his existence, he cannot see the movement of the *Kabtsansker* or the *Glupsker* as anything but a senseless parody. After all, it takes them nowhere; they wriggle, swarm, buzz, run "like poisoned mice" and stay exactly where they have been. (The whole comedy of *Benjamin the Third* is based on the detection of this *semblance* of movement, from which the work derives its mock-heroic effect.) As the voyager, whose own movement is effective and purposeful, Mendele can always observe and present the frenzied movement he encounters in the Jewish towns he visits either as an aesthetic gesture, a ballet, or as a mechanical reaction, a spasm. This immediately gives away the sense of dissociation, of self-alienation with regard to the Jewish community, which he may otherwise try to conceal.

Another characteristic of Mendele's descriptions of the Jewish communities, which gives away his fundamentally alienated attitude, may also be connected, perhaps indirectly, with his experience of the road. As an itinerant he has an opportunity—a rather rare one for a traditional Jew at the time—to observe nature, to study its manifold phenomena, even to "commune" with it. For all his satirical references to himself as a traditional Jew, whose Jewishness stands between himself and a real attachment to nature, he certainly lets himself, as he often confesses, "be allured" by its charms, which he personifies in the figure of a seductive beauty.[14] He both intimately knows the world of open fields, groves, brooks, and hollows and is able not only to savor its more conventional beauties but also to share the vibrant vitality which informs it; he actually senses its mystical unity, which establishes concord between himself and nature's tiniest and humblest creatures. The proof of this is the series of nature descriptions for which Abramovitsh's works have been justifiably praised for more than a hundred years by critics of all literary and ideological persuasions. This lyrical communion with nature, which in itself dissociates Mendele's sense of himself as well as of his environment from the sense of self and world formed within the framework of the traditional culture of the *shtetl* is obvious and does not need further comment here. What should be emphasized is its projection into Mendele's descriptions of Jewish life as a negative reflection. What I have in mind is not Mendele's openly satirical attacks on the traditional Jewish detachment from nature, but rather his way of portraying Jewish life as a vicious parody of nature. For it is quite clear that on arriving in a Jewish town from the open world of the Ukrainian plains, what Mendele often finds is a direct continuation of the fauna and flora he has encountered on his way. But what in the field was a part of the proper, divinely prescribed order of things—the hum and buzz of insects, for instance—becomes in the town an improper and debased version of nature; indeed, a vitiation of it. A Jewish community that hums and buzzes like a swarm of insects or attacks a newcomer like locusts presents, as we have seen, an existence of diminished humanity; sometimes a downright dehumanized existence.

Although Mendele's "bestial" analogies and similes, which are perhaps the most prominent figurative features of his descriptions of Jewish life, are not always exactly his own literary property (the numerous comparisons of people to locusts or to "poisoned mice" are current idiomatic similes still widely used by speakers and even by writers of robust, "folksy" Yiddish), they certainly add up to a highly individualized and conscious metaphorical system; that is, they are employed in an orderly and consequential manner as a device that expresses Mendele's quintessential experience of Jewish communal life as well as his most characteristic attitude toward it (an attitude in which the biological–positivistic bias of Abramovitsh and his age is concomitant with the old literary traditions of "bestialization" in satire and fable). In any case, nothing strikes his fancy more readily than to visualize a Jewish community as a herd of cattle, a flight of poultry, a population of mice, bugs, gnats, etc. The similes and metaphors by which this visualization is conveyed may differ in their connotations. They may attribute to the Jewish people hopeless, mindless apathy (see the list of dramatis personae which Mendele prepared for the play *Di takse* [*The Tax*]: "a poor Jew, a poor Jewess, . . . slaughterers, women, geese, hens, turkeys, ducks, and a population of fifty thousand human cattle heads, shorn like sheep"),[15] or insatiable greed (locusts); they may emphasize their rashness, their aimless hustling about ("like poisoned mice"; this is another idiom Mendele makes ample use of), or impute to them the cold, cruel determination of egotism (bugs). Whatever their specific emphasis, these metaphors always dehumanize the Jewish people and render them both repulsive and ridiculous. Take, for example, the passage in which the effect of Hershele's sudden appearance among the people of Tuneyadevke is figuratively delineated:

> The sleepy Tuneyadevke was startled from its slumber, gaped at him, and wondered how such a person could appear in its dream. It looked as if somewhere at night in a distant place, a person carrying a faggot had suddenly entered a miserable hole where fowl doze perched on a roost. The fowl, half asleep, their eyes blinking, ask themselves how anybody can be stirring at such a late hour and thereat, heaving a sigh, look quite stupid.[16]

This is an overwhelmingly malicious description. What saves it artistically from the gross excess of caricature is the calculated elaboration and realism of the pictorial representation. The fowl are not caricatured as fowl. They are observantly and objectively depicted. It may be noted that Mendele employs here what is technically known as a Homeric, or epic, simile (an elaborate, richly pictorial comparison of two actions). As is often the case with such similes, the long and circumstantial description of the figurative vehicle (e.g., storm clouds in movement over a hillside) overshadows the tenor (e.g., the Greek army marching toward Troy) and makes us disregard the former's dependence on the latter. We may be inclined to enjoy the description of the dozing fowl as an autonomous piece of pictorial poetry and ignore its bearing on the reality to which it is correlated. This tendency checks or mutes somewhat the violent effect of Mendele's analogy, but it does not eliminate it. In fact, it may be argued, the precision, the artistic balance, the air of epic expansiveness convey an intensity of contempt as no metaphorical frenzy could have. Moreover, through his Homeric simile Mendele creates a tiny but extremely effective piece of mock heroic: Hershele (a man), carrying the torch of knowledge (the faggot), comes as a veritable Prometheus into ignorant, benighted Tuneyadevke (a miserable hole) and encounters his brethren—a flight of dozing fowl. The satirical impact of this scenic arrangement is obvious.

    It should also be remembered that with this simile Mendele is sounding only the first note of what will be developed into a dominant metaphorical motif in his narrative. *Dos vintshfingerl*, at least in its first part, teems with figurative comments such as, "Of all the people of the world, Jews are like roosters who always lie on the boards over the stove near their females and little ones";[17] or, "His [Hershele's] mother did what was expected of her with no ifs, ands, or buts: she conceived and gave birth. For what purpose is she a Jewish woman if not for breeding, when even a common hen obeys God's will, lays eggs, clucks and does not ask too many questions. . . ."[18] Or,

> In his family circle, his father was the true rooster who always leads his hen and their progeny around the courtyard, looks for food, digs worms for them from under the earth; but let a chicken somehow disobey him, and immediately he pecks its tiny head, then resumes walking, his head raised up, his fiery eyes sweeping haughtily around. To show how important he is, he beats his wings and makes a great, a royal cock-a-doodle-do, which means "Behave yourselves, chickens! Remember who you are and who I am!"[19]

The cumulative effect of these similes, no matter how pictorially balanced they may be, is devastating.

Such similes and metaphors have a direct bearing on the problem of Mendele's identity, with which our present discussion deals.[20] The pictorial conception of the common Jewish people that they convey could not have originated from within the world of "the Jew." Indeed, they argue a far-reaching dissociation from this world. Hershele's metaphors, we have seen, reduce the Jewish people to mechanical objects; but Hershele is a stranger. The point that his metaphorical *faux pas* are meant to make is that, although he would like to regard himself as "one of the people," he is completely isolated from them. By the same token Mendele's metaphors must also be regarded as indications of isolation from the Jewish people. If Hershele renders the people of Kabtsansk and Tuneyadevke inanimate, Mendele bestializes them. Both treat them with a pronounced sense of superiority. Of course, there are many differences between the use the two characters make of metaphorical language. Hershele blunders with his metaphors, contradicts himself, gets entangled in his analogies, while Mendele uses his with consummate skill. With the former, they work like a boomerang; with the latter, like arrows shot by the best of marksmen. This, however, only proves that what in the case of Hershele is a state of involuntary, perhaps unconscious isolation, is with Mendele a perfectly

conscious and deliberate although well-concealed act of self-dissociation. Hershele cannot help his alienation; Mendele celebrates it.

ii

The extent of Mendele's alienation from the world of "the Jew"
can be best gauged by an examination of the first paragraphs in some
of his best prologues. Mendele opens his prefatory addresses, as befits
a traditional Jew and a disseminator of prayer books and other accessories of holiness, by celebrating the glory of God. In his mouth,
however, the praise of God sounds more like blasphemy. Take, for example, the opening paragraph of the prologue to the play *The Tax*:

> Omar Mendele Moykher-Sforim—quoth Mendele the Bookpeddler.
> Praised be the Creator, Who has created great oceans and many rivers:
> the Nile, the Teterev and the renowned Gnilopyatke; praised be the
> Creator of the Mountains of Darkness, the deserts, the wastelands,
> many wild places, and the big Jewish town of Glupsk. Praised be His
> beloved Name for choosing us, Jews, out of all the people of the world,
> to confer on us a Tax, a money-box,° inspectors, communal leaders, at-
> torneys, arbitrators, persons of high principles, intercessors, and very
> many idlers. Praised be the Creator for everything He has created:
> praised be He for the wild animals, lions, leopards, wolves, bears, and
> for the tax-farmers; praised be He for the cattle, the oxen, the horses,
> the asses, for the fine gentlemen of Glupsk, and for the whole pack of
> public benefactors. . . . But this is beside the point. I thank and praise
> God for giving me courage and helping me to publish this terribly inter-
> esting story.[21]

Here Mendele is preparing the background for a play which, more
than any other work of Abramovitsh's, subjects the reader to a shock
treatment. *The Tax* is one of the most radical, shrill, and effective ex-
posés of social injustice within the Jewish community to be found in
Yiddish literature, and throughout it employs the technique of the
shocking equation. Of course, Mendele's equations in the prologue are
intended to strike us as funny. Mentioning in one breath the Nile—the

---

° The tax referred to was the special tax levied on Jews in czarist Russia for the right
to consume kosher meat. Its professed purpose was to supply the Jewish congregation
with funds for the public services it was supposed to offer. The tax was collected either
through private tax-farmers or through the agents of the congregation, and as the
amount was never fixed, it could be exploited by corrupt communal leaders. The
"money-box" mentioned by Mendele is the congregational treasury.

grandest river in Jewish mythical geography (it is the biblical river par excellence, symbolized by the serpent or the huge whale and remembered as the grave of all Jewish male offspring in Eygpt)—with the Teterev and particularly with "the renowned Gnilopyatke," Mendele employs the rhetoric of intentional bathos. He lists as equals the "highest" and the "lowest"; he crosses with one acrobatic step the distance between Africa and Barditshev, between biblical grandeur, remote and poetic, and ugliness and puniness close at hand. (The "Gnilopyatke" was the satirical name Abramovitsh gave to the little marshy rivulet—a tributary of the Teterev, itself a tributary of the Dnieper— that flows near the town of Barditshev, the model of the fictional Glupsk. The name connects the Russian equivalents of "heel"—an indication that the river, especially during summer, can be crossed on foot—and putrefaction—a reference to its smell. In the Hebrew versions of Abramovitsh's stories "Gnilopyatke" was translated into "Sirkhon": "Stinkriver".) This, especially when the three rivers are mentioned as God's wonderful creations, for which He deserves ecstatic praise, cannot but yield a comic effect. The same goes for the equation of the mythological "Mountains of Darkness" (the remote and wild area that according to the legendary geography of the Midrash separates Asia from Africa; in Yiddish the expression designates "the end of the world." According to the Jewish legend Alexander the Great had to ride an eagle and feed it with the flesh he carved from his own leg in order to cross these terrible mountains), the Asian or African deserts and wastelands, and the "big Jewish town of Glupsk." However, this equation of the mythologically remote and the all-too-familiar, of the Bible and the Midrash with present-day Glupsk, is obviously more than a bathetic gag. Mendele is also dead serious when he compares the frightfulness of remote deserts and of the monsters of the Nile with the cruelty and misery inherent in the familiar scene of Glupsk and the smelly Gnilopyatke. This is his way of driving home—with a rhetorical shock—his idea of what present-day Jewish life is like. Thus the quintessential Jewish town is compared to a slaughterhouse (toward the end of *The Tax*), to Sodom and Gomorrah, to a wilderness, a jungle. Its leaders are referred to as wild, predatory animals; its poor population are portrayed as defenseless, stupid sheep. This is done from the start, from the very first sentence of Mendele's prologue. What makes this prologue particularly significant in connection with our present discussion is that in it the shocking equations are couched in the phraseology and forms of Jewish liturgy. The opening sentences, with their insistent repetition of "praised be the Creator," sound like a rhythmic incantation. They constitute, in fact, an antipsalm. The Psalmist praises God for His infinite goodness and for His fatherly love for all creatures (e.g., Psalm 104); Mendele insolently uses the same rhythms to praise God for the brutality of an amoral Creation. Mendele uses phrases and forms which come naturally to "the Jew," but with them he evokes something like a Darwinian vision of universal ferocity. God's entire Creation—not only the town of Glupsk and its tax-farmers—is referred to in his equations as a vast, arid, dark arena of murderous activity; and the reference is disguised throughout in the conventional language of the Jewish religion. Can this be an authentic expression of the world of "the Jew"? Doesn't this ironic subversion indicate a profound dissociation from this world?

For another example, let us examine the more subtle opening of Mendele's preface to *Masoes Binyomin hashlishi (The Travels of Benjamin the Third)*:

> Praised be the Creator Who fixes the destiny of the heavenly spheres and the fate of all His earthly creatures. Even the least blade of grass will not sprout unless some angel urge it on: "Grow, now! Come forth!" How much more so in the case of man, whom an angel most certainly must urge on: "Grow on! Come forth!" And still more with our praiseworthy little Jews. Among us no oaf dare open his mouth out of turn; a simpleton doesn't step into a sage's shoes, an ignoramus into a pietist's, a boor into a learned gentleman's, until such time as each oaf, simpleton, ignoramus, and boor is goaded and urged by some angel. It is likewise the angels who urge on our paupers of every sort, admonishing them: "Grow, ye poor, ye beggars—beggars born, beggars broken-down, plain-spoken and close-mouthed—sprout, spring up like grass, like nettles! Go ye forth, ye Jewish children—go ye begging from door to door!" [22]

Mendele conveys his ironic intentions not through a pseudopsalm but rather through a pseudo-Midrash. If it is not the Midrash itself that he mimics, then it is the Midrash-imbued style of the traditional Jewish preacher. The long, complicated sentences, the parallelism, the insistence on the mediatory task of the angels in the husbandry of the universe (in the Bible angels are hardly mentioned; in the Midrash they become the all-important agents of God) are all perfectly in character. The sound of the passage, its stylistic flavor, its rhythm are familiarly

traditional. Even its contents are overtly in line with Jewish tradition,
for on what does the passage elaborate, if not on the commonplace
idea that life in general and human life in particular are directed,
guided, and protected by the divine omniscience? Yet Mendele manages to let this idea, as he develops it, become self-defeating. Here this
is brought about not by the technique of the shocking equation but by
that of *reductio ad absurdum.* Opening with a reference to the cosmic
incidence of God's providence (from "the heavenly spheres" to "the
least blade of grass"), Mendele's statement progresses with what seems
to be flawless logic toward the conclusion that Jewish indigence and
beggary are direct manifestations of God's benevolent care. Thus he
devises a "theological" framework for Benjamin's journey of discovery, for it is as a simple beggar that Benjamin sets out to discover the
lost Jewish tribes of biblical times. Once again Mendele employs the
stylistic and religious conventions of "the Jew" only to dissociate himself from them.

Most revealing are Mendele's religious effusions in the opening
paragraphs of his 1888 prologue to *Dos vintshfingerl*:

> Omar Mendele Moykher-Sforim—quoth Mendele the Bookpeddler:
> Praised and glorified be God's name for the holy congregations of Kabt-
> sansk and Tuneyadevke in the vicinity of Glupsk—three towns with
> which He has adorned His universe and in which He has established His
> beloved children of Israel to test them there, out of His love for them,
> and see whether they can stand His trials and not collapse under the
> burden of Judaism; whether they can sever themselves from this lowly
> world, conquer their craving for food and similar gross appetites, with-
> out which other people, ordinary mortals, cannot exist; thus to reward
> them at last and make them the happiest of people here on earth, and
> there, in the spiritual world. Kabtsansk and Tuneyadevke have mar-
> tyred themselves for the sanctification of His name, passed the test with
> the greatest honors, and showed the whole world *who* they are, *what*
> they can achieve, and what they are good for. . . .
>
> Praised and revered be His holy name also for the great privilege
> which He has conferred on me, poor sinner, to be His messenger and
> hasten to bring to these holy congregations the good tidings. Congratu-
> lations, Kabtsansk! Congratulations, Tuneyadevke! You are both to be
> made fortunate and happy. Your warfare is accomplished, and you will
> soon find favor; indeed, very soon. . . .[23]

The confrontation of Hershele and the people of Kabtsansk and Tuneyadevke is interpreted here against a wide historical and metaphysical background, and the symbolic roles of both the confronted parties and that of the mediating Mendele are vastly augmented. Kabtsansk and Tuneyadevke are made to represent not only the contemporary, actual "Jew" but also the whole history of Jewish suffering and privation. Their ordeal of hunger, of economic superfluity, is commented upon in well-established theological terms. It is the ordeal of the chosen, the suffering of God's servants, of His martyrs, the despised and the rejected whom God is now to reward with His blissful favor. The three "holy congregations" which adorn the whole of creation like dazzling jewels, are implicitly compared to the bejeweled Zion of Isaiah's prophecies of redemption and to the medieval congregations of martyrs who withstood the supreme trial of faith and proved by religious suicide that they could sever themselves from the lowly world of the body and conquer all life instincts in order to support the full weight of their Jewish persuasion. Like those congregations, Kabtsansk and Tuneyadevke are referred to as manifestations of God's presence on earth. Their very existence is to be given thanks for, since it indicates the benevolence of the Creator.

Mendele is explicitly described as a godly messenger; in other words, as a prophet. A "poor sinner" (i.e., a mortal), he cannot be said to be taking the place of the half-human, half-angelic Elijah, to whom the role of the divine harbinger, the announcer of the imminent coming of the Redeemer, is traditionally assigned. But he certainly can be equated with other prophets, such as Isaiah, who also referred to himself as a mortal, a sinner, and "a man of unclean lips" (6:5), and who was made worthy of carrying the divine message by God's special favor. It is not accidental that Mendele evokes through his Yiddish text the language of Isaiah's most famous prophecy of redemption: "Speak ye comfortably to Jerusalem and cry unto her, that her warfare is accomplished, that her iniquity is pardoned," etc.[24] Doesn't he bring "good tidings"? Isn't he that beatific messenger whose feet look "beautiful upon the mountains" as they hasten to bring comfort to Zion?

As for Hershele, although he is not explicitly mentioned, he must be associated with the Redeemer himself, since his plans for the redemption of Russian Jews constitute Mendele's "good tidings." His imminent appearance, perhaps the appearance of his book, *Dos vintshfingerl*, are announced here. It is through him that the destitute *shtetlekh* will find favor and at long last be rewarded for their loyalty to the Jewish faith. The triangle Hershele-Mendele-*shtetlekh* is thus invested with eschatological grandeur. Kabtsansk and Tuneyadevke, the representatives of biblical Zion, are addressed by Isaiah-Mendele, who heralds the coming of Hershele the Messiah.

Mendele's messianic ardor is, of course, not meant to be taken seriously, or to be exact, it is meant to be taken seriously as a prophetic parody. In the prologue to *Dos vintshfingerl* we are presented, then, with a gigantic messianic farce. What Mendele performs here would, in Christian terms, amount to a Black Mass. The most hallowed symbols are turned topsy-turvy; the supreme act of faith in Jewish history is being subverted into an act of mockery; the language of faith is made to turn on itself and be exposed as so much humbug. If that has not been made clear enough by the dissonance of the prophetic declaration itself, it is being made so as Mendele suddenly precipitates his readers from the messianic heights to the lowliness of an everyday colloquy:

> Do not press me to reveal at once what my tidings are. You are kindly requested to have patience. For so many decades of sorrow and misery you have waited, that now you can afford to wait a little more. Haven't you already become accustomed to delays? Indeed, haven't you proved many a time that you and you alone of all the people of the world possess that ironclad patience without which nobody could suffer as you do and still go on waiting . . . waiting . . . waiting. . . . Well, to tell you the truth, I am not much concerned whether you can or cannot wait. I do not care to go hastily about my business. Whatever I do, if it interests you, I do in good order, slowly, unhurriedly. Even my horse will hardly move from his place, hardly raise a hoof, without much deliberation; he just will not be rushed. First you must listen attentively to the whole story. Only when you have heard it through, will you learn what my good tidings are and what happiness is in store for you. The story itself, regardless of all other things, is also worthy of your attention, and it is, indeed, necessary for you to know it. Ah! How well I know you, brothers! What you want to know is only the sum total, the practicable upshot of the matter. You have use for a person only as long as he has not divulged what you want to get out of him. Once you have touched upon his secret he is for you no better than a squeezed lemon; you cannot get rid of him soon enough! Much do you care then for his stories, jokes, uncalled-for tricks, and superfluous witticisms. . . . It is the Passover dumplings you have in mind, not the Passover *Hagode.*° Not with me,

° The *Hagode*—the old mishnaic compilation of the tale of Exodus plus Midrashic interpretations and additions. It is read on Passover night. A considerable part of it must

brothers! Let me tell you once more, and in plain words: whatever you
may have in mind, with me you will read the *Hagode* through! First, if
you don't mind, fill yourself with the *Hagode* to the point of bursting.
Only then will you live to see the dumplings. But this is beside the
point.[25]

The tone of the discourse has changed with a sharp twist. The voice of
Isaiah has been replaced almost in mid-sentence by the voice of the
bookpeddler, and the lofty address suddenly has shrunk into a chat.
This is a perfect maneuver of intentional bathos. Here climax and anticlimax noisily collide, and we are dazzled by the violent rhetorical
effect. We must, however, remember that Mendele's feats of deflation
and precipitation are not performed for their own sake. It is not just a
show of rhetorical acrobatics that we are being treated to. If Mendele
uses drastic rhetorical means, it is because he has something quite
drastic to convey. What better way has he to express his attitude toward Kabtsansk, Tuneyadevke, and their redeemers than to set them
in a traditional messianic framework and then destroy this framework
with one blow? Endowed with religious significance, the passivity of
Kabtsansk and Tuneyadevke in the face of hunger is almost monstrous.
Equated with messianic tidings, Hershele's plans are exploded even
before they are concretely described (and they are never concretely
described). The whole traditional structure of Jewish life—spiritual
and nonspiritual—is being smashed here again and again. God himself,
no matter how richly decorated the allusions to Him are, is subjected
to sarcasm, and the more tremulous Mendele's tone is, the more bitter
and biting the sarcasm. If, Mendele implies, the people of Kabtsansk
and Tuneyadevke have failed to preserve their human dignity, it is because the historical ordeal which they were forced to undergo had
from the very start been grossly unfair. Given a human constitution,
they should not have been required to transcend its limitations, and of
course, they have not really transcended them. Their martyrdom of
hunger was senseless and arbitrary; it did not call for any positive
faith, just for numbing endurance. Is it to be wondered that endurance
has developed with them into something of a vice? Here they are, grotesquely impatient over each trivial matter and endlessly patient in

---

be read before dinner is served, and this sometimes causes an understandable impatience. To have in mind the Passover dumplings rather than the *Hagode* means therefore
to prefer physical compensation to spiritual edification.

matters which concern their basic needs as human beings. Their historical experience has distorted in them the true proportions of humanity, and it is at the door of the divine Creator that Mendele lays the blame for the resulting deformity.

Whatever and whoever else Mendele is, he is also a humanist and an apostate. He can by no means be regarded as a genuine member of the traditional Jewish community. His beard, sidelocks, and old-fashioned gabardine are a mask, his biblical and rabbinical phraseology, a clever parody. Playing the role of the pious bookpeddler, he never misses an opportunity to express what the Midrash calls *khutspa klapey shmaya* ("insolence against heaven"). *Dos vintshfingerl* being what it is—an anatomy of the degradation of the Jewish people—can Mendcle's declaration that he publishes it "to the glory of the holy Creator who lives forever, and to His beloved people of Israel," [26] mean anything other than insolence? With this sanctimonious declaration Mendele brings the prologue to its conclusion, giving the finishing touch to an ingenious literary trap. Intricate, taut, and ready to close with unexpected violence on its victim, the prologue stands at the opening of the novel, itself both a guide and a riddle.

iii

What, then, is the true identity of Mendele? Most readers of Yiddish literature give this question an answer as simple as the question itself is complex. In fact, it is not too often that the question is asked, so self-evident seems its answer. There is nothing problematical about the identity of Mendele as far as the general reading public and the majority of the critics are concerned. Who is he? For whom does he stand? He stands for the author, of course; he *is* the author.

For more than eighty years now, Mendele and Abramovitsh have been treated as if, for all practical purposes, they were one and the same. I say for more than eighty years, because the process of amalgamating the two, like so many other important developments in modern Yiddish literature, began around 1888 and under the auspices of Sholem Aleichem. Prior to 1888 the situation had, in this respect, been quite different. Not only Abramovitsh's Hebrew works but also his Yiddish ones, although they had been connected with the name of Mendele since 1864, were never referred to in print as having been written by Mendele. Reference in print to the works of Yiddish writers

could not, for reasons already discussed, be numerous before the
1880s. Still, to the extent that Abramovitsh's Yiddish works were mentioned by writers, they were invariably described as Abramovitsh's. In
1875, for example, Perets Smolenskin, the well-known Hebrew novelist, back from a tour of south Russia, informed the readers of his
monthly, *Hashakhar* ("Dawn"), that, in the Volhynian town of Zhitomir, among other *maskilim* and men of letters, lived Mr. Sh. Y.
Abramovitsh, "who was for many years well-known as a Hebrew
writer but has lately divorced the Hebrew language, with which one
cannot make a living, and preferred to it the spoken Jewish language.
In this language he has written excellent artistic compositions that give
much pleasure to their readers and are full of witticisms which can
both pierce one's bowels and delight one's heart." [27] A year later
Linetski mentioned Abramovitsh by his proper name in a list of prac-
ticing *zhargonistn* (Yiddish writers), although in the same list he referred to another writer (Sh. Bernshteyn) by the name of his literary
persona (Shilshom Bar Yente).[28] In 1884 the twenty-fifth anniversary
of Abramovitsh's literary activity was celebrated in some Russian-Jewish newspapers (characteristically, not one Yiddish article was dedicated to the event); the author was, of course, referred to by his
proper name. In 1885 and 1886 *The Travels of Benjamin the Third* and
The Nag, respectively, appeared in Polish translations under the name
of Abramovitsh, not of Mendele. As late as 1888 Y. Dinezon, in his article "The Yiddish Language and Its Writers," took issue with "Mr.
Abramovitsh" for allegedly betraying the bright promise of his early
Yiddish works and committing (in *Benjamin the Third*) "artistic
crimes." [29] Even Sholem Aleichem, although in his *feuilletons* he had already treated the figure of Mendele as a living person,[30] took care up
to that time to refer in his critical articles to "our great zhargonist
Abramovitsh." [31]

In literary circles, then, nobody confused Abramovitsh with Mendele. As far as the popular reading public is concerned, we may assume that a considerable part of it was totally unaware of the existence of an Abramovitsh. Another part was aware of him only as a
Hebrew writer and a *maskil*. Moreover, we may assume that the majority of this public swallowed wholesale the fiction of Mendele exactly as it was served, that is, they believed in the reality of Mendele,
but they did not attribute to him the direct authorship of the works he
allegedly published. There were reasons (which will be discussed in
the next chapter) why Abramovitsh wanted his Mendele to be re-

garded not as the actual writer of the stories but merely as their publisher or editor, and he largely succeeded in this. We can learn something of this from the memoirs of Y. Dinezon, the same Dinezon who in 1888 was so dissatisfied with the development of Abramovitsh's writing. In his youth, he tells us, he could by no means associate the Hebraist Abramovitsh with the delightful but somehow disreputable Yiddish narratives published by Mendele the Bookpeddler:

> I envisaged Abramovitsh as a middle-aged scholar of vast erudition, whose Hebrew writing, although not as purely biblical in its style as that of Mapu or Kalman Shulman,° was always readable and always made sense. He could at times be witty and biting and show disrespect for established writers older than himself, but he was always perspicacious and in the right. He knew much, and of what he knew he wrote. For him I had much respect. I thought him too proud to answer a letter, if I would have dared to send him one.
>
> Reb Mendele I envisaged as a completely different figure. Mendele the Bookpeddler, I assumed, must be fairly advanced in years, let's say in his sixties, and may he live to be a hundred and twenty! °° He must also be tall and skinny, with a deeply lined forehead and with eyes full of wisdom and good nature; eyes that look at everybody with love and compassion. . . . He has seen much and heard much of people in general and of Jews in particular. Usually he tells his stories in a melancholy tone, with a sigh, although sometimes he pretends to be jocose and sound cheerful.
>
> Reb Mendele, I thought, was not a writer at all. Those stories of his he, indeed, told himself, but somebody else has put them in writing. Him I loved with all my heart. . . .[32]

We need not, for the purposes of our discussion, take much notice of the cloying sweetness of this Mendele figure, for it only reflects the incorrigible sentimentalism of Dinezon. This most lachrymose of all Yiddish writers probably could not envisage a storyteller, and a Jewish one at that, whose eyes were not "full of love and compassion" and who was not constantly on the verge of tears. Skimming off the sentimental excesses, however, we may have here something like the image that most of Abramovitsh's unsophisticated readers of the 1860s and

---

° Kalman Shulman (1819–1899), a popular Hebrew compiler, adaptor, and translator famous for his "pure" pseudo-biblical style. He scored his greatest success as the adaptor of Eugene Sue's *Mystères de Paris*.

°° A traditional Jewish formula of wishing longevity, used especially when mentioning a person's age.

the 1870s had in mind as they read the early versions of *Dos kleyne mentshele, Fishke der krumer, Di takse,* and *Di klyatshe.* Of special interest is the fact that Dinezon, though he believed in Mendele's actual existence (once, he tells us, he even thought he recognized him in an old bookpeddler he saw in the courtyard of his town's synagogue), did not credit him with the writing of the stories. As I have pointed out, this was Abramovitsh's intention, and young Dinezon probably represents in this respect the common reader of the time.

We have reason to believe that Abramovitsh thought it was in his interest to protect this innocence on the part of the common reader and to keep the literal trustworthiness of his Mendele intact. This, he felt, would ensure his rapport with the Jewish masses. As long as the belief of these masses in the actuality of Mendele was not in danger, he was unconcerned about the references to his authorship of his Yiddish works. When these references were made in a commendatory context, he most probably relished them as any other writer would. He very much enjoyed the moderate publicity he got in 1884–1886 in the Russian and Polish press, and, of course, he wanted to be known to its reading public by his proper name. In various ways he indicated a wish not to be confused with his Mendele Moykher-Sforim in the minds of his "European" (i.e., non-Yiddish) readers. He regularly inserted his proper name (S. Abramovitsh) into, and eliminated Mendele's name from the Russian title pages, which from the 1870s on followed (according to a regulation prescribed by the government) the Yiddish title pages of his works. Even more telling in this respect is the fact that he made his friends, who reviewed his Yiddish works for the Russian-Jewish magazines, remind their readers of the difference between himself, the author, and Mendele, "the distributor of Mr. Abramovitsh's works" (*rasprostranitel' proizvedenii gospodina Abramovitsha*).° Russian, Polish, and even Hebrew newspapers could, on the one hand, spread the fame of the author throughout wide segments of the "respectable" Jewish (and possibly also non-Jewish) intelligentsia, whose respect would gratify his vanity. On the other hand, they were inaccessible to the "simple" Jewish reader, whose naive confidence he did not want to lose.

° This phrase is from the long and highly recommending review of *Fishke the Lame,* written for the prestigious *Voskhod* by Abramovitsh's close friend, M. Margolis (to whom, by the way, the reviewed novel was dedicated). See the *Voskhod,* ninth year (1889), the January–February issue, section of literary reviews, p. 32 (the whole article seems to have been written under the supervision of Abramovitsh himself).

When, however, the name Abramovitsh began to be mentioned
and quite frequently in such a popular Yiddish magazine as *Dos
yidishe folksblat*, and especially when Sholem Aleichem made him one
of the "good" heroes of his *Shomers mishpet*, he was somewhat
alarmed. Sholem Aleichem already enjoyed a considerable popularity
with the "common reader," and *Shomers mishpet* was not a work of
formal criticism; it was an informal, dramatic pamphlet. Informing
Sholem Aleichem of his reactions to *Shomers mishpet*, Abramovitsh
therefore added among his other reproofs: "You have also done wrong
by referring to me as Abramovitsh instead of Mendele the Bookpeddler." [33] His "grandson" did not need much encouragement in this direction. In a few months he published his *Stempenyu*, dedicated not to
"the great zhargonist Abramovitsh" but to his "dearly beloved grandfather, Reb Mendele Moykher-Sforim." Following Abramovitsh's
wish, he did not bother to preserve the original image of Mendele; he
much improved upon it. As the reader may remember from the first
chapter, Mendele Moykher-Sforim of the introduction to *Stempenyu* is
neither the Mr. Abramovitsh known to writers and *maskilim* before
1888 nor the real bookpeddler of Abramovitsh's imagination. He is a
fictional figure in his own right, a new character in whom features
drawn from both Abramovitsh and Mendele are combined with others
which Sholem Aleichem had no difficulty in supplying from his own
teeming imagination. Thus, the confusion was artistically initiated.
Sholem Aleichem's creation, although mythically compelling, is historically completely unreal and misleading. Mendele of the introduction
to *Stempenyu* is, of course, a bookpeddler in name only. How can he
sell books and still remain the middle-class savant and the "grandfather" of Yiddish letters? If he is still the outwardly traditional Jew (as
the title "Reb" may suggest), it is a very well-kempt version of the
same that he represents. He is certainly not the man who pitches the
wheels of his old wagon, spends his nights in filthy inns, treads heavily
beside his horse in the knee-deep bogs of the roads of old Russia, and
wears clothes which, according to the evidence of one of Abramovitsh's protagonists, are "ragged and tattered, besmeared and, forgive
my expression, befouled." [34] On the contrary, his gabardine, if he
wears one, is almost as immaculate as Hershele's dress. Yet he cannot
be the "Frenchified" Odessa gentleman whom Fishke the Lame encounters, the gentleman who takes care to speak Russian whenever he
is functioning in the capacity of the *Talmud-toyre* principal. It is not

only the appellation "Mendele the Bookpeddler" that is out of character. The tone of the dedication as a whole, its familiarity, coyness, and that particular sweetness of Sholem Aleichem when not at his very best, does not agree with it either. Sholem Aleichem wanted his hero to be both a "good" Jew and a respectable bourgeois, both the conscientious artist and the "folksy" storyteller. He created an impossible, hybrid image, and this image still dominates the consciousness of the Yiddish reading public.

Sholem Aleichem's Mendele superseded Abramovitsh himself and drove him out of the public eye in a very short time. For some years the shift created irregularities. Articles on Abramovitsh during these years were characteristically given such double titles as "Sh. Y. Abramovitsh (Mendele Moykher-Sforim)" or vice versa. Soon, however, Mendele emerged victorious from this nominal twilight, first in Yiddish and then in Hebrew, though it took somewhat longer. By 1900 the name Abramovitsh had all but disappeared from public use. Henceforth, it was resorted to only by the most pedantic of critics, and even they would drop it as soon as they had finished with the purely biographical parts of their articles. Eventually, even the full name Mendele Moykher-Sforim was felt to be too cumbersome and formal, and the shorter, familiar Mendele was preferred. Perets summed up this evolution in a few sentences:

> The people call him "Mendele." Had he written only one book, the people would have called him by the name of this book. But he has written many, and the pivot on which all of them turn is Mendele the Bookpeddler—and this will remain his name forever: Mendele Moykher-Sforim —and for the sake of brevity, just Mendele. The name Sholem Yankev Abramovitsh is known to few people. It is his private name, and it will certainly find a place in the histories of Jewish literature. The people, however, will call him "Mendele." That is his name for posterity, and that is his glory.[35]

Perets himself, it should be noticed, did not confuse Mendele and Abramovitsh (in another place he referred to Mendele as "Abramovitsh's best creation"),[36] but he welcomed the same confusion in others. His prophecy (made in 1910), has, of course, been proven true. He was wrong in only a single detail: even in the histories of Jewish literature, at least in most of them, it is Mendele and not Abramovitsh who looms large.

Not a few critics tried to establish some renewed awareness of the differences between Abramovitsh and Mendele.[37] Their influence on the general public was, however, negligible. Nor were most of them always clear about their distinctions and ready to sustain them all the way through Abramovitsh's work. Quite often they would dwell on "Mendele the author" versus "Mendele the character" in one chapter or paragraph in an article, only to let the distinction slip through their fingers later on, so that the "character" they had referred to imperceptibly resumed the role of the author.[38] Clearer and better sustained distinctions were drawn in the Yiddish criticism by some of the more scholarly and responsible Soviet-Yiddish critics. M. Mezheritski chided the critics, in an article written as early as 1927, for "having in the meantime forgotten to differentiate the author Mendele from the character Mendele the Bookpeddler, the narrator and protagonist of Abramovitsh's major work [Mezheritski was referring to *Fishke the Lame*], which should by no means be identified." [39] In 1929 Y. Goldberg clearly defined the role of Mendele as a character in *Fishke the Lame*, although he was quite unsure whether many of Mendele's rambling comments (to which he referred as his "causerie") should have been attributed to the character, the author, or to both, and even suggested the launching of a special literary–biographical study, which would decide how much of his authorial self Abramovitsh had invested in his Mendele.[40] In the 1930s the distinction between author and character was elaborated by the two major historians of nineteenth-century Yiddish literature in Soviet Russia, M. Viner and M. Erik.[41] Hebrew critics were, on the whole, less clear-sighted in this as well as in many other matters pertaining to the understanding of the Mendele phenomenon than the better Yiddish critics. Nevertheless, the distinction was drawn in Hebrew too, and with considerable clarity, in 1954 by Y. A. Klauzner in a rarely mentioned article, which should be considered an important step forward in the development of the Mendele criticism.[42] More recently Klauzner's insights have been elaborated by some of the younger Hebrew critics.[43] However, no sooner was the distinction made than new errors crept in (some of which will be discussed later). Even the best critics left in their analysis much to be desired in clarity and consistent reasoning. Most critics, both Yiddish and Hebrew, when they bothered to make the distinction at all, actually blocked the way to a real comprehension of its meaning by separating Mendele from Abramovitsh not as a fictional character from an author but as the mature Abramovitsh from the young *maskil*, the "artist" from the "ideologue." The tendency to view the distinction in this way was much reinforced by the battle over the legacy of Abramovitsh between Yiddishists and Hebraists (with the former claiming Mendele for themselves and leaving the meager, unattractive Abramovitsh to their opponents), but it did not originate there. It originated in the erroneous doctrine according to which Abramovitsh's literary career must be viewed as a sequence of conflicts between "art" and "ideology"—two allegedly pure, separate, and mutually inimical categories that somehow found themselves fighting over the soul of one writer. This doctrine, initiated by D. Frishman[44] and developed by many others, sometimes to the point of constituting a theory of two completely separated personalities operating within one literary consciousness,[45] basically expressed the wish of nationalistic critics to have their cake and eat it too; that is, to reject the *Haskala* and yet let a favorite author who happened to have been a *maskil* retain his seat in their pantheon. For this purpose nothing could be more propitious than the splitting of the author's personality in two. Needless to say, this operation could not help but further confuse an already confused issue. To the understanding of the artistic identity of Mendele, it added nothing.

iv

The accepted official solution of the Abramovitsh–Mendele problem hangs by the thread of a technical term. Mendele, as one learns from lexicons, encyclopedias, textbooks, etc., was Abramovitsh's pen name. This we have been accustomed to read and regard as one of the irrefutable facts such as dates of birth and death and titles of major publications.[46] Indeed, this seems to settle matters very neatly, at least as far as those whose duty it is to see that facts fall into their proper pigeonholes are concerned. Wasn't Abramovitsh entitled to use a device which, for one reason or another, so many other writers have used? To mention only a few of these writers, who like him were popular nineteenth-century novelists and whose real names are all but unknown even in their native countries: Jean Paul (J. P. Friedrich Richter), George Sand (Aurore Duderant), George Eliot (Mary Ann Evans), Shtshedrin (M. E. Saltikov), Mark Twain (Samuel Clemens), Anatole France (Jaques Thibaut). Why shouldn't Abramovitsh–Mendele be able to peacefully join this respectable list?

From a critical point of view, this "solution" is even less satisfactory than the confused image of Mendele as a bookpeddler, a grandfather, an artist, and the archetypal Jew all huddled together. Misleading as it is, this image does contain some measure of reality. If it does not add much to our understanding of the author, at least it can add to our understanding of his readers. The pseudonym "solution" is nothing but a terminological arrangement.

The phenomenon of the literary pseudonym, especially as it has been used in the last two hundred years or so, is immeasurably more complex and interesting than writers of lexicon and encyclopedia items or of textbooks of the common type usually present it. In every single case where the use of pen names has been deeply probed (even in cases where it was supposed to have originated from sheer practical necessity), our understanding of the basic premises upon which the writer concerned based his artistic activity is greatly enriched. Reading such a biographical study as Justin Kaplan's *Mr. Clemens and Mark Twain*, for example, we not only enrich our knowledge of the writer but also bring our perception of the structure of his work into better focus. What the use of a pen name (at least from the Romantic period onward) usually indicates is the writer's deep-rooted urge to differentiate his literary self from his personal self, to objectify his notion of himself as an artist in order to be able to function as one; sometimes, even in order to discover himself as one. In the preface to his above-mentioned book Mr. Kaplan comments: "The central drama of his [Samuel Clemens'] mature literary life was his discovery of the usable past. He began to make this discovery . . . as he explored the literary and psychological options of a new, created identity called Mark Twain." [47] This, with proper qualifications, is applicable to many, perhaps to most, pen-named writers. Of course, each individual pen-name case differs from all others in the extent to which artistic self-discovery depends upon self-alienation through disguise. In some cases the disguise may remain quite thin; in others nothing short of a complex system of revolving masks can ensure the writer's relatively unhampered artistic functioning. Harry Levin writes on the greatest of all pen-named novelists, Stendhal:

> The incessant clash of reveries and realities, idealistic aspirations hidden beneath ironies, raillery shielding a wounded heart—in such phrases he is characterized by his acquaintances. Their antitheses suggest neither a dual nor a multiple personality, but a single elusive person masking

under many disguises. He himself could not have been more conscious of playing a role, more irrepressibly addicted to cults and poses, shrugs and quick changes, masquerades and mystifications. By uncompleted count, he seems to have employed at least two hundred different pseudonyms, including peradventure the modified name of Winckelmann's Prussian birthplace, Stendhal—a name which because of the supererogatory *h*, has been a shibboleth halting many a printer.[48]

The mere classification of a name like Stendhal or Mark Twain or Sholem Aleichem as a pseudonym is therefore almost meaningless. Only when the specific artistic uses to which the names were put, the functions they fulfilled, the meanings they acquired in different social and psychological connections—only when all these are properly elucidated, can the classification become something more valuable than a mere technical conveyance. However, even to classify Mendele the Bookpeddler as a pen name is technically untenable. Whereas in other cases it may at least mark out an avenue for study, here it leads to a blind alley. Mendele Moykher-Sforim cannot be defined as a pseudonym in the accepted sense of the term. It simply does not meet the technical criteria for a pseudonym, that is, it does not involve an attribution of authorship to a false name. Mendele, as we saw, is not supposed to be the author of the works he presents to the public. On the title pages of most of Abramovitsh's works in their nineteenth-century editions,[49] the relation of Mendele to the stories is usually indicated by formulas such as "Printed through the endeavors of Mendele the Bookpeddler" or "under the supervision of Mendele the Bookpeddler." On the title page of the 1865 *Vintshfingerl*, for example, the long title itself is followed by this list of credits:

This book was written in the German language by

HIRSCH RATHMANN FROM RUSSIA

and was published for the first time in Leipzig

by Brockhaus, 1864.

Now it has been translated into Yiddish and printed

for the benefit of the public by

MENDELE THE BOOKPEDDLER

by
A. Y. SH.

the author of DOS KLEYNE MENTSHELE

158 A Traveler Disguised

Here two different names are listed as responsible for the authorship of
the book. "Hirsch Rathmann" is, of course, Hershele, the protagonist
of the story and its imaginary author. "A. Y. Sh." are the initials of
Abramovitsh's full name (Abramovitsh, Yankev Sholem), reversed so
that they form the Hebrew word *ish*, "man" (this procedure was customary with the Hebrew *maskilim*, many of whom were known by initials tortured into recognizable Hebrew words). Mendele, however, is
not described as having anything to do with the writing of the book.
His name certainly does not figure here as a pseudonym.

This may seem to be an overly formalistic approach, but formalities are of great importance in the matters we are dealing with here.
Conscious disguise, in one way or another, is always formalistic, and it
is precisely through the differentiation of various literary formalities
that we can get at the nature of the specific literary disguise under
consideration. We must, therefore, register clearly that the formal
status of Mendele is different from that of George Eliot or Anatole
France. Whereas these fictitious personalities are said to be writers,
Mendele is not. Moreover, the names of these personalities, whatever
associative or symbolic meanings may be attached to them, are not
supposed to convey anything directly but themselves. Mendele's name
conveys a host of social and economic facts. It conveys a profession
and a certain social setting within which this profession makes sense.
It points to what may properly be designated as a way of life, a mode
of physical and mental existence. It indicates connections, dependen-
cies, advantages, disadvantages—in short, much of what goes into the
creation of a dramatic character.

Abramovitsh himself fully recognized these implications and also
made them amply clear from the very start of Mendele's career in
1864. All twelve installments of *Dos kleyne mentshele* in its first version were run in the *Kol-mevaser* unsigned.[50] Instead of the author's
name the first installment offered a short monologue of self-introduction, which was not formally separated from the narrative itself and
which, in fact, merged into it. It ran as follows:

> Tsviatshits° is my native town, and I am called Mendele the Bookped-
> dler. I am on the move most of the year; at one time I am here, at an-
> other, there. I am known everywhere. I make my rounds throughout Po-

° This name may mean "Town of Hypocrites." As Mendele's birthplace, it perhaps
deserves its name.

land ° and carry all sorts of books from the Zhitomir printing press. Aside from books, I carry prayer shawls, *tales-kotns*, eightfold *tsitses*, *shofars*, leather straps, amulets inscribed with the letter *Hé*, *mezuzas*, wolves' teeth.°° Sometimes you can also buy from me brass and copper wares; and yes, in fact, since the *Kol-mevaser* began to be published, I sometimes carry a few issues as well; but never mind, this is beside the point. What I want to tell you has nothing to do with this. This year [5624 = 1863–1864]—and it happened in *Hanukkah*°°°—I drove to Glupsk, where I counted on making a little sum by selling wax candles. Never mind, this too is beside the point. Arriving in town—it was Thursday, after the morning prayer—I drove, as I am used to, straight to the synagogue. . . .[51]

Here it is quite clear that the author wants to put his readers as quickly and as summarily as possible on firm ground. He supplies the most concrete details concerning the time and place of the story, and he is also anxious to make the person who tells it as concrete as he possibly can. Mendele informs the readers not only of his name, birthplace, and occupation but also of every item in his inventory, brassware and all. This makes his opening sentences seem somewhat dry and matter of fact, although actually they are not. Even in this preliminary self-introduction, Mendele exhibits his characteristic techniques of insinuation and equivocation. Simple as this short monologue is, it is not devoid of some of the features which render Mendele's later monologues so exquisitely and intricately ironic. Take, for example, his "this is beside the point" trick, which was to remain Mendele's most conspicuous trademark throughout Abramovitsh's career. It is employed here with considerable effectiveness. The mechanism of the

---

° "Poland" here and elsewhere in the nineteenth-century Yiddish literature should not be confused with the post-1918 political unit, or even with what contemporary Poles regarded as their historical homeland. It is the "Jewish Poland," i.e., the southern and eastern regions of the Jewish pale in czarist Russia (including the Ukraine). "Polish" Jews were all those Jews who lived in the vast territory that had been part of the Polish Empire in its days of expansion, and not necessarily those who lived among Poles or who spoke Yiddish in its "Polish" dialect. Thus, Linetski's *Poylish yingl*, for example, lived in Podolia, a southwestern province of the Ukraine.

°° *Shofar*—the pierced ram's horn blown in the synagogue on the "Days of Awe." *Hé*—the fifth letter of the Hebrew alphabet. It stands for the ineffable name of God. *Mezuza*—the small parchment attached (in a wooden or metal case) to doorposts in Jewish houses. It contains excerpts from Deuteronomy, chapters 6 and 11.

°°° *Hanukkah*—the feast commemorating the rededication of the Jerusalem temple to the God of Israel after it was purified from the pollution of the Greek idol which had been forced upon it by the order of the Syrian Antiochos Epimanes.

trick—a typical ironic device—is rather simple. Creating the impression that he is unable to concentrate on his story and avoid whatever is
beside the point, Mendele builds up a façade of simple-mindedness,
which is essential to his function as an *eiron*. With his irrepressible circumstantiality he perfectly illustrates what Coleridge, in his famous
comment on the Nurse in *Romeo and Juliet*, defined as "the uncultivated mind." ("The cultivated mind will be found to recall the past by
certain regular trains of cause and effect; whereas, with the uncultivated mind, the past is recalled wholly by coincident images, or facts
which happened at the same time.")[52] But with Mendele this lack of
cultivation is deceptive. He is never at the mercy of an associative, coincidental memory. The "this is beside the point" dismissals are his
means of drawing attention to an ironic point that has just been made.
Whenever we are asked to consider something he has told us as immaterial, we are in fact alerted to look for its hidden meanings. The first
dismissal of this kind in our passage concludes the list of the commodi-
ties which Mendele carries. Of course, we are not supposed to regard
this list, a rather transparent maneuver of advertisement, as an unintentional digression; but that is not all. The "beside the point" draws
our attention to the methodical order of the list; an order which may
be described as a gradual descent from the holy to the profane. The
list opens with the books of the Zhitomir printing press. As this press
was for decades controlled by the *hasidim* and, in contradiction to the
concurrent Vilna press, was known to be "uncontaminated" by the
Haskala, the books which Mendele carries must be "holy" and probably hasidic in tenor. The books are followed by objects of legitimate
ritual use, such as *shofars*, leather straps for the *tfilin* (phylacteries),
etc., and we are still in the sphere of holiness but perhaps one rung
down in its hierarchy. By further descent we reach the level of illegitimate ritual, that is, of magic. Here, listing his amulets and protective
charms, Mendele unobtrusively equates the cabalistic amulets of the
hasidic rabbis, which presumably carry divine powers (the letter *Hé*),
with such stock-in-trade items of rustic non-Jewish conjurers and
witches as wolves' teeth. At this stage brass and copper wares intrude
upon books and ritual objects, with which they may have only a slight
connection (they probably include *Hanukkah* lamps and Sabbath can-
dlesticks, but Mendele himself, in a later version of this monologue,
confesses, "exactly how brass and copper wares fit in with religious
books, I am not quite certain myself").[53] It is this incongruity, how-

ever, which makes them a proper *pareve* ("neutral") barrier between
the Zhitomir books, the amulets, and other ritual accessories and the
profane, maskilic *Kol-mevaser*. Mendele smuggles the *Kol-mevaser*
into his inventory at the very end as if against his better judgment,
which shows how cunning an advertiser he is. The *Kol-mevaser* is a
popular success,[54] and Mendele must inform his customers that they
can get it through him. Still, it is nothing to be proud of and to talk
loudly about. In certain influential circles it may prove harmful. That
is why Mendele makes every possible effort to minimize the importance of this item in his inventory. First, he pretends to have forgotten
all about it; then, as if he is incidentally reminded of it, he does not
confess to more than carrying "a few issues" of it "sometimes." Having
made this minimal confession, he immediately dismisses the whole
matter as immaterial and "beside the point." What he wants to tell, he
argues, has nothing to do with it. In fact, what he is about to tell has
everything to do with the maskilic magazine. Not only is his story
being published in it, but it is also firmly committed to its cause. Like
the *Kol-mevaser* and through it, it is intended to bring the ideas of the
Haskala to the Yiddish reading masses and thus combat the coercing
influence of those powers to which, overtly, Mendele bows. The second "beside the point," although of comparatively minor importance,
illustrates the same technique. Explaining how he happened to arrive
in Glupsk at *Hanukkah*, Mendele emphasizes the connection between
ritual and commerce, holiness and money, which he has already
pointed out. *Hanukkah* is the best time for selling wax candles (no less
than forty-four candles will see a Jew through the eight days of the festivity), and Glupsk, with the largest Jewish population in Volhynia (it
represents the town of Barditshev), offers the best market. Mendele is
quite explicit about his commercial expectations; he "counts" on
making a snug little sum of money in Glupsk. He makes it clear that, as
far as he is concerned, prayerbooks, prayer shawls, amulets, and candles, very much like brassware, are so many vendibles, objects one can
make "a little sum" on, provided one hits the right market at the right
moment. In so doing he adds an ironic afterthought to the distinction
between the holy Zhitomir books and the profane *Kol-mevaser*, reminding his readers that the conflict between the *hasidim* and the
maskilim has commercial as well as spiritual aspects. The Zhitomir
printers, his remark may suggest, shy away from the *Haskala* because
they know in whose hands their market is. As for the hasidic rabbis

themselves, aren't they selling their holiness in every marketplace? Aren't they offering the mystic powers of the ineffable Name to any person, honest or crooked, who can afford the few pennies which add up to huge sums in their coffers? Aren't they fighting the *Kol-mevaser* because it threatens their commercial interests?

All these are ironic overtones which most of the readers of *Kol-mevaser*, thoroughly acquainted with the contemporary Jewish scene and presumably sympathetic to the *Haskala*, were sure to catch. Mendele's self-introduction reveals the young Abramovitsh as a quite proficient manipulator of the art of subversive conformity and predicts the far-reaching heresies to which, as we have seen, he was letting his Mendele drift. It also reveals him, however, as a dramatic poet of considerable ability. An ironic understanding with his readers, it should be observed, was not the only thing Abramovitsh wanted to establish through Mendele's prefatory remarks. These remarks also establish the presence of a complex fictional character. Voluble and yet calculated, digressive and yet meticulously deliberate, open and yet attentive to commercial advantage and disadvantage, the figure of Mendele throbs with the pulse of full dramatic life. His fictional reality is immediate and unquestioned. It is much more than matter-of-fact information that he transmits to us in his opening sentences. Scarcely have we read the first paragraph of his monologue through and we already have received an impression of the way his mind works. We have already gained some insight into the intricacies of his shrewdness, and we know him for the calculating, observant, and down-to-earth fellow he is. This knowledge is being enriched throughout the introductory section of *Dos kleyne mentshele*. Going about his business of setting the background for the "little man's" confession (of which the story mainly consists), Mendele asserts his dramatic presence and independence in a constant flow of observations and remarks, asides and digressions, all perfectly in character and unmistakably authentic.

Consider, for example, his reaction to the excitement with which he is received at the house of the *rov* of Glupsk, to which he was summoned as soon as he had parked his wagon in the synagogue courtyard. Called thus unexpectedly, he nevertheless did not forget to take with him some samples of his merchandise, for he might do some business with the *rov* or with his wife. However, the moment he confronts the *rov*, his commercial hopes evaporate. The *rov* is too eager; he seems to have been expecting his arrival, and that cannot be a good omen:

> Another bookseller would have concluded that it was his wagonful of wares that caused all this impatience, but I am not such a simpleton as not to know better than that; nor was I hatched yesterday from my egg. You can take it from me as a rule: It is cheating that makes the world go round. A person who is about to buy something he really needs pretends to have no use for it whatsoever, so that you will let him have it for a song. For instance, somebody who needs a *makhzer* will haggle with you over a *kine*, a *slikhe*,° or a bundle of *tsitses*. In the meantime, he will casually, just for the fun of it, pick up a *makhzer*, and hardly looking at it, put it down again with a shadow of a smile wrinkling his face: this, he says, for some small change, he would perhaps buy. Believe me, the whole world is a market. Everybody wants the other guy to lose so that he can find. Everybody hunts for bargains; but this is beside the point. By the *rov's* face I could tell that he had not the slightest intention of buying anything from me; otherwise he would not have let his eager expectation show. True, the *rov* is an honest, kosher person, so help me, but in this world one cannot do without cheating. Even the angels on their visit to Abraham had no choice but to adapt themselves to the order of our lowly world. "And they ate," the book says, and that must mean: and they pretended to be eating . . . well, never mind; this is beside the point.[55]

I have quoted this mélange of common sense and commonplaces in full not only because of its sheer brilliance as a piece of characterization through monologue but also because it so clearly and definitely establishes the status of Mendele as a dramatic character and not as a pseudonymic cover. It must be clear that Abramovitsh was not trying to reconstruct his own mentality and ideas in these conventional reflections on the lowly nature of the world. On the contrary, in his early works, and to a certain extent also in some of his later ones, he made his Mendele function not as his mouthpiece but rather as his opponent, the cynical *homme moyen sensuel*. With his commonsensical, if often "low" comments, Mendele undermines the high idealism of the protagonists. The moralistic tenets they recommend as well as their harangues on the usefulness and enlightening influence of the sci-

---

° *Makhzer*—a prayer manual for the festivals; *kine*—a lamentation for the ninth of Ab, the day on which both the first and the second Jerusalem temples were destroyed; *slikhe*—a penitential prayer for the "Days of Awe."

ences are infinitely more in line with what Abramovitsh himself
thought and wrote (in his nonfictional prose) at the time than Mendele's "philosophy of the little man." This function Mendele fulfills as
an anti-idealistic, practical *raisonneur*, whose presence in the stories
counterbalances the ideological flights of the protagonists, is particularly prominent in the first version of *Dos vintshfingerl*, where the author allows him to deflate the protagonist's paean to science, to the
wonderful technical innovations of the West, etc., in a rude but very
effective manner.[56]

In a less explicit way Mendele performs the same deflating services
in *Dos kleyne mentshele*, where the protagonist, after amassing a huge
amount of money during a lifetime of swindling, dies repentant, proclaiming in his will, that "riches cannot buy happiness. Happiness is
reached only through a good heart and good deeds. It is preferable to
suffer and pine away, as long as one is an honest man, than to enjoy
the rarest luxuries and be *a kleyn mentshele*"[57] ("a little man," a
petty, unscrupulous egoist). Mendele's dictum that, after all, it is still
"cheating that makes the world go round" even where the honest and
good-natured rabbi is concerned, is a timely reminder, that it is easier
to recommend perfect honesty from the vantage point of a deathbed
than from that of the daily struggle for bread.

That Abramovitsh saw fit to include these sobering views in his
early stories, while in his nonfictional prose he was adhering to the
high idealism of his protagonists without qualification, proves how
right he was when he gradually shifted the main thrust of his literary
activity from nonfiction to fiction, until the latter became his major
medium. The room fiction left for polyphony, for ambiguities, ironies,
paradoxical juxtapositions, for tentative, even self-contradictory argument, was essential for the free and natural movement of his mind. It
allowed him from the very start to become a more perceptive and humane writer than he would ever have become had he continued writing nonfictional, discursive prose. It even allowed him to do full justice
to the limited truth contained in Mendele's cynicism. He took care to
make such "truths" as "cheating makes the world go round" as in-
offensive as possible by putting them in the mouth of a petty peddler
struggling for mere survival and also by garnishing them with "folksy"
Jewish humor. For instance, Mendele does not neglect the opportunity
to parade his erudition, and he quotes—out of context, of course—
Rashi's commentary on the biblical description of the angels, Abra-

ham's guests, eating the meal the patriarch prepared for them. The
medieval Rashi could not accept the idea of angels indulging in ani-
mal-like activity such as feasting, and he commented: "They pretended to be eating; that proves that the manners of the place should
be adhered to," even by angels.[58] This spiritualizing rendering of the
Scripture is interpreted in a farcical way by Mendele, who quotes it as
an illustration for his contention that cheating is essential even for
spiritual beings, when they descend to our world.

All this notwithstanding, it is perfectly clear that Abramovitsh is
far from identifying with Mendele and from accepting his "truths." As
a matter of fact, it is precisely this cynicism that he attacked in his
Kleyn mentshele and that he abhorred in the Jewish bourgeoisie to the
point that it "turned my soul into a volcano throwing flames and vitu-
peration all around," as he wrote at the time in a letter that has become a basic document in the history of the social consciousness of the
modern Jewish intelligentsia.[59]

v

Mendele's self-introduction at the opening of *Dos kleyne mentshele* should be regarded as a formal introduction to the whole Mendele
cycle, in other words, to almost all of Abramovitsh's Yiddish works,[60]
and to a considerable part of his Hebrew ones. Indeed, Abramovitsh
himself regarded it as such, and consistently opened his various "Collected Works" with it. In 1879, when he planned a systematic republi-
cation of his early works that were to be enlarged and completely refashioned, he developed it into an elaborate conversation between
Mendele and his readers. He published it once again with *Dos kleyne
mentshele*, but regarded it as a separate and independent work, a general overture to the whole projected series.[61] This is indicated by the
fact that nine years later, as he announced the publication of his collected works, Abramovitsh did not hesitate to sever this self-introduction of Mendele's from *Dos kleyne mentshele* and use it to open the
first volume of the new series, which happened to be *Fishke der
krumer*. In a further enlarged (and, alas, somewhat diluted) version, it
again preceded *Dos kleyne mentshele* in 1907, opening a new (also discontinued) collected edition. The plan of the "Jubilee edition" unfortunately detached the overture from the major works, squeezing it
between an introductory essay and some minor, late short pieces,

where it failed to attract attention. It was mysteriously deleted from the "new, improved" posthumous edition, and the omission (although merely the result of slipshod editing) reinforced the pervasive unwillingness to acknowledge Mendele's dramatic independence. Abramovitsh himself, as much as he protected his Mendele mask, never lost sight of the dissimilarity between it and his own authorial face. He remained perfectly aware of the duality and of the opportunities for artistic play it offered. For example, one of his late series, *Seyfer habeheymes* ("The Book of Cattle"), was presented as written by Sh. Y. Abramovitsh "in honor of Reb Mendele the Bookpeddler, and as the author's present to him." It was also preceded by a long introduction, which instead of being one of the regular "Quoth Mendele" addresses was a letter addressed *to* Mendele by the author.[62] Abramovitsh never ceased to indulge in games of this kind, although he never again emphasized the character's independence as explicitly as in Mendele's 1879 self-introduction. In it he went out of his way to make the fictional independence and separateness of Mendele as clear as such separateness and independence can be. He crammed the piece with concrete details concerning the personal history, the characteristics, and even the physiognomy of his chief character. To support all these details with a proper rhetorical structure, he devised a highly characteristic scheme, which enabled Mendele to say whatever the author wanted him to say by stating its opposite.

As a starting point, Mendele brings up the proposition that a Jew is usually indecent in his curiosity; he thinks that it is his right to know the most personal details about any other Jew he happens to come across:

> The first question one Jew asks another, even a total stranger, as soon as they have met and shaken hands, is: "And what is your name?"
>
> It occurs to neither of them that his response might be as follows: "Tell me, brother, why is it so important for you to know my name? Are we going to discuss the betrothal of our children? I'm called by the name that I was given—and let me be!" But the question "And what is your name?" is a natural one.[63]

Elaborating on this (notice how Mendele's deliberations immediately take the form of a dialogue, a little theatrical piece), Mendele is able to play the role of a reluctant person who, under the circumstances, has no choice but to let strange people pry into his private affairs. A merchant must satisfy his customers whatever the price he pays. As much as Mendele regrets the loss of his privacy, he must indulge his inquisitive readers. Mendele's monologue is therefore constructed around groups of imaginary questions, and its tone is one of pretended impatience. Assuming that the readers are anxious to know more about himself and his family, Mendele unwillingly goes on disclosing one detail after another. From time to time he stops to chide his imaginary audience. Even his wife, he says, was not half as curious about him and as interested in all these "petty details" when her father let her know that she had been betrothed, as his readers now seem to be. "Whose concern is it what kind of nose I have or what kind of face?" he pleads. "Whose business is it and why should it bother anyone?" Isn't it enough to know that he is "a person like most other people and neither a tomcat nor an ass, God forbid?" [64] Apparently not, for Mendele keeps answering these self-imposed questions at great length and with barely concealed relish. Thus we learn, for example, that he was named Mendele after a maternal great-grandfather, a person who in his day had been much esteemed as a *Moskver*, because he traveled once to the capital to purchase some wares. We are also informed of Mendele's doubtful birthdate. His mother and father could not agree on this point. While the former insisted that the birth took place two years after the great fright[65] in Tviatshits, the latter connected the uncertain date with a certain frost, severe enough in itself to be remembered as a chronological milestone (the one idea that never occurred to his parents, Mendele insinuates, is that they were not necessarily contradicting each other).[66] We further learn that Mendele's surname is Yudelevitsh; that his wife's name is Yente; that they have had together many children—exactly how many he will not reveal lest the evil eye harm them, but there can be no less than half a dozen, for "who has ever heard of a Jew who is married and does not have a minimum of half a dozen little ones, especially a poor Jew?" [67] We hear that Mendele's forehead is high and wrinkled, that he has rather large and coarse nostrils, and that when he parts his lips, he appears to be smiling "very acidly" (that is, his face goes well with his evident satirical inclinations). Concluding the monologue, Mendele offers his readers his address. Should any of them be impatient for further personal information, he is welcome to write to him privately, and he will "soon receive a clear answer." For his part, he promises to fill in any missing details in his future publications.

All this was perhaps too obvious and crude for the old Abramovitsh. Still, whatever were his reasons for blurring (in 1907) the sharp
lines of the 1879 monologue, it is still the best entrance to the world of
his works. With perfectly good sense, Solomon A. Birnbaum made it
the opening piece of his German edition of Abramovitsh's works,[68] and
Gerald Stillman wisely retained it in his English version of *Dos kleyne
mentshele*.[69] Indeed, many of the Abramovitsh scholars might have
done well to follow these two translators in paying attention to this introduction, which they should have regarded as their primer.[70] One
wonders how many of the obnoxious errors which critics continue to
commit by treating Mendele as if he were the author and the author as
if he were Mendele would have been avoided had the 1879 monologue
kept its prominent place as the formal introduction to Abramovitsh's
works.

CHAPTER SIX

THE MENDELE MAZE

II. The *Folkstip* Fallacy

FROM THE VERY start Mendele was conceived of as a fictional character, and he is certainly one of the best, the most lively and rounded
characters ever created by a Jewish writer of fiction. But what kind of
"lively" character is he? To designate him as "full-blooded," "true to
life," or even as "three-dimensional" is not nearly enough. The distinction between "flat" and "rounded" characters or between "two-di-
mensional" and "three-dimensional" ones, so popular with critics of
fiction until our present generation, may at times prove quite useful
(although one rather doubts the validity of the assumption that what
E. M. Forster calls "the nations of fiction" or "Homo fictus" can really
be divided into two neatly contrasted and completely differentiated
subspecies: "round people" and "flat people");[1] however, in itself the
distinction cannot take us very far. In fact, the exclusive interest in the
psychological thickness or thinness of fictional characters has been,
and in many cases still is, one of the gravest shortcomings of the criticism of fiction. The alleged roundness or flatness of a character means
very little unless it is interpreted as an indicator of the character's
function in the fictional work as a whole. The case of Mendele illustrates this point rather strikingly. Mendele certainly meets most of the
requirements imposed by the rank of fictional roundness, but so do
Fishke the Lame and Hershele, and yet Mendele is fundamentally
different from them. What differentiates him is not his specific psychological make-up (in this respect every one of the three is unique) but

his mode of literary existence. We feel that he lives, talks, knows, and thinks on a plane altogether separate from the one on which Fishke and Hershele live, talk, know, and think. Like them he is an actor, in the sense of "a man in action" (or *prattōn*, the proper subject of literary mimesis, according to the Greek theory of literature);[2] but unlike them he is also an actor in the current sense of the word, that is, a man consciously acting a part in front of an audience. We have already realized this: there is something unmistakably histrionic about him; about his speech, his gestures, even about his beard and sidelocks. We can almost see a heavy layer of make-up on his face. The 1879 version of his self-introduction perfectly illustrates this theatrical quality of his (and of nineteenth-century Yiddish fiction in general, as I have suggested in Chap. 3). Its whole rhetorical structure presupposes the dualism of an actor and an audience, of an individual in the limelight versus a physically present public. This self-introduction clearly suggests a theatrical première, an atmosphere of curtains rising.

I dwell on this point rather lengthily because it seems to me vital and too often neglected. If we are ever to reach a clear definition of the nature of Mendele, we cannot afford to let our awareness of this special dimension of his fictional existence fade away. We must fix it in our minds that whatever Mendele says or does, he says or does with us, his audience, in mind; that his is a stage presence that has no reality outside of its theatrical framework. Failure to take account of this almost ensures that we will stumble against the error which may be referred to as the *tip* ("type"), or the *folkstip* ("folk-personage," or "folk-archetype") fallacy. It is the counterpart of the "pseudonym fallacy," and although somewhat more difficult to perceive, not a whit less fallacious. Especially vulnerable to this fallacy were, as experience unhappily proved, precisely those critics who had enough presence of mind to see the difference between Mendele and Abramovitsh and to insist upon its importance.

The logic of this fallacy—for errors do not become fallacies unless they have a certain logic of their own—is this: Mendele is not Abramovitsh; he is also not a "normal" character. What is he then? A collective character, an archetype, or even a symbol (when critics refer to Mendele as a "symbol," they usually mean to present him as archetypal). The propagators of this fallacy often differ with each other on significant points, but they all agree on one basic proposition: Mendele's identity can be defined by his position as a representative of the Jewish people. In him an inherent trait of the nation finds expression. Some critics express this proposition in vague, "metaphysical" formulations, according to which Mendele represents a quintessential "Jewishness." "He is a higher *folkstip*, who speaks for the Jewish community as it widens into the whole nation," comments one of those critics.[3] Others usually put it more conventionally: "He is the essential Jew," or "The soul of the people speaks through him."[4] Other critics were much more concrete in the delineation of Mendele's nature as a collective figure. The Soviet Yiddish critics, for example, being uncommitted to the idea of an all-embracing Jewish national "identity," were quick to recruit Mendele to the army of the "democratic" Jewish proletariat and to place him very accurately on the historical map between the old and the new in Jewish life. M. Viner commented:

> Mendele the Bookpeddler is the embodiment of the cordiality and cleverness of the masses. He is the people's prosecutor, the conscience of the masses—one of the common people in every way. . . . He is more intellectual, better educated, more sharp and severe, and more serious than Sholem Aleichem's Tevye the Dairyman; less good-natured, more burdened with the worries which a conscious examination of life involves. But he shares with Tevye the same cleverness of the simple folk, the same tendency to let other people into his thoughts, the same creative talkativeness.[5]

Max Erik went even further than Viner. To him Mendele embodies "the positive plebian" and is "very materialistic and very critical in his attitude toward the old Jewish junk." Erik also places Mendele historically with much more "scientific" rigor:

> The figure of Sholem Aleichem's Tevye represents the idealized apologetics of the bourgeoisie. Tevye shies away from reality; Mendele, on the contrary, faces the new times. Like his creator he stands on the line which separates two epochs: that of Feudalism and that of Capitalism. His eyes are turned with interest and curiosity toward the new epoch. Both in Tevye and in Mendele the old is locked in conflict with the new. Mendele, however, leans toward the new and draws from it the strength to combat the old, while Tevye, frightened, turns his face toward the old. . . .[6]

I quote these two Soviet critics at some length because the *folkstip* theory lends itself to examination in their formulations. Arguments such as "the soul of the people speaks through him" are immune to criticism, being unverifiable by their very nature. Nor am I sure whether one can prove or disprove such statements as "Mendele the Bookpeddler is the embodiment of the cordiality and cleverness of the masses." The comparison of Mendele and Tevye, however, offers a firm point of reference. Indeed, such a comparison must be the test by which the *folkstip* theory as applied to Mendele is tried out. It is not accidental that both Viner and Erik drew this comparison with Tevye, for he is the most celebrated *folkstip* in Yiddish literature. There can be no doubt that Sholem Aleichem meant him to represent symbolically the common Jewish man. If Mendele is a *folkstip*, he must belong with Tevye in one literary category; he must be, as Viner put it, "Tevye's elder brother." [7] By this I do not imply that the two characters must belong to one social milieu, or that they must represent one social position. They may, as Erik suggested, represent different "plebeian" attitudes toward social change (although I am not certain that Mendele can be defined as a "plebeian"). They may, indeed, differ in this respect in a manner even more radical than the one Erik suggested; but this, as Mendele so often says, "is beside the point." The point is that as literary creations, as dramatic presentations of an allegedly symbolic nature, the two characters must resemble each other closely if the *folkstip* theory is to have any substance. Both Mendele and Tevye are supposed to represent "the common Jew" and both are supposed to do it through their "creative talkativeness," through their free-ranging monologues. What each of the two thinks, feels, and says can and even must be distinctively different from what the other thinks, feels, and says. The rhetorical procedures by which the thoughts, feelings, and language of the two are conveyed to us must be similar. Do Tevye and Mendele share the same dramatic status or don't they? This is the one question relevant to the purposes of our discussion. The answer is that they definitely do not.

Mendele, Viner says, shares with Tevye not only the cleverness of the simple folk but also the tendency to let other people into his thoughts. This must be true, for otherwise how could we have known what his thoughts were? However, there is a further question: Who are the people with whom he shares his thoughts? Can they be expected to belong to the same category of listeners? I submit that they cannot. Tevye is telling his stories to a personality known as Sholem Aleichem; Mendele talks directly to us. We face here a rhetorical difference of cardinal importance, which perhaps can best be realized through a theatrical analogy. Tevye, like an actor in a realistic drama on a room-minus-one-wall stage, talks to a fellow actor. Their conversation is not supposed to be overheard. We, the readers, are only incidentally present, or rather, we are not present at all. Sholem Aleichem is willing to repeat Tevye's monologues for our benefit, and as his memory is faultless, he can repeat them without any deviation from the original. Actually, we cannot even be sure of that. As Tevye himself is not supposed to be present at any of these repetitions, we can never be sure whether Sholem Aleichem has or has not altered his stories. Sholem Aleichem is protected from the danger of refutation by Tevye through the very narrative procedure that he has chosen to bring Tevye's words to our attention. Mendele's position is completely different from that of Tevye. He is not an actor in a realistic drama but rather a *conférencier* or a one-man chorus, and his stage is the open arena. While Tevye is not supposed to be conscious of our existence, Mendele never loses his awareness of our presence for one moment. Both Tevye and Mendele are telling something, or "monologizing," but their modes of telling or monologizing differ in many ways. First, there is a difference in *place*. Tevye tells his stories against a concrete backdrop. He sits with Sholem Aleichem in a forest nook near a Ukrainian summerhouse or in a railway compartment, etc. In his story he evokes, of course, other places and other scenes, but as he speaks, he always remains anchored in a specific place. Mendele evokes in his monologues scenes of great variety: Glupsk, Kabtsansk, a Ukrainian cornfield shimmering in the summer sun, the noisy streets of Odessa, trains, inns, etc. But where is he at the time he is telling his story? He is nowhere in particular, or rather, he is in that secluded, abstract spotlight where the presence of the *conférencier*–storyteller is supposed to hover as he addresses his reader. The noisy streets of Glupsk or the sleepy marketplace of Tuneyadevke are presented as theatrical worlds from which he, Mendele, *as he narrates*, is exiled, not to other, unseen parts of the stage but rather to the ramp in front of the curtain, from which he announces—with the full awareness of his special position—"Now the curtain rises and here is the scene. Take a good look, ladies and gentlemen!" [8]

Second, there is a difference in *time*. As we read Tevye's monologues, they are already a thing of the past. I refer here, of course, not to the historical but to the narrative past. We assume that sometime in the not-too-distant past Tevye met Sholem Aleichem and told him his story. Sholem Aleichem himself, in the first version of Tevye's first monologue, made this chronological condition quite clear in an expository preface (later deleted), which began thus:

> "It was summer, sometime around Pentecost that is, why should I tell you an untruth, it was a week or two before Pentecost, and then perhaps it was a few weeks after Pentecost. . . ."
>   This is how Tevye began the story which he had long promised to tell me in the most minute detail. He had parked the horse and the wagon nearby, in the shadow of a tree, and sat himself near me in the green grass on a warm and fragrant summer day, one of those rare, numbered days in Boyberik, when the vacationing people who have come to this place from Yehupets "to catch a breath of fresh air" dare stick their noses outside without imminently expecting a bad cold. . . .[9]

We are explicitly referred here to four different "times": (a) the summer of Tevye's story ("around Pentecost"); (b) the time when Tevye promised Sholem Aleichem to tell him his story "in the most minute detail"; (c) the time of the actual telling of the story ("a warm and fragrant summer day"); and (d) the time of the present retelling of the story by Sholem Aleichem. To these we may even add a fifth time, occurring between (c) and (d), in which Tevye wrote the letter to Sholem Aleichem that, in this version of the story, separates Sholem Aleichem's introduction from Tevye's monologue.[10] Essential to the mechanisms of the narrative, however, are only three of these times: two pasts (of the story itself, of its telling by Tevye) and the present (the retelling by Sholem Aleichem). Whenever Sholem Aleichem repeats one of Tevye's monologues, he evokes this chronological scheme with the three levels of happening, telling, and retelling. Mendele, like Tevye, can evoke several pasts, but he is always telling his stories in the present. His chronological position, then, resembles the position of Sholem Aleichem, not that of Tevye; but here too an important difference should be noted. Sholem Aleichem tells us in the present a story that is in itself a finished thing. Since he is supposed to be repeating Tevye's monologues, he cannot be assumed to be creating them on the spot. Mendele's monologues are offered to us as they evolve. Theoretically, as Mendele monologizes, there is no telling (even he himself cannot tell for sure) how he is going to terminate his address or whether, indeed, he is going to terminate it at all. The basic assumption upon which his art of monologue is constructed is that we, the

readers, are to accept his speech as instantaneous, free to take any
form that may strike his fancy and to explore any avenue he may come
across. If we do not accept this assumption, we must discard Mendele's most characteristic ironic stratagem, that of "but that is beside
the point." I already explained how this stratagem, which obviously
presupposes the fiction that Mendele's ramblings evolve as we hear or
read them, is essential both as an individualizing feature of Mendele
qua fictional character and as a vehicle for his satire.

Third, it is not true at all that Mendele, like Tevye, tends "to let
other people into his thoughts," for we, the readers, cannot be regarded as "other people" in the same sense that Sholem Aleichem, in
his relation to Tevye, can. For Tevye, Sholem Aleichem is the collective *les autres,* the representative of general humanity, to whom he
can communicate his sorrows and joys. Talking is to him an act of faith
in human brotherhood. As for Mendele, does he share his sorrows and
joys with any of the other human beings he communicates with in
Abramovitsh's stories? Rarely. His talkativeness is in reality the talkativeness of an actor in a soliloquy or an aside where, as far as the other
actors are concerned, he is not talking at all. Mendele does not unbur-
den himself, as Tevye does; he *performs.* With the other characters in
the stories, he usually converses infrequently and unwillingly. I can remember only one instance in which he "lets himself go" and talks to
other characters at length and with zest. That occurs in *Fishke the
Lame,* first when he tells Alter about Fishke and his bizarre marriage,
and then when Fishke's description of the beggars spurs him on to an
agitated speculation about the extent of beggary among the Jewish
people. Here Mendele communicates to two fellow characters, Fishke
and Alter the Bookpeddler, what amounts to an anatomy of Jewish
paupery. This burst of talkativeness is referred to in the story itself as
obsessive and unusual. It is as if Fishke's story had struck a hidden
vein that immediately began to pour forth its pent-up contents and
could not be stopped. Ironically, the other two characters are not in
the least interested in this communication, and indeed, as far as they
are concerned, to listen to it is nothing more than a nuisance. As Mendele keeps interrupting Fishke's story in order to add new divisions
and sub-divisions to his already extensive catalogue of Jewish beggar-
types, his creative talkativeness elicits in the other characters an impatience bordering on open rudeness. Usually, however, forcing his conversation on unwilling listeners or even granting it to willing ones is

not at all in Mendele's line. If we ignore for the moment his function as public monologist, we must pronounce him a definitely taciturn and even curt person. He listens much, talks little, and when he talks, is seldom straightforward and openhearted. It is only when he faces *us*, his audience, that the tide of his creative talkativeness flows. Upon his turning toward the other characters, it immediately ebbs to a mere trickle. With them Mendele is an observer; with his public he is the greatest speaker of all.

Mendele exercises the art of the monologue in a completely different fashion than does Tevye. The difference is manifest in whatever the two characters say, and consequently there is not a single aspect that they can really be said to share. Take, for example, their common tendency to quote the biblical and midrashic sources. In Tevye this tendency offers Sholem Aleichem endless comic opportunities, for the former is a great master of the malapropos. His quotations are often comically distorted and even when they are correct, his translations and interpretations of them are hilariously wrong. In any case, they never truly suit the context to which they are applied. Mendele is never guilty of this. It is not that his quotations are never distorted and applied to the wrong context; they are, and with relish. (This happens in Abramovitsh's Hebrew renderings of his stories and particularly in his stories originally written in Hebrew[11] much oftener than it does in his Yiddish works. The reason is obvious: the very use of the holy tongue for description of contemporary "low" life involved a stylistic paradox or a built-in discrepancy between levels of decorum.) However, Mendele's mishandling of the holy sources is totally different from Tevye's. The difference can be explained on various levels. Viner would have us believe that it is basically a quantitative difference; Mendele is better educated than Tevye, and his Jewish scholarly erudition is wider by far. This is undoubtedly true. While Tevye quotes those parts of Jewish lore that any simple Orthodox Jew would know (the daily prayer, the liturgy of the high holidays, the Pentateuch with Rashi's commentary, Psalms, *Pirkey-avot*),° Mendele's quotations indicate a *Yeshiva* education and a lively scholarly interest. This, though it certainly indicates the difference between Tevye's and Mendele's respective social and intellectual make-ups, is

---

° *Pirkey-avot*, a moralistic–epigrammatic section of the *Mishna* which Orthodox Jews used to read and teach their children every Saturday afternoon.

hardly an essential aspect of the distinction we must draw between the two characters in general and in the matter under discussion in particular. More far-reaching are the discrepancies between Tevye's and Mendele's attitudes toward the quoted and distorted texts. Mendele— we have already learned from the opening passages of his prologues to *Dos vintshfingerl, Di takse,* and *Masoes Binyomin hashlishi*—is a "spoiled" theologian. His erudition is scholarly, and his handling of the hallowed texts indicates his familiarity with the Jewish homiletic tradition. He possesses all the virtuosity of the experienced scholiast who has lived all his life with quotations from and references to the texts. But he is the insidious, subversive scholiast; the "black" rabbi who enjoys the subtle desecration of the Scriptures; who dexterously mingles the holy with the profane and then offers the explosive mixture to his readers, expecting it to blow up in their faces. He wallows in his erudition in the mood of a scholar's unholy holiday. Unfortunately, these feats of his, these little gems of scholasticism turned upside down, which for sheer brilliance are unsurpassed in Jewish literature and which can even stand the test of comparison with the parodies of Rabelais and Sterne, cannot be illustrated here. They defy translation, and in order to understand them one must be well versed in the texts they mock. Tevye's malapropos are also a translator's despair, but for a different reason. With Mendele it is the perfect—but subversive— fitting of the old quotation into the new context that evades reproduction; with Tevye it is the hilarious discord between the two that does the trick. For Tevye never tries to explode the old text by quoting it. Nothing can be more alien to his attitude toward the Scriptures or the liturgy than the cunning destructiveness of Mendele. Whatever his distortions, they are never malicious. The question whether they are intentional or unintentional is a delicate one, and in many cases cannot be settled with any certainty. There seems to be little evidence for the current notion that the comic effect of his misquotations and mistranslations stems *solely* from his ignorance, or from his genuine misunderstanding of the Hebrew and Aramaic expressions he hears and constantly repeats but is hardly able to decipher. This notion is undoubtedly correct in several specific cases, but as an overall explanation of this aspect of Tevye's comicality it is a gross simplification. A strong case can be made for a contrary notion claiming that in most cases Tevye is aware of his "mistakes"; he well understands at least a part of his quotations but chooses not to acknowledge the fact out of

sheer high spirits, or in some cases, from a desire to overcome the de-
pressing effect of the terrible histories he relates. However, what this
little good-natured game of hide-and-seek indicates is a kind of familiarity, which is the reverse of Mendele's. Tevye is on such intimate
terms with his Psalms or with those parts of the Bible he hears read
every Sabbath in *shul,* that he can twist their sentences a little bit. He
can afford to treat them with the cordial and rough camaraderie that,
by the way, he also allows himself in his frequent conversations with
God. This does not for a minute diminish our feeling that belief in God
and in His holy word (the texts) is the very source of Tevye's spiritual
existence. Tevye's mishandling of the texts does not give the faintest
hint of sacrilege.

The aspect of the difference between Tevye and Mendele clearly
puts the former on one side of the fence between "the Jew" and "us,"
while the latter is left sitting on the fence in a most ambivalent position. Moreover, it clearly puts Tevye behind yet another fence, which
separates him, the archetypal folksy Jew, from "us," and that is the
presence of Sholem Aleichem, his interlocutor and our reporter.
Whether Tevye mishandles the texts intentionally or not, it is never he
who sets *our* norm of the comic in his monologues. It is the persona
"Sholem Aleichem" who performs this service. When Mendele talks,
his consciousness constitutes the fictional world to which we are introduced. It fills this world entirely. Smaller entities within this world can
be found faulty and faltering; Hershele blunders, Fishke is naive and
sometimes silly, etc. Mendele is never silly without sufficient presence
of mind to realize and report his silliness.[12] There is nothing higher or
more comprehensive than his judgment. What he knows, we can aspire to know, but never more than that. In the course of the story itself
Mendele can have doubts, be misinformed, commit errors (though infrequently); in the telling of the story the erroneous, doubting, misinformed Mendele never exists. In fact the assumption is that the Mendele of the present is omniscient; only the Mendele of the past is
subject to human error. With Tevye it is Sholem Aleichem's consciousness that constitutes the fictional world to which we are introduced.
Even when Sholem Aleichem is not supposed to have added a single
word of his own to the story, in retelling it he becomes its master.
Tevye's story becomes a part of his consciousness, but only a small
part of it. Since Sholem Aleichem knows better than Tevye and can
see his limitations, we also know and see. Tevye's and Mendele's mis-

quotations can be said to resemble each other inasmuch as they indicate the presence of a superior knowledge that is setting the norms of the correct and the incorrect (every error intended to be regarded as error indicates this presence). In the case of Tevye, however, the superior knowledge is external to the speaker of the monologue; in the case of Mendele it is the speaker's knowledge. In the first case the comic "harm" caused by misquoting is, if I may borrow a grammatical term, intransitive, that is, the harm originates from Tevye and is inflicted upon himself. In the latter case the harm is transitive. It originates from Mendele and is inflicted upon the quotations themselves, upon the context to which they are applied, and occasionally upon us, the readers, who are not quick and erudite enough to catch their full meaning.

The same distinction can and should be made between every sentence Tevye and Mendele utter. Tevye's sentence is measured by criteria external to itself and then offered to us for our examination. As Sholem Aleichem delivers it, he is already smiling. Mendele's sentence is offered to our understanding and judgment without any mediation, and if we can imagine Mendele smiling while delivering it, we can only assume that he smiles at our expense. This differentiates Mendele not only from Tevye but also from all the numerous speakers of Sholem Aleichem's brilliant *monologn* (the monologue was Sholem Aleichem's *maitresse forme*). When his simple Jewish women, who pour their hearts out in such masterpieces as "Dos tepl" ("The Small Pot") or "Gendz" ("Geese"), endlessly digress from their stories, it is really the "uncultivated mind" à la Coleridge that we encounter, the uncultivated mind of coincidental, associative, obsessive memory in all its delightful circumstantiality. When Mendele oversteps the proper line of the story and says something which he dismisses as "beside the point," his mind is revealing itself at the peak of its intricate cultivation. That is why to pronounce Mendele "the elder brother" of any one of Sholem Aleichem's characters is to misrepresent both Abramovitsh and Sholem Aleichem. One may find points of meaningful resemblance between Mendele and the persona Sholem Aleichem, or between Tevye and some of Abramovitsh's characters, but no resemblance between Mendele and Tevye is possible. The speakers of Sholem Aleichem's monologues and Mendele belong to different orders of literary existence. The former can really be regarded as "types" or even as *folkstipn*. The latter cannot.

ii

Something must also be said about the "quintessential Jew" version of the *folkstip* theory, although, as I have already remarked, the argument that Mendele somehow expresses the totality of "Jewishness" is virtually outside the ken of criticism. This argument draws its strength, however, from some element inherent in Mendele's monologues. Mendele himself often encourages his readers to regard him as a Jewish Everyman, a universal Jewish commoner. He insistently points to a certain generality, even to a certain abstraction about his nature, and he does this while continually reminding us of his particularity and individuality. Such contradictions should not surprise us; they are part of the very texture of Abramovitsh's thought. Abramovitsh was always attracted to phenomena of a dual nature or to things which were, as his Mendele often said, both "kaylekhdik un shpitsekhdik" ("well-rounded and yet pointed"). He often let Mendele's monologues run simultaneously in different, even in opposite, directions. The 1879 version of Mendele's self-introduction offers an interesting illustration of contrary progression on a two-way avenue. As we have seen, it lays overwhelming stress on the reality of Mendele as an individual character. But it would be wrong to assume that this reality is the only aspect of himself that Mendele is trying to convey in it. Particularity and fictional separateness are repeatedly affirmed in this monologue; yet, perhaps because the affirmation *is* so vigorous, it is also calling for its opposite. With Mendele a statement almost inevitably begets a counterstatement. Thus, while strongly proclaiming his uniqueness, he stealthily undermines his proclamation. Much of the specific, indeed, intimately personal data in which the monologue abounds only seems specific and personal. The surname "Yudelevitsh," for instance, may mean "the son of Yudl" (Yudl being the diminutive of the name Yude); but it may also mean "the son of a Jew" and thus point to a generality that in the framework of Abramovitsh's works is almost as broad as the generality suggested by the biblical "son of man." In any case, it is a name so widespread among Eastern European Jews as to indicate the average Jew or the common man, just as names like Jones, Brown, or Smith indicate the common man in English fiction. "Mendele" itself as has already been pointed out, is a Tom-Dick-and-Harry sort of Jewish name,[13] as is "Yente," the name of Mendele's wife, which is employed as the stereotyped denomination of the old-fashioned, old-world, uneducated Jewish woman. As the 1879 monologue reaches the point at which Mendele is about to enter upon a physical description of himself, it submits passport specifications, which are the specifications of Everyman around his fiftieth birthday: "Height—medium. Hair and eyebrows—gray. Eyes—brown. Nose and mouth—ordinary. A gray beard. An unmarked face. No distinguishing features." [14]

Of special interest in this connection are the details concerning Mendele's commercial activity. From this introduction we learn that bookselling was not Mendele's original occupation. Instead, it was a last resort to which he applied himself after he had failed in all the other occupations open to an unskilled person in the Jewish world of his time:

> I have had many different jobs. Soon after leaving the room and board of my in-laws, I became a money-changer, a spice dealer, an innkeeper, a grain dealer, a peddler, and a *melamed* [teacher]. I went from one type of trade to another, as most Jews do, and remained a pauper. As the old saying has it: "a sakh melokhes un veynik brokhes" ["many trades and little profits," or "many jobs and no luck"]. [15]

Mendele, then, is also the Jewish Everyman in his "progress" through economic disasters. On his way from his bed and board with his in-laws° to minimal economic security, he went through "all the reincarnations that every Jew must undergo, one after another, during his life" (to quote a part of the elaborate title of one of Abramovitsh's lesser-known short stories). [16] His history, in this respect, calls to mind the progress of Sholem Aleichem's eponymous *Menakhem-Mendl*, that great drifter of Jewish literature, who endlessly changes his occupations in a dizzying cycle of disasters. Menakhem-Mendl, we may remember, is a Jewish Everyman in his own right. Sholem Aleichem himself emphasized the general quality of this character in his preface to the 1910 edition of Menakhem-Mendl's collected letters, where he suggested that those letters could be used by Jewish merchants as a *brivn-shteler* (letter writer) with suitable models for all possible com-

---

° Most young Jewish couples in Mendele's day stayed with their parents for some years after the marriage (usually with the bride's parents). Their *kest* (free bed and board) was considered a part of their marriage settlement, and its duration was stipulated in the marriage contract. The economic history of the young Jewish man began as his *kest* drew toward its end. Then, already the father of two or three children, he had to make the best use he could of the ready money he had also been given at his marriage.

mercial occasions (since "Jewish businesses are, thank God, the same everywhere; that is, they all start with a bang and end with a whimper").[17] This, however, takes us immediately back to the point made in examining the comparison of Mendele and Tevye. It reminds us of the basic literary difference between an Everyman of the order of Menakhem-Mendl and one of the order of Mendele. It is through the eyes of Sholem Aleichem that we see his hero as a symbol. Although Sholem Aleichem is not supposed to have added anything to the authentic letters of his hero except the short preface to which I have just referred, it is through his judgment of these letters that we regard them as characteristic or as indicating a wider and more general message than the very personal and limited one they seem to convey. The letters, we should remember, are supposedly private. Like Tevye's monologues, they were not originally meant to reach us, as they eventually and quite mysteriously did. Unlike Tevye's monologues, the letters were not meant to reach even Sholem Aleichem.[18] Moreover, they were certainly not meant to be collected, culled,[19] arranged in series, and contrasted with the letters of Sheyne-Sheyndl, Menakhem-Mendl's shrewish wife. In short, whatever elements of overall structure, of formal unification, and hence, of general significance we find in *Menakhem-Mendl* originates not from the hero but rather from the fictional personality of Sholem Aleichem. He is a personality Menakhem-Mendl supposedly knows, though not intimately, and with whom he occasionally corresponds. This fictional Sholem Aleichem somehow obtained the hero's correspondence with his wife (Menakhem-Mendl himself wonders how that happened),[20] and it is through his arrangement and exposition of this correspondence that it has acquired its universal significance. The hero himself never dreams of being universally significant. He is alternately hopeful and crestfallen, silly and sometimes naively smart, but he is never consciously symbolical. Were he capable of examining himself objectively enough to become aware of his symbolic role, he would not have been what he is. He is prisoner for life in the cell of his dream of quick and easy riches, the most narrowly subjective of fictional characters. If he is a Jewish Everyman, it is not because he is in any way conscious of the wider implications of his humanity or of his "Jewishness" (in fact, Menakhem-Mendl, a grotesque *Homo oeconomicus* but a *Homo oeconomicus* nevertheless, is quite indifferent to his national or religious Jewishness). With Mendele, the opposite is true. If he is a Jewish Everyman, it is because he himself decided that he is one, for it is his comment upon himself that constitutes our final frame of reference for judging him. Thus, even if he is actually symbolic, as many critics insist, he is completely different as a symbol from Menakhem-Mendl. The latter innocently plays his universal drama of imagined success and real bankruptcy. His symbolic significance originates from a certain correspondence which Sholem Aleichem finds between his obsession and the human situation in general and the "Jewish" situation in particular. Mendele's universal significance originates from his rhetorical position. He is symbolic not because in what he did or wanted to do—in his hopes, fears, and follies —he is profoundly human, but because his very position as a commentator on the human situation in general and on the Jewish situation in particular makes him so. If Menakhem-Mendl represents eternal human folly and hope, Mendele represents the universality of common humanity in its reaction to folly and hope, in the judgment it passes on them. Mendele, it should be remembered, never claims for himself the status of an archetype. What he does claim is the status of the average man, and he may be that not because as a character he is common and average but because by his artistic function he expresses the common human experience and sets the limits of human "normality." A leader of the chorus in a Greek drama represents the citizenry of Thebes or the common experience and wisdom of the people of Corinth not by being a Theban or a Corinthian *folkstip,* but by his official function as a representative and a commentator.

iii

One of the results of the *folkstip* fallacy was an almost general inattention to Mendele's role as the structural spine of Abramovitsh's works. In his highly influential essay on Abramovitsh, David Frishman, the leading Hebrew critic at the beginning of the present century, commented thus on *Fishke the Lame*:

> Apparently we find in this story nothing of what we call composition. What we find are loosely combined events, episodes, reflections, actions. . . .
> Not the *chain* but the *single links* are the important things here. Why, of course, we have no intention of demanding a regular plot here. . . . For we deal here with Mendele, that Jew whose yellowish and pointed beard is already somewhat graying, and such a Jew, were I to

tell him about rules of composition and accepted norms, would listen but pay no attention. "This is beside the point," he says quite often, and this is what he would also say to me.[21]

Here the logic of the *folkstip* fallacy is pursued to its disastrous end. If Mendele is a "common Jew," a folk-personage, the embodiment of the heartiness and cleverness of the Jewish masses, etc., how can he be expected to bother with matters of composition and to function as the structural coordinator of Abramovitsh's works? Consequently, Abramovitsh's stories, the structural burden of which obviously lies on him, must be formless; they are even welcome to be so. The argumentation is utterly false. None of Abramovitsh's works can be legitimately separated into independent episodes, reflections, descriptions, etc., and wherever such a separation has been attempted, it has yielded critical results as trivial and as flippant as the above-quoted passage from Frishman's essay. One can legitimately argue that not all of Abramovitsh's structures were fully realized, that we can detect structural intentions that at a particular stage of the composition of a story (for instance, *Fishke the Lame*) were upset or thwarted by elements within the story he had insufficiently or ineffectively controlled.

However, the structural problems of Abramovitsh's works are not in themselves the subject of this discussion. They interest us here inasmuch as they have a bearing on the problem of the identity of Mendele. The harmful results of the *folkstip* fallacy in this direction are important to us because they hamper the detection of the links between Mendele's structural functions and his fictional identity. Even Viner, a critic who, in spite of his Soviet-Marxist persuasion, paid much attention to the "formal" aspects of the works of nineteenth-century Yiddish writers, manifested a general indifference to these important links. Having represented Mendele as "one of the common people in every way" and as "Tevye's elder brother," he quite logically went on to belittle the significance of Mendele's "ancillary" technical services in Abramovitsh's stories. He commented on these services in a note:

> The ancillary "storyteller" Mendele the Bookpeddler was meant at the beginning to serve as a mere technical auxiliary, a narrative device. With this storyteller, it was assumed, the strongly idiomatic language, the thinking and imagery of the common people, will sound natural, not fabricated. The creation of the character Mendele was, then, influenced

by a "rationalistic" motive.* However (these things happen quite often in Abramovitsh's works), the character soon outgrew its "functional–technical" framework and developed into an independent figure, with a life of its own.[22]

In this there is undoubtedly some truth. Mendele's role cannot be equated with the technical services he performs. It certainly grew richer and more complex than that. Yet the truth of Viner's remark is vitiated by a basic error. Mendele never grew completely "independent" of his "functional–technical" framework. However much richer his role became, it always remained rooted in this framework. Even when, toward the end of Abramovitsh's career, Mendele became almost the sole hero of the drama, it still remained his business to set the stage and raise the curtain. It is precisely this duality of character and *conférencier* that must be grasped if we are to achieve a full understanding of Mendele. We must start with a recognition of his significance as a "device" rather than as a character, *folkstip*, symbol, etc. Only a recognition of this primary aspect of his fictional reality forms the basis for an adequate understanding of its other aspects, of his being as a whole, with its overwhelming vitality as well as its severe limitations. For Mendele is in many ways a severely limited fictional entity. Fully and vividly realized as he is, he is not capable of absorbing experience to the extent that it would change him in a significant way. His technical and rhetorical functions in the different stories are constantly being stretched and broadened, as we shall see, but his character changes very little, if at all. Almost from the start, his character is a given entity, of which the author keeps making more and more extensive use, but which he hardly changes. This is why Mendele never ages. When we encounter him for the first time, in 1864 (the first version of *Dos kleyne mentshele*), he is already a man of mature age, fifty years old or so. When we take leave of him in Abramovitsh's late works, written during the first fifteen years of the twentieth century, he is still the same man. He does not grow older, although he may complain from time to time of his aching back and refer to himself as "weak and old." He is extremely vigorous, although we can never detect in him the impatience of youth. On the contrary, his vigor is always mitigated by experience, "knowledge of the world,"

---

* It seems to me that Viner employed the word "rationalistic" here in the sense of "intellectual" or "calculated."

mature deliberation. As a matter of fact, we cannot even imagine what he could be like as a young man or as a very old one. Indeed, he has scarcely any personal existence that transcends the limits prescribed by his function as a caretaker of the machine that sets Ambramovitsh's stories in motion. Within these limits he is as flexible as a fictional character can be, but he is never allowed to cross them. He moves with an amazing, almost acrobatic skill, but he must balance himself on a very narrow thread hung high up in the air, for he is a living fictional figure confined to a particular technical function as a "device." It is the duty of the critic to mark with as much precision as he is capable of the exact position of Mendele as such a device and to differentiate between his role as a person imitated or represented in a story and his role as a persona through which imitation and representation of a particular kind are carried out. One should, however, be on one's guard against the alluring convenience which the employment of mere new labels (e.g., "narrator" or "persona" instead of "pseudonym" or *folkstip*) seems to offer. What is called for is not a new label but rather a full descriptive definition of the technical function of Mendele, which is the root of his existence in the different stories of Abramovitsh as well as in the different phases of his career. Some well-intentioned recent efforts to differentiate between Abramovitsh and his Mendele have failed to uncover this root precisely because critics rely with unjustified confidence on terms such as "narrator." [23] To be sure, Mendele *does* fill in characteristic instances (most notably in *Fishke the Lame*) the traditional functions of a character–narrator, but then in other, equally characteristic ones (such as *The Travels of Benjamin the Third*), his function is altogether different. Here he is presented as the translator and compiler of the work, or even as its coauthor.[24] No one technical term can cover the common denominator of these (as well as other) functions of Mendele, but a description of his development as a device in Abramovitsh's works can.

The technical function of Mendele at its simplest and most essential is that of a fictional agent or vehicle through which "true stories" are transmitted to the public. This is Mendele's function not only "at the beginning" but throughout Abramovitsh's literary career. In most of Abramovitsh's Yiddish works and in many of his Hebrew ones, one basic fiction is constantly maintained, that of a literal, nonliterary veracity. Every one of the longer narratives (with the exception of the early Hebrew novel *Ha'avot vehabanim*) is presented as the history of a "real" person, written or told by himself either in a free monologue (Fishke) or in a formal will (Yitskhok Avrom, "the little man"), an autobiography (Hershele, Shloyme Reb Khayims), a travelogue (Benjamin), etc. The stories are presented as "true" in two senses: first, what is being told in them "really happened," and second, they are recorded in their "true," authentic form. This second aspect of the truthfulness of the stories must, however, be somewhat modified. Most of the stories are presented as having been prepared for publication by Mendele. For the purposes of public presentation, Mendele insists, style and sometimes structure must be corrected and improved upon. We shall see later on that during the development of Abramovitsh's career this tendency of Mendele's to improve upon his originals steadily grows until it reaches a point where the whole fiction of literal truth is in danger of imminent collapse. Still, Mendele does not cease to be the intermediary. As an occasional publisher he prints stories; as an editor or even a writer of sorts, he prepares them for publication; as a bookpeddler he sells them; as an experienced man of the book trade he sometimes makes comments on them. One thing he is not supposed to do—he is not to create the stories. As important as his additions to them may be, he is not supposed to be their author.

The selling of books may seem the least important in the list of mediatory functions. After all, Mendele's main responsibility, as far as the maintaining of the fiction of nonliteral veracity is concerned, is that of publishing the true stories, not of circulating them. The truth, however, is that Mendele's activity as a bookpeddler is absolutely essential to his successful functioning in all the other capacities. If he is effectively to perform his structural duties under the given circumstances of time and place, he must be an itinerant bookseller. The profession perfectly suits his task of literary transmission in a society with almost no other channel for such transmission. As a member of the Jewish book trade, he is the natural repository for manuscripts and documents which, for one reason or another, people want to see published. He is known to be connected with books and printing, and so manuscripts reach him by hand (*Di klyatshe*), by mail (*Di takse*), by accident (the first *Vintshfingerl*), by commission (*Shloyme reb Khayims*), or even posthumously by a stipulation in a will (*Dos kleyne mentshele*). As a traveling man, always on the move in a relatively immobile world, he is more exposed to the extraordinary and to the abnormal in Jewish society—and in this society, at the time, the writing of one's life story, or

for that matter the writing of stories in general, was an extraordinary
and sometimes quite abnormal activity (at least one of the imaginary
authors of Abramovitsh's stories, Yisrolik from *The Nag* is supposed to
have lost his wits). Above all else, Mendele will be entrusted with
manuscripts for publication simply because, as a bookpeddler, he is
connected with the Jewish printers (and we should remember that
many of Abramovitsh's stories take place in a time when there were
only two such printers in all of Russia),[25] he has some knowledge of
printing, and he is able to give the printed book the widest possible
circulation. These technical advantages are straightforwardly stated by
Abramovitsh's first protagonist, "the little man" himself. Yitskhok
Avrom concluded his will with the instruction that his confession is to
be handed over after his death to Mendele, "because he is well versed
in matters of printing; besides, he constantly drives throughout Poland, so he will be able to sell it." [26] Other depositors of manuscripts
added to these two basic reasons—mercantile mobility and professional know-how—reasons bearing on Mendele's moral character.
The people who sent Mendele the manuscript of *The Tax*, for example, wrote in their anonymous covering letter that they chose to address the play to him not only because they knew that "he drives with
his wagon to all Jewish towns and hamlets, and he sometimes under-
takes to publish stories at his own expense," but also because "he is
known in their parts as an upright, honest person." [27] The depositor of
the manuscript of *The Nag*, who is not the imaginary author himself
but one of his friends, flatters Mendele in a similar way. With customary irony, however, Mendele lets us understand that these compli-
ments are not intended to be implicitly believed. The senders of *The
Tax* know very well (as they indicate by remaining anonymous) that
the play is explosive and its publication may compromise Mendele in
many ways. Besides, they want him to publish it at his own expense.
How can they expect him to comply with their wish without referring
to his high morals? As for the depositor of *The Nag*, he wants Mendele
to publish the manuscript of a person who, as the sender himself puts
it, "has bees in his bonnet." [28] Mendele may well refuse to deal with it
(indeed, we are allowed to suspect that Mendele would not have un-
dertaken this publication were he not, by an unhappy accident, forced
to snatch even at the small amount that was offered him as an advance
toward his fee and the coverage of his expenses).[29] Thus, we may or
may not take seriously the references to Mendele as a minor regional

celebrity. The hard core of his professionalism, to which the richer and disinterested Yitskhok Avrom refers without complimentary round-abouts, is certainly the more important element in his role as the literary entrepreneur of the Jewish world.

This is the reason Mendele is never allowed to abandon his occupation of bookselling. It is only through this occupation that he can be useful. We saw, that like Menakhem Mendl, he had run the gamut of Jewish occupations and in his day had been a jack-of-all-trades. Unlike Menakhem Mendl, however, his economic drifting ended as soon as he hit the bookselling business. Menakhem Mendl could conceivably have become a bookseller for a time. In some preposterous way he would have convinced himself—by facts and figures—that there are millions to be had in this miserable trade, and he would have applied himself to it with all the ardor of his indomitable optimism. But by no means would he have remained a bookseller as Mendele does. The inevitable disaster would have come; Sheyne Sheyndl would have rescued him with money for train tickets and personal expenses, but on his way home another brilliant idea would have occurred to him, and a new business entanglement would have ensued. We can see how different the mode of Mendele's fictional existence is from that of Menakhem Mendl's. It is not only that they are different characters. They exist literarily in different ways. Were Mendele to change his *métier*, he would simply cease to exist. Only once in all of Abramovitsh's works is he allowed, very briefly, and for the purposes of anti-Zionist satire, to dissociate himself from bookselling. This happens in the Hebrew short story "Bymey hara'ash" ("In Days of Tumult"), in which Mendele, under the temporary influence of Zionist propaganda, suddenly wishes to become a colonist in Palestine. "I came to loathe my trade," he confesses. "Why should I keep on dragging myself through all the scattered Jewish habitations. . . ." [30] This, however, is only a momentary aberration. For Mendele to loathe his occupation is for him to loathe that particular form of the human situation which is his destiny. He himself diagnoses this sudden loathing as a symptom of both a personal and a public spiritual malady. In the turgid atmosphere of the "days of tumult" (i.e., the years following the pogroms of 1881), the Jewish people, he says, became sickly in every way, even in their reading habits. Like sick people who loathe wholesome food, they lost their literary taste. Mendele, infuriated by this, becomes sickly in his own way and decides to ask the Odessa Zionists to settle him as a comfortable farmer in the pastures of Judea "under his vine and under his fig tree." As the story reaches its conclusion, however, he is on his way back from Odessa to Glupsk and Kabtsansk; he repurchases his old horse and once again becomes the bookpeddler he must be. With "the relief of the frog when he returns weary and jolted to his native bog from a long journey on dry land," [31] he relapses into his old habit of driving through the small Jewish towns and carrying books for their small-town inhabitants.

This is how he remains to the very end. Never again is he to talk disrespectfully of his trade. On the contrary, he constantly develops his professional pride. When Hershele passes a harsh judgment on Jewish books, Mendele will have none of it because, as he says, it "destroys my whole trade." [32] In the prologue to *Shloyme reb Khayims*, Abramovitsh's last major work, Mendele expresses his credo as a bookseller in the clearest terms. The question of whether it is worthwhile to write and publish for the Jewish public is discussed at length in this prologue, and the writer Shloyme (Abramovitsh's self-portrait) voices his doubts. He is requested by his friends to write and publish his memoirs, but he cannot see the value of such a work. The writing, he concedes, may have a personal relevance, but why publish? Why go through the whole ordeal of publication when there are no interested readers? At this, Mendele feels as if his whole existence is being undermined, and he makes his very existence the answer to Shloyme's misgivings. "Loudly" and with "the pride and arrogance of the expert," he tells the writer to keep out of the business of publication and circulation: "You forget, Reb Shloyme, that there exists a Mendele the Bookpeddler, whom God could not have created for no purpose at all. . . . Don't you worry. You, Reb Shloyme, write. All the rest I take upon myself." [33] Thus Mendele identifies himself with his occupation and indeed *becomes* his occupation. He refers to the printing and selling of books in existential terms. They are the mode and the destination of his existence, and if he is to exist, they too must exist. Without them he would evaporate into nothingness.

Mendele knows that his trade is on the wane; that the sale of old-fashioned Jewish books, haphazardly printed by old-fashioned printers, and circulated in an old-fashioned mode (i.e., by the *pakntreger*, or *moykher-sforim*—the itinerant bookpeddler) is a doomed profession; that his territory is shrinking; that his merchandise and he himself are being superseded. This awareness supplies him with yet

another outlet for his irony and satire, and throughout his long career
he never gets tired of making the Jewish book trade the butt of his
witty comments. As early as 1865 he made this trade (in the prologue
to the first version of *Dos vintshfingerl*) the subject of a little comedy:
two Jewish bookpeddlers, involved in an accident, resolve their quarrel by striking a deal—they sell and buy each other's stock (without
exchanging a single penny). Each of them thinks that he is cheating
the other. Actually, they are both self-deceived—the Jewish book
trade being what it is.[34] In 1869 this ironic motif was repeated in the
first version of *Fishke the Lame*, which starts with Mendele relating
how, after having renewed his stock in trade and packing his wagon
full of books, he once again set out on his way

> to those places, where Reb Mendele and his merchandise are still worth
> something, thank God. One should know those Jews. They like the
> pages of a book to be of different colors as well as of different sizes, the
> print to be a little blurred, and each page to contain different typefaces:
> *rashi, diment, perl, cicero.*° Chapter heads should be printed both in
> large and in small *velish.*°° Errors are also not taken amiss. A Jew has a
> head on his shoulders and can guess what was meant. . . .[35]

Digs and thrusts of this kind were, from then on, seldom missing from
Mendele's prologues. He always finds an opportunity to comment either on the suspicious quality of books or on their deficient marketabil-
ity. However, at the same time one always notices the sense of belonging, the love of the *métier* that permeates his sarcasm, when it is aimed
at his profession. Note the familiarity with which he mentions the
name of the Hebrew typefaces; his ease when he converses about the
technical aspects of book production. His identity and his profession
are one and the same. After all, it is for "those Jews" and in "those
places, where Reb Mendele and his merchandise are still worth something, thank God," that he exists.

iv

The selling, editing, publishing, introducing, and announcing of
books represent Mendele's mode of existence. What he does is, basi-

---

° *Rashi, diment, perl,* and *cicero* are different Hebrew typefaces.
°° *Velish* means Italian. Mendele refers to the old Hebrew typeface inherited from
the great Jewish printers of Italy.

cally, what he is. What he does, however, gradually changes, as I have already intimated. It is not, as Viner suggested, that he outgrows his technical functions. It is rather that his technical functions gradually outgrow their initial form. Fundamentally, Mendele is always the same: a literary mediator. The nature of his mediation varies. Between the two extreme positions of mere publisher and full-fledged coauthor there is a wide range of entrepreneurial possibilities, and Mendele gradually covers this range. As the years pass the literary activity that his occupation involves steadily increases, and although he never ceases to be a book merchant, he becomes more and more of the professional *littérateur*.

This process is worth tracing in some detail. As a graphic frame, I will use the earliest (1864) and the latest (1907) versions of *Dos kleyne mentshele*. In 1864 Mendele was commissioned to publish Yitskhok Avrom's confession for purely technical reasons, as we have seen. He was not supposed to apply any editing to it; nor did he seem very concerned about its contents. By 1907 the nature of his commission had changed considerably. In the late version, this is how Yitskhok Avrom phrases his instructions with regard to Mendele:

> For properly putting these my papers in order, for correcting my crude errors, for adding to the chronicle some pepper and spice, so that it will make a tasty dish, for printing it in book form and then circulating it everywhere—for all these tasks I know no better man than Reb Mendele the Bookpeddler, whom I remember from Tsviatshits as a young married man. You will submit these papers to him, and he, I hope, will abide by my wishes to the best of his ability. It goes without saying that his efforts must be handsomely rewarded.[36]

In a postscript to this version, Mendele himself adds, "I immediately applied myself to my assignment and made haste to publish the book. I did not spare any effort to make it turn out tiptop, well-rounded, and yet pointed. . . ." [37]

The metaphorical terms in which this change in Mendele's function is conveyed are, as is always the case in Abramovitsh's work, highly suggestive. In 1864 Mendele was a mere technical contractor. His skills, whatever they were, had nothing to do with the story itself. In 1907 he is referred to as an expert *chef de cuisine*. Although he cannot supply the chronicle itself, it is his treatment of it, his spices and sauces, which will transform it from the raw piece of "real life" it must have been into a "tasty dish." Of course, Mendele must also perform the cruder, preliminary parts of the cooking. He must put the papers in order, correct crude errors, etc. He is still responsible for the technicalities of printing and circulation; but he is more than a printer and an editor. He is the master about whose "finishing touch" there is always some air of wizardry. The reader may remember the "spell" with which Mendele "charmed away" the stitches and patches from Hershele's resewn manuscript. It is the same spell that he is required here by Yitskhok Avrom to apply to his chronicle, except that the metaphor of the sartorial genius has been replaced by that of the culinary connoisseur. Both metaphors suggest a basic ambiguity in the relationship between Mendele and the manuscript he is supposed to doctor. The question arises, Is he still the vehicle, the intermediary between the "true" story and the public, or does he in a sense stand above the story and use it as the artist has used *his* raw materials?

This is the general framework of Mendele's development as a literary go-between. Within this framework we can now divide his development into three or four phases. The first begins in 1864 and extends to 1869. This is the purely "technical" phase. It is represented by the first versions of *Dos kleyne mentshele* and by the first version of the *Vintshfingerl* (1865). In this second work Mendele is already an independent publisher with initiatives of his own. He is not commissioned to publish the work; he happens to get hold of it (in the form of a German book) in a trade he has made with another bookseller, and he decides to translate it into Yiddish and publish it. Ironically, this only proves how incompetent he still is to do anything beyond printing and selling. Unable to read the German original, he mistakes it for a story of romance and witchcraft, of magic rings and supernatural apparitions, only to find that the "magic ring" of the title is metaphorical. It is "the natural magic ring," i.e., natural science, and not some entrancing legend that the book purports to offer its readers.[38] Mendele also tries here for once to exceed his limitations and instruct the translator of the book (obviously a *maskil*) how to go about his business.[39] For this he is promptly and quite properly rebuffed, after which he consents to limit himself to matters of printing and subscription.

The second phase may be described as one of ordinary editorial work with occasional authorship. It begins in 1869 with *Fishke the Lame* (first version) and *The Tax*. Mendele's roles in these two works differ from each other in nature as well as in scope. Fishke's story is the only one of Abramovitsh's major works that Mendele is supposed to have heard rather than received in some written form. This, of course, allowed him considerable elbowroom. Not only could he, within this framework, repeat his own exclamations and comments, which had allegedly interrupted the story while it was being told, but he could also, was even obliged to, describe in detail how he happened to hear the story, upon what occasion and under what circumstances, etc. Thus the thematic and structural relationships between Mendele's part in this story (it can no longer be described as a mere prologue) and that of its protagonist and chief narrator could, and indeed had to, become stronger and more involved than the equivalent relationships in most of the other stories. In its later versions *Fishke der krumer* became the most "Mendelean" of all Abramovitsh's longer narratives, i.e., Mendele's part in it reached such proportions as to almost render Mendele rather than Fishke the major figure in the story.[40] Even in the rudimentary version of 1869 Mendele's part is unusually intricate, as he welds—by contriving a super-plot of melodramatic coincidence—*four* different narrative monologues into one coherent story.[41] However, this does not change his basic function, which at this stage is, as I said before, that of the editor–publisher who occasionally allows himself the rights of authorship. Editorial duties and even authorial license are given to him in this story because of its very nature as a true rendering of life in the Jewish beggar-world and underworld (which is indicated by the subtitle: *A mayse fun yidishe oreme-layt* "A Story About Jewish Poor People"). Fishke is a creature of the lowest depths of Jewish contemporary society, and it goes without saying that he is illiterate. Moreover, we are informed that even his speech is most irregular both in pronunciation and in syntactical order (he is said to be telling his tragic story "with a lisp and in broken phrases").[42] So much so that a considerable amount of editorial smoothing in the rendering of his story can be taken for granted, although there is no specific reference to it in this version of the story.[43] Except for the reference to Fishke's lisp and "broken phrases" there is no indication here that the story is more than a verbatim repetition of his original monologue. However, the regularity and, indeed, the felicity of the narration, its rhythmic and syntactical texture indicate Mendele's intervention. In *Di takse* this intervention is openly admitted. Allegedly written by a frightened and harassed author, this work reached Mendele in the most disorderly form. The writing on the sheets "was crowded onto both sides" and in a very bad hand. The sheets were also in utter confusion. Mendele almost "lost his eyes" trying to link the scenes of the play into something like a coherent order. Then he discovered that some scenes were missing, and these he had to fill in by himself. Mendele, however, does not conceal that the play intrigued him to such extent that "he could not refrain from adding to it a few words here and there from what he himself had seen and heard in his voyages." [44] Thus, Mendele entered the sphere of authorship, though still in a very minor way. His editorial work as yet has nothing of the wizard about it. It is a common, workaday job. And it remains so in *The Nag* (1873), where again the manuscript is said to have been in sad disorder (the author is a madman). Mendele describes his editorial labor on the work thus:

> I applied myself with zeal to *The Nag*; put its parts in their proper places; arranged it in chapters to which I also gave appropriate titles—a work for which some claim the authorship of other people's compositions and proclaim themselves writers. . . . To cut a long story short, I spared no labor and did my work with all my heart.[45]

This awareness of his limitations is characteristic of Mendele in this interim phase of his career. On the one hand, he already claims recognition as a professional and hard-working editor. On the other hand, he has no pretensions to know better than his author. He would not join certain of his colleagues in claiming authorship where only the credit of editorship is due, and he does not deem himself a writer.

This reticence on the part of Mendele is dissipated by 1878. In that year, with the publication of *The Abridgment of the Travels of Benjamin the Third*, Mendele the chef, the wizard, makes his public debut. In the prologue to the *Travels*, Mendele explains the method by which he collected, arranged, collated, and unified the story. The book is said to be based on Benjamin's own travelogues and memoirs (excerpts from which, like the excerpts from Hershele's original autobiography that Mendele found "pertinent" enough to quote, occur from time to time in the text of the story). It is also said to include information derived from the reports about Benjamin's travels and discoveries to be found in the European press. Benjamin's story, Mendele explains, has been available for some time in all European languages. Only Benjamin's brethren, the Eastern European Jewish people, cannot "savor

. . . the honey overflowing from the Jewish hive" and take due pride in their eminent coreligionist, who, like themselves, was born and raised in a small *shtetl*, in fact, in the very *shtetl* of Tuneyadevke:

> So I, Mendele, whose aim it has been all his days to do for his brethren all that was within his power and his ability, could restrain myself no longer, and I said to myself: "Before the writers of Hebrew—whose little fingers are broader than my loins!—before they awake to the task of rendering the narrative of Benjamin's travels into the Holy Tongue, let me try to give at least an abbreviated account of it in my plain everyday Yiddish." So, despite my years and aches—may you be spared the latter—I girt my loins as if I were a giant and attempted to gather from the great treasure, things likely to interest the children of Israel and to retell them freely, in my own fashion. . . .[46]

Here Mendele claims, then, to have done the actual work of composition; he wrote, or rewrote, the book as he puts it, "freely, in my own fashion." As we already know, he was going to repeat this claim, perhaps even in stronger terms, in the 1888 prologue to *Dos vintshfingerl*. Hershele's manuscript and Benjamin's memoirs and travel books are treated in a similar manner. In both cases Mendele uses originals supposedly written in the first person and tailors them in his adaptation to the third person (leaving only the short, "pertinent," direct quotations already mentioned). In both cases he also abbreviates the original texts and consequently has to reconstruct them. Actually, the resemblance goes much further. The ironic structures of the two announcements are very much alike. Both begin with overt praise for the discarded originals. If in *Dos vintshfingerl* Mendele refers to Hershele's story as "a very good one" and even confers on it the supreme honor of describing it as "well-rounded and yet pointed," [47] in *Benjamin the Third* he euphemistically refers to Benjamin's original books as "the honey overflowing from the Jewish hive" (a conventional literary formula of praise in the Jewish rabbinical literature) and as "the great treasure." Yet in both cases he decides to offer his readers not the allegedly excellent originals but rather his own versions of them, and in both cases he insinuates, through different techniques of mock modesty, that because of his intervention, his readers can expect much better fare than they would have been served otherwise. In *Dos vintshfingerl* the covering excuse is the impatience of the readers. A mere Jewish publisher, Mendele has to accommodate his uneducated customers. In *Benjamin*

the Third it is the humble position of the Yiddish language, in which
only works of a temporary value can be written, ephemeral books for
the "common people" to enjoy until they know better. Mendele's account of Benjamin's travels is therefore only makeshift. The proper
and permanent Jewish version of the history of Benjamin must be written by the understandably slower but definitely more respectable Hebrew writers, "whose little fingers are broader than my loins" (here
Mendele uses the language of "the young men" who gave King Reho-
boam the intemperate counsel which cost him the better part of his
kingdom).[48] Mendele, in fact, is employing here the logic of the "aesthetics of ugliness" for his ironic purposes and thereby evokes the
apologetic tone of Yiddish writers—of Abramovitsh himself—only to
turn it into mockery. All this cannot and is not meant to conceal Mendele's true assessment of his literary ability. It only prepares the way
for allowing this assessment to buoy up in the closing sentences of the
announcement (as it buoys up in *Dos vintshfingerl* when Mendele
suggests that the reader regard the story "as if it were mine"). Mendele explains that he adapted the story "freely and in my own fashion"
and that his criterion was the appeal which certain events in Benjamin's history may have for Jewish readers ("things likely to interest the
children of Israel"). From this, two conclusions must be drawn: first,
he has developed a distinctive style of his own, a personal "fashion,"
or manner, which is so good, so superior to the style and the manner of
the adapted original, that it justifies the uninhibited freedom of his
treatment of them. Second, as the Jewish connoisseur, Mendele is the
expert in matters of Jewish taste. In *Dos vintshfingerl* the same assumption was conveyed through a sartorial metaphor (as an expert
Jewish tailor, Mendele knew how to refashion Hershele's manuscript
"in the Jewish style"). Here it is emphasized by an amplified version of
the culinary metaphor we have already encountered. Mendele refers
to himself as the wizardlike chef, only the cuisine is now explicitly
Jewish:

> Somehow I felt as though I were solemnly adjured from above:
> "Awaken, Mendele, and crawl out from your snug nook! Bestir thyself
> and gather handfuls of Benjamin's precious fragrant herbs and prepare
> them into such viands as your brethren may delight in!"
>
> And so, with God's help, crawl I did, and I did as I was bidden.
> Here, then, is the delectable repast, and may it prove, my dear friends,
> to your taste! [49]

Asserting Mendele's literary competence, his authoritative knowledge
of the pleasures of the Jewish palate, these sentences also remind us of
his mastery of the ambiguous reference. Perhaps he was never more
subtly equivocal than he is here. He defines his literary mission in religious terms, and as we have seen, his use of such terms is always a sign
of extraordinary ironic tension. "I felt," he says, "as though I were solemnly adjured from above: 'Awaken, Mendele. . . .' " The reference
to divine inspiration is quite explicit, and the language is befittingly
heavy with biblical allusions. We hear in it the echoes of numerous divine or divinely inspired imperatives: the "Arise!" and the "Awaken!"
sentences that mark the moment of transition from the slumber of
common, undemanding existence to the strenuous wakefulness of the
spiritual mission in the lives of the Patriarchs and the Prophets. Appropriately, perhaps, we may detect here the echo of that ecstatic call in
the Song of Deborah: "Awake, awake, Deborah; awake, awake, utter a
song";[50] appropriately, because the call to Deborah, like the call addressed to Mendele, has to do with poetic composition ("utter a
song"). Yet the one biblical allusion that dominates all others contains
no reference to spiritual inspiration of any kind. It cannot but strike us
as ironic that Mendele chooses to convey the meaning of his literary
mission through allusions to the story of Jacob and Esau and the stealing of Isaac's fatherly blessing. Jacob, we should remember, was also a
superb cook (cf. the story of the red pottage),[51] who knew how to prepare such viands as would sharpen the appetite of his brother. Not unlike Mendele, however, he had to make use of ready-made or easily
obtainable materials, for unlike his brother Esau, he was not "a cunning hunter, a man of the field," but rather "a plain man, dwelling in
tents." When the blind Isaac sent Esau, his beloved son, to take his
quiver and his bow, go out to the field to hunt venison, and prepare
him "savory meat" so that he would give him his blessing, Rebecca
sent her beloved son Jacob to the flock to bring two good kids from the
flock of goats with which, by proper seasoning, she intended to fool
the old man, as in fact she did. Preparing the "delectable repast" for
his brethren out of Benjamin's herbs, or the "tasty dish" out of
Yitskhok Avrom's raw chronicle, by applying everywhere his salt and
pepper, spices and sauces, Mendele is somehow comparable to the patriarch Jacob, the most "Jewish" of biblical figures, in his hour of disgrace and disguise. Like him, he offers something which is not his "as
if it were mine." Like him, he must disguise himself. (Are his gabar-

dine, beard, and sidelocks the equivalents of Esau's goodly raiment
and of the skins of the kids that the subtle Rebecca put on Jacob's
smooth skin lest his father feel him and detect his deception?) We
must relate the command "Bestir thyself and gather handfuls of Benjamin's precious fragrant herbs" not only to God's imperatives but also
to Rebecca's "Go now to the flock, and fetch from thence two good
kids of the goats." [52] Through one allusion Mendele both claims to
have been divinely inspired and confesses to having committed an act
something like the stealing of a birthright. These ambiguities, I suggest, are not accidental. In the next chapter I shall try to explain their
meaning as indicators of the direction which the entire development
of Mendele both as a fictional character and as a rhetorical persona
had, under the historical circumstances, to take.

That phase in the progress of the entrepreneurial functions of
Mendele, which I have half-heartedly enumerated as the fourth one
and which actually began even before the appearance of the first parts
of the 1888 *Dos vintshfingerl*, can be described as a phase of retreat.
After a period of perilous "brinkmanship," Mendele withdraws from
the danger zone in two directions. First, the direction he takes in his
last major work, *Shloyme reb Khayims*, and also in some other more
ambitious pieces such as *Seyfer habeheymes*, leads him back to the un-
pretentious initial status of mere publisher. The regressive aspect of
the other direction, that taken in most of the short stories which
Abramovitsh published (mainly in Hebrew) from 1886 onward, is less
obvious. At first appearance it seems that here, in such short stories as
"Beseter ra'am" ("In the Secret Place of Thunder," 1886–1887),
"Shem vayefet ba'agala" ("Shem and Japheth in the Train Compartment," 1890), "Lo nakhat beya'akov" ("There Is No Good in Jacob,"
1892), "Bymey hara'ash" ("In Days of Tumult," 1894), "Byshiva shel
ma'ala uvyshiva shel mata" ("In the Heavenly Assembly and in the
Earthly One," 1894–1895), etc., Mendele finally breaks into full authorship. All of these stories are presented as originating from Mendele
himself. Not only is he supposed to have written them; he is also supposed to have conceived of them. There is no reference in them to any
written or oral source. Yet these stories do not introduce any new rhetorical element into Abramovitsh's work, and in fact what they suggest
is, as I have said, a retreat from any experimentalism in this respect.
What Mendele does in them he has been doing for a long time, practi-
cally since his first version of *Dos kleyne mentshele*; he continues to

weave the chatty, informal monologues which until now preceded and sometimes concluded the longer narratives in the form of "Quoth Mendele" prologues and epilogues. Almost from the very beginning these monologues showed a tendency to expand and to grow into dramatic narratives in their own right, a tendency which at a very early stage brought about the intricate concentric form of "a story about the story" versus "the story itself" (see the 1865 version of *Dos vintshfingerl*). Now, in the late short stories, the duality of a framing and a framed narrative was circumvented and replaced by what amounted to uninterrupted "quoth Mendele" addresses. What proves that these stories, or at least most of them ("Lo nakhat beya'akov" may be considered an exception), are extensions of the earlier addresses is not the mere fact that they are allegedly written or recited by Mendele. Their whole tenor, the very grain of their rhetorical and narrative texture retains the basic qualities of the prologues to *Dos kleyne mentshele* and *Dos vintshfingerl* or of Mendele's extensive story framework in *Fishke the Lame*. Like these prologues and story framework, the late short stories deal only with events which Mendele personally witnessed and mainly with events in which he took a major part. Like them, they include lengthy portions of dramatized discourses. Like them, they evolve in the narrative present, are directly addressed to an audience (see especially the first chapter of "Beseter ra'am"),[53] etc. In short, these stories are monologues in which Mendele narrates personal reminiscences to a present public. In them he stands near the footlights, halfway between the audience and the fictional action, exactly as he did before. It is only that what formerly constituted the curtain raiser now fills the entire show.

This account of the development of Mendele's alleged technical and literary involvement in Abramovitsh's work covers, of course, only one aspect in what may be described as Mendele's Progress. It is my belief, however, that through a clear perception of this single aspect, one can get very near to a full understanding of the phenomenon of Mendele, and perhaps of other significant phenomena in the history of nineteenth-century Yiddish fiction. Mendele's progress, we have seen, although it drives him from relative simplicity toward complexity, does not proceed from one unequivocal stage to another but just as unequivocal one. Mendele does not grow from a mere "technical–functional" auxiliary into an "independent figure," a *folkstip* as easy to place as Tevye the Dairyman. From the very beginning he is the compound of a rhetorical device and a very lively fictional character, and he remains such a compound even as he keeps growing more complex and tricky. In him the person and the persona are always interdependent, if not altogether indivisible. That is why, by tracing in detail his progress and retreat as a literary mediator, we can chart with some measure of precision his extent and limitations, thus gaining a better insight into his historical significance as the center of nineteenth-century Yiddish fiction. We can understand why with his appearance in 1864 this fiction emerged from its erratic infancy and established its own characteristic manner: a limited manner, but one richly creative and on many occasions extraordinarily effective.

For this purpose all the facts concerning Mendele which have been hitherto assembled must be gathered together and placed in focus against the background of the general historical situation discussed in the first chapters of this study. This I shall attempt in the next two chapters. At this point, however, it may be useful to summarize some of the main points that have been made with regard to Mendele. They can be divided into two groups: negative and positive points.

The negative points are that, first, Mendele the Bookpeddler is not a pseudonym; he does not merely echo his master's voice. Second, Mendele is neither a *folkstip* nor is he "the essential Jew," in the sense of a representative of "the Jewish character." Far from being that, he cannot even be regarded as a loyal, "common" Jew. His attitude toward the Jewish religion, the holy texts, the eschatological interpretation of Jewish history, even toward the Jewish people themselves, is extremely ambiguous. Third, Mendele is not an independent character who has outgrown his initial limitations as a technical storyteller. Fourth, a description of him as a mere "narrator" is partially correct but basically misleading.

The positive points correspond more or less to the negative ones: First, Mendele is a fictional character with his own biography, attitudes, and mental constitution. Above all else, he possesses a most distinctive individual dramatic voice, easily separable either from the voices of other characters or from that of the author himself. Second, Mendele is a fictional character of a special order. His status as a rhetorical medium between the action and the readers distinguishes him from all other characters in Abramovitsh's work and also from such characters as Tevye the Dairyman and Menakhem Mendl. Third,

Mendele's rhetorical peculiarity originates from his double role in Abramovitsh's stories. On the one hand, he is one of their heroes, perhaps their main hero. On the other hand, he is a means through which Abramovitsh was able to maintain throughout his career the fiction of nonliteral veracity, i.e., Mendele is used as a vehicle for transmission of "true stories," supposedly written by their protagonists, to the reading public. Fourth, this function of his grows in significance and reaches the verge of full authorship. From there, however, it recoils back into mediation. The verge is never really crossed.

CHAPTER SEVEN

THE MENDELE MAZE
III. The Outlet

AT THE BEGINNING of the present century, when both Hebrew and
Yiddish literature were under the impact of the then newly dominant
Jewish nationalism, critics denied vehemently the relevance of a European context to the understanding of Abramovitsh's art. With the exception of *Don Quixote*, it was generally agreed that European literature in general and the traditions of the novel in particular had no
bearing whatsoever on his writing, which allegedly was utterly original
and purely "Jewish." Abramovitsh himself, now playing the role of the
"grandfather" for all it was worth, was well satisfied with this conception of his work. As a young man, however, he used to take pride in
his extensive reading of German literature,[1] and once he even let his
characters Mendele and Sender, the bookpeddlers, drop the names of
Cervantes and Lessing (though in a properly blundering fashion).[2] Yet
now he used every means that his almost royal prestige placed at his
disposal in order to crush any critical attempt at integrating his writing
into the framework of European literature.[3] As effective as they were,
these efforts would have proved of no avail without the help of the
contemporary Jewish intelligentsia. The intellectuals were eager to retain their Abramovitsh—or rather Mendele, for by now these two had
become a *unia personalis*—"untainted" by any blot of foreign influence or connection. "Is there such a thing as Jewish art?" the na-
tionalist intellectuals had asked themselves with scarcely concealed
anxiety, and they were all relieved to hear that, indeed, there was such

a thing and that, furthermore, it was represented by their own Mendele. "His is a unique art, with nothing to compare with it in any language . . . a Jewish art . . . the art of the essential Jew," they were told by no less a critic than David Frishman.[4] As a writer who was himself regarded as the ambassador of European culture in Hebrew literature and who wrote articles on Schiller and Byron, Tolstoy and George Eliot, Baudelaire and Oscar Wilde, he was supposed to know what he was talking about. When he pronounced Abramovitsh "not a fiction writer at all, that is, not a fiction writer in the sense that one who has read much fiction in foreign languages would attribute to the term," he was taken at his word. Abramovitsh "received nothing from others; he did not draw upon any precedent; he had no use for any other writer as a model. Whatever he did, he did by himself. . . ."[5] His art was a phenomenon that sprang directly from the anima of the nation; it gave a pure expression to "the spirit of the people." To compare one of his works or a certain aspect of his works to anything outside the native traditions was more than an error; it was an act of contamination tantamount to intellectual treason. Readers and critics were not prone to look for links and parallels even within the boundaries of the Jewish tradition. Comparison, it was said, was not the right method to study and judge Abramovitsh, for above all else, he was a "first," an original, "an almost natural artist," as Frishman put it with some uneasiness.[6] Byalik, the great poet, in an essay written in a beautifully balanced Hebrew prose, depicted Abramovitsh as a primeval, titanic sculptor, who had hammered and forged his own tools and then took them to the mountain "to hew his sculptures out of the wild rock itself."[7] The poet warned his readers "not to forget to forget the rules and theory of literature" when they come to study Abramovitsh, and even more urgently, "not to study him by comparison," for he constituted a separate category of literature.[8]

By and large, Byalik's warning was and still is heeded.[9] The notion of Abramovitsh as a self-made artist who is also the Jewish artist par excellence hardened into a critical orthodoxy that is still quite influential. As with all literary orthodoxies, however, it also bred its own heretics. As early as 1919 (two years after Abramovitsh's death), the Hebrew critic Sh. Tsemakh judiciously argued that Abramovitsh's art, if Frishman's definition of it was to be trusted, could "either be an art originating from the deep jungles along the banks of the Congo River . . . or not exist at all." Moreover, if one must believe that such an art "was created in Europe in the latter part of the nineteenth century by an artist who had written zoology textbooks and believed in the progress of civilization," one had every right to regard it with suspicion.[10] He suggested that Abramovitsh's place in the development of Jewish literature could be understood *only* by comparison. The revolution Abramovitsh introduced to this literature, he argued, was the change traditionally initiated in most European literatures by the emergence of the picaresque novel from the status of subliterature; a change which he interpreted as a historically necessitated deflation that violently brought literature from a conventionalized idealism back to the reality of common human existence. Whether this interpretation has a real bearing on Abramovitsh's fiction or not, the idea that his art was connected with the picaresque tradition took hold and was in time made much of,[11] perhaps too much. It is my belief that even in the case of such works as *Fishke the Lame* and *The Travels of Benjamin*, where the influence of the picaresque tradition is undoubtedly present, a mere comparison with the great models of the tradition would not take us far unless it was immediately and severely qualified. However, the comparison does have at least one value. It points the correct way to a comparative study of Abramovitsh, inasmuch as it indicates that his works should not primarily be compared or linked with those of his contemporaries in European literature but rather should be related to the pre-nineteenth-century traditions of the European novel. Both Frishman and Byalik implicitly based their erroneous notion of Abramovitsh's originality upon the dissimilarities between his structural techniques (which they regarded as the "lack" of and disrespect for structure) and the conventions of the rounded, psychological novel of the late nineteenth century.[12] Of course, Abramovitsh did not conform to the structural conventions of Turgenev and Tolstoy. The question is, however, whether or not there is any similarity between his techniques and those of the tradition of Sterne, for instance.[13] Were Frishman and Byalik to read him against the background of eighteenth-century or early nineteenth-century fiction, some similarities in technique and manner could not have been overlooked. They might have even discovered that the very idea of a Mendele was inherent in these earlier traditions, i.e., that the fictional device of a "publisher," "editor," or "bookseller," whose task it was to transmit genuine "true histories" to the public, was indeed an inevitable technicality in all European literatures at a certain stage of their development.

ii

With the idea of presenting his "true histories" through the agency of a fictional publisher, Abramovitsh was certainly treading a well-worn path. The urge to present works of fiction as "true histories" has manifested itself everywhere during the development of the novel and is peculiarly typical of its earlier stages. Readers of English literature will remember that Defoe tried to impose all his novels on the public as "true histories," in which only "the names and other circumstances of the person are concealed" and the style "a little altered," especially where the story was supposed to be told by a thief or a whore whose language had to be improved to render it "fit to be read" [14] (the same is said by Mendele with regard to Fishke's language).[15] Even Richardson presented his *Pamela* as a collection of genuine letters and, posing as a mere editor, firmly maintained "that the story has its foundation in truth; and that there was a necessity, for obvious reasons, to vary and disguise some facts and circumstances, as also the names of persons, places, etc." [16]

In the early development of the French novel the insistence on the literal veracity or the nonfictional authenticity of the story was common enough to invite Rousseau's challenge in the first preface (1761) to his *Nouvelle Héloïse:* "Ai-je fait le tout, et la correspondance entière est-elle une fiction? Gens du monde, que vous importe? C'est sûrement une fiction pour vous." [17] Thus the readers of this famous epistolary novel were left suspended between their belief in the alleged authenticity of the protagonists' letters, and the possibility that they might after all be "the editor's" fabrication. In the meantime "the editor" cunningly proclaimed full authorial responsibility for the novel in case it was considered a failure and declined authorial credit in case it proved a success. In 1782 the convention Rousseau had challenged was ridiculed by Laclos in his *Liaisons dangereuses,* where it was put to use with all its attendant cliches as "the editor" asserted the authenticity of the work, apologizing for its allegedly crude style and insufficient selectiveness, only to be contradicted and undermined by "the publisher," who advised the public to be on its guard and take the editor's words *cum grano salis*.[18] Nevertheless, this convention of "authenticity" in fiction was kept alive in France throughout the eighteenth century and well into the nineteenth even by writers as sophisticated as Benjamin Constant.

This need to present fiction as literal truth, although enhanced and qualified in different literatures by specific circumstances and traditions (e.g., the objection of Puritan morality to "romances" and even to fiction as in the cases of Defoe and Richardson), was, generally speaking, postulated in the early stages of the development of the modern novel by the very nature of its generic principle, which Ian Watt has defined as "formal realism" ("formal," because the term "realism" refers only to the techniques and procedures of narration). Since the writing of these new novels was conceived of as "the production of what purports to be an authentic account of the actual experiences of individuals," [19] it had, at least during the period before the genre established itself, to extend as far as possible the pretense of truth. Later on, when novels were written under the impact of the cult of sensibility, the fiction of literal veracity was maintained for purposes of emotional immediacy and authenticity of sentiment (see, for instance, Henry Mackenzie's *The Man of Feeling*, Goethe's *Werther*, Constant's *Adolphe*, Alexandr Radishtshev's *Journey from Petersburg to Moscow*, etc.). When historical and regional fiction began to be written, literal veracity was simulated in order to insure the reader's belief in the reality of remote time or place (the best examples are Scott's novels of Scottish history and of the half-civilized Scottish countryside).

Wherever the pretension of literal truth has appeared in the development of the novel, it has always involved—ironically perhaps—the creation of two or even of several fictions instead of one, since to the initial fiction, i.e., the story itself, a fictional frame had to be added. Thus, throughout the eighteenth century and the first decades of the nineteenth century, a legion of imaginary editors, publishers, literary executors, etc., were indefatigably producing for this purpose prefaces, proems, advertisements, and diverse notes *ad nauseam*. Again and again manuscripts were "discovered" in distant places by serious, solitary people who felt it their duty to make them public and, for the occasion, describe with all proper modesty under what strange circumstances they had come by them and how they did or did not change a word of the original (the suppression of proper names was often mentioned in these introductions). Reams of memoirs, letters, and diaries reached the shops and cabinets of booksellers and publishers who thought "they may be printed with a good prospect of success" and who also found that the difficulties involved in "printing the

private correspondence of persons still living" were not insurmounta-
ble (cf. the prefatory letters of Jonathan Dustwich and Henry Davis at
the opening of Smollett's *Humphrey Clinker*).[20] These booksellers and
printers, in one way or another, also made their appearance before the
public and tried to present the intent in their publications in the most
favorable light. Some of the prefatory addresses of publishers, editors,
etc., were written with an unmistakable flair for lively characterization
and authentic speech. We may, for instance, compare the liveliness
and volubility of Mendele with that of Jedediah Cleishbotham, the deliciously garrulous "schoolmaster and parish clerk of Gandercleugh"
who is the "collector and reporter" of some of Scott's allegedly true
Scottish novels and tales. Indeed, the comparison might reveal more
points of resemblance than one would have thought possible. Like
Mendele, Jedediah is a man of good sense and naive shrewdness who
sometimes likes to conceal his very practical common sense (especially
in pecuniary matters) behind homiletic formulae. Like him, he is lo-
quacious and given to the employment of traditional stylistic conventions. Like him, he is a parochial representative of "culture," the "literary" mentor of a small backwater world, and as such is entrusted
with manuscripts that he makes public for the benefit of "his loving
countrymen" (Mendele's "dearly beloved children of Israel"), and not
for anything as gross as financial gain. Finally, like him, he finds the
writing of his proems too great a pleasure to be quickly done with. He
obviously enjoys the position of a literary entrepreneur, and he lets his
natural chattiness carry him far beyond the mere call of a publisher's
or editor's duty.

I am not trying to suggest that Abramovitsh was directly influenced by Scott. In fact, the problem of direct or even indirect influence has but little bearing on my argument. It is quite possible that,
for all Scott's international fame, Abramovitsh did not read his novels
and was not aware of the existence of Jedediah. He was, however,
probably well-acquainted with some of the Jedediah-like figures in
Russian literature, created by the host of "Scott's followers" who
flooded the Russian book market during the 1820s and 1830s with regional tales collected and edited by chatty, literate villagers and provincial raconteurs. At least in one case, that of Gogol's Rudi Panko, the
garrulous old narrator of the tales in both volumes of *Evenings near
the Village of Dikanka* (in whom contemporary critics were quick to
recognize Scott's influence),[21] his awareness of this conventional figure

cannot be doubted, since his interest in Gogol and his satirical techniques is well known. And, indeed, it would not be an illegitimate
practice to examine possible similarities between Mendele and the
Ukrainian beekeeper, who although he knew what it meant "for a vil-
lager like me to poke his nose out of his hole into the great world" and
stumble into print when "so much stuff gets into print . . . that one
has more wrapping-paper than one can use," [22] decided nevertheless
to publish the folk tales he allegedly collected and edited. However, a
comparison between Mendele and Panko or Cleishbotham can prove
helpful to the student of Yiddish fiction, and perhaps also to the student of modern European prose fiction in general, not because of any
succession of influences that the traces of similarity may indicate. The
comparisons are relevant because affinities between Mendele and
these figures can be regarded as demonstrating the autonomous logic
of the genre at work. They seem to prove that, as a poetic form, prose
fiction in general and the novel in particular were motivated by an intrinsic logic that made writers, in mutual ignorance of each other,
come up with similar answers when they are faced with similar problems. That is why affinities are possible not only between phenomena
close to each other in time, place, and cultural milieu but also between
phenomena as distant from each other as Cleishbotham's introductions
to Scott's novels and tales (e.g., the introduction to the *Tales of My
Landlord* series)[23] and the "Quoth Mendele" prologues. As much as
Abramovitsh differed from Scott in his artistic temper, concepts, and
traditions, and as much as his Kabtsansk, Tuneyadevke, and Glupsk
were alien to Gandercleugh and Glasgow, still the two novelists confronted difficulties of a somewhat similar nature: they both applied the
forms and the norms of art to a world that knew little of them and
cared less. They both described a society with a traditional, provincial,
deeply religious, and highly individualized culture from the vantage
point of a different culture—metropolitan, partly secularized, and allegedly more sophisticated. They both tried to render in a generalized
literary idiom the particularities and robustness of a dialect. In order
to retain in their works at least a semblance of the naiveté of the world
they described, both had to resort to special artistic devices. In short,
both had to employ a fictional agent who functioned as a mediator between the subject matter and their estranged selves. The possibility
that the agents they devised for this purpose are in some ways similar
is not surprising and, *pace* Byalik, should be looked into. Abramovitsh

as well as other Jewish writers should be studied in comparison to writers of other literatures, for comparison is the only method of study by which their works and the tradition they represent can be properly located on the map of European literature. Not a whit of their originality and peculiar "Jewishness" will be lost in the process. On the contrary, it is only by comparison of similarities that the uniquely dissimilar or the meaningful difference that often lurks behind the similar can be pointed out.

The very conventionality of the function performed by Mendele indicates, on the one hand, that the tradition of nineteenth-century Yiddish fiction which blossomed in the works of Abramovitsh and Sholem Aleichem is not a literary rod of Aaron, but rather a branch of modern European fiction. As such it is bound to be connected with, and, to a certain extent, to resemble, the other branches. On the other hand, the similarity between Mendele's monologues and those of imaginary publishers and editors in earlier European novels is in itself also a sign of historical dissimilarity. By the time Abramovitsh came to use the fictional mechanism of the imaginary publisher, it seems to have gone out of fashion in most European literatures. Although by no means extinct, it was seldom resorted to by respectable novelists during the second half of the nineteenth century. (The only outstanding exception I can think of is Dostoevski, who in *The House of the Dead*, employed the mechanism in quite a conventional manner as late as 1859–1862. Dostoevski, however, was generally notable among the great novelists of the second half of the century for his tendency to employ the techniques and conventions of the cruder forms of the sentimental novel.) The very fact that Abramovitsh clung throughout his long career, well into the twentieth century, to a convention which in other literatures had exhausted its vitality at least two, and perhaps three generations before his shows that the circumstances under which he developed his art must have been different from those under which most of his European contemporaries developed theirs. He could not have found the conventions of the eighteenth-century novel more useful and acceptable than those of contemporary novels without being somehow conditioned by a literary situation in many respects unique.

The uniqueness of this situation is variously reflected in the fiction of Mendele. It is even demonstrated by the very vitality of this fiction. Mendele's prefatory addresses differ from those of other imaginary booksellers, publishers, and editors not only in their chronological place in the development of the modern European novel but also in their degree of artistic excellence. If such prefaces can be regarded as an autonomous dramatic subgenre with its own gradation of merit, then, I think that Abramovitsh must be pronounced one of its greatest masters. Indeed, it may well be that in his works this subgenre reaches its apex. The first criterion of merit in a fictitious preface must be that of dramatic self-sufficiency. If the preface is not to be dismissed as a mere technical accessory, it must have a life of its own. It must certainly be closely related—thematically and structurally—to the story, and yet it must also justify its existence by sublimating the technicalities of a fictional mechanism into a fictional reality. The imaginary editor, publisher, etc. should have dramatic life. No matter how few his sentences, they are either charged with that suggestiveness that makes the presence of a personality immediately felt, or they do not count. In this regard some of the greatest novelists failed; Abramovitsh gloriously succeeded. Even Jedediah Cleishbotham's "proems" and Panko's introductions, which certainly stand the test of dramatic self-sufficiency, seem quite dull beside the virtuoso performances of Mendele. Every one of Mendele's introductions—even the shorter and the less important—is an independent dramatic unit, complete in its rhetorical structure and sustained throughout in tone and manner. It is immediately effective. The ceremonial Hebrew phrase "Omar Mendele" ("Quoth Mendele") is no sooner uttered, and already we are under the spell of a living voice, which is certain, whatever it is made to say, to convey a supreme vividness. It may even breathe life into that most tedious of literary technicalities, the list of the dramatis personae (cf. his introduction to the play *The Tax*).[24]

This extraordinary success cannot, I submit, be explained by superiority of talent. Abramovitsh was a highly gifted writer of fiction, but if he succeeded in pursuing the technicality of the fictional publisher perhaps more vividly than any other novelist, it is not necessarily because he was more talented but because certain conditions inherent in the literary context in which he functioned made him channel an unusually large portion of his creative vitality into this technicality. We saw how the importance of the fiction of Mendele gradually grew to overwhelming dimensions; it can, indeed, be said that this growth indicates a major shortcoming in Abramovitsh's art. As much as the Mendele fiction demonstrates the brilliance of his talent, it also implies that there was a certain narrowness, a certain limitation that forced this talent to expand disproportionately in one direction. This one-sided expansion is of broad historical significance. The pressures that narrowed the range of Abramovitsh's art and brought about the lop-sided prominence of Mendele were historical; they were brought to bear not only on Abramovitsh but also on many other nineteenth-century Yiddish writers. The expansion of the figure which was originally meant to serve as an auxiliary into a dominating archetype (which re-peated itself in the case of Linetski, Sholem Aleichem, and others) reflects the dynamics of an unusual literary development. The circum-stances under which modern Yiddish fiction was created must have in-volved strong modifying conditions or differentiating influences; other-wise, it is hard to explain how a conventional novelistic mechanism of secondary importance, which had been transplanted from one Euro-pean literature to another with no significant changes, became the most memorable feature in the works of at least two great writers to the extent that it absorbed and usurped the very reality of these writ-ers' personal existence and submerged Abramovitsh and Rabinovitsh in a Mendele and a Sholem Aleichem.

iii

To comprehend the full purport of the fictional Mendele, we must see how different historical principles immanent in the development of nineteenth-century Yiddish literature were brought, through the agency of a great writer, into a fructifying relationship.

First, something must be added concerning the problem of literal veracity in Abramovitsh's works. At its beginnings the need in modern Yiddish fiction for pretended veracity was as urgent as it was in the corresponding stages of the development of the novel in other Euro-pean literatures. We encounter its manifestations everywhere. Aksen-feld, for instance, insisted on the literal truthfulness of his plots in al-most every one of his doggerel verse introductions. Introducing his play *Di genarte velt, oder der oytser* ("The Duped World, or the Treas-ure," probably written in 1842), he assures his readers that his is "an emese mayse" ("a true story"), having nothing "disguised or dis-sembled" in it, with only the style somewhat smoothed:

> In Shpitsenits iz alts emes; un in Sharivke—akurat.
> Alts, azoy vi si'z bashribn, nor dertseylt glat.[25]

("What happens in Shpitsenits is all true; in Sharivke—true to a word;/ Everything—exactly as it is described, only told in a smoother manner." Shpitsenits and Sharivke are the names of the town and the village in which the action of the play takes place.) In the introduction to *Dos shterntikhl* Aksenfeld seems for a moment to be playing with other possibilities, only to revert with double emphasis to the pretense of complete veracity:

> Oyb der bashrayber fun der mayse hot zikh dos oysgetrakht,
> Iz es nokh mer tsikave, vi azoy er hot azelkhes gemakht.
> Nor, az me vet oysleynen in gantsen gor,
> Veln ale moyde zayn, az alts vos shteyt iz vor.[26]

("If the recorder of the story has fabricated all this,/ Then it is even more interesting to know how he did such a thing;/ But once you have read it through,/ Every one of you will concede that whatever you find here is true." It should be noted that in both of the quotations from Aksenfeld the verb *shraybn*—"to write," "to compose"—and its derivatives are replaced by *bashraybn*—"to describe." Aksenfeld, for instance, refers not to "the writer of the story," but rather to what I translated as "the recorder of the story," for lack of a better gloss. The word *bashrayber* means literally "describer" and the word *mayse* may mean not only "a story" but also "an actual event." These shades of meaning are important. Aksenfeld does not present himself as a writer, a composer of stories, but rather as a "describer" of real events, although he confesses to some literary smoothing of the stories.)

In the long and often rhyming subtitles that Dik gave to his numerous novelettes, the nonliterary veracity of the plots is endlessly emphasized. Many of the stories are referred to in these opening announcements as "an interesting and true story" (here, too, the word "story" may be read as "event," "occurrence") or as "very important and very true" ("zeyer vikhitik un zeyer rikhtik"). In fact, Dik can be quite redundant and tiresome on this subject; one complete illustration will have to do. This is how Dik announced his story "Yekele Goldshleger" (1859):

> Dear readers, I will tell you an interesting story about an incident I myself witnessed when I stayed in Ssuria [an anagram of Russia]; but don't think that you are being told one of those stories which the *kheyder* boys tell each other on winter evenings, before their teacher is back from the evening prayer. No. This is a true story. From it you can learn how you yourself should behave.[27]

Linetski presented each of his three longer stories—*Dos poylishe yingl*, *Der litvisher bokher* ("The Lithuanian Lad," 1875–76), and *Der vorem in khreyn* ("The Worm in the Horseradish," 1888)—as his "true" autobiographies, although each tells a different story and only the last actually contains a significant autobiographical element). In *Der litvisher bokher* the hero discourses about the superiority of auto-biographies as compared to novels. With no embarrassment he refers to *Dos poylishe yingl* as a glorious example of autobiography, "the tremendous usefulness of which is known to every reader." [28] "Having to do with facts," autobiographies must be more "useful" than mere fiction.[29] This constant harping on the advantages facts have over fiction continued late into the 1880s. (See Abramovitsh's emphatic reference to *Dos vintshfingerl* as "a *history* of Jewish life" rather than "just another story," and Sholem Aleichem's persistent references to his early novels in terms such as "undzer rikhtike, nisht oysgetrakhte geshikhte '—"our true, unfabricated story.")[30]

The reasons for this insistence on nonfictional veracity were numerous. Modern Yiddish fiction was as susceptible to the pressures forcing it toward "formal realism" as other branches of modern European fiction had been in their phases of initial formation. The literary dialectic which had driven Western European writers of fiction a hundred or a hundred and fifty years earlier to reject the conventionalized romance fiction of the Renaissance and develop the disreputable, "low" genres of the picaresque, the criminal "history," etc., into the new genre of the realistic novel, re-created itself in Yiddish. If the writers of Yiddish fiction had no romance literature of the de Scudery type to reject, they had to oppose the popular legendary literature and the hasidic hagiography. In Perl's *Megale-tmirin* the entire thematic and structural unity of the work depends on an ever-expanding "battle of books," which is the battle of truth against falsehood and fact against fable. Truth and verifiable fact are represented by the maskilic *bukh*, which the hasidic protagonists of the story are so anxious to destroy (i.e., Perl's own German tract on "the hasidic sect"). Falsehood and outrageously impossible fable are represented by *Shivkhey-ha-besht* ("The Praises of the Bal-Shem-Tov," the legendary cycle on the life of the founder of hasidism) as well as by other standard hasidic works, which are constantly referred to in the mock notes and are thus linked to the criminal chicanaries unfolded in the epistolary text.

Yiddish writers had also to reject the still-popular romances of the seventeenth century (cf. Elye Bokher's *Bovo-bukh* in particular).[31] The rejection of this type of literature was often offered as a justification for the creation of new Yiddish fiction[32] and remained a living issue much later than is usually assumed.[33] Young Abramovitsh subjected the popular Yiddish romances to the irony of Mendele, who as a bookpeddler knew only too well how much they still appealed to the common reader. In the prologue to the early *Vintshfingerl* Mendele explained how he purchased the original work from another bookpeddler:

> I bought for a song a slim German book called (as its title was translated to me) something like *The Magic Ring*. That's a bargain, I thought; that's just the thing for Jews to have. It is just that stuff which makes a hit like *Bovo-mayse* and *The Arabian Nights*.[34]

He willingly barters several *Haskala* pamphlets for it, confessing that he "would gladly trade all the *Haskala* books in the world for a single *mayse* or a couple of *Magic Rings*." [35] It turns out, of course, that the *Magic Ring* itself is a *Haskala* pamphlet, which the other bookpeddler was only too glad to get rid of. As usual, Mendele's irony here cuts both ways. He satirizes not only the Jewish readers and their craving for the bizarre and the unreal but also the *maskilim* writers whose lugubrious, arid pamphlets do not stand the slightest chance of outselling such popular hits as the *Bovo-mayse*. Nevertheless, through Mendele's ironical remarks, Abramovitsh dialectically asserts the position of *his* "magic ring" as opposed to that of the legendary magic ring in terms of fact versus fiction. His is a "true story," a document, the real and perfectly plausible autobiography of a *shtetl*-born Jew, not the strange adventures of the imaginary prince *Bovo*. Besides, his "magic ring" is supposed to introduce a book on natural science, a sort of a popular encyclopedia full of scientifically verifiable facts.

This, of course, indicates the relation between the pretense of literary veracity in the writings of nineteenth-century Yiddish novelists and storytellers and their general intellectual commitment to the ideas of the *Haskala*. The disciples of the Jewish Enlightenment were imbued with rationalist and positivistic respect for logical analysis and for verifiable facts—hence their immense interest in natural science and the numerous books and articles they wrote on subjects ranging from chemistry and zoology to geography. (The first maskilic narratives in Yiddish were adaptations of books regarded as geographically and ethnographically edifying: Campe's version of *Robinson Crusoe* and his story of the discovery of America by Columbus, Cortés, and Pizarro.)[36] Moreover, the *maskilim* understood their bitter struggle against the *hasidim* as the struggle of truth against fancy and of fact against fiction. The great Hebrew satirist Y. Erter (1791–1851), who profoundly influenced many Yiddish writers, defined fiction in his satire "Khasidut vekhokhma" ("Hasidism and Enlightenment," 1836) as one of the major allies of hasidism. His allegorical embodiment of Enlightenment (a beautiful young woman, of course) promises to teach her followers geography, history, logic, psychology, political science, algebra, geometry, architecture, astronomy, meteorology, zoology, botany, even ballistics and navigation—in short, anything capable of verification by measurement or logical analysis.[37] The allegorical embodiment of hasidism (naturally, an ugly, noisy *yidene*) promises her adherents the deceptive charms of fiction, by which, she suggests, they will be able to rule and exploit the common people:

> I know, my son, the nature of people, the constitution of their minds. The common people have an overpowering desire to hear wondrous tales, and they relish hidden things, which no eye has seen. This is so because even before the child knows to refuse the evil and choose the good, his nurse tells him her tales of wonder, and with them she coaxes him to sleep in her lap when he cries. With the breath of her lips she creates in the heart of the boy or girl new heavens and a new earth; she fashions according to the wheel of her heart new creatures with which to populate the world she has called into being out of the void, and she arbitrarily regulates this her word-created world, as she wishes. Then the parents and the teachers strengthen this world in the heart of the child until it is established and cannot be moved for the rest of his life. When he grows up and becomes a man in the world, his eye yearns to see strange sights and cannot find a single one; he is overjoyed when he thinks he sees something wonderful, and his heart is sore saddened when he can see only his real surroundings. Then he complains of the Creator of all things on account of the order He imposed on the world and the compass He set upon it to check its tribulations.[38]

Fiction as such, not mere supernatural fiction, is branded here as an intellectual corrupter, an evil apostate. Indeed, the nurse referred to in this indictment of the imagination can be regarded as the allegorical representative of the art of fiction bent on corrupting minds and souls in the service of hasidism. This strongly negative attitude toward fiction was deeply rooted in the hearts of the *maskilim*. A. Mapu, the Hebrew novelist, was probably the only eminent *maskil* who cared to distinguish between "true fiction" and "false fiction" and who contended that only true fiction (i.e., rational, didactic, but still imaginative, colorful, and inspiring narrative) would stand a chance of curing the dangerous tendency of the Jewish people toward false fiction (i.e., supernatural, improbable narratives).[39] Most other *maskilim* believed that only exposure to scientifically asserted facts could have the necessary therapeutic effect.[40] It was not accidental that Mapu's novels, the first Hebrew novels, as much as they were enthusiastically received by what may perhaps be described as the Hebrew-reading public of the 1850s and 1860s, were frowned upon by some of the official exponents of the *Haskala* and were considered potentially dangerous merely for being fictitious.[41] Adult and reasonable people, it was argued, should not indulge themselves "in colorful soap bubbles—a proper plaything for silly urchins—which dissolve and evaporate even as they come into existence." [42]

If Hebrew fiction had to face such opposition, Yiddish maskilic fiction was in an infinitely worse position to assert the rights of its fictionality. Hebrew novels could always be justified on account of the dignity and self-sufficiency of the language or as demonstrations of the suitability of Hebrew to modern usage.[43] These justifications could not be applied to Yiddish. Here, as we have seen, the aesthetics of ugliness postulated the need for literal veracity. Allegedly lacking in stylistic dignity and barred from artistic self-sufficiency, a Yiddish narrative at least had to possess the merit of being unequivocally "true." Then again, maskilic Yiddish fiction was conceived of by its apologists as a subversive literary means whose mission was to explode the bizarre and heady mysticism by which the hasidic leadership allegedly drugged the masses. Was there a better stratagem for carrying out this mission than the fabrication of "true documents," secret correspondences (*Megale-tmirin*), confessions of a repentant, high-placed *hasid* (*Dos poylishe yingl*), a record of the chicaneries of the *tsadik* and his henchmen written by a member of the inner circle (*Gdules reb Volf*), etc.?

One can clearly see how all these mounting pressures were brought to bear on Abramovitsh as he began to develop his art of

Yiddish narrative. As a Hebrew writer, he was esteemed primarily for his textbook on zoology and for his numerous pseudoscientific articles. Expatiating in his first Hebrew novel on matters of literary ideology, his mouthpiece, David, the son of Elkana, mentions the popularization of the natural sciences as the first and major duty of Jewish literature and recommends, not without some reservations, a strictly realistic fiction based on precise knowledge of "the ways of nature" and directly corresponding to the realities of Jewish life.[44]

In shifting from Hebrew to Yiddish, resort to the fiction of literal veracity was, therefore, almost inevitable. What was necessary in Hebrew was doubly so in Yiddish, where the dubious protection of the pretension to immediate didactic usefulness was considered the only justification for writing at all. If he was to write fiction and do so in a "disreputable" language with no respectable literary tradition he could associate himself with, it was at least to be an immediately "useful" fiction and hence an obviously "true" one. He was going to bring the Jewish people to the world of facts (initially he planned to include in this world not only social and psychological facts but also biological, chemical, and geographical ones), and his stories in themselves were to be facts—given, indisputable pieces of reality, authentic social documents. "Whatever is written here is true; we swear by our *tales un kitl*," ° the senders of the manuscript of *The Tax* insist in their anonymous letter, and Mendele in his prologue adds his solemn protestation, "The story is true, I swear; I have added nothing to it from my imagination!" [45]

iv

These historical considerations bring us nearer to but do not reach the heart of the matter. What this study sets out to elucidate is not the mere creation of the fiction of Mendele but also the historical significance of its extraordinary development. The pressing need for a semblance of nonliterary factuality might have brought Abramovitsh to conceive of a Mendele mechanism as necessary for maintaining the fiction of literal veracity, but of itself it could not have brought him to conceive of Mendele as the rich and complex amalgam of character

---

° *Tales,* prayer shawl; *kitl,* the white garment worn on festive occasions. Having to do with prayer and holiness, these garments are fit objects on which to swear a solemn, binding oath.

and mask that he is, a figure consistently instrumental yet equally as consistent in transcending his instrumentality. As far as the mechanical needs of fictional veracity were concerned, Mendele could have been born as pale and as insignificant a fictional being as one of the imaginary editors of Defoe's novels, and like them, he could have repeated his little performance at the opening of each new narrative with little gain in significance or interest. But this, as we know, was not the case.

One may assume that at least for some time Abramovitsh actually wanted the readers to accept his Yiddish works as literally "true" as well as to believe in the historical reality of Mendele himself. We have his own word for the current notion that he molded the figure of Mendele after the model of a living Jewish bookpeddler, who "used to drag at that time [the early 1860s] with his horse and wagon in the neighborhood of Barditshev, which is none else than the well-known Glupsk," and he did it with the explicit intention of confusing the readers (of *Dos kleyne mentshele*) and making them identify the fictional character with the living person.[46] As we have learned from Y. Dinezon's memoirs, he succeeded in this, and at least some readers —probably many—were taken in.[47] The question of how long he was interested in maintaining this naive belief and at what point he started to sustain the Mendele fiction for artistic purposes (primarily or exclusively) cannot be answered with certainty. Perhaps we may be allowed to regard one of Mendele's little stratagems, which was employed by the author for several years and then dropped, as an indication of the duration of that phase in his career in which he insisted on the literal "authenticity" and historical truthfulness of the story and was maneuvering the simple reader into a position of unqualified belief in them. This stratagem, obviously intended to encourage such a belief, was Mendele's tendency to be specific in terms of place and particularly of time. This became evident in the opening passages of *Dos kleyne mentshele* (first version, 1864), where Mendele disclosed the date on which he was trusted with the manuscript of the story (upon his arrival in Glupsk on a Tuesday, Hanukkah, 5624). Of course, Mendele's calendar is Jewish; he "places" the story chronologically by relating it to the holidays.[48] Similar specific references to place and time occurred in *Dos vintshfingerl* (first version, 1865; the Sunday following *Shabes-nakhmu,*° in the summer of 5625; on the highway leading from Kabt-

° The Saturday following 9th Av.

sansk to Glupsk),[49] *Di takse* (1869, Sukkoth 5629),[50] and *Fishke der krumer* (first version, 1869, 17 Tammuz 5628).[51] The last evidence of this tendency of Mendele's toward chronological accuracy can be found in Abramovitsh's unfinished and unpublished story "Mayn (letste) nesie" ("My [Last] Trip"), written probably in 1870–1871.[52] From then on Mendele becomes vaguer in his chronology and volunteers no more precise dates. If this signifies the change in Abramovitsh's attitude toward the Mendele fiction, then it is from the early 1870s on that he did not as persistently demand the reader's belief in his hero's historical reality.

This, however, does not mean that even in his earliest appearances during the 1860s was Mendele employed as a mere automaton. From the start he was endowed with a vitality far in excess of the demands evoked by the sheer mechanics of his role. Later on, as we have seen, his importance constantly increased, and his technical functions were stretched and augmented to the point where they threatened the very mechanism of veracity which Mendele was supposed to operate. In order to understand this development historically, we have to look for motives, influences, and pressures which, if not altogether unrelated to those originating from the need for veracity, are yet distinctly different from them.

At this point we must re-examine the progress of Mendele as the entrepreneur of Abramovitsh's works and concentrate on one of the four phases, or stages, sketched in the preceding chapter; to wit, the third, the critical phase. We have already discerned that by 1878 Mendele had been raised from a "low" and relatively simple to a highly ambiguous position. What was his status now? Was he more than an author or less than one? He himself suggests that without his treatment the stories would remain devoid of literary interest, of taste and zest; he announces that they have been rewritten "freely and in his fashion"; he is to insinuate (in the 1888 *Vintshfingerl*) that they should be read "as if they were his." Yet he is still not prepared to support the full burden of genuine authorship. What can his literary brinkmanship, his acrobatics on the verge of authorship mean? We can break this question into two, more specific ones: first, Why did Abramovitsh elevate Mendele from the comfortable "lowness" of the two first phases to the perilous ambiguities of the third? and second, Why did Abramovitsh—once he had elevated him to these uncomfortable heights—not

let him take the next logical step and openly become a full-fledged
author?

The second of these questions seems to me more easily tackled,
and I shall begin with it. A simple and certainly not incorrect answer
to this question would be that, even in the advanced stages of his artistic career, Abramovitsh could not detach himself completely from the
fiction of literal veracity. The need for this protective fiction had been
so overwhelmingly impressed upon his literary consciousness, that it
had become an integral part of it; he could not, even if he wished, ignore it. This, however, is at best a partial answer, or rather, it is only a
restatement of the question in other terms, for in itself it implies a new
question: What made the impression left by the allegedly indispensable semblance of veracity so indelible? After all, Abramovitsh did not
remain prisoner to all the literary conventions he conformed to in his
youth; he had outgrown many of them. What prevented him from out-
growing this particular convention?

For a more satisfactory answer, we have to look more closely at the
nature and at the consequences of Abramovitsh's artistic experiments
in those two major works in which Mendele totters on the brink of authorship: *The Travels of Benjamin* and the 1888 version of *Dos
vintshfingerl*. What immediately strikes one as pertinent in this connection is that in these two works Abramovitsh, for the first time in his
career as a writer of Yiddish, shifted from first-person narrative to
third person. While, as already noted, he did introduce into the two
narratives short excerpts from the allegedly discarded originals (written, of course, in the first person), the bulk of the two texts was written
by the semiomniscient Mendele in the third person. This was for
Abramovitsh a bold experiment, a departure from his established manner into a literary area that until then had been explored in Yiddish
mainly by writers of limited or of no artistic sensibility, such as Dik,
Dinezon, and Shaykevitsh. What were the consequences of this experiment?

In *The Travels of Benjamin,* the third-person narration was handled with great success; the more ambitious experiment made in *Dos
vintshfingerl* began triumphantly, but after a short, felicitous progress,
sank into quicksands from which almost twenty years of grinding labor
did not really extricate it. Of course, this inequality of consequences
can be generally said to correspond to the difference in nature and

scope between the intentions Abramovitsh wanted to realize in the two works. *The Travels of Benjamin* is a relatively short, closely knit, perfectly sustained satire; in *Dos vintshfingerl* Abramovitsh attempted "an epic," a "history of Jewish life" in Russia. However, to bring this general difference to bear more directly on our discussion, we must isolate one aspect of it and concern ourselves only with the particular rhetorical quality of Mendele's narrative in the two works.

The Travels of Benjamin, if not necessarily the most interesting and meaningful of Abramovitsh's works, is certainly the most dazzling and absorbing rhetorical *tour de force* the author ever attempted. Its texture is extraordinarily tight and rich, varied yet yielding a unified effect. Its different threads crisscross each other, forming minute patterns, which in turn inform the whole work with larger unifying patterns that—thematically and philosophically—are perfectly in line with the author's satirical message. At the same time they exhibit an almost geometrical precision, as they relate formally to each other in parallelisms, symmetrical curves, tangential motions, and intersections.[53] The only aspect of this structural complexity that can be discussed here concerns what may be described as the "polyphony" or rhetorical parallelism of the work. In other words, it concerns the multiplicity and quick interchangeability of the authorial "voices" in it. That the story is being told by different voices and from different vantage points must be obvious to any reader with the slightest awareness of "the rhetoric of fiction." The author has no intention of camouflaging his shifts from one narrator to the other which occur throughout the story in quick succession. On the contrary, he almost calls attention to them as one realizes while reading the two first paragraphs of the first chapter:

> "All my days (so says Benjamin the Third himself)—until my great journey, that is—I have lived in Tuneyadevke. There I was born, there I was raised, and there I had the great good fortune to marry my spouse, the virtuous Zelde, may her days be long in the land!"
>
> Tuneyadevke is a little town, far, far out in the hinterland, so far removed from the great world that whenever, once in a blue moon, some traveler does chance to come, all the windows and doors are flung wide and people swarm to gawk at the newcomer. Leaning out of their windows the neighbors ask one another: "Who can this stranger be? Where does he hail from? Why has he picked out our town, of all places? What's behind all this? Nobody's going to come here without a good

reason! Something must be up; we've got to find out what's what!"
Whereupon each one becomes anxious to show his cleverness; conjectures of all sorts fly thick and fast. Old folks recall other strangers who
had visited their town in the past, in such and such a year. . . .[54]

The English translation hardly does justice (and perhaps cannot be expected to do justice)[55] to the stylistic differences between the two
paragraphs. Later on it will in many cases flatten the rich fusing of
voices of the original to a single stylistic pitch. Nevertheless, it sufficiently indicates two contradictory attitudes toward the story about
to be told. The voice of Benjamin himself, who launches the narrative,
is respectful and somewhat pompous. Obviously Benjamin takes himself and everything which has to do with his biography very seriously.
Mendele's attitude is openly satirical. Thus the first paragraph refers to
Tuneyadevke—in a grand Hebrew sentence (in the Yiddish original) as
the birthplace of a hero, which nourished and educated him, supplied
him with his "virtuous wife" (she is also referred to in Hebrew), prepared him for his great enterprise, and earned its fair place in the an-
nals of history. The second paragraph precipitates Tuneyadevke from
these heights. Its status is very low indeed, that of a backwater hamlet,
almost completely forgotten by the rest of humanity. Concentrating
on the description of the commotion caused in Tuneyadevke by an
unexpected visit of a stranger, Mendele emphasizes, as he does in
other descriptions of small *shtetlekh*, the static, almost paralytic quality of Tuneyadevke-like existence by contrasting it with its "opposite":
exaggerated, purposeless, and senseless activity. So far from being another Macedonia (Benjamin constantly compares himself with his
ideal: Alexander the Great) or Tudela ("Benjamin the First," a famous
medieval Jewish traveler, hailed from this Spanish town), the town is
ridiculously small and provincial.

This bivocalism is sustained throughout the story. It is constantly
being enriched and complicated by additional rhetorical elements,
such as a "low" element, supplied by a series of dialogues realistically
rendered in spoken, contemporary Yiddish, and a grotesquely "high"
one, supplied by systematical reference to old Hebrew books of legendary and mythological lore. Thus to the narrating voices of Mendele
and Benjamin other voices are added: those of living people in casual
conversation and those of "ancient authorities," which offer interesting bits of information, such as:

> There is a race in Brittany that has tails like animals, and in their
> midst one will come upon women tall and stalwart as Amazons, and
> their skins having bristles like unto those of swine.[56]

or a description of the terrible Kileyna:

> This monstrously huge fish becomes so encrusted with earth and
> grass that it takes on the aspect of an island. Voyagers, cruising by and
> deceived by its appearance, often beach their boats upon its back and
> even kindle a fire to cook their food. When the Kileyna feels the pene-
> trating heat, however, it dives to the very bottom of the ocean and all
> those encamped upon it find a watery grave.[57]

To all this one should add that each of the two principal narrators
in the story (Mendele and Benjamin) employs not one, but rather several "styles," according to the occasion. Benjamin expresses himself on
at least four different stylistic levels: (a) Describing moments of great
tension in his adventures he may resort to a clumsy, redundant version
of the poetic "sublime" (see, for instance, his rendering of the anxiety
and relief he experienced while waiting for his "mate," Senderl, who
was late for their rendezvous on the morning scheduled for their secret
departure from Tuneyadevke and, seeing him coming, at long last:
"Even as the hart panteth after the water of the brook, . . . as the
desert-parched traveler rejoiceth when he cometh upon fresh waters
of a mountain stream, so did I pant after and rejoice over Senderl, my
tried and true companion").[58] (b) More common in his narrative is the
style of the ceremonial biography, which was already illustrated by the
opening paragraph of the story. (c) Long passages allegedly quoted
from Benjamin's "works" are imitations of "scientific" travelogues. In
these Benjamin imparts geographical, historical, and ethnographic "information," supplementing it with observations and comments that
smack of medieval scholasticism (since Benjamin's models are the famous Hebrew medieval travelogues) and the rhetoric of "scholarly"
polemics. It is in these passages that most of the quotations from medieval literature occur. (d) From time to time Benjamin loses control
over his narrative and fails to preserve the dignity of tone befitting the
history of a world-famous traveler. On these occasions he may stoop to
such petty complaints, insignificant details, and low style as one encounters, for instance, in his description of the techniques of harass-
ment one of his enemies in the town of Teterivke used against him:
"No sooner would I doze off in the synagogue than he would tickle the
soles of my feet with a straw, or blow smoke up my nose through a
paper squib. I would start awake, frightened out of my wits, coughing
and wheezing from the vile smoke. . . ."[59]

Benjamin's stylistic versatility is, however, a mere trifle when compared with that of Mendele, who incessantly changes rhetorical masks.
As a matter of fact, Mendele's "voice" rarely stays the same for more
than one paragraph at a time, and very often the voice is drastically
changed within one and the same paragraph. The following list of
eight(!) different Mendelean "styles" in *The Travels of Benjamin* is by
no means exhaustive. It illustrates only some of the variations of Mendele's mimicry in this work.

1. The grand style of the epic poet or of the writer of a grandilo-
quent romance. Mendele employs here various mock-heroic devices.
He abounds with "Homeric" or "epic" similes. When Benjamin,
stranded in the sluggish town of Teterivke, loses momentum under the
influence of the place, Mendele comments: "He was in great danger of
getting lost there, even as a ship which has strayed into the motionless
sea,° and he would still have been there, wasting his life in slumber,
were it not for an incident which—fortunately for him and for the rest
of the world—chased him out of there like a gale and forced him to
continue his voyage." [60] He indulges in mock-allusions, such as the
comparison of Benjamin and a calf, who happen to sleep side by side
in a squalid inn in the village of Pyevke, to Saul and Jonathan, whom
David in his lamentation described as "lovely and pleasant in their
lives and in their death they were not divided." (II Sam. 1:23.) Benjamin and the calf are referred to as "lovely and pleasant in the corner
and in the puddle they were not divided." [61] Above all else, Mendele
in his capacity as a poet of the mock-epic is the master of the heightened situation, of the aggrandizement of gesture. One illustration can
sufficiently establish this. Here is the description of the morning of
Benjamin's departure from Tuneyadevke. Having sneaked away from
his sleeping wife, Benjamin waits for Senderl with a glowing feeling of
achievement and with the greatest expectations:

> Meanwhile the glowing sun gradually came up on the horizon,
> brightening the entire countryside. Its radiance had an exhilarating
> effect on all things. The trees and grass welcomed it, smiling through
> their tears of dew, like children bursting into laughter when shown a
> gaudy plaything. Birds were wheeling and chirping around Benjamin, as
> though in salutation:

° "The motionless sea," or (interchangeably) "the frozen sea" indicates a specific
lethal sea in legendary Jewish geography, and is mentioned several times in modern Jewish literature.

"Come, let us cheer and sing a paean of triumph to the great person-
age standing near the windmill—let us sing to Benjamin of Tuneyadevke, the Alexander of Macedon of his time, who is leaving his wife
and children behind him to embark on a holy mission, going wherever
his eyes may lead him! There he stands, the great Benjamin who, like
the sun, has left his night's shelter, anxious to set foot on the path of adventure! With the prowess of a leopard and the swiftness of an eagle he
is prepared to do the will of our Father in heaven! Warble and trill,
break into song, so that his heart may be gladdened and rejoice!" [62]

We cannot enter here into the host of allusions upon which this rather
obvious piece of mock-heroic depends for its effect (for example, the
prowess of a leopard and the swiftness of an eagle are traditional attributes of God). Nor does the quality of the translation justify an elaborate analysis. A general impression of Mendele's posture as the Virgil
of Benjamin's mock-*Aeneid* will have to suffice.

2. In direct opposition to this posture stands Mendele in his role as
the avowedly satirical observer, whose function is to reduce Benjamin's "adventure" to its tiny, insignificant dimensions, not by blowing
it up to the point of bursting but rather by making it shrink and shrivel
under his corrosive examination. This has already been illustrated by
the description of Tuneyadevke in the opening paragraphs, and it can
be further illustrated by passages from every episode in the story (see,
for instance, the encounter of Benjamin and Senderl with the peasant
after their "triumphant" departure from Tuneyadevke in Chap. 5).

3. Different from both the mask of the bard and that of the satirical
observer is Mendele's mask as the author of a traditional Yiddish
mayse-bikhl; a naive and conventional storyteller of the old school,
who connects the different parts of his fable with such formulae as
"Let's leave now the princess, that is, Senderl, to her talk with the innkeeper and turn to the prince, Benjamin, to see how he fares and what
he is doing." [63] It is he who opens new paragraphs with formulaic
pseudobiblical Hebrew sentences as "Ish ekhod hoyo betuneyadevke,"
"There was a certain man of Tuneyadevke," "ushmoy Senderl," "and
his name was Senderl" [64] (cf. I Sam. 1:1); and who indulges in conventional gestures of "professional" coyness: "No pen would be able to
describe how happy, how overjoyed they were at that time." [65] It is
the task of this storyteller to express naive admiration for Benjamin
and develop a respectful intimacy between him and the reader; an intimacy totally different from the condescending and contemptuous

one expressed by the satirist in his constant references to Benjamin
and Senderl as "undzere parshoynen" (an expression that can be understood in many ways: "our people," "our beauties," "our person-
ages," "our characters").

4. Diametrically opposed to this author of a *mayse-bikhl* is a modern, secular author who from time to time comes to the fore, forces the
story out of its world of mock-mythology or naive fable, and places it
within a modern historical and psychological framework. This is the
author who pinpoints the date of Benjamin's voyage and relates it to
current historical events (the date is 1855–56, as we learn from the attitudes of the different factions in the synagogue of Teterivke toward
Benjamin. These attitudes are determined by their "political" bias toward one of the powers taking part in the then raging Crimean War
(see the opening paragraph of Chap. 7). His is the pathetic comment
on the atrocities perpetrated by the Jewish *kahal* and its henchmen
the *khapers* ("kidnappers"), who kidnapped boys as well as defenseless
adults and delivered them to the authorities of the Russian army in
lieu of the richer members of the community whose turn it was to be
drafted (see Chap. 12). His are also the seriously meant comments on
the protagonists' characteristics (see, for instance, the comparison between Senderl and Benjamin—a home-bred turkey and a real migra-
tory bird—in Chap. 13).

5. Another authorial voice manipulated by Mendele expresses ob-
tuse "psychological" and "philosophical" observations, which of
course are not meant to be taken seriously. In fact, the "reflections" of
this pompous ass are often made to conceal a satirical hint, which he
himself is not supposed to understand (see, for instance, the elaborate
and deliciously stupid argument on the connection between seemingly
insignificant causes and their "important, very important consequences," which follows the discussion of the trivial causes which subsequently brought about Benjamin's decision to leave his home town
and set out to visit the Ten Lost Tribes. It concludes the first chapter
of the story).[66] This is the voice of an author of Benjamin's history who
allegedly believes in the historical importance of his subject and of his
own task and who takes upon himself to accompany this history of an
illustrious personality with edifying comments on the nature of human
greatness and the difficulties and misunderstandings it must encounter
in our lowly world (see the opening remarks in Chap. 9 starting with

"Reading the histories of illustrious intellectuals one cannot but sigh and groan," etc.).[67]

6. In long stretches of his narrative Mendele seems to do no more than repeat Benjamin's own words in the third person and in indirect speech, allowing himself from time to time to shorten or condense his original and on occasion even to leave out sections of considerable length that deal with matters he considers immaterial or too offensive to merit repetition.[68] In this role he seems faithfully to copy all Benjamin's various styles, from the poetic and florid through the obtusely "learned" to the conversational and "low." However, he manages, of course, through various and subtle techniques, which cannot be adequately illustrated without reference to the Yiddish original, to distort Benjamin's prose, to slightly "heighten" it and make it more pompous than it should be, or to present it in such a selective manner as to make bathetic falls from higher to lower levels of decorum even more crass and ridiculous. On the face of it, this mask of Mendele is that of the faithful editor, i.e., the one Mendele said in his prologue he was going to adopt in order to present his "Jewish brethren" with at least a concise version of Benjamin's own books. Actually, this mere repetition is one of his sharpest satirical tools.

7. At the same time Mendele is also the observer and commentator, who stands far above everybody else in the story, "explains" and evaluates the characters' behavior. He may do this in various ways, such as a direct, discursive evaluation ("One must also say that the inhabitants of Tuneyadevke, to their credit, are . . .")[69] or occasionally, in a reporter's interview:

> Just ask a Tuneyadevke Jew (do it suddenly, however): "How do you get along?" He'll seem flustered, not knowing what answer to make at first, but on regaining his composure he'll answer you in all seriousness: "How do I get along, you ask? Ours is a kind Lord, I'm telling you, Who never forsakes His creatures! He supplies their needs and, I'm telling you, He'll go on supplying them!"
> "Yes, but just what do you do for a living? Have you a trade of any kind, maybe, or a little business?" . . .[70]

8. Finally, with all these tasks on his hands Mendele does not forget his old, well-established manner of chatting with the readers, straying "beside the point" of his narrative, making his witty, seemingly superfluous remarks, and even waxing epigrammatic ("Death is

the end of man and taxes the end of the Jew").[71] Admittedly, he cannot indulge here in such pleasant off-the-record chats as often as in some of Abramovitsh's other works. He is too busy for that.

The Travels of Benjamin is obviously a hilarious rhetorical feast, a work as playful (while being almost deadly in its satirical ferocity and saeva indignatio)[72] as any in Jewish and perhaps world literature.[73] To realize the full extent of Abramovitsh's rhetorical virtuosity one has to keep in mind that, on the one hand, all the above listed "voices"—not only those of Mendele but also those of Benjamin and others—are in constant flow and mutual interpenetration, and on the other hand, the whole noisy orchestra is perfectly tuned. It never gets out of hand, never violates the strict, formalistic rules of the author's composition. By realizing this one also realizes what the position of Mendele in this composition actually is. By assuming in part the responsibilities of direct authorship in The Travels of Benjamin and with them some of the functions of the omniscient narrator (such as knowledge of dreams, inarticulate feelings of the protagonists, etc.), Mendele never for a moment ceases to be the theatrical performer par excellence that he has always been. On the contrary, never in his whole career is he as wholeheartedly the aktyor ("actor," "impersonator") or the circus acrobat as he is in this opus, the most spectacular of all his "numbers." For who lets Benjamin talk, only to undercut him with a sarcastic remark? Who constantly pits one quotation against the other? Where does the narrator stand while the wise birds of Tuneyadevke encircle Benjamin with the crown of their paean in a scene of mock-adoration? What are the purposes of this ventriloquist who constantly changes his manifold voices? Obviously, it is Mendele the conférencier who does all this. He stands, as ever, near the footlights of the stage on which the brilliantly lit scenes follow each other in quick succession, he faces us, his audience, with a significant smirk and a knowing wink and manipulates us as well as the characters who are going through their parts behind his back. His purpose here, as everywhere, is to make his presence (whenever he appears) the basic reality of the story. He is immeasurably more vital than the objects and the people he describes. While he is the wizard, they are mere puppets and scenery.

Thus, so far from being forced in The Travels of Benjamin to face the basic artistic problems of the third-person mode (which in his case were all pointing to one need: the need for a narrative voice more abstract, less dramatic than that of Mendele the monologist, of Fishke, or

of Yitskhok Avrom; the need, in short, of replacing the dramatic mode
of narration by an epic one), Abramovitsh developed it as his ultimate
and most successful dramatic performance. This, however, did not
happen in *Dos vintshfingerl*, his second major work in which Mendele
assumes authorial responsibilities; or rather, it did happen, to a much
lesser extent in the first and most vital books of *Dos vintshfingerl*, and
then somehow the dramatic vivacity of Mendele's tone gradually pe-
ters out. As the story progresses toward wider historical prospects and
more complex psychological situations the need to establish the more
abstract, nondramatic narrative tone becomes imperative. Mendele attempts to do it—halfheartedly—and is often caught off his guard. This
is for him a foreign and unfriendly territory. One can see why his long
voyage through it never reaches its destination.

Superficially there seems to be no sufficient reason for such a difference between the two works. In both Mendele allegedly uses texts
which he quotes wherever they are "pertinent"; the basic rhetorical
structure of the stories could, therefore, be the same. But it is not.
Compared with the complex polyphony of *The Travels of Benjamin*,
the vocal orchestration of *Dos vintshfingerl* seems confined, rigid, and
unimaginative. In the first book, concentrating on the description of
Hershele's childhood in Kabtsansk, Mendele *does* quote the "original"
autobiography of Hershele several times. Later on, however, he seems
to have no use for this quotation technique, and he lets himself as well
as the reader forget about the alleged existence of an "original" text
and lose awareness of the particular status of the novel as an adaptation of that original. Never, not even in the first book, does he use the
quotation technique as vivaciously and successfully as he has used it in
The Travels of Benjamin. The reason for this becomes obvious once a
comparison is attempted between the quotations from Benjamin's
works and those from Hershele's autobiography. While the thematic
and stylistic relationships between the original Benjamin excerpts and
the Mendelean context which surrounds them are always those of innocence versus experience, naive, if not downright stupid, use of language and ideas versus the crafty machinations of a mastermind with
all the resources of language and techniques of argument at its command, the equivalent relationships between the Hershele excerpts and
their Mendelean contexts are by far duller and less useful. What are
the basic distinctions, one may ask, between Hershele's direct memoiristic description of his father as a rooster who (with all his love for his

family) vehemently protects his dominant position in the pecking order of the family,[74] and Mendele's satirical reference to the sexual intercourse that resulted in the conception of Hershele as the mounting of a quacking, submissive hen by a domineering rooster?[75] Or what is the essentially new element that Hershele contributes to Mendele's satirical description of Kabtsansk as a human factory, producing human merchandise for export,[76] with his own satirical rendering of the grotesquely "economic," *do ut des* relationship of the *Kabtsansker* and God? [77] Isn't he actually extending Mendele's satire, developing its well-known motifs, rather than qualifying it by applying a different perspective to the description of his home town? At the most he adds to the satire some softening lines, one or two redeeming features, but even in these he only echoes Mendele's bursts of compassion, which in this novel accompany the satire from the very start (compare the satirical first chapter of the first book with the pathetic, at times sentimental, second chapter).

While in the prologue to *Dos vintshfingerl* Hershele and Mendele represented totally different approaches to Jewish life, thus providing the author with many opportunities for subtle and hilarious juxtaposition, in the text of the novel itself they are rarely antagonistic. The fact is that here Hershele's view of his life is too similar to that of Mendele, and therefore it could not be of much use. This becomes truer as the novel develops. Gradually the subtle differentiation between Mendele and Hershele, so brilliantly worked out in the prologue, disappears. This makes a distanced account of Hershele's development more and more difficult for Mendele, who is subsequently edged out of his habitual track of satire, parody, and double talk into the path of straightforward third-person narrative. With him this path of the righteous narrator cannot be but somewhat dull. This does not mean that he cannot, from time to time, set off little fireworks and rekindle for a moment the old brilliance. However, he can do this only when his attention is turned from his protagonists—Hershele, Beyle, Rephoel, Moyshele, etc.—to the community. The first book of *Dos vintshfingerl* is so well written because in it Mendele is required to comment very little on Hershele as an individual. Instead he portrays the grotesque "world" of Kabtsansk as the milieu that molded Hershele's consciousness. As long as he is doing that he can sustain beautifully his dramatic presence as commentator and raconteur. The whole first book and large sections of the second can be felt and believed in as monologues of

Mendele. They are more restrained and narrative than Mendele's monologues usually are, but they still are unmistakably his, spoken by his own voice. However, as the line of the story emerges from the early childhood of Hershele and from the exclusive world of the Jewish community, Mendele begins to falter; his voice becomes depersonalized, but he cannot really settle for the unobtrusive existence of a concealed narrator. He cannot cease to be his voluble, interfering, commenting, monologizing self, but his loquacity is no longer artistically reliable. On short holidays from the task of regular narration, he may still come up with a delicious little paean to the crooked Jewish nose (Part IV, Chap. 1) or compose a brilliant mythological tale about the origins of the town of Glupsk, which allegedly was founded by Mercury, the God of Commerce, and was then inhabited by bankrupt Jewish merchants from India, who cruised along the river Gnilopyatke.[78] But then, turning back to the protagonists and their story, his artistic presence becomes a thing indistinct and undistinguished. He goes on talking, but he leaves firm ground behind; occasionally, he falls into an artistic void. Whose voice recites this elementary, textbook lecture on recent Jewish history in Russia?

> At that time—forty, fifty years ago—the long, dark night of Jewish life in our country [i.e., in Russia] began to draw toward dawn. A fresh breeze began to blow lightly from the West, to drive away the heavy clouds from above the narrow streets of the Jewish ghetto, and the Enlightenment, like the morning star, began to reach even there with its rays. At this hour of dawn a small part of the Jewish people rose early and began to study; among them some whose eyes were still filmy with sleep, their thoughts still confused. Like crazy people, they began to rush, struggle, and in their hustle they knocked things over, broke, caused damage. The majority of the people did not bother to move from their place; they only got angry and grumbled because their sleep was disturbed. . . .[79]

This is surely a piece of very poor, indeed, of inferior writing. Not a sentence is free of clichés; the metaphors and similes are unbelievably stale. The whole passage develops the hackneyed equations used and abused thousands of times by numerous maskilic writers: the time prior to the *Haskala*—a "long, dark night"; to become a *maskil*—to be roused from a heavy slumber; to oppose the *maskilim*—to persist in slumber. And then the long line of well-worn threadbare expressions: "the long, dark night," "to drive away the heavy clouds," "the narrow

streets of the Jewish ghetto," etc. Not one ironic wink enlivens this pedantic repetition of maskilic formulae, which for all its concessions to
the critics of the *Haskala*, is smug and pompous, and because of its
stale language, utterly unreal. Is this the shrewd, ironic, equivocating,
superbly intelligent Mendele we encountered in the prologue to *Dos
vintshfingerl*? The truth is that Abramovitsh had no adequate instruments for the epic, "historical" novel he wanted to write. His Mendele
would not suffice for it, and to create another, more suitable instrument was beyond his artistic means. One is allowed perhaps to guess
that this was the main reason for his inability to finish the novel. The
further he got the more bewildering his task became, the poorer and
more arbitrary the results. Abramovitsh's art could not survive the loss
of dramatic immediacy. It is not to be wondered then that Abramovitsh recoiled from the cold world of the concealed author and of the
third-person narrator and retreated to more familiar territory, where
his Mendele could occupy his natural position of ironic commentator
and witty entertainer.

v

This, it seems to me, answers the question of why Abramovitsh had
to check the development of his Mendele at the ambiguous phase between editorship and authorship. Now, however, we can raise the
more acute question of why he allowed him to go even this far.
Granted that having reached a certain stage in Mendele's development, Abramovitsh could not go on widening his function without
risking the effectiveness of the fictional machine, which it was Mendele's task to activate; but why had he begun to widen it in the first
place? Why had he not left his Mendele in the position he had held in
the early versions of *Dos kleyne mentshele* and *Dos vintshfingerl*?
What made him tamper with the simple and seemingly convenient arrangement he had devised in these early stories and lead his Mendele
to an impasse?

The answer to these questions must be that the initial arrangement, simple though it was, did not satisfy him artistically because it
left the bulk of his stories confined within the narrow sphere of the
consciousness and style of their protagonist. In both the first *Kleyn
mentshele* and the first *Vintshfingerl*, once Mendele has done with his
introduction, the story depends on Yitskhok Avrom or on Hershele and

on them alone. Since both are supposed to be autobiographical documents they cannot transcend their limitation. They can possess only the vitality and wisdom their characters can impart to them, and that, Abramovitsh must have realized at quite an early stage, was not sufficient. Reading the two early stories, one cannot but be struck by the artistic gap between the excellent prefatory addresses by Mendele and the stories themselves. The former are so vivid that they are inevitably followed by a gradual but disastrous anticlimax. In both stories the fall from Mendele's prologues is somewhat cushioned by the initial sections or units in the protagonists' stories, which are by far more vivid and artistic than those to follow. Both stories deal in different ways with the problems of traditional Jewish education and its allegedly pernicious consequences, and they tend to fall into three sections: the first describes the "world" or the educational system that molded, and allegedly distorted, the protagonists in their childhood; the second describes the protagonists' adolescence or "maturing," when they finally grasped the basic presuppositions inherent in their education (in *Dos kleyne mentshele* the hero finally learns the meaning of the title: in order to survive and succeed one must become a ruthless egoist; in *Dos vintshfingerl* the hero religiously adopts the concept of "the magic ring"—i.e., of a passive expectance of a miraculous change in one's life—and is ready to accept the poverty and helplessness of his parents and home town); the third section shows the consequences of this "educational" process, explains in what way the protagonists came to realize how distorted was the world into which it introduced them, and recommends radical changes in Jewish education. This third section, being written in both stories in the form of a homily, is where the anticlimax is reached and where the tone of crass maskilic propaganda prevails. In the opening sections of the narratives the narrators are allowed to assume a somewhat distanced position, from which they can describe the world of their childhood with empathy restrained by a sense of humor. Nevertheless, it is even in these opening sections with their relatively successful combination of sentiment and comedy that we realize the artistic inferiority of the protagonists when compared with Mendele. As soon as we leave Mendele's prologues behind us and start to read the autobiographies, we experience that sense of "power failure," of dimming lights, that was to follow, even in Abramovitsh's most mature works, the exit of Mendele from the narrative arena. This is particularly obvious in the early *Vintshfingerl*, where the possibilities dormant in the Mendele fiction were developed with astounding dexterity. In *Dos kleyne mentshele*, published only a year before, they had been only half realized. Now Mendele suddenly flourished, and his prologue (which occupied more than a quarter of the entire work) strongly indicated the artistic dimensions he was to achieve later on. Brilliant nature descriptions, ironic ambiguities, subtle insinuations, seemingly free and natural movement of "idealized" spoken Yiddish, as well as other prominent Mendele features—they are all there, although in a rudimentary form. The protagonist's story, however, remained here as simplistic, primitive, and rigid as that of the early *Kleyn mentshele*, and the contrast between the "story about a story" (as Mendele's prologue was titled in this instance) and "the story itself" became so pronounced as to make their coexistence in time and place enigmatic; it seems that the introduction was written by a different artist, an artist more talented and maturer by far. The reason is not merely that Mendele is so much more lively a character than Hershele, but rather that Mendele and Hershele, as dramatic characters, belong to different orders. The positions and attitudes that can be assumed by a character like Mendele cannot be assumed a priori by a character like Hershele. Take, for example, their respective stands on the matter of books and learning. It is Hershele's function to "seriously" recommend books and learning; it is Mendele's privilege to treat them ambiguously. Hershele must perform the maskilic task the author assigned to his book; Mendele can afford to remain aloof; he can even afford to deflate Hershele's scholarly pathos. Bringing his autobiography to its conclusion, Hershele indulges in a long sermon on the importance of learning that culminates in the following recommendation:

> In this book I took it upon myself to describe in a simple, easy language all the sciences and all the branches of knowledge through which every man can obtain the true, natural magic ring. Study it, Jewish people! Study and you will be happy, as King Solomon said: "Ashre odem matso khokhme"; that is, "Happy is the man that findeth wisdom." [80]

This display of pomposity is immediately deflated by a postscript of Mendele's that opens with the urgent demand, "Zhid, davay hroshi" (a Ukrainian phrase: "Jew, hand over your pennies"), a fitting antidote to the biblical Hebrew of Proverbs. The word *Zhid* and the employment of a rude expression (the equivalent of a highwayman's "Stand and deliver") suddenly bring the subject of books and learning down to its economic preliminaries: to have books and learning, one must pay for them. "I am a poor Jew," Mendele explains, "I have been now a Jewish bookpeddler for thirty years and I'm still a pauper!" Then he instructs the interested subscribers how to send their money so that he can go on with the printing of Hershele's compilation, warning them not to send him their torn bills, etc.[81] Mendele does not contradict Hershele; he reduces his flourishes to their commercial value, and thereby he achieves not only a livelier and a more entertaining tone but actually a much wider and more balanced exposition of the subject of books and their importance. We have already seen how Mendele's confession in the prologue to the early *Vintshfingerl*, that he would "gladly trade all the *Haskala* books in the world for one *Mayse-bukh* or a couple of *Magic Rings*," scourges both the readers of the popular legendary literature and the incompetent writers of the *Haskala* books. There can be no doubt that Mendele with his keen, double-edged intelligence probes into the problem of the value of books in general and of the maskilic literature in particular much more deeply than Hershele. The difference is not so much one of sheer intelligence as it is one of position. Mendele, we feel, is a freer agent than Hershele. Printing and selling Hershele's book, he can also pass judgment on it; in his comments he can imply a scale of values wider than the one inherent in the book itself; as the commentator, the chorus, the masked *eiron*, he represents a more comprehensive understanding than any of the characters who take direct part in the story.

It is quite obvious that, as Abramovitsh matured artistically, he found the comprehensiveness of Mendele's understanding more necessary and the confinement to the directly dramatic presentation of the stories through their protagonists more cramping. We can mark the years 1867–1869 as a time of major crisis in this respect. During these years Abramovitsh embarked on several literary projects, all of which indicate his impatience with this narrowly dramatic system of representation.

First, he revised for publication his early Hebrew novel *Limdu hetev* (now entitled *Ha'avot vehabanim*), a narrative written throughout in the third-person mode under the full control of an omniscient author and without any mediatory intervention of Mendele or another persona.

Second, he wrote his first play, *The Tax*. Here too he was, of course, confined to direct dramatic representation, but at least he was not at the mercy of one dramatic character; or even a small group of dramatic characters. *The Tax* is not a drama of individuals; in it vast groups chant their lines in choral fashion, assigning the expression of their attitudes to their numerous members. Nothing further from the narrowness of the single consciousness of a Yitskhok Avrom or a Hershele can be imagined. One can easily see how much duller *The Tax* would have been had it been presented as an autobiographical document written by Shloyme Veker, its *maskil* protagonist.

Third, he wrote *Fishke der krumer*, a narrative constructed in such a way as to enable Mendele largely to dominate it even while letting the protagonist tell his story. The basic technical differences between *Fishke* and the earlier works, which made this new position of Mendele possible, have already been discussed.[82] One should add here, however, that it is not only through his ability to interrupt Fishke in order to edit his story and to contrast it with other stories, that Mendele is able to project himself here into the whole structure of the work and condition its texture. He does this in many other, subtler ways. For instance, he prepares the background for Fishke's story, which forms the second major structural unit in this bipartite work, with a change in the weather. While the first unit, which includes a mercilessly comic description of Fishke and his marriage (as well as a host of sarcastic remarks on Jewish matchmaking, weddings, bathhouses, etc.), was dominated by a blazing sun and was full of aridity, thirst of man and cattle, sweating bodies, and hot, stagnant air, the second unit—in which Fishke will tell his story "from within"—is announced with a description of the influence of a cool evening breeze. Nature is being transformed; its harsh lines are softened, even blurred in the twilight. Its thirst is quenched by the settling dampness. With nature we too are being softened, prepared for a new, sympathetic, or even sentimental attitude toward Fishke. Here Mendele, who brings to the fore his acclaimed talent for description, obviously conditions the tone of the work as a whole.[83]

Fourth, Abramovitsh embarked during these years on a project about which little is known, and that little was almost never made use of. He attempted to create a new *eiron*, one that was destined to employ ironic devices entirely different from those of Mendele, to use a totally different style and address himself to matters by and large beyond Mendele's reach. This projected *eiron* was to be an intellectual, a *maskil*, who unlike Mendele would have been both able and willing to discuss in abstract terms problems involving the whole history of the Jewish people, their religion and historical institutions, to offer new and (from the vantage point of a *maskil*) heretical observations on the *positive* role of the hasidic movement in the historical process of liberation from the dead letter of the rabbinical law in Jewish life, and also to re-examine the current maskilic prognosis concerning the allegedly benevolent intentions of the czarist regime toward the Jewish population of the Russian Empire. In order to be able to function—both as an ideological and an artistic vehicle—this *eiron* had to be mad. His madness seemed to offer the author a whole series of ironic stratagems that could not be employed within the framework of the Mendele fiction and that would have allowed him to extend the intellectual scope of his works without falling into the trap of sheer discursiveness and loss of the all-important maneuverability between the differing positions of "the Jew" and "us," of tradition and modernism. Thus Abramovitsh was preparing himself for the writing of a whole cycle of new works dominated by either several mad *eirons* or by the one, who finally was called *Yisrolik der meshugener* ("Yisrolik the Madman," Berl and Hershele were earlier, tentative names) and who eventually became known to the readers only as the protagonist of *Di klyatshe* (*The Nag*). Actually *Di klyatshe* was supposed to form only the first volume in an extensive series of Yisrolik's "Complete Works," where he would have superseded Mendele as an ironic commentator and monologist, although he would not necessarily have eliminated him altogether. (A long monologue of Yisrolik's was published in 1875, signed not by Mendele but by "A. Y. Sh.," the pseudonym Abramovitsh used both in the first *Kleyn mentshele* when published in book form and in the first *Vintshfingerl*).[84] The significance of this only half-realized plan of Abramovitsh's should be quite clear. It indicates impatience on his part with the limitations of Mendele as an *eiron* who had to protect his "folksy" mask from the intrusion of any easily detectable "foreign" or "modern" feature. He also wanted to create a figure who, unlike Mendele, would be able to hold the position of the main or perhaps the sole speaker in his works, not merely their announcer. That the plan remained for the most part unrealized is, however, also significant.

vi

During the 1870s Abramovitsh discovered that his Mendele was more essential than perhaps he himself had formerly imagined. He could not be safely superseded by another *eiron*; nor could he be replaced by an omniscient narrator. Whenever he tried to break away from him altogether (in the *feuilleton* "Yidishe kinder," in the long allegorical poem *Yidl*, 1875), the artistic consequences were disappointing (the poem, perhaps the only Yiddish work the author published under his full name, Sh. Y. Abramovitsh, without any reference to Mendele, proved a most embarrassing artistic *faux pas*). Little wonder, then, that he let Mendele grow. Rewriting *Dos kleyne mentshele* (a much-enlarged version appeared in 1879), he broke into Yitskhok Avrom's story several times to make room for Mendele's comments. He also added to the story the detailed self-introductory Mendele prologue, which has already been mentioned several times. Slowly extending and complicating *Fishke der krumer* (second version, left unpublished, 1876;[85] third version, 1888) he steadily developed Mendele's part in it until the "frame" became larger and more conspicuous than the picture itself. Above all else, he decided, as we have seen, to make Mendele the cowriter of *The Travels of Benjamin* (1878) and the 1888 *Vintshfingerl*, so that he would not have to rely solely, or even mainly, on Benjamin and Hershele.

We can detect here two forces or pressures forming the artistic development of the Mendele fiction: on the one hand, a force driving Abramovitsh to get as far as he could from the narrowness of direct dramatic presentation, from protagonists telling their own "true" stories; on the other hand, the force confining him to direct dramatic presentation because of the lack of instruments for a successful artistic employment of the third-person narrative. In other words, Abramovitsh aspired to more than dramatic monologues, but he could not offer anything better; he tried to move away from utter subjectivity, but he had no means of detaching his story completely from the fictional consciousness of his heroes. When he tried to overreach himself and assume the position of the omniscient narrator (in *Dos vintshfingerl*, 1888) his sure artistic grip began to slacken. This was his dilemma; between these two pressures his art was caught. But Abramovitsh was an expert in dealing with difficult situations and in detecting the point where two contending forces would neutralize each other and allow him free play. If he could not bring the two circles into congruence, he could at least locate the tiny dot at which they were tangent: Mendele the Bookpeddler.

An ironic commentator, removed from the narrative itself, Mendele had the power to widen the horizons of the stories he introduced, to counterbalance their subjectivity with his equivocations, to neutralize their affirmations by his doubts. A superb monologist himself, he could, however, also ensure Abramovitsh's works a margin of artistic safety by retaining them within the familiar sphere of the dramatic. Thus, he brought to these works an optimum measure of freedom and objectivity without breaking their dramatic mold. That is why whenever he comes into a story (except for the few cases where Abramovitsh forced upon him tasks to which he was unequal), he brings with him a gust of fresh air, a flow of vitality. With his entrance, the stories warm up, move more freely, their heavy, clogging subjectivity melts away.

It is now perfectly understandable why his presence in these works becomes steadily more prominent, and why at last Abramovitsh let him inundate entire narratives. No Jedediah Cleishbotham was ever as necessary as Mendele. No imaginary editor or publisher offered so much where so little was available. That is why the dot was allowed to cover the picture. What I referred to in the preceding chapter as the fourth phase in Mendele's development was virtually the corollary of tight, unremitting artistic mathematics: if the story could not be narrated in any but the monologue form and yet the author aspired to achieve it in a maximal freedom, then he somehow had to come up with a narrative recited dramatically by a character who (a) was thoroughly familiar with the subject of the narrative; yet (b) was capable of detaching himself from the subject; and (c) was capable, to a considerable extent, of detaching himself from himself. In other words, he needed a character who was an insider and yet an outsider; a character who was endowed not only with irony but also with self-irony. In short, he needed someone very like Mendele the Bookpeddler.

As we have seen, Abramovitsh felt this need from the very start. Having had the great luck of discovering his Mendele in his first Yiddish story, he immediately employed him beyond the call of technical duty. Later on, he ceaselessly sought ways and means to let Mendele play bigger parts. He ended by constructing his entire literary world around him. It should, however, be remembered that he also knew where to stop him. The fiction of Mendele became the liberating force in nineteenth-century Yiddish literature not only because of its vitality and sheer force, but also because on the whole it was kept within proper limits; because Abramovitsh did not persist in trying to do with it more than he safely could. This too was one of his great contributions to the education of Yiddish literature as it grew to maturity. As he went on experimenting with Mendele, exploring and enlarging his functions, he had the sense to discover in time the limitations of his innovation, and thus he taught two or three generations of fiction writers an invaluable lesson in literary economics, in the art of distinguishing the possible from the impossible, the proper from the improper under given circumstances.

vii

At this point, a comparison between Mendele and the ironic persona employed by Linetski in his *Poylish yingl* will be edifying. *Dos poylishe yingl* is written in the form of a monologue addressed to the readers of *Kol-mevaser* by a persona, who in many ways resembles Mendele (he was, of course, to a certain extent modeled after Mendele). The speaker is supposed to be a person who had spent most of his life as an ardent *hasid* but who has finally seen the light. Now he is bent on exploding hasidism and on unmasking it in all its corruption. For this purpose he assumes the mask of a still-loyal *hasid* and ironically pretends to defend all those values which he is out to destroy. Since the story is being published in the *Kol-mevaser*, it is supposed to be addressed to an audience of scoffers and infidels, and thus it is rhetorically conceived of in terms of mock-polemics. The persona pretends to attack the Enlightenment, to ridicule the *maskilim* and to glorify the cult of the *tsadik*. Its most common ironic trick is to compare at length the "normality" and "pleasantness" of the hasidic life with the perversity and gloom of the *daytshunes* (the "Germanized ones," i.e., the *maskilim*) and in this manner catalogue all the horrors of a hasidic childhood, education, marriage, etc. We have here, then, a feigned innocence somewhat similar to that encountered in the Mendele fiction. We also have similar subversive intentions and a similar tension between overt loyalties and implied self-dissociation. The technical devices that Linetski employed also resemble the ironic devices of Abramovitsh. The basic fictional reality of *Dos poylishe yingl* is that of an actor or an entertainer facing his public. The Polish Boy is liable to digress from the story at any moment for a chat with his audience, for a sarcastic remark, for a joke or an aside. His contact with them is, if anything, even more pronounced than that which is assumed in the monologues of Mendele. Like Mendele, the Polish Boy chides his readers, ironically flatters them, lays traps for them, and gleefully watches them succumbing to them. His irony can often have that double edge so characteristic of Mendele's witticisms. While briskly going about his business of undermining the *hasidim*, he can suddenly turn on his maskilic readers with an unexpected ferocity and suggest that some of the criticism he aims at them while in guise of a *hasid* should be taken quite seriously. For all their orderliness and good sense, he insinuates, their lives *are* rather gloomy and stale. He even attacks them where they are supposed to be strongest: in the sphere of knowledge and rational judgment. They can be as ignorant and as irrational as their opposites, he argues. For example, he describes his first encounter with his intended wife—a disfigured, miserable child. Attacking the entire system of traditional Jewish matrimony, he nonetheless stops to settle some accounts with his maskilic public:

> I was left rooted to my place in great consternation and looked even in my own eyes as my *feuilleton* must look to a Jew "Frenchified" from his cradle, who, when told for once about a Polish *tsadik*, gapes at you as wide as he can and envisages to himself a *tsadik* in the form of a werewolf with bear's feet. When you read the *feuilleton* to him, he laughs all right, but ask him what he is actually laughing at, and immediately he is reduced to utter stupefaction. Let me be frank with you, dear editor. I really don't understand what right such people have to exist. Besides, how do they beget children without the *tsadik's* help, etc.[86]

The last two sentences represent the usual antihasidic bantering of the Polish Boy (especially the remark concerning the indispensable help of the *tsadik* in the continuing of the species; one of the most common and vulgar allusions recurrent in the antihasidic literature refers to the alleged virility of the *tsadik* and to his possible participation in the begetting of his adherents' progeny). However, within this usual bantering the persona succeeds for a moment in turning the rhetorical tide of his speech in the opposite direction, or perhaps he even succeeds in dividing his rhetorical flow into two contradictory channels. The passage is also highly interesting from other aspects. In it the storyteller

manages not only to offend his readers but also to chat intimately with
them, to refer to his own *feuilleton* (that is, to the very story he is telling; *Dos poylishe yingl* was published in the *Kol-mevaser* in the *feuilleton* section), and even to have a heart-to-heart conversation with the
real editor, Tsederboym. One can see how completely uninhibited
Linetski was in his use of the monologue form. Not one technical convention that he employed was adhered to with any consistency. His
only rule was never to let the Polish Boy's flow of dazzling sentences
flag for a moment. Like a vaudeville entertainer, he can allow himself
to say almost whatever comes into his mind, as long as his audience remains interested. He can impersonate a character and yet stop for a
talk with the electrician, or pick a theatrical quarrel with somebody
behind the scenery and then remind his audience that he is only acting, or suddenly become tearful, almost tragic, etc.

This already indicates the great difference between the Polish Boy
and Mendele, who is always calculated and purposeful and who even
during his zaniest escapades maintains some measure of restraint.
Mendele's double irony is, of course, far more subtle and meaningful
than that of the Polish Boy. When he turns his sword upon his readers,
he has it honed so sharp and wields it with such agility, that it takes
the reader some time to realize that he has been run through his very
vitals. With Linetski's persona the brandishing of the sword or, rather,
the swinging of the bludgeon is more conspicuous than the cutting—
which is no less than butchery—or the heavy clubbing itself. Moreover, Mendele controls his rhetorical moves with superior foresight.
When he intends to perform a rhetorical precipitation, an abrupt rais-
ing or lowering of his tone, he prepares for this effect ever so carefully.
He knows that he must maintain himself on one level for quite a long
time for his rhetorical fall to make the proper splash. Linetski's Polish
Boy continually jumps, falls, pirouettes, stands on his head, and is incapable of sustaining anything but the state of incessant movement.
Mendele, even at his wildest, does not possess anything like the
breathtaking effervescence and nervous garrulity of the Polish Boy.
This, on the one hand, made a great many readers of the 1860s and the
1870s prefer Linetski to Abramovitsh. (The two sensational hits scored
by the *Kol-mevaser, Dos kleyne mentshele,* and *Dos poylishe yingl,*
were often paired and compared.) Linetski's brilliance was so much
more obvious than Abramovitsh's, so much more abundant and so
much easier to absorb, that for the simple-minded to prefer him was

only natural. On the other hand, this is also the reason that in the long run Mendele proved so much more useful and workable, so much more capable of growth. It is not simply that the Polish Boy's restlessness can become tiresome so quickly, although that in itself is also significant. The difference between Mendele and the Polish Boy is mainly a structural one.

As we have seen, in all Abramovitsh's longer narratives Mendele supplies the framework of the story. His importance is ever increasing, but he never figures as the formal protagonist. In *Dos poylishe yingl* the ironic commentator figures as the hero himself. The Polish Boy fulfills the functions which in Abramovitsh's stories are fulfilled both by the confessing protagonist (Yitskhok Avrom, Fishke, etc.) and by the commenting *eiron*. This gives *Dos poylishe yingl* another advantage over the early stories of Abramovitsh. We saw how in the early versions of *Dos kleyne mentshele* and *Dos vintshfingerl* the narrative is dimmed as soon as Mendele leaves the field for the proper protagonists to have their say. This does not happen in *Dos poylishe yingl*. Here the ironic persona very rarely allows anybody else more than a short say;[87] no pedestrian Hershele of Yitskhok Avrom has to be accommodated, and the fireworks can go on without interruption.

This advantage is, however, dearly paid for. The entire rhetorical structure of *Dos poylishe yingl* is undermined by it. An external indication of this undermining can be detected in that the nominal identity of the persona is not clear. The story is signed by "Eli Kotsin Hatskhakueli" (an anagram of Linetski's full name, which may also mean something like "Eli the Jocose Dignitary" or "The Joking Magnate"), but is it his voice that the readers are supposed to hear talking in it? Is he the representative of the Polish Boy, or is it somebody else, who is referred to on several occasions as "Ephroim," who does the talking? We may, I think, assume that Linetski himself was not clearly aware of a possible distinction in this respect. In fact, it is quite probable that he never really bothered to decide precisely who his persona was. This led to graver inconsistencies. Although this seems to have escaped the notice of the critics, the protagonist of *Dos poylishe yingl* is supposed to be telling his story from the world of the spirits. During the narrative present, the voice of the Polish Boy is that of a dead man, since his story is concluded with a full description of his terrible death and even with an epitaph that he has allegedly composed *after* his death. This is not an indication of sheer eccentricity on the part of

Linetski. *Dos poylishe yingl*, like *Dos kleyne mentshele*, is a satire written in the tradition of Y. Erter's "Gilgul nefesh" ("The Metamorphosis," 1845), a tradition which was kept alive throughout the literature
of the *Haskala* and which can be characterized as the line of "posthumous truth" or of the "sermon from the grave." [88] In "Gilgul nefesh" a
naked spirit, just freed from a dead man's body, unfolds all the sins
and follies it has committed in its numerous reincarnations. This is basically what happens both in *Dos kleyne mentshele* and in *Dos poylishe
yingl*. Although the motif of metempsychosis was not developed in
these stories, they both consist of confessions made by sinners who,
after having been freed from all worldly obligations, can now "tell the
whole truth." Abramovitsh, however, took care to make his Yitskhok
Avrom write his confession before his death. Linetski let his protagonist perform in the capacity of a disembodied spirit, walking more
conservatively in the wake of Y. Erter. This in itself can be perfectly
legitimate. There is no reason whatsoever why disembodied spirits
should not have their say in literature, provided they have it within the
framework of a proper convention. Linetski, however, did not abide
by the rules of the convention. He did not and he could not, for instance, let his spiritual Polish Boy speak the beautifully formal, balanced, crystal-clear Hebrew which Erter had let his spiritual protagonist employ. The style of the Polish Boy was, on the contrary, as earthy
as it could be. Moreover, Erter took care to make his spirit describe its
numerous bodily lives in a generalized, succinct way. Linetski preferred an all-too-vivid, detailed, physical pictorialism, which could
hardly be believed to represent a meta-sensual consciousness. Of
course, he had to do it because his protagonist was not only a dead
man but also a theatrical entertainer, a brilliant *conférencier*. The artistic damage which this duality caused becomes more obvious if we
ask ourselves what kind of memory the Polish Boy is supposed to have.
Allegedly, he had died a broken-hearted, dissipated man, a human
shadow. The victim of a system of swindling in which he had played a
part, he spent several years in prison both for the crimes he himself
had committed for the sake of the *tsadik*'s interests and as a "cover"
for the crimes of the *tsadik* himself. Once out of prison, the *hasidim* no
longer had any use for him. In the meantime, he had lost his hasidic
faith. The *maskilim* offered to help him, but he was already beyond
the reach of help; his hasidic youth had ruined him completely and
forever. This is how he describes the last stage of his dismal decline: "I

had faith in nobody, not even in God himself. Somehow I managed to while away the few dark years, with troubles, with worries, with anger, with licentiousness, with boredom." [89] Yet it is this victimizer and victim who is supposed to share with us (until the last section of the story) his exuberant high spirits, to play his ironic part with an alarming gusto, and to overwhelm us with his dazzling mimicry. In Abramovitsh's stories protagonists like Yitskhok Avrom or Fishke convey throughout their tales the full weight of their somber experiences. They can have a consciousness with a real psychological past. Linetski's hero cannot afford that. Telling his reminiscences, he is not allowed to have a psychological past. He must be born anew every narrative moment, as fresh and as bursting with verbal energy as he supposedly had been in his early days. Otherwise he would not be able to perform his ironic–theatrical part.

These two roles—the protagonist telling his autobiography and the ironic entertainer—are irreconcilable. This becomes even more apparent as we realize that the Polish Boy cannot sustain his ironic tone through even a single chapter in his story. While Mendele keeps a cool head, Linetski's hero cannot contain his irony. Disguised as the common Jew, Mendele sustains the tension of feigned naiveté with painstaking care. True, it is his special delight to tease his readers by approaching from time to time the point of unmasking, yet he always remains the master of the situation. He is always able to retire elegantly into the brittle armor of his innocence without flawing it with so much as a scratch. Not so the Polish Boy. With him the brittle armor is shattered to pieces every few pages. He upsets the ironic balance of his story so often that before we have gone through its opening sections he has no more secrets with which to lure us; his mystery has been all but spent. This happened not only because, unlike Abramovitsh, Linetski had no sense of artistic consistency and no awareness of irony as a binding principle but also because Linetski had unwittingly weighted his hero down with two burdens, each pulling in its own direction. On the one hand, he made him a victim who must get the story of his sordid life off his chest, and on the other, he made him play the *eiron*. As a victim and a public-minded dead man, the Polish Boy had to cry out the truth in the streets; as an *eiron*, he had to let the truth speak indirectly for itself. As both, he could not help falling between two chairs. By contrast we can see now how cautious and well controlled Abramovitsh was in his experiments with Mendele. He al-

most never put him in a position where he was in danger of losing his
self-control. In Linetski's story the victim undermines the *eiron*, the
protesting *maskil* destroys the mask of "the Jew." With Mendele the
double burden of Jewish familiarity and maskilic stratagem was so
evenly measured as to constitute the double-headed pole with which
the ropedancer balances himself in the air.

The most significant difference between Mendele and the Polish
Boy is even more elementary and far-reaching. As the protagonist of
an autobiographical story, the latter progresses along "the way of life":
childhood, education, maturity, decline. As the chorus of Abramovitsh's dramatic stories, the former progresses along the roads of the
Russian-Jewish pale, but he does not become subject to the laws of the
biological cycle. If he is not ageless, he is at least able, as we have seen,
to remain middle-aged or elderly for more than fifty years. The hero of
Dos poylishe yingl is finished with the conclusion of his life story, and
Linetski is very much finished as a writer with both. The speedy decline of Linetski, whose writings were for a short time even more ap-
preciated and relished than those of Abramovitsh, was caused not, as
has often been said, by the fact that in *Dos poylishe yingl* he had told
his autobiography and had nothing more to tell about. This notion is
contradicted by the facts of Linetski's biography. It also indicates a
basic misunderstanding of the satire. Both *Dos kleyne mentshele* and
Dos poylishe yingl represent not personal confessions of the author but
confessions of the Jewish average man, the point of the two stories
being that the sins the protagonists confess to are those which average
people would commit under the same circumstances. Nor is it true
that Linetski declined so quickly because in *Dos poylishe yingl* he had
used all his ideological "ammunition"; actually, he reached his ideological maturity only in the mid-1870s. What really happened was that
in the *Poylish yingl* he had used all the rhetorical resources he could
command, and he irretrievably associated them with a figure who
could not be brought back to literary life. The Polish Boy was the only
rhetorical mask Linetski could devise, but he was also the hero of a
story that terminated with his death. Linetski went on using the voice
of the Polish Boy, or of Eli Kotsin Hatskhakueli, employing his ironic
devices, doing his best to radiate the same nervous brilliance, but
there was something distinctly passé about his exuberance, something
which evokes the "we have already heard all about that" feeling. No
matter how different was the story he was trying to tell, how changed

were his ideas (later in his career he even became a Zionist), his performance, his rhetoric, remained that of the dead and gone Polish Boy.
Mendele's performance and rhetoric also remained basically unchanged, but they were *expected* to be so. He was the old acquaintance that people were glad to meet, not the shadow of a dead man.
Thus, while the art of Eli Kotsin speedily declined, Mendele had all
the time he needed to realize his great achievements. The mask of the
feigned *hasid* wore thin and began to shred on Linetski's face. Soon
enough he could not use it any longer, and he had to replace the voice
of his Polish Boy by the very pathetic but utterly ineffective and nondramatic voice of Linetski himself. Mendele's mask only gained in vitality until it ended by absorbing—in the popular imagination—the
face of Abramovitsh himself.[90]

Now we can perceive why Abramovitsh's plan to make Yisrolik the
Madman an *eiron* in competition with Mendele did not materialize.
The one monologue of Yisrolik's that Abramovitsh published after the
publication of *The Nag* indicates that what happened to Linetski could
have very well happened to him, for this monologue reads as a diluted
repetition of *The Nag*. In order to develop freely, the *eiron* must remain a somewhat abstracted figure with no heavy biographical chains
to drag after him; he must be something of an Everyman (and we have
seen that even while pretending to tell "all about himself," Mendele
managed to remain an Everyman). While Linetski's *eiron* was imprisoned in his life story, Mendele was supplied only with that amount of
biography necessary to endow him with credible fictional reality. It is
through comparison with Linetski—who until the appearance of Sholem Aleichem, was the only real competitor Abramovitsh had in the
employment of the ironic persona—that we can realize how intricate
was the progress along the avenues of the Mendele maze, how many
dangers Abramovitsh had to circumvent, and what a superb sense of
propriety and limits he possessed. This comparison can also prepare
the way for a final glance at the place of Mendele in nineteenth-century Yiddish literature. The resemblances between Abramovitsh and
Linetski indicate the basic uniformity of the artistic problems with
which the two artists were grappling; the differences explain why the
solutions worked out by Abramovitsh became the strongest force in
the development of Yiddish literature.

CHAPTER EIGHT

THE DISGUISED TRAVELER
Conclusion

> It is much more difficult to converse with the world in a real than a personated Character. That might pass for Humor, in the *Spectator*, which would look like Arrogance in a Writer who sets his Name to his Work. The Fictitious Person might condemn those who disapproved him, and extoll his own Performances, without giving Offence. He might assume a Mock-Authority; without being looked upon as vain and conceited. The Praises and Censures of himself fall only upon the Creature of his Imagination.
>
> (Richard Steele, *The Spectator*, No. 555. December 6, 1712)

WE ARE NOW in a position to examine the Mendele phenomenon against the background of nineteenth-century Yiddish fiction as a whole and to perceive some of the reasons for its unique historical significance.

The Mendele phenomenon with all its intricacies and ambiguities can be best explained as a great artist's answer to the central artistic problem of nineteenth-century Yiddish literature in general and of its fiction in particular—the problem of the possibilities and the limitations of the dramatic mode of writing. The following may be considered as a rule with very few exceptions: Yiddish literature in the nineteenth century is more clearly and exclusively dramatic in progressive ratio to the ideological and artistic self-consciousness of its writers. The more a writer was committed to the struggle of the *Haskala*, the more sensitive he was to the artistic possibilities of the language, the more prone he was to write dramatically, that is, to employ one or more of the following dramatic modes of composition. (a) The full-fledged drama, usually either straight comedy or the characteristic middle-class *comédie larmoyante;* an example of the former would be Gotlober's *Dektukh*; of the latter, Etinger's *Serkele*. (b) The argumentative dialogue or symposium, either in prose (e.g., Levinzon's

"Hefker-velt"—"Where Might Is Right";[1] Linetski also contributed
copiously to this subgenre)[2] or in verse (e.g., A. Fishelzon's *Teater fun
khasidim*[3] or Linetski's famous "Der erev-yonkiper," "The Eve of the
Day of Atonement").[4] (c) The "recited" monologue of a character (i.e.,
a monologue we allegedly hear; as distinct from the "written" monologue. Mendele's monologues are "recited"; Yitskhok Avrom's confession in *Dos kleyne mentshele* is a written monologue). An early example of this genre is Khayim Malage's *Gdules reb Volf.*[5] Later on many
writers contributed to it. Linetski was perhaps the most popular writer
of the short, independent monologue during the 1870s (see "Di khsidishe damf-mashin,"[6] "The Hasidic Steam Engine," a characteristic
monologue of a *hasid*, who takes it upon himself to reveal the mystical
source of the workings of the steam engine). From the late 1880s on,
Sholem Aleichem became the indisputable master of the genre.
Abramovitsh, as we have seen, developed the full-fledged monologistic
story or novel. (d) The "recited" and "written" monologue of an authorial "persona," which unlike the monologue of a "character" is addressed to the readers (the difference between Mendele's and Tevye's
monologues) and would often begin with a direct appeal to the "dear
readers." Almost all Yiddish writers of the nineteenth century used
this form in one way or another. Mendele Moykher-Sforim and Sholem
Aleichem are the best-known personae of this kind. Linetski's Eli
Kotsin Hatskhakueli was for a short time as well-known and as popular
as they were. Linetski's collections of *feuilletons* and *kartines*
("sketches") are full of monologues of this type (see *Dos meshulakhes,
Der pritshepe, Der statek, Der plapler*, etc.), and it was in his *Poylish
yingl* that the type was developed into something like a novel. (e) The
comic or parodic letter. The great master of this form in the first half
of the century was Yosef Perl, in whose *Megale-tmirin* parodic and
comic letters of various types form a delightful and most complex narrative sequence. The single epistolary unit was also used independ-
ently[7] or inserted into a nonepistolary narrative context. Toward the
end of the century the comic letter, like the monologue, became Sholem Aleichem's major vehicle. From the appearance of the sentimental
and lachrymose school in modern Yiddish fiction in the 1870s on, the
emotional, "lyrical," and "tragic" letter became as common a feature
as the comic-parodic one (see, for instance, *Der shvartser yunger-
mantshik* by Y. Dinezon). (f) The "primitive" dramatic novel or novelistic drama. The main exponent of this genre was Y. Aksenfeld, whose

four surviving dramas are constructed as scenic-melodramatic stories and were not meant to be staged (but rather "to be read in company on a winter night." [8] One of them is referred to on its German front page as a "Komisch-tragischer Roman").[9] This does not mean that the dramas do not contain strong theatrical elements as well as a basically dramatic construction (exposition, dramatic entanglement, peripeteia, a long denouement with many "recognitions," etc.). These, however, are also to be found in Aksenfeld's single surviving novel, *Dos shterntikhl*, which in large parts is nothing but camouflaged drama, a series of scenic episodes cemented by a narrator and structured, to a very large extent, along the lines of comic melodrama. Aksenfeld's art, as far as we know it, always mingles the dramatic with the narrative. Needless to say, all these modes are often employed in various combinations.

In the same way, and almost as categorically, one may say that the less radical a writer was in his commitment to the *Haskala* and the more marginal and superficial the influence of its ideology was on him, the less sensitive he was to the artistic possibilities of the language and the more prone to employ the epic mode in narrative and the straightforward, dialogue-free homily. This rule holds true from the beginnings of modern Yiddish literature in the last decades of the eighteenth century until the 1890s.

This is not the place to elaborate fully on this generalization. For the purpose of our argument, a sweeping survey of some of the most characteristic developments of nineteenth-century Yiddish fiction will, perhaps, suffice. Although Yiddish fiction did not acknowledge the fact at the time, one can detect in it two fairly continuous "traditions," or lines of development, differentiated according to geographical-cultural regions as well as intellectual and literary criteria: the attitude toward Jewish society, stylistic "purity" (i.e., use of idiomatic, un-Germanized, Eastern European Yiddish) or "impurity," and mode of narration ("dramatic" versus "epic"). The geographical-regional demarcations involve distinctions that cannot occupy us here. The very general notion that one of these traditions flourished mostly in the northern part of the Jewish pale in the Russian Empire (particularly in Lithuania; to some extent also in Warsaw during the 1860s and 1870s), while the other one was developed mainly in the south (the Ukraine, and the Austro-Hungarian Galicia), where Jewish society was very strongly influenced by the hasidic movement, will have to suffice. One should, however, be reminded that Abramovitsh, the most prominent figure in nineteenth-century Yiddish literature, was a northerner who settled in the south. This indicates the manifold qualifications which the generalization just offered calls for. With the intellectual and literary criteria we are on firmer ground. Generally, the exponents of the two "traditions" differ among themselves according to all three of them, although cases of intermixture are, to some extent, also not rare. Thus we can characterize one group of writers as radical *maskilim* who employ colloquial, idiomatic Yiddish in what are basically dramatic narratives. Another group of writers can be characterized as marginal *maskilim*, whose employment of the language is less consistent (they may use colloquial, idiomatic Yiddish in the more dramatic sections of their works and shift to heavily Germanized, or at a later stage, Russianized, prose in other sections) and whose narratives are basically nondramatic. The first group of writers sees an inevitable connection between the evils that plague Jewish society and its own specific social and cultural structure; the second group, although they may qualify perfectly as *maskilim* in the sense that they favor some measure of Europeanization and secularization in Jewish life, do not, on the whole, criticize Jewish society as such. When they do find fault with it, they interpret it in terms of general morals. For them it is because people are "good" or "bad," not because they are conditioned primarily by the circumstances of Jewish life, that they act in either a praiseworthy or a blameworthy manner. Often they seek the correction of moral defects in the name of traditional Jewish values. In any case, their works seldom imply the need for a far-reaching, revolutionary change in Jewish life. This is precisely what the works of the other writers most often *do* imply. The method of education and correction that these more radical writers employ is mainly that of punitive satire. They are primarily interested in forcing upon the Jewish people an awareness of their imperfection. The other writers prefer softer exhortations. Their method of education is mainly homiletic. They are interested in a general moral improvement and refinement of the Jewish people, and they also tend to promote education in the informational sense of the term. While the subject matter of the "radicals" is almost exclusively contemporary, daily life in the towns and hamlets of the Jewish pale in Russia, the nonradicals often carry their readers not only throughout Europe but also to America, Africa, and the East.[10] They also resort from time to time to the pseudohistorical narrative and introduce their readers to the horrors of the Spanish Inquisition or to the alleged simplicity and innocence of Jewish life in Eastern Europe during the seventeenth or eighteenth centuries.[11] The radicals, thoroughly influenced as they might have been by foreign literary and intellectual trends and values, are usually original artists. The nonradicals often work as adaptors and compilers. The more we study the sources of their works the more we discover them to be translators or, more correctly, transplanters rather than writers of original fiction. The radicals are bent on the description of the ordinary. The supernatural or the bizarre, when it appears in their works, is sure to prove deceptive. Their means of pleasing and attracting their readers are parody, satire, comedy. The means employed by the writers of the other group are often those of epic suspense. Instead of liveliness of character or authenticity of speech, sheer storytelling is their forte; they often manifest a journalistic interest in the exotic, the bizarre, the wondrous, and even in the merely freakish.[12] The radicals are represented by the most attractive names in nineteenth-century Yiddish fiction—Perl, Aksenfeld, Abramovitsh, Linetski, Shatskes, and in most of his work, Sholem Aleichem. The others are usually less important writers. Their best-known representatives are Dik, Dinezon, and Shaykevitsh. To these one may add numerous background figures, from the anonymous adapter of *Robinson Crusoe* and Kh. Kh. Hurovitz (the adapter of Campe's *Entdeckung von Amerika*) in the early part of the century, through the Warsaw school of fiction writers of the 1850s and 1860s (Gedalye Beloy, A. B. Ruf, etc.),[13] to Bekerman, Bukhbinder, Bloshteyn, and the other disciples of Shaykevitsh who flourished in the late 1880s and particularly in the 1890s.

The sweeping polarization of nineteenth-century Yiddish fiction calls, of course, for some immediate qualifications. First, it should be remembered that the groupings do not automatically imply literary merit or lack thereof. Nor do they impart in any way an equality of sorts to the "members" within any group. Among the so-called radicals we can certainly find the most talented Yiddish writers of the century, but we can also find among them writers whose names are mentioned by, or perhaps even known to, only a few exhaustive historians. Second, the groupings should not be understood to stand for monolithic unities either in matters of ideology or in the art of storytelling. There is certainly a very considerable difference, for instance, between the cultural aims and the storytelling of Dik and those of Shaykevitsh, as there is a no less considerable difference between, say, Abramovitsh and Linetski. Third, although the two traditions I have delineated certainly represent different levels of artistic and social consciousness in nineteenth-century Yiddish literature, they do not necessarily, or in all cases, represent a "truer" and a "less true" understanding of Jewish life. While most of the radicals offer a better insight into the overall social structure of the Jewish community, Dik, in his more naive way, catches the variety of Jewish existence, the minutiae of manners, as no other writer before Sholem Aleichem. The Jewish world that his novelettes portray is much more diverse and probably much more faithful to the minutiae of history than the one created in the works of Abramovitsh. Fourth, and most important, my groupings correspond to the historical literary reality as such means of generalized exposition always do—like a diagram. Their expositional neatness should not be accepted as an indication of any neatly groomed reality. It should be remembered that the dividing line is often crossed within the work of a single writer. Dik at a certain stage of his development (the late 1850s and the early 1860s) drew very near to the "radicals." In novelettes such as *Khaytsikl aleyn* ("Khaytsikl All by Himself," 1856), *Yekele Goldshleger* (1859), or *Reb Shmaya Aliter, der gut-yontev biter* ("Reb Shmaya Aliter, The Happy-Holiday Greeter," 1860) his narratives grew to a considerable extent more critical of Jewish society, more pugnaciously satirical, more colloquial in tone, and much more dramatic than they had formerly been or than they were to be in the later phases of the author's career. It has been proved that even the notorious Shaykevitsh divided his writing between the sensational novels, which in plot and style represent the "epic" (or rather "romantic") line of nineteenth-century Yiddish fiction at its most uninhibited, and his short stories, in which the wide geographical amplitude, adventure-filled plots, and the lexical vicissitudes are brought under control. Here, as the stories are put in the mouth of one Yudke Shmerkes the Idler, a mini-minor Mendele figure (his stories actually open with "quoth Yudke Shmerkes" monologues), they become dramatic in form, their subject matter is confined to contemporary daily Jewish life, and their attitude to Jewish society becomes comparatively critical and satirical.[14] On the other hand, young Sholem Aleichem can be said to have begun his career as a sentimental storyteller (in his puerile novels, to be distinguished from his early *feuilletons,* in which he can be said to have revealed his "other" self) in the line of Dinezon or even, heretical as this may sound, in that of Shaykevitsh, rather than in the line of his heroes, Abramovitsh and Linetski.[15] Even Abramovitsh contributed to the nonradical fiction in adaptations such as the *Luftbalon*, or some of the more sensational parts of *Dos vintshfingerl* (especially the brothel episodes). Linetski made his contribution in the adaption of a Jewish-German historical novel, in which a Portuguese Marrano who escapes to England talks to Queen Elizabeth and Lord Burleigh in a strange, formal Yiddish, full of official Russian expressions. (Linetski announced that he had adapted the story in "refined Yiddish"—by which he may have meant either that he had purged the style of colloquialisms or that he did not employ the Germanisms so characteristic of Shaykevitsh and his school. Probably he did not think that blatant Slavicisms could form as foreign a body in a Yiddish text as Germanisms.)

Some writers never settled down to any of the two "lines" and kept fluctuating between them. M. Spektor, for example, would write one novel (for instance, his first success, *A roman on a nomen*, "A Novel Without a Title," 1883–1884) in the epic-homiletic line; another (*Reb Traytl*, 1884–1885), clearly in the dramatic-satirical line. Some of his other novels (for example, *Aniyim ve'evyoynim*, "The Poor and the Destitute," 1885), are in this respect hybrid compositions.

ii

In spite of these and, no doubt, many other necessary qualifications, the distinction on the whole is valid and is of the highest importance for understanding the artistic development of nineteenth-century Yiddish fiction. It has been customary in Yiddish criticism to distinguish between writers or even between different phases in the career of a single writer (Dik, for instance), according to lexical criteria: those who wrote "pure" idiomatic Yiddish were set apart from those who alloyed the language with Germanisms. As we can see now, this distinction is only one aspect of a much wider distinction. The writers who employed foreign lexical elements were, strangely enough, not the tough *maskilim* but rather the milder ones. The explanation is that the tougher *maskilim*, as dramatic satirists, concentrated on contemporary, daily Jewish life and could confine themselves to colloquial Yiddish, while the milder *maskilim*, as "epic" writers of a wider range, included in their descriptions elements for which the tra-

ditional Jewish world and its vocabulary had fewer equivalents, forcing them to resort to foreign expressions. In other words, it required
the decision to remain within the boundaries of the dramatic and familiar in order to retain a stylistic "integrity" in Yiddish. This decision
was, of course, prompted by a keener artistic sensibility, but it also
reflected a firmer ideological commitment. The reader who has kept in
mind the gist of my speculations on the problematical commitment of
nineteenth-century Jewish writers to Yiddish, on the "aesthetics of
ugliness," and on the theatrical tendencies which Yiddish writers developed, can easily see the logic of this combination. Those speculations, although they are partially applicable to almost all Yiddish writers of the time, are especially and most significantly applicable to the
writers of the radical tradition; that is, those whose style is designated
as critical, colloquial, and dramatic: Perl, Aksenfeld, Abramovitsh,
Linetski, Shatskes, and Sholem Aleichem. In other words, they are
more applicable to those writers whose contributions to the artistic development of Yiddish fiction were the greatest. This is not a coincidence. In contradiction to the notion propagated by many critics from
Frishman onward, the artistic mellowing of nineteenth-century
Yiddish literature was not independent of or even contradictory to the
ideology of the *Haskala*. It is not true that Abramovitsh "the artist"
functioned with no reference, or even in opposition, to Abramovitsh
"the *maskil*." On the contrary, wherever we find a firmer commitment
to the social and educational values of the *Haskala*, there we also find
a more pronounced readiness for artistic experimentation combined
with a surer knowledge of the writer's artistic limitations. It is in
Perl's, Abramovitsh's, and Linetski's works that we can detect, on the
one hand, a social and cultural radicalism, and on the other hand, an
unmistakable tendency toward artistic play. It is also in these works
that we find the artistic limitations of nineteenth-century Yiddish
fiction more clearly recognized, reconciled, and even made use of;
within a narrower scope, a freer movement; within a smaller scale, a
demonstration of virtuosity. It is not the more conservative and supposedly less *engagé* writers that allow themselves free artistic play in
Yiddish. On the contrary, it was precisely the sort of writer like Dik or
Dinezon, the nonradicals, who found fault with Abramovitsh for his
sheer artistry and who propagated strict utilitarianism in Yiddish letters.

   Strange as that may seem, those fiction writers who took more seriously the aesthetics of ugliness in all its far-reaching implications were

better equipped to develop the art of Yiddish storytelling. This is only an apparent paradox. The aesthetics of ugliness implies that enduring art cannot be created in Yiddish, and this implication, as we have seen, brought about serious inner conflicts, discrepancies between theory and practice, and required constant self-vindication; it certainly exerted an inhibitory influence on many writers. But the aesthetics of ugliness also imposed on Yiddish writers, especially on fiction writers, a strict discipline, which invariably proved helpful. It taught them to confine their art to the dramatic and thus oriented them toward the one and only direction in which, under the circumstances, their artistic urges could find successful outlet. Given the historical-cultural rupture between the writer ("us") and the common Jewish people ("the Jew"), the only method of sustaining artistic literature in Yiddish involved a conscious detachment from "us" as well as a conscious mimetic dramatization of "the Jew." Any other method inevitably led to a violation of the language (through the introduction of excessive foreign elements) as well as to enervating homiletics.

To this even the earliest works of the Yiddish maskilic literature bear evidence. In the late eighteenth-century dramas of Volfzon and Aykhl, and also in Etinger's *Serkele*, a linguistic barrier divides the characters into two groups: first, the opponents of the Enlightenment, those who stubbornly stick to the traditional way of life and speak fluent, idiomatic Yiddish. The harsher the judgment passed on them the livelier the language; the more ruthlessly satirized they are the more vital their dramatic presence becomes. Second, there are the exponents of the Enlightenment, those who are obviously mouthpieces for their creators and who speak "educated," bookish, anemic German. The more grammatical their language the paler their presence; the more righteous their sentiment, the less dramatic its expression. There exists in these plays a smaller, third group who seem to adhere to the ideas of the *Haskala* but who are mere fellow travelers. Frivolous, superficial characters that they are, they befittingly try to speak German, only to prove themselves to be neophytes; their German is ludicrously incorrect. In *Serkele* the maskilic hero, Gutherts, who speaks all his asides in the most respectable German clichés (that is, his consciousness is supposed to function in German), even reprimands a young woman who belongs to this group and suggests that she get off her German stilts and speak plain Yiddish.[16] In that he does not, however, as Max Weinreich has suggested, manifest a positive attitude toward Yiddish;[17] he simply shows the young woman her proper place in the linguistically and ideologically divided world of the play.

This division of characters and language in the early maskilic Yiddish dramas established a distinctive pattern which was to recur in different variations in the development of Yiddish literature. It implied the choice that later Yiddish writers had to make between vital, "negative" (that is, satiric or parodic) dramatic representations and bland, "positive" (that is, homiletic) nondramatic ones. As artists they could either imitate the "unenlightened" and express their maskilic message in a negative but vivid way or express themselves directly through positive but weak Gutherts-like characters. The need to make the choice became pronounced as the *maskilim* began to write fiction. The playwright had a considerable advantage over the fiction writer in this respect. He could always rely on his villains, the sharp-tongued shrews and the glib hypocrites, to transfuse enough lifeblood into his play and yet to let the positive *maskilim* have their say too. If he managed to construct the play so as to let the *maskilim* occupy a comparatively small but strategic part of it (the denouement), he could have the best of both worlds. The writer of fiction had to choose the voice that he was about to employ in his work. It had to be either the positive but artistically barely audible voice of his enlightened self or the dramatic, very lively voice of his opponent. The first of these alternatives led to the adaptation of *Robinson Crusoe*, to the early novels of Dinezon, Shaykevitsh, and the early Sholem Aleichem; the second led to *Megale-tmirin, Dos shterntikhl, Fishke der krumer, Dos poylishe yingl,* and the Sholem Aleichem of *Menakhem-Mendl.* Characteristically, when in these latter works the typical positive representatives of the *Haskala* appear, they figure as silent partners; they are idealized but kept offstage (see the figure of Mordekhay Gold in *Megale-tmirin* and that of Gutman in *Dos kleyne mentshele*). They are not allowed to interfere with the dramatic handling of the work.

Choosing the dramatic solution, however, Yiddish fiction writers had to face the two related problems of ideology and artistry. Ideologically, how was the writer going to deliver his full, positive maskilic message through a negative medium? He could, of course, do it through parody, let the unenlightened speak for themselves and invite, with the help of the author's parodic accentuation, the criticism they deserved. The Yiddish language itself, as I have already suggested, was conceived of as capable of drawing out and pointing to defects in the national character. This, however, left much to be desired in respect to ideology. After all, parody is a rather limited medium of criticism. Within its limitations it can be, when handled by a man of parodic genius, wonderfully effective. But even Perl, the greatest of Jewish parodists, saw fit in *Bokhen-tsadik* ("He That Triest the Tsadik," 1838), the (Hebrew) sequel to *Megale-tmirin*, to temper his parody by introducing into it an idealized farmer from one of the few Jewish colonies the Russian government had half-heartedly included in its colonization plan for the southern provinces it had snatched from the Ottoman Empire (an experiment which the *maskilim* enthusiastically welcomed). Levinzon had to bring into his "Hefker-velt" a traveler who, coming from the northern Russian provinces, where the social behavior of the leaders of the Jewish community was allegedly more restrained than in the south, could represent something like a positive principle. (Levinzon, himself a southerner, idealized the northern communities somewhat, for, being much poorer than those in the south, they probably offered fewer opportunities for corruption.) Somehow this traveler is also supposed to represent international Jewry (especially the Western European Jews) as a positive entity.[18] Aksenfeld, in *Dos shterntikhl*, let his protagonist move to Germany for a while and there absorb "positive" norms through direct experience as well as through the teachings of Oksman, Aksenfeld's chief *raisonneur* in the novel. Linetski concluded *Dos Poylishe yingl* with the appearance of the archangel Michael, accompanied by an operatic chorus of lower angels (this occurs in the protagonist's dream), intending thereby to represent his positive maskilic ideas with all the authority of angelic clairvoyance.

Dramatic parody was, then, hardly a sufficient medium from the ideological point of view. It was even less so from the artistic one. Again, within its limitations dramatic parody can achieve dazzling artistic brilliance, as it did under the hand of Perl; but the limitations it involved left the writer a very narrow space for artistic maneuvering. Besides, parody defeats itself by sheer excess. Even Perl, who was as clever a parodist as any in European letters, and who took care to introduce into his *Megale-tmirin* as many shades of parodic tone as he could possibly command, overreached himself. Reading his masterpiece we feel more than once that sensation of imminent suffocation which a ceaseless, merciless demonstration of brilliance can cause almost as effectively as an unremitting demonstration of dullness. With less-gifted writers this shortcoming became much more oppressive.

Aksenfeld's *Shterntikhl* illustrates the limitations of the dramatic mode in fiction. As mentioned, the better part of the novel constitutes a camouflaged drama. At least most of the sections that are set in the Jewish towns and hamlets of Eastern Europe consist of an endless flow of dialogue pieced together with drab, matter-of-fact, conjunctive sentences. M. Viner, in his study of this novel, described its style as "raw" and its syntax as haphazard. He convincingly illustrated his argument with some badly mangled sentences, utterly unattractive, even incomplete.[19] Viner, however, did not notice that Aksenfeld's erratic and negligent sentences occur only in those connective passages I have referred to. It is as if Aksenfeld were impatient with those interfering, technical passages, which he may have regarded as mere stage directions bracketed between the units of the dialogue. The moment he lets his heroes talk, there is nothing arbitrary or inefficient about his use of the language. On the contrary, the dialogues are often extremely well-written. Viner explained the rawness of Aksenfeld's style by the fact that in the first half of the nineteenth century, modern Yiddish had no stylistic canons. This explanation, if true, reinforces the assumption that only through direct dramatic mimesis could the language be artistically employed. Indeed, most of the vitality Aksenfeld's novel possesses is attributable to dramatic mimesis of colloquial Yiddish, which of course, is not to be confused with mere imitation on the level of scrupulous accuracy. Aksenfeld manipulated the language, intensified and exaggerated some of its elements (such as dialectological differences); he caricatured it and developed in it a parodic momentum that, as the novel unfolds, carries us on the crest of a grotesque wave. For example, by sheer insistence on the employment of a recurrent, irrelevant, and sometimes meaningless phrase in the speech of almost every one of the "unenlightened" characters (an obvious continuation of a practice common among Yiddish dramatists and used by Aksenfeld in his own plays), he methodically detached the language of the dialogues from any semblance of logical order and endowed it instead with a staccato order of its own—obsessive, illogical, rhythmic, haunting, and utterly crazy. In some sections of the novel this employment of a relatively primitive parodic device proves almost unbelievably funny. Yet the novel as a whole, although not very long, seems at times almost insufferable. We are saturated with the effect of the parodic dialogues before we have read a third of it, and we all but welcome the dull sections in which Oksman expatiates on the nature of the educational theater and on the tactics of the *Haskala* in general. These sections, undoubtedly the least vibrant in the novel, supply the necessary breathing space and brace us for the plunge into the final, hilarious, and most histrionic section, set in the court of the *tsadik* and containing brisk theatrical business with numerous noisy appearances and exits of various characters as well as no less than six unrelated "recognitions." As a matter of fact, we had been supplied with shorter, though no less necessary, breathing spaces even in the earlier section of the novel, before we reached the German intermission that separates its two more dramatic parts from each other. Aksenfeld made it the narrator's duty not only to form the connections between the scenic sections dominated by dialogue, to follow the action with short descriptions of gesture and grimace (which are very much like stage directions), and sometimes even summarize it for the purposes of accelerated narrative movement (see, for instance, Chap. 8). He also trusted him with the task of explication—of the psychological causation in the story (which is very slight and skin-deep) as well as of historical and cultural background features, which the readers, already far removed from the time of the action (the Napoleonic wars in Russia) or from its particular hasidic milieu, may not be familiar with (comments of this kind are much more thorough and interesting than the "psychological" ones). More importantly, he also makes him from time to time assume an autonomous dramatic role, become an authorial "persona," and accompany the action with his own ironic remarks. When this happens the stylistic drabness, which is usually characteristic of the narrator (as opposed to the characters), disappears, and we feel that what we face may be a primitive, very rudimentary Mendele. The narrator comes up, for instance, with a whole series of ironic remarks on the nature of Loyhoyopoli, the *shtetl* in which the action in the first section of the novel takes place (the meaning of the name is "a town that never was"), as *a shtot*, a big town. The people of Loyhoyopoli are very proud of the size of their town, and thus the narrator can point out their provinciality by seemingly concurring with them, echoing again and again their credo: "Loyhoyopoli is a [real] town. In Loyhoyopoli everything must happen." [20] He can also forget himself, refer to Loyhoyopoli as a *shtetl*, and immediately apologize,[21] as well as use other forms of sarcasm. This endows him with some kind of dramatic presence. However, his appearances under this mask are too short, fragmentary, and irregular to allow it to become an important factor in the novel. It is only once (as some critics have noticed)[22] that the narrator is able to sustain a whole "Mendelean" paragraph:

> What did Mikhl see in the big city of Barditshev? Ten Loyhoyopoli swamps joined into one; the same Loyhoyopoli mud-bespattered women and dirt-covered men, only fifteen times more; thirty-eight times more beggars clinging to one's coat tails; forty times more wagons and horses. Pushing and shoving, scurrying, one person chases another. One curses, another delivers blows, ten engage in a quarrel, five shout: "Sholem Aleykhem! How do you do?" Nobody has a free moment. One is caught by a wheel, which tears half a coat off his back. On the other side he is congratulated with "Good luck!" Tin boxes rattle: "Charity delivereth from death!" * and on top of all this people follow the wedding musicians carrying holiday hallah to the bride and dancing in the street. Jews with tall bamboo canes demand alms, and nearby ten Jews pass chasing somebody, with a hue and cry: "Catch the thief! He is getting away." [23]

It is while reading a passage like this that one's sense of the artistic limitations of the scenic mode of narration, which by and large dominates the novel, is particularly heightened. As the narrator suddenly finds his own dramatic voice, one realizes how much could not be conveyed through accentuated, often parodic dialogue and what an enormous step forward in the development of Yiddish fiction was taken when Abramovitsh, only three years after the publication of Dos shterntikhl, developed what with Aksenfeld seemed to be only a happy accident into a systematic mode of narration and representation. And it is not only the quantity and the parodic accent of the dialogue that is responsible for the breathlessness of Dos shterntikhl and for the rather narrow limits of its artistic effectiveness. It is the melodramatic structure of the story itself, the forced movement toward a theatrical denouement, the monotonous permanence of its one dominant scenic dimension that accounts for that, although the parodic exaggeration certainly adds to the cumulative asphyxiation. Again we realize that

---

* This biblical saying (Prov. 10:2; 11:4) is quoted many times during a funeral. The Authorized Version reads: "Righteousness delivereth from death." But in Hebrew "righteousness" and "charity" are designated by one word, and thus the quotation is here interpreted as an appeal to charity.

the danger of self-defeat through excess was inherent in the compulsive dramatics of radical nineteenth-century Yiddish fiction. It originated in the very artistic premises upon which this fiction was constructed. Thus, it seems unlikely that sophisticated fiction could have been created under the circumstances, unless some means for widening its range could be devised.

Of course, we cannot be really sure. A major part of the Yiddish fiction of the first half of the century has never reached us. It was only recently when a new, important bilingual work by Perl was discovered in manuscript and published, that we learned how adeptly this master of parody could imitate and manipulate not only the hasidic letter, discourse, and conversation—i.e., the dramatic modes of hasidic expression—but also the hasidic fable at its highest "epic" achievement: the tales of Nakhman of Bratslav.[24] Perl penetrated the style and manner of Nakhman's tales like a fierce enemy in order to "explode them from within."[25] None of the latter-day neoromantics—Perets, Berditshevski, or even Buber and Agnon—caught the style and spirit, the most minute nuances of the tales, as expertly and as sensitively as Perl; nor did they succeed in re-creating the epic continuity, complications, suspense, and final solutions, the sheer complexity of their *fabula*, as he did. Of course, even in that Perl remained restricted within the limits of parody. But one wonders how he handled the narration in *Antignos*, his long, historical novel which was discovered in manuscript after World War I only to be lost again during World War II.

Aksenfeld's numerous novels (some of which, subtitled "A Jewish Gil Blas," ran in manuscript to 1500 or 2000 pages)[26] were probably destroyed before the beginning of the present century.[27] Therefore we cannot know how or if the limitations of the direct dramatic representation were circumvented in these works. From the little we do know about Aksenfeld's first novel, *Seyfer khasidim* ("The Book of the Hasidim"), we can, I think, assume that it did not differ fundamentally in its artistic methods from *Dos shterntikhl*.[28] In any case, we must base our notion of the development of nineteenth-century Yiddish fiction on what we have, for even with the possible discovery of new manuscripts (and the publication of the unknown tale by Perl certainly whets the appetite for more), our historical perspective cannot change, at least on the one point which is central to this study: in 1864 Abramovitsh liberated the art of Yiddish fiction by bringing Mendele into it.

iii

Introducing Mendele to the readers of *Kol-mevaser* in his *Kleyn mentshele*, Abramovitsh was grappling with the very problem I have been discussing. Whether he consciously posed it to himself or intuitively grasped it without conscious formulation, the question that he was trying to answer was crucial to the continuing development of artistic Yiddish fiction: How could this fiction both be broadened in scope and remain firmly anchored to its dramatic foundation, grow and yet not detach itself from the sources of its artistic vitality? The answer he developed as he explored the possibilities of the Mendele fiction was all that could be expected at the time. Within the framework of this fiction a dramatic mode of narration was evolved that was richer in structural possibilities, more susceptible to diversity of tone, more elastic, and more capable of control than any before it. From his very first experiments with this mode, Abramovitsh was in a much more advantageous position in many respects than that of Aksenfeld in *Dos shterntikhl* or Perl in *Megale-tmirin*. They had been restricted throughout their stories to one narrative gear; they had no reliable mechanism for shifting narrative dimensions. Abramovitsh had from the start such a mechanism to count on. Perl could, of course, introduce a new tone to his narrative by including in it some letters written by the opponents of the *hasidim*, but he remained imprisoned within the limits of parody and, largely, also within those of the epistolary system. Aksenfeld could shift his dramatic narrative from the court of the *tsadik* to the company of westernized Jewish contractors in Breslau, but on the whole he remained imprisoned within his scenic system of dialogues. Abramovitsh had two systems to play one against the other, that of the writing protagonist and that of the commenting Mendele. Both systems were dramatic, but they were so in different ways, for the dramatic quality of Mendele, as we have seen, was completely different from that of Yitskhok Avrom, Hershele, and Fishke.

Thus, a new element began to circulate through the budding, still half-embryonic body of modern Yiddish fiction. The achievements of the earlier part of the century were not discarded. The farcical scene and the epistolary parody were to remain two of the most popular conventions in Yiddish fiction to the end of the century, but through the agency of the new element they were integrated into a broader framework. In Linetski's *Dos poylishe yingl*, for example, we can find entire sections in which the technique and tone of *Megale-tmirin* (in its Hebrew version, of course) and those of *Dos shterntikhl* are closely imitated.[29] Yet this technique and tone do not dominate the story. The author is free to make as much use of them as he wishes, knowing all the time that he has other means to fall back on. Perl was undoubtedly a more careful and resourceful artist than Linetski, but Linetski had the benefit of having the fiction of Mendele for a model. Thus, the lesser craftsman, he was better equipped. And Linetski was by no means the only fiction writer who made use of Abramovitsh's innovations. Throughout the 1860s and the 1870s the principles of the Mendele fiction were put to use by several writers and journalists; a veritable "Abramovitsh school" flourished then, a school which, I believe, will be found to have been quite extensive and of much artistic interest when scholarly attention is drawn to the lesser-known publications of these decades. (See, for instance, the highly interesting *Briv fun Galitsyen*—"Letters from Galicia"—which the scholar N. Oyslender discovered in the forgotten magazine *Kol-la'am*. The letters were signed by "Dr. Tsigenzon," a still unidentified pseudonym.)[30] Even Shaykevitsh, whose command of the Yiddish fiction market began toward the end of the 1870s, was influenced by this school, as we have seen. In the 1880s the incentive to develop Yiddish fiction in the direction set by Abramovitsh was reinforced as the "leadership" of the school shifted away from such writers as Linetski and Sh. Bernshteyn (better known by the name of his persona, "Shilshom Bar Yente") to the indefatigable Sholem Aleichem, who canonized Abramovitsh and by making a cult of him created the historical consciousness of modern Yiddish literature. During all this time Abramovitsh himself continued to experiment with his Mendele, stretching him in every direction and enlarging his capacities as much as he could. He even tried to join him in leaping beyond the verge of the dramatic, only to prove how impossible such a leap still was at that stage.

The best of Yiddish fiction remains confined to the dramatic until well into the twentieth century; but the confinement was now much less cramping. It had enough "living space" to allow two or even three generations of talented fiction writers to develop an art of storytelling which, in spite of the great achievements of twentieth-century Yiddish fiction, is still one of the most memorable achievements of modern Yiddish literature. This "living space" can be described as the space surrounding the ironic persona. Every use of ironic language involves the creation of artistic space. Contrasting an overt meaning with a hidden one, juxtaposing the speaker and the subject of his speech, ironic language inevitably makes room, multiplies possibilities, enhances free movement. Abramovitsh's great contribution to Jewish literature was the introduction of the freedom of narrative movement through the employment of an ironic persona. Of course, Abramovitsh was not the first modern Jewish writer to discover this device. To some extent he can be said to have learnt his secret from the Hebrew satirists of the first half of the nineteenth century, especially from Y. Erter, who constructed the entire cycle of his work around *Hatsofe leveyt Yisrael* ("Watchman to the House of Israel"), which concerns a maskilic ingénue whose calculated innocence proved a very effective medium of satire. Even in Yiddish fiction of the first half of the century, as we now know it, writers did occasionally hit upon the idea of the ironic speaker. An excellent example of such an early discovery is Khayim Malage's *Gdules reb Volf* (which Abramovitsh could not have known), a parody in which a *hasid,* one of Reb Volf's adherents, records with all the trappings of feigned innocence how his adored leader climbed out of his obscure position as an insignificant and rather ignorant *dardeke-melamed* ("teacher of abecedarians") up to the status of a famous *tsadik*—through lies, dissimulation, clever warfare and timely armistices with other *tsadikim,* and even through criminal acts; all this told in a perfectly sustained tone of blind confidence in the sanctity of Reb Volf. Aksenfeld, we have just seen, managed to develop in his *Shterntikhl* the first rudiments of a Mendelean persona. It is quite possible that in his longer picaresques (*Mikhl der oyzerkes, Leyb Fridland,* etc.), now lost, he further developed it. In some of Dik's more satirical novelettes of the late 1850s the rudiments of ironic personae are present. The speaker in *Yekele Goldshleger,* for example, is definitely not Dik himself. From the few references he makes to himself, we learn that he is a stranger in Vilna (where the story takes place), a well-to-do businessman probably from Austro-Hungarian Galicia (he mentions acquaintances among members of the "aristocratic" families of Jewish Vilna whom he met in Vienna).[31] His interest in Yekele, the protagonist, who is a swindler and a merry rogue (he keeps marrying and divorcing women at the rate of one every few months), is characteristically "superior." To him, Yekele is both a despicable vagabond and an interesting "character." His narrative tone is imbued with quiet, almost subtle irony.

With the appearance of Mendele, however, these earlier intimations were combined and organized into something new; they became a "system." No more were they to emerge sporadic and half-intentional, allowing writers only fleeting moments of narrative freedom. Now they were developed into a useful, reliable set of artistic devices, the nucleus of an artistic manner or "fashion," as Mendele himself referred to it ("written freely and in my own fashion"). They were unified in the figure of Mendele into something even more organic than a "system," for in Mendele, Yiddish fiction found not only a liberating manner but also a symbol of liberty. In more than one way the itinerant bookpeddler represents the principle of freedom. His very physical mobility symbolizes this principle. From *Dos kleyne mentshele* onward we see him drive into one or another Jewish town as the story opens and out of it as it draws toward its conclusion, or vice versa. Never left stranded, he is always on the move. He may witness events, even take part in them to some extent, but basically he remains uncommitted. He is free to depart. He is free to leave for the open, to compare one town with another, to compare the entire Jewish or human world with "nature," with the field, the beast, the river, the forest, the ravine. He represents the freedom of the road. To compare Mendele to a picaresque hero is wrong because he has never been rejected from "normal" society (which, in the terms of the picaresque novel, is an immobile society). Outwardly he still forms a part of it. He is also not intended, as most classical picaresque heroes are, to find his way back to blissful immobility in the lap of society. He will always look like a perfectly acceptable member of traditional Jewish society, and yet he will always dissociate himself from this society and subject it to his ironic, distanced observation. His is not the conditional, degrading, and temporary freedom of the *picaro*, but rather the unconditional and permanent freedom of the insider–outsider. In the Jewish town he looks so misleadingly intimate, that he never comes to a showdown with the world in which he lives; intimate as he is, he is nevertheless a traveler disguised, much more so than Hershele. Hershele is not a real traveler. He has made his one great, successful trip (from his home *shtetl* to the West), and his one great fiasco of a trip (from the West back to his home *shtetl*), but he is not a man of the road. Traveling is not his "walk of life." His involuntary disguise reflects the historical breach between "the Jew" and the Europeanized "us." With Mendele, traveling *is* a way of life, and his voluntary disguise reflects the effort of Jewish literature to find an artistic means to reconcile—at least within the realm of art—"the Jew" to "us" and "us" to "the Jew." Thus, he is the most significant symbol of nineteenth-century Jewish literature in general and of Yiddish literature in particular. Intimate yet strange, speaking the language of "the people" and yet saying in it something the people have never said, confined to the Jewish world and yet strangely free to move among its contending parties, he is one of those flashes of the ironic spirit which seem to reconcile the irreconcilable.

As a disguised traveler, Mendele set Yiddish literature on its way toward maturity. As such he was studied, imitated, elaborated on by a host of writers. We should not forget that the figure of Sholem Aleichem, based on the foundations of Mendele, came to the world a traveler disguised, opening many of his monologues with the biblical quotation (originally uttered by Satan): "Mishut bo'orets umihishalekh bo"—"From going to and fro in the earth, and from walking up and down in it." (Job 1:7; 2:2.) [32] Until the very end he kept driving in trains, roaming between Odessa, Yehupets, Boyberik, Kasrilevke, London, New York. His very appellation, "Sholem Aleichem," is a greeting offered to a stranger coming from afar.

But this is the beginning of a new story. The story of the "being" Sholem Aleichem, its development, its mode, or rather modes, of literary existence, its kinship with Mendele, and its points of departure from him—all this calls for a separate analysis[33] and might be the subject of a sequel. Then there remains to chart the progress of the dramatic persona in modernistic Yiddish fiction, from Perets to Y. Bashevis Singer with his manifold masks of prattling innocence and garrulous, rather Mendelean devils. Our present study must, however, end here.

NOTES

Chapter One: The Commitment to Yiddish

1. See Gordon's introductory poem to his collected poems, *Kol shirey Y. L. Gordon*, Vol. I, 1884, p. xiii.

2. When A. Mapu, the first Hebrew novelist, decided to write a novel on contemporary Jewish life, he realized that adherence to pure biblical Hebrew —the stylistic ideal of Hebrew writers at the time—would rule out any real dialogue. In an open letter to a friend, appended to the second volume of the novel, he claimed that the Hebrew language itself gave him permission to take with him "on his way from the pastures of Eden and from ancient days to the habitations of her people in our time" another language, "her friend and follower," the Aramaic; i.e., he had to give up the purity of his biblical style and resort from time to time to the language of the Talmud and Midrash (see his *Ayit tsavua*, Vol. II [Vilna, 1861], pp. 204–5). Many Hebraists of the time objected to this compromise (see Mapu's introduction to *Khozey khezyonot* [Warsaw, 1869], p. 5; see also "In Search of the Vernacular," in David Patterson's *Abraham Mapu—The Creator of the Modern Hebrew Novel* [London, 1964] pp. 78–85).

3. See Abramovitsh's *Limdu hetev* (Warsaw, 1862), p. 4.

4. Ibid., pp. 5–6. See also my "Der onheyb fun aktueln hebreishn roman," in *Limdu hetev fun Sh. Y. Abramovitsh, araynfir, heores un hoysofes fun Dan Miron* (New York, 1969), pp. 80–84.

5. See Mapu's letter to Norov, the Russian minister of education, in *Mikhtevey Avraham Mapu*, ed. by B. Dinur (Jerusalem, 1970), p. 284. See also Sh. Ginzburg's article "Tsu der geshikhte fun yidishn drukvezen," *Historishe verk*, Vol. I (New York, 1937), pp. 60–61.

6. See Mapu's letter to his brother of January 5, 1858, in *Mikhtevey A. Mapu*, p. 24.

7. See Dik's introduction to his Hebrew novelette *Makhaze mul makhaze* (Warsaw, 1861), unpaginated. To these facts concerning the circulation of Hebrew books as opposed to Yiddish ones during the 1850s, 1860s, and even the 1870s (in the 1880s the situation changed considerably) a qualifying note must be added: The number of Hebrew readers at the time should not be equated with the number of copies a Hebrew book (even a successful one like *Ahavat tsiyon* or *Misterey Paris*) sold. From many contemporary sources—belletristic, memoiristic, and others—we know that a copy of a Hebrew book or magazine would travel among scores of readers, who either could not afford to buy it (because of the comparative costliness of Hebrew books and the extreme poverty of a large part of the Hebrew readership) or would not dare to have it in their possession and be stigmatized as "heretics" if found out by their orthodox relatives or neighbors. Thus, a single copy of a Hebrew novel sometimes served a whole town, and was surreptitiously and avidly read by generations of young yeshiva scholars succumbing to the attractions of modern secular literature. Mapu may have been right when he complained in one of his letters (to M. E. Beylinson, written in 1858), "And what is the fate of my books? The more readers and admirers they have—the less buyers" (see *Mikhtevey A. Mapu*, p. 180); or when, in another letter (to A. L. Mandelshtam, May 5, 1857), he sarcastically referred to "my books, which the young generation adores but never buys" (ibid., p. 19). Yiddish publications, such as Dik's novelettes, appeared at the time in the form of slim brochures, and were sold, thanks to their wide circulation, for only two or three *kopeks*. They were usually purchased not by the penniless young but by married women for their entertainment in the free hours of Saturdays and other holidays. These Yiddish *mayse-bikhlekh*, or "story books," even when written by a "modern" writer like Dik (provided that he was not associated with the radical *Haskala* movement and did not ridicule the *hasidim*) were tolerated by the orthodoxy as unworthy but harmless stuff, fit to be consumed by uneducated, silly women. (See Sh. Niger's study of the intimate relationship between nineteenth-century Yiddish literature and the Jewish female reader: "Di Yidishe literatur un di lezerin," in *Bleter geshikhte fun der yidisher literatur* [New York, 1959], pp. 37–107.)

8. See Abramovitsh's literary ideology at the time in his Hebrew novel *Ha'avot vehabanim* (Odessa, 1868), pp. 17–20.

9. Sh. Ginzburg, *Historishe verk*, Vol. I (New York, 1937), pp. 77–78.

10. See Tsederboym's introduction to *Dos poylishe yingl*. Published for the first time in the 1869 Odessa edition, it was republished in all the following ones. It was even included in the enlarged version of *Dos poylishe yingl* entitled *Dos khsidishe yingl* (Vilna, 1897), p. 3.

11. See Y. Sh(atski), "Notitsn vegn Linetskin," in *Pinkes*, Vol. I (New York, 1927–1928), pp. 270–71.

12. M. Spektor, *Mayn lebn*, Vol. II (Warsaw, 1927), pp. 14–15.

13. On the problem of the number of the editions of *Dos poylishe yingl*, see Y. Reminik, "Tsu der geshikhte fun Poylishn yingl," *Tsaytshrift*, Vol. V (Minsk, 1931), p. 194.

14. See Leonard Forster, *The Poet's Tongues—Multilingualism in Literature* (Cambridge, 1970).

15. See Maks Vaynraykh, "Ineveynikste tsveyshprakhikeyt in Ashkenaz biz der haskole: faktn un bagrifn," in *Di goldene keyt*, No. 35 (1959), pp. 80–88.

16. A first sketch of a theory of bilingualism in modern Jewish literature was drawn at the beginning of the twentieth century by the critic Bal-Makhshoves (Isidor Elyashiv), whose article "Tsvey shprakhn—eyneyntsige literatur," *Geklibene verk* (New York, 1953), pp. 112–23, remained for several decades the only coherent and general statement on the subject. Sh. Niger's *Di tsveyshprakhikeyt fun undzer literatur* (Detroit, 1941) broadened the scope of the discussion but added few analytical insights to it. A highly original and thought-provoking theory of bilingualism in Jewish literature was formulated by Dov Sadan in his short "Prolegomenon" to the study of modern Jewish literature "Masat mavo," in *Avney bedek* (Tel Aviv, 1962), pp. 9–66. All these sketches consist largely of theorems and generalizations, the relevance of which has not yet been manifested through consistent application of the body of historical data. They also do not treat the aesthetic problems involved.

17. The first important Hebrew work of prose fiction in the nineteenth century, *Megale-tmirin*, was found to have been written in Yiddish as well. The Yiddish version (published in Vilna, 1937), is in every way as stylistically brilliant as the Hebrew one, though its stylistic principles are different (see Z. Kalmanovitsh, "Yoysef Perls yidishe ksovim," in the Vilna edition mentioned above, pp. c–cvii). Another major parodic work by Perl, recently discovered in manuscript and published (Yosef Perl: *Ma'asiyot ve'igrot mitsadikim amitiyim ume'anshey shlomenu*, edited by Sh. Verses and Kh. Shmeruk, Jerusalem, 1970), is also written in Hebrew as well as Yiddish, both languages being employed with the same consummate mastery, though in different manners (see the discussion in the editors' introduction of the stylistic problems and quality of the Hebrew and Yiddish versions of the stories, ibid. pp. 42–75). Thus, throughout the century, from Perl, whose creative period started in its second decade, to Y. L. Perets, whose creative period in Yiddish started in the 1880s, works of the highest stylistic standard were written simultaneously in Hebrew and Yiddish.

18. See Berditshevski's article "Tishtush hagvulim," *Kitvey M. Y. Bin Goryon (Berditshevski): Ma'amarim* (Tel Aviv, 1960), pp. 191–92.

19. See, for example, N. M. Shaykevitsh's Hebrew novels *Hanidakhat* (Vilna, 1886), and *Mot yesharim* (Vilna, 1887), and see also short stories such as *Akhrit tsadikim* (Vilna, 1881) and *Mumar lehakh'is* (Vilna, 1881).

20. See Sholem Aleichem, *Yidishe folks-biblyotek*, Vol. I, belletristic section, p. 155. See also Y. L. Perets, *Ale verk*, Vol. I (New York, 1947), pp. 20–22.

21. The other two did explain the decision to write in Yiddish. For Aksenfeld's explanation, see above, p. 4 and also Ginzburg's *Historishe verk*, Vol. I, pp. 77–86. For Spektor's account see *Mayn lebn*, Vol. I, p. 281.

22. For details on this interesting adaptation, see M. Viner's *Tsu der geshikhte fun der yidisher literatur in 19-tn yorhundert*, Vol. I (New York, 1945), pp. 255–64.

23. This anonymous comedy, titled *Di genarte velt*, was republished in Moscow in 1936. For details, see ibid., pp. 49–63.

24. See S. Etinger's *Ksovim*, ed. Max Weinreich, Vol. I (Vilna, 1925), p. xxviii.

25. See Dik's introduction to *Makhaze mul makhaze*.

26. Abramovitsh liked to remind his admirers that he went on writing articles and essays almost exclusively in Hebrew. See Klozner's *Historiya shel hasifrut ha'ivrit*, Vol. VI, 2d ed. (Jerusalem, 1958), p. 346.

27. Sh. Abramovitsh, *Kol kitvey Mendele Mokher-Sfarim* (Tel Aviv, 1947), p. 4.

28. Cf. Ecclesiastes 1:16, 2:22, 4:8.

29. Cf. Proverbs 5:20, 31:3.

30. Cf. Hosea, 2:21, 23.

31. Cf. Esther 2:9.

32. See *Kol kitvey Mendele*, p. 5.

33. See Sh. Niger, "Ven hot A. M. Dik ongehoybn shraybn yidish?" *Pinkes*, Vol. I (1927–1928), pp. 289–93.

34. *Kol kitvey Mendele*, p. 4. Lefin, by the way, did publish one of his Yiddish works, the translation of Proverbs, in 1814.

35. Etinger, *Ksovim*, Vol. I, pp. xxxii–xxxvi.

36. See Aksenfeld's letter to Gotlober in *Y. Aksenfelds verk*, ed. M. Viner, Vol. I (Kharkov and Kiev, 1931), pp. 352–54.

37. See Ginzburg's *Historishe verk*, Vol. I, pp. 75–78.

38. This was due especially to the decision of the Russian government under Nicholas I to allow only two Jewish printers to operate in Russia. The monopoly, which was given for 25 years (1836–1861), made it extremely difficult for the Yiddish-writing *maskilim* to publish their works.

Ironically, this measure of the authorities was triggered by the campaign of some *maskilim* against the expanding literary activity of the *hasidim*. As it turned out, the monopolization of the Jewish printing business gave the *hasidim* virtual veto power in all matters relating to Jewish printing and publishing inside Russia. One of the two monopolistic presses (in Zhitomir) was completely controlled by the *hasidim*. Even those *maskilim* who taught in the governmental Rabbinical Seminary in Zhitomir, "reliable" as they were, had to send their manuscripts to the other press in Vilna, where many books of the Hebrew *maskilim* were printed; but the *hasidim* were quite influential here, too. Since the printer's business was founded on the large and constant demand for traditional Jewish books of learning and ritual, it was vulnerable to hasidic pressures. The hasidic leaders, who did not hesitate to issue orders of excommunication, could easily sever the printer's connections with the better part of his market. The Vilna printers published Hebrew books of the *Haskala* because the *hasidim* chose in most cases to ignore them, but they were reluctant to publish Yiddish books of *maskilim* (unless their *Haskala* was of the mildest brand, like that of Dik), especially if they attacked the *hasidim* or ridiculed them. See the letter of the Vilna printers to the Russian ministry of education concerning their refusal to publish Aksenfeld's *Seyfer khasidim* in Sh.

Ginzburg's *Historishe verk*, Vol. I, pp. 81–82. See also Ginzburg's article "Tsu der geshikhte fun yidishn drukvezn," ibid., pp. 48–62.

39. For differing conjectures concerning the dates of Aksenfeld's compositions see Max Erik, "Vegn sotsyaln mehus fun Aksenfelds shafn," in *Tsaytshrift*, Vol. V, pp. 125–27. Erik dates *Dos shtentikhl* "after 1841." See also Viner's *Tsu der geshikhte*, Vol. I, pp. 195–97. Viner dates the novel "not later than the 'twenties'."

40. Perl, who lived outside of Russia, could certainly have published his Yiddish compositions if he had had a mind to. The same goes for Levinzon, who published his Hebrew antihasidic pamphlets out of Russia (among them, one written in Yiddish as well as in Hebrew and published in Yiddish as the second part of *Hefker-velt*). From Gotlober's reminiscences (published in *Di yidishe folks-biblyotek*, Vol. I) we do not learn that he did in fact have a mind to publish his Yiddish compositions before the 1860s.

41. Characteristically the only instance in A. A. Roback's *The Story of Yiddish Literature* (New York, 1940) where the widespread usage of pen names is mentioned as a historical problem which calls for further investigation occurs in a chapter which the editors preferred to leave out of the printed book. It was subsequently published in the author's *Supplement to the Story of Yiddish Literature* (Cambridge, Mass., 1941). See p. 40.

42. Leo Wiener, *The History of Yiddish Literature in the Nineteenth Century* (New York, 1899), pp. 383–84. Wiener's list attributed to Sholem Aleichem six pseudonyms, to Perets ten. However, both writers had not yet reached the zenith of their careers when Wiener's *History* appeared. Throughout their careers they used many pseudonyms which the historian at the time could not have known. Saul Chajes' lexicon of pen names in Hebrew and Yiddish literature (*Otsar bduyey hashem—Thesaurus pseudonymorum quae in litteratura hebreica et judaeo-germanica inveniuntur*, Vienna, 1933) ascribes seventeen pen names to Perets, and twenty-three to Sholem Aleichem.

43. Hebrew writers of the nineteenth century also resorted very often to pseudonyms, but their motives for this were, in most cases, quite different from those of Yiddish writers. For a Hebrew writer of the time employing a pen name was usually a matter of decorum. His real name, of Germanic or Slavonic origin, was not regarded as worthy of being incorporated (as the author's signature) into the pure biblical Hebrew text of a poem, a story, an article, etc. The stylistic etiquette he so ardently adhered to demanded from the Hebrew writer a Hebrew name. It was not, however, his intention to conceal his personal identity and to disassociate himself from his literary work, and therefore he made every effort to retain in his pen name a part of his real name or an indication of it. Thus he either translated his name into biblical Hebrew (as in the case of the poet Gotlober who published the edition of his collected poems under the pen name Mahalalel, both names, the German and the Hebrew, having the same meaning: "one who praises God"), or he resorted to clever anagrams, weaving the initials of his or his father's name into something resembling a Hebrew word (as in the case of the poets Lebenzon senior—Adam hakohen, and Lebenzon junior—Mikhal, and scores of others), or he simply re-

constructed his name according to the rules of Hebrew grammar (as in the case of the novelist Semolenskin, who had only to delete from his name its last 'n' in order to change its Russian form into a Hebrew one). Yiddish writers very rarely used such methods in constructing their pen names, although some of them did play the anagram trick (A. M. Dik—Adam; Yitskhok Yoyel Linetski—Eli Kotsin Hatskhakueli, etc.). Basically they employed "folksy" nicknames which had nothing to do with their real names and which were meant to be "funny" as well as to conceal their identity. Many of them were quite successful in this. There still exist pseudonyms of Yiddish writers the identification of which is doubtful.

44. *Ale verk fun Sholem-Aleichem*, Folksfond edition, Vol. XV, *Yidishe shrayber* (New York, 1918), p. 156.

45. See Dik's introduction to *Makhaze mul makhaze.*

46. See Kh. Liberman, "Der mekhaber fun yidishn farpeysakh," *YIVO-bleter*, Vol. XIX (1942), pp. 130–34.

47. *Dos Sholem-Aleichem-bukh*, ed. Y. D. Berkovitsh (New York, 1926), p. 4.

48. Ibid.

49. *Kol kitvey Mendele*, p. 4.

50. Linetski noticed that in the early 1870s. See his *feuilleton*, "Di kurtszikhtige shrayber," in his *Dos meshulakhes* (Zhitomir, 1875), pp. 48–57.

51. See, for example, M. Y. Berditshevski, *Yidishe ksovim*, Vol. II (New York, 1951), pp. 187–90.

52. See D. Bergelson, *Bam Dnyeper*, Vol. II (Moscow, 1940), pp. 118–19. See also Sh. Niger's interpretation of this episode in Penek's literary development in his article "Di tsvey Bergelsons—der kinstler un der politiker," in *Yidishe shrayber in Sovet-Rusland* (New York, 1958), pp. 313–14.

53. *Bam Dnyeper*, Vol. II, p. 119.

54. See, for instance, the opening poem in Y. L. Gordon's collection of Yiddish verse, *Sikhes-khuln*, 4th ed. (Vilna, 1899), p. 7.

55. See, for instance, Sh. Niger, *Dertseylers un romanistn*, Vol. I (New York, 1946), p. 72.

56. See the introduction to Dik's *Makhaze mul makhaze.*

57. See below, Chap. 7, p. 215.

58. See Sholem Aleichem, *Shomers mishpet* (Barditshev, 1888), p. 4.

59. The Yiddish-writing *maskilim* were connected with each other in a complex net of personal relationships formed by wandering and pilgrimage. For a partial illustration, see Gotlober's *Memuarn* in *Gotlober un zayn epokhe*, ed. A. Fridkin (Vilna, 1925), Vol. I, first part, Chaps. 22–23, pp. 164–78, Chap. 28, pp. 205–12; second part, Chaps. 2–3, pp. 268–80, Chap. 7, pp. 304–10.

60. See Tsederboym's bibliographical note on Etinger, *Kol-mevaser*, 1869, No. 23.

61. See Tsederboym's note to Y. M. Lifshits' article "Di fir klasn," *Kol-mevaser*, 1863, No. 25.

62. See Max Erik, *Etyudn tsu der geshikhte fun der haskole*, Vol. I (Minsk, 1934), pp. 138–58.

63. See Dik's introduction to *Makhaze mul makhaze*.

64. *Kol kitvey Mendele*, p. 4.

65. Ibid., p. 5.

66. See Sh. Niger, *Dertseylers un romanistn*, Vol. I (New York, 1946), p. 55.

67. See Lifshits' introduction to his *Yidish-rusisher verterbukh*, (Zhitomir, 1876).

68. See *Dos Sholem-Aleichem-bukh*, p. 4.

69. See Abramovitsh's letter to Sholem Aleichem of June 28, 1888, in *Shriftn*, Vol. I (Kiev, 1928), p. 255.

70. See Y. Dinezon, "Di yidishe shprakhe un ire shrayber," in *Hoyzfraynt*, Vol. I (1888), pp. 9–10.

71. The scope of this study does not allow any discussion of the change in the attitude of Russian-Jewish intellectuals toward Yiddish, which took place in the 1880s. How this change occurred and what were its diverse (and sometimes contradictory) manifestations—these questions must be answered in a detailed study, which has still to be written. In most histories of Yiddish literature this change is said to have emanated from the state of shock into which Russian-Jewish intellectuals were thrown by the series of pogroms triggered by the assassination of Alexander II in 1881. Complacently tolerated, or, in some cases, even instigated by the representatives of the czarist government, those pogroms shattered the high hopes for political and economic emancipation of Russian Jewry, which the early liberalism of the regime of Alexander had inspired in the heart of the *maskilim*, and they, the *maskilim*, went bankrupt so to say, both morally and intellectually. Out of their great disillusionment sprang the new Jewish nationalism with its different branches, particularly Zionism and Jewish Socialism. A mood of nationalistic (and sometimes chauvinistic) repentance swept the intelligentsia. The common Jewish people and the values inherent in the traditional and communal Jewish life began to be cherished as the source of the national genius. Thus the way was laid open for the recognition of Yiddish as a value although some elements in the emerging Zionism reinforced the deprecation of Yiddish. Formerly Yiddish had been incriminated as the language of the uneducated, superstitious masses. Now it became the language of the Diaspora, one of the blemishes added to the national physiognomy by long centuries of exile and persecutions. This historical explanation, though basically correct, must be revised. A detailed re-examination, which will take into account all the relevant facts, will reveal, I suspect, that it overemphasizes ideological-nationalistic factors (which undoubtedly played an important role in the development discussed here), while neglecting other factors of decisive importance (mostly those connected with the economic and social development of Yiddish-speaking Jewry in Russia and overseas in the last two decades of the century; the emergence of a new Yiddish market, etc.).

72. See *Dos Sholem-Aleichem-bukh*, p. 326.

73. See Sholem Aleichem's "Der yidisher dales in di beste verke fun unzere folks-shriftshteler," in *Dos yidishe folksblat* (1888), the literary supplement, No. 39, p. 1076, and No. 42, p. 1149.

74. See Sholem Aleichem's *Shomers mishpet* (Barditshev, 1888), p. 4.

75. *Dos yidishe folksblat*, 1888, No. 40, p. 1107.

76. See Sholem Aleichem's series of book reviews, "Oyfn literarishn mark," *Folks-biblyotek*, Vol. I, p. 353.

77. I translate "popular writers" for lack of a better gloss. Actually, the term *folks-shriftshteler* used by Sholem Aleichem (a term central to his conception of literature; later changed to *folks-shrayber*) should be rendered "a writer of the people." Sholem Aleichem himself stated that mere popularity did not make a real *folks-shrayber*. A *folks-shrayber* writes for the people, about the people, and in order to educate the people while entertaining them.

78. See Abramovitsh's letter to Sholem Aleichem of June 28, 1888. *Shriftn* (Kiev, 1928), Vol. I, p. 255.

79. See *Di yidishe folks-biblyotek*, Vol. I, p. 250.

80. See Levinzon's "Hefker-velt," in *Di yidishe folks-biblyotek*, Vol. I. See also Sholem Aleichem's promise to publish Aksenfeld's *Der fraymar* and Lefin's *Der ershter khosid*, ibid., pp. 251, 258.

81. See E. Shulman, *Di geshikhte fun der zhargon literatur*, in *Di yidishe folks-biblyotek*, Vol. II.

82. The first *Hoyz-fraynt* included the first historical survey of nineteenth-century Yiddish literature (by Y. Dinezon) and an extensive biography of Abramovitsh (by M. Spektor). Many of the older writers contributed to it.

83. See *Dos Sholem-Aleichem-bukh*, p. 182.

84. Ibid., pp. 166–67, 190–91.

85. Leo Wiener, *History of Yiddish Literature*.

86. See *Vegn der yidisher literatur, Ale verk fun Perets*, Vol. XI (New York, 1948), p. 299.

87. See N. Mayzl, *Y. L. Perets—zayn lebn un shafn* (New York, 1945), pp. 214–21.

Chapter Two: A Language as Caliban

1. This was explicitly asserted as early as 1784 in what is regarded by many as the first document in the history of the so-called new Hebrew literature, *Nakhal habsor*, the manifesto-like prospectus which the founders of the Hebrew monthly *Hame'asef* had circulated before they published the first issue of their epoch-making periodical (see an analysis of this document in Kh. N. Shapira, *Toldot hasifrut ha'ivrit hakhadasha*, Vol. I [Tel Aviv, 1940], pp. 173–76). Throughout the nineteenth century this proud and defiant assertion of the role of the new literature as a revolutionary and a restorative cultural phenomenon remained the core of the literary ideology to which most Hebrew writers adhered. It was expressed again and again in many forms and styles. A documentation and analysis of the development of this literary ideology would necessitate a separate and rather extensive study.

2. See Sh. Niger's "Vegn dem onheyb fun der nayer yidisher literatur," in his *Bleter geshikhte fun der yidisher literatur* (New York, 1959), pp. 207–79; and M. Viner's "Di yidishe literatur baym onheyb funem nayntsentn yorhun-

dert," in *Tsu der geshikhte fun der yidisher literatur in 19-tn yorhundert*, Vol. I, pp. 23–63.

3. In 1875 P. Smolenskin, a major Hebrew *maskil*, published his *Et lata'at* ("Time to Plant"), which included an iconoclastic attack on Mendelssohn and his disciples. A heated controversy followed. For details see Y. Klozner, *Historiya shel hasifrut*, Vol. I (Jerusalem, 1930), pp. 73–79.

4. See H. Graetz, *History of the Jews*, Vol. V (Philadelphia, 1895), pp. 300, 328ff. For example, this is what Graetz had to say about education through Yiddish in Germany in the eighteenth century:

> Polish school masters—there were no others—with rod and angry gestures, instructed Jewish boys in their tender youth to discover the most absurd perversities in the Holy Book, translating it into this hateful jargon, and so confusing the text with their own translation, that it seemed as if Moses had spoken in the barbarous dialect of the Polish Jews. (p. 328)

5. This happened in the 1880s, as Yiddish literature was beginning to gain in self-consciousness and in self-esteem, and Graetz's expressions of contempt for Yiddish drew sharp reactions from some writers. See E. Shulman, "Di geshikhte fun der zhargon literatur," *Folks-biblyotek*, Vol. II, *Visenshaftlekhe opteylung*, p. 118.

6. See Mendelssohn's letter to August von Hennings of June 29, 1779, in M. Kayserling's *Moses Mendelssohn, sein Leben und seine Werke* (Leipzig, 1862), p. 522.

7. Ibid.

8. See David Friedländer, "Sendschreiben an meine Mitbrüder," in the *Auserordentliche Beilage* to *Hame'asaf* (1888), unpaginated. See also Z. Reyzen, *Fun Mendelson biz Mendele*, Vol. I (Warsaw, 1923), p. 19.

9. R. Maler, *Hakhasidut vehahaskala* (Rekhavya, 1961), p. 83.

10. Mendelssohn's translation was used throughout the century by aspiring Eastern European *maskilim* as a textbook for the study of German. For an example, see Max Erik's *Etyudn*, Vol. I, p. 81. In the 1860s all Jewish teachers in some of the provinces of the Russian Empire were required to purchase the translation. However, only a few of them, the most "advanced" and "modern," made any use of it. Others saved the books by tearing the German pages (which were printed facing the Hebrew text) out of them. See Ab. Kahan's *Bleter fun mayn lebn*, Vol. I (New York, 1926), pp. 73–74.

11. See the Introduction to Dr. Markuze's *Seyfer-refues* in Reyzen's *Fun Mendelson biz Mendele*, Vol. I, p. 85.

12. For preliminary details on Lefin and his life's work see R. Mahler, *A History of Modern Jewry* (New York, 1971), pp. 588–600.

13. Lefin made his recommendations in a pamphlet he wrote in French (because it was intended to be read by the "enlightened" Polish nobility): *Essai d'un plan de reforme ayant pour l'objet d'éclairer la Nation Juive en Pologne et de redresser par la moeurs*.

14. See R. Mahler's *History of Modern Jewry*, pp. 590–92.

15. For details on Lefin's biblical translations see Mahler's *History*, pp. 596–600; Reyzen's *Fun Mendelson*, pp. 147–62; M. Erik's *Etyudn*, Vol. I, pp. 151–56.

16. From Lefin's introduction to his translation of Psalms, preserved in manuscript. See Mahler's *History*, p. 596.

17. See Kh. Shmeruk, "Vegn etlekhe printsipn fun Mendl Lefins Mishley iberzetsung," in *Yidishe shprakh*, Vol. XXIV (1964), No. 2, pp. 33–52.

18. For the first excited reaction see E. Shulman, "Mendl Satanover in yidish," ibid., No. 3, pp. 82–90. See also an earlier article by Y. Mark, "Di hoypt-eygnshaftn fun Mendl Satanovers Mishley-iberzetsung," in *Yidishe shprakh*, Vol. XVI (1956), No. 4, pp. 108–14.

19. The only relevant argument in Shulman's critique of Shmeruk seems to be his contention that, written for "export," i.e., for non-Jews interested in the polonization of the Jews, Lefin's French pamphlet (and particularly his insisting in it on the speedy replacement of Yiddish by Polish) should not be accepted at its face value. This should certainly be taken into consideration. Although we have no reason to suspect Lefin's sincerity in his pamphlet, which is a typical maskilic document (its recommendations, including the one concerning the replacement of Yiddish by the official language of the state, were repeated by dozens of *maskilim* who wrote for a Jewish audience—in Hebrew and even in Yiddish), it is quite possible that had he written about Yiddish for a Jewish audience he would have expressed himself in a different, more positive, way. The fact that he referred to Yiddish as "our Jewish tongue" in his unpublished preface to his translation of Psalms can be regarded as a slight corroboration of this. The importance Shulman attributes to this tiny bit of evidence is, however, blown out of all proportion. The important fact is that Lefin did *not* care to mention in any of his various Hebrew books the possible usefulness of Yiddish, a fact that can be construed as signifying that he was far from willing to encourage a positive appreciation of the language among those who spoke it. Had Lefin wanted to dwell on the possible merits of Yiddish as a literary language in an article or a book addressed to the Jewish audience, he had ample opportunity of doing so; but he did not, even when he found himself vilified and exposed as a "traitor" to the *Haskala* (by the Hebrew *maskil* Tuvya Feder) for translating into Yiddish a part of the Holy Scripture. The vindication of his translation was left for the alienated and quite uncharacteristic *maskil* Y. Sh. Bik, who certainly did not express the ideas of his fellow *maskilim*, including Lefin. In any case we have no positive proof that Lefin thought of the literary use of Yiddish in any but pragmatic terms and that he foresaw a development of a Yiddish literature not strictly subordinate to the *Haskala* tactics.

20. See, for instance, the evaluation of Lefin's achievement in Y. Klozner, *Historiya shel hasifrut ha'ivrit hakhadasha*, Vol. I (Jerusalem, 1930), pp. 199–225. Klozner did not realize that there existed a close relationship between the stylistic concepts Lefin had developed in his Yiddish translations of the Bible and what he (Klozner) considered Lefin's lasting contribution to modern Hebrew literature—his new flexible prose style based on a dexterous "mixture" of early (biblical) and late (mishnaic, midrashic, even medieval) linguistic elements.

21. See Erik's *Etyudn*, Vol. I, pp. 147, 151.

22. See below, for example, the quotation from Levinzon's *Te'uda beyisra'el*, pp. 45–46.

23. See Erik's *Etyudn*, Vol. I, pp. 158–62. See also Sh. Verses, "Y. Sh. Bik —der blondzhnder maskil," in *YIVO-bleter*, Vol. XIII (1938), pp. 505–36.

24. See Y. Sh. Bik's letter to Tuvya Feder in *Kerem khemed*, Vol. II (1836), p. 97.

25. See, for example, Gotlober's contradictory utterances concerning Yiddish in *Gotlober un zayn epokhe*, ed. B. Fridkin, Vol. I, pp. 311–14.

26. See Kayserling's *Mendelssohn*, p. 283.

27. See Kh. Borodyanski, "M. Mendelson un zayne yidishe briv," *Historishe shriftn*, of the YIVO, Vol. I (1929), pp. 297–346.

28. See *Or lanetiva*, a Hebrew pamphlet Mendelssohn published as an introduction to the translation of the Pentateuch (Berlin, 1783). The brochure is unpaginated.

29. Kayserling, *Mendelssohn*, p. 283.

30. *Kerem khemed*, Vol. II, p. 98.

31. From N. H. Vayzl's poem "Mehalel re'a," opening the brochure *Alim litrufa*, published as a prospectus to the translation of the Pentateuch (Amsterdam, 1778). See also Klozner's *Historiya shel hasifrut*, Vol. I, p. 99. N. H. Vayzl is often referred to in English as N. H. Wesseley.

32. Aykhl's comedy was circulated at the time of its writing in handwritten copies and during the nineteenth century very few people had first-hand knowledge of it, and its description as "a biting satire on Yiddish" (probably originating from the German-Jewish historian Y. M. Jost) was repeated unqualified (see E. Shulman, "Di geshikhte fun der zhargon literatur," *Folks-biblyotek*, Vol. II, section of criticism, p. 118; see also Reyzen's *Fun Mendelson*, p. 20). In the 1920s attention was drawn to the comedy again. Now critics decided that it contained no ridicule of Yiddish at all. The assumption that it was an anti-Yiddish satire was pronounced "a legend" (see N. Shtif, "Literatur-historishe legendes," in *Di royte velt*, 1926, Nos. 7–8, pp. 152–57; No. 10, pp. 96–105. In 1930 the play was published by Reyzen in *Arkhiv far der geshikhte fun yidishn teater un drama*, Vol. I. Reyzen in his introduction accepted the "legend" theory (see ibid., p. 86); but now that the text was available it became clear that Shtif and Reyzen were as wide off the mark as the nineteenth-century scholars had been. While the play can by no means be considered a pamphlet against Yiddish—it is much too rich and complex for that—it also cannot be doubted that Yiddish was made fun of in it, as a provincial, barbarous dialect. The whole comic structure of the play is based on the differentiation between "pure" German and deviations from it (see Erik's *Etyudn*, Vol. I, p. 110).

33. In the Authorized Version, Nehemiah's complaint ends "could not speak in the Jews' language, but according to the language of each people" (Neh. 13:24). This reading, however, would not substantiate Levinzon's commentary. I have therefore digressed for once from the Authorized Version and translated the biblical text as Levinzon read it.

34. See Y. B. Levinzon's *Te'uda bayisra'el* (first edition 1828), 4th ed. (Warsaw, 1901), pp. 33–38.

35. The different names of Yiddish and their various meanings have been studied by several scholars. See, for instance, Y. Shatski, "Vegn di nemen far yidish," in *YIVO-bleter*, Vol. VIII (1935), pp. 148–54; E. Spivak, "Di grunt-nemen fun Yiddish," in *Fragen fun der yidisher shprakh*, ed. M. Viner and A. Zaretski (Moscow, 1938), pp. 71–86.

36. See Mendelssohn's *Or lanetiva*.

37. See, for example, the dedication of A. D. Lebenzon's *Shirey sfat ko-desh*, Vol. I (Leipzig, 1842), to "the fair inhabitant of God's house, chosen by the God of Israel and his prophets' dear one, the queen of languages, whose holy name is *Hebrew*, God will establish her forever, Selah."

38. For typical "poetics" of the Hebrew writers of the early phases of the *Haskala* literature see N. H. Vayzl's introduction to *Shirey tif'eret* (first edition 1789) and Sh. Levizon's *Melitsat yeshurun* (first edition 1816).

39. See Y. M. Lifshits' introduction to his *Yidish-rusisher verterbukh* (Zhi-tomir, 1876). See also Linetski's article "Ovinu-malkeynu" in *Der statek* (Odessa, 1876), pp. 90–118.

40. See *Shirey Shomer vezikhronotav* (Jerusalem, 1952), pp. 175–76.

41. See Abramovitsh's *Eyn mishpat* (Zhitomir, 1867), pp. 35–36. Abramo-vitsh argued here that although Yiddish, "the language of stammerers," should be eliminated as soon as possible, some use can temporarily be made of it by the *maskilim*. He praised Tsederboym for his activity as editor of *Kol-mevaser* but added this qualification: "We should be grateful to the *maskil* Tseder-boym for publishing the Yiddish magazine *Kol-mevaser*, the aim of which is not to improve the mixed Jewish-German language but to communicate through it with the masses, who for the time being still do not understand any other language, and thus draw them nearer to the *Haskala*" (p. 36).

42. See Sh. Ginzburg's *Historishe verk*, Vol. I, p. 83.

43. See E. Shulman's *Di geshikhte fun der zhargon literatur*, p. 122.

44. The language was referred to as "dos yidish loshn" ("the Jewish lan-guage" in Yiddish) or "die jüdische Sprache" (in German, "the Jewish lan-guage") by as early a figure as M. Lefin. The second reference is to the title of a German brochure on the possible usefulness of Yiddish for the enlighten-ment of the Jewish people, no copy of which has survived. Y. Lifshits was, however, the first nineteenth-century *maskil* who referred to "Yiddish" con-sciously and more or less systematically. In the ninth issue of *Kol-mevaser* (first year, 1862–1863) he began his campaign for Yiddish with a versified dialogue between the Jew and his despised language. The dialogue was titled "Yidl un Yehudis" and in a note it was explained: "Dos meynt men yidn mit zeyer yidish loshn" ("This is meant as the Jews and their Jewish language"), thus designating the language as Yiddish, i.e., as Jewish, not as *Yidish-daytsh* (Jew-ish-German), the common appellation at the time. In further publications, Lifshits kept referring to the language as "di yidishe shprakhe" or "dos yidish loshn" (see his article "Di fir klasn," in *Kol-mevaser* [1863], No. 21). In the ti-tles he gave his two dictionaries, the language is referred to as *yidish*. How-ever, even Lifshits was not always consistent. He announced the publication of his *Rusish-yidisher verterbukh* in an article titled "Di daytsh-yidishe brik" ("The Jewish-German Bridge," see *Kol-mevaser*, Vol. V [1867], No. 31).

45. See "Di fir klasn," in *Kol-mevaser*, Vol. I, No. 21–23.
46. Ibid., No. 21.
47. See "Di daytsh-yidishe brik," *Kol-mevaser* (1867), No. 31.
48. See the introduction to Lifshits' *Yidish-rusisher verterbukh* (Zhitomir, 1876).
49. This parody was found in Tarnopol, in Perl's archive, attributed to him and published with the Yiddish version of *Megale-tmirin* in Perl's *Yidishe ksovim* (pp. 221–24). It was discovered, however, that the real author of the brilliant piece is not Perl but one Khayim Malage, of whom we know only that he lived in the Podolian town Bar during the 1820s, was, like Perl, one of Lefin's disciples (letters from him to Lefin were found), and, evidently, a loyal, antihasidic *maskil*. See S. Kats, "Naye materyaln fun dem Perl-arkhiv," *YIVO-bleter* Vol. XIII (1938), pp. 561–65.
50. See Erik's *Etyudn*, Vol. I, p. 145.
51. Y. Aksenfeld, *Dos shterntikhl*, ed. by M. Viner (Moscow, 1938), p. 117.
52. Of course, I do not suggest that this modest "theory," a working hypothesis of an unsophisticated writer, is to be compared with the intricate theoretical structures which some professional philosophers, especially the German post-Hegelians, erected in their discussions of the place of the ugly in art. Still, naively as nineteenth-century Yiddish writers dealt with theoretical problems, they touched in their attitude toward the alleged ugliness of Yiddish upon philosophical principles (see Karl Rosenkranz, *Aesthetik des Hässlichen* [Königsberg, 1853], pp. 35–47).
53. This was made amply clear by his own practice as a novelist and playwright to the extent that we know it, for in his novel and surviving plays a practical joke of disguise, recognition, and unmasking is under way at almost any given moment. Indeed, the typical development of his comic fabulae is that of an elaborate practical joke or of a protracted hoax.
54. See Ginzburg's *Historishe verk*, Vol. I, p. 78.
55. See Y. Klozner, *Historiya shel hasifrut*, Vol. III, 2d. ed. (Jerusalem, 1952), pp. 300–4. See also my article "Der onheyb fun aktueln hebreishn roman," in Sh. Y. Abramovitsh, *Limdu hetev*, pp. 28–41.
56. *Dos shterntikhl*, p. 117.
57. See Y. Kh. Ravnitski's "Shalom Ya'akov Abramovitsh," in *Kol kitvey Mendele Mokher-Sfarim*, Vol. VI (Tel Aviv, 1936), p. 147.
58. Y. Y. Linetski, *Der statek* (Odessa, 1876), p. 117.
59. Ibid., p. 115.
60. Ibid., p. 118.
61. See *Yisrolik*, No. 0. (Strangely enough, Linetski and Goldfaden began to enumerate their magazine only from its second issue).
62. See Perets' letter to Sholem Aleichem on May 17, 1889. The letter was written in Hebrew. *Kol kitvey Y. L. Perets*, Vol. X, second part (Tel Aviv, 1960), p. 226.
63. See his letter to Byalik of January 30, 1906. Ibid., p. 250.
64. See *Folks-biblyotek*, Vol. I, p. 155. I quote from the first version of *Monish*, published in 1888 in the *Folks-biblyotek*. For the second version (1892) see *Ale verk fun Y. L. Perets*, Vol. I (New York, 1947), pp. 20–21.

65. See *Monish* in its first version, the *Folks-biblyotek*, Vol. I, p. 155.
66. See *Ale verk fun Perets*, Vol. XI, p. 7.
67. Shortly before publishing *Monish*, Perets directly defined his notion of what poetry was (or rather of what the poet was) in one of the sections of his Hebrew poetic cycle *Manginot hazman* ("The Melodies of Our Age," 1887). This is how he characterized his "brothers" (i.e., the poets, distinguished from nonpoetic, ordinary human beings), whose alleged "waywardness" he defended:

> Im yismekhu akhay, ve'im nafsham ne'ekeret,
> Im akev yagdilu veyashuvu ad daka,
> Lo vam hatmura, lo rukham akheret,
> Hem kesef khay bikne zkhukhit zaka.
>
> Av kal ki yakhlof katsel al shamayim,
> Keren or yeta, ru'akh tsakh shfayim,
> Tal orot ki yipol . . . bemar midli day
> Leha'alot ulhapil hakesef hekhay,
> Hu gilgul hameshorer bikne hashfoferet,
> Lo teda margo'a neshama ne'ekeret!

("If my brothers rejoice, or they are dejected,/ If they soar to the sky or become utterly depressed,/ It is not they who change, they remain the same,/ They are but quicksilver in a tube of crystal-clear glass.

"Let a light cloud pass like a shadow on the sky,/ Let a lightbeam stray, a fresh wind blow,/ Glimmering dew fall . . . one drop of water suffices/ To raise or precipitate the living silver,/ Which is the poet metamorphosed in a tube;/ An excitable spirit will have no peace.") See *Kol kitvey Perets*, Vol. IX, second part (Tel Aviv, 1957), p. 240.

Perets conceived of the nature of the poet as essentially impressionistic, and therefore in a constant flux. It is the poet's fate to be "excitable," to react to every "atmospheric" pressure, and it is his vocation to express as sensitively as he can the constant emotional fluttering he experiences under the unceasing rain of new impressions. Obviously, this could not be adequately done in a language tuned only to the emotions of the national "giant." Perets, of course, proceeded to write many poems in Yiddish, but he had to qualify his notion of poetry. See, for instance, his highly suggestive Yiddish poem *Mayne muze* ("My Muse," 1891), which begins with a negative definition of the poet's source of inspiration. The Yiddish poet's muse is not a flower; she does not grow on the lawn; nor is she a butterfly or a nightingale, and she has no sweet trills. She is rather "an old Jewish woman, shriveled and ugly. A deserted wife with orphaned children, she is scattered over the whole world, and she is a destitute pauper, whose shouts and curses never stop" (see *Ale verk fun Y. L. Perets*, Vol. I, p. 28). The opening negative analogies dissociate the Yiddish muse from natural beauty, i.e., from the traditional characteristics of the lyrical muse: bloom ("flower"), color ("flower," "butterfly"), free and graceful movement ("butterfly"), and the most important of all, vocal sweetness ("nightingale"). The old and shriveled woman who replaces the more conventional personification of the muse is obviously a collective symbol of the Jewish people in their fallen state as an exiled nation, the Zion of Lamentations, who in her grief "sat solitary—like a widow" and whom the *Midrash* described as a woman deserted by her husband. She is designated in our poem as "a yidene," i.e., a vulgar Jewish woman of the old generation, uneducated and noisy. Clearly, she represents here not only the degraded Jewish nation but also the Yiddish language. Hence her shrillness (she shouts and curses), her deficiency in vocal sweetness.

68. See his *Te'uda beyisrael*, 4th ed., p. 34.

69. See *Gotlober un zayn epokhe*, ed. A. Fridkin, Vol. I, p. 312.

70. In the phrase "sensations and emotions," I have rendered the Hebrew word *hamurgash*, which applies both to sensory and to emotive experiences. Perets' intentions may have compassed either, or both.

71. See Perets' letter to Sholem Aleichem, May 17, 1889. *Kol kitvey Perets*, Vol. X, second part, p. 226.

72. See the *Folks-biblyotek*, Vol. I, p. 476.

73. See *Igrot Y. L. Gordon*, ed. Y. Y. Vaysberg (Warsaw, 1894–1895), Vol. II, p. 310.

74. See Sholem Aleichem's "Vegn zhargon oysleygn," in the *Yidishe folks-biblyotek*, Vol. I, p. 476.

75. See his letter to Sholem Aleichem of June 17, 1888. *Kol kitvey Perets*, Vol. X, second part, pp. 211–13.

76. See Tsederboym's note to Lifshits' "Di fir klasn," in *Kol-mevaser*, Vol. I (1863), No. 25.

77. A. Tsederboym argued, for instance, that the so-called Lithuanian Yiddish dialect was so "corrupt" and confused in its grammar and syntax because the Lithuanian Jews, "though they still use certain words and expressions in accordance with the rules of pure, grammatical German, use others without any attention to their correct gender, person or even number." Lithuanian Jews according to this absurd explanation simply did not bother to preserve the purity of a language they had supposedly brought with them from Germany hundreds of years ago, a language which must have somehow conformed to the "correct" grammatical norms of late eighteenth-century and nineteenth-century literary German. (See Tsederboym's "Memshelet hakohanim," in *Hamelits*, Vol. VI [1866], No. 44. See also Max Weinreich's "A polemik tsvishn Tsederboymen un Perets Smolenskinen vegn yidishe dialektn," in *YIVO-bleter*, Vol. V [1933], No. 2, pp. 401–4; and the chapter "Reyn daytsh bay yidn," in Max Weinreich's article "Ikrim in der geshikhte fun yidish," first part, in *Yidishe shprakh*, Vol. XIV [1954], No. 4, pp. 106–10.)

78. A. M. Dik, "A maskils utopye," ed. Sh. Niger, in *YIVO-bleter*, Vol. XXXVI (1952), p. 157.

79. Tsederboym's words on this matter are especially revealing: "In such cases we abide as much as we can by the true German language. What harm can it do, if we have at least in our books a real language?" (*Kol-mevaser*, Vol. I, No. 25).

Chapter Three: The Mimic Writer and His "Little Jew"

1. See *Dos Sholem-Aleichem-bukh*, p. 326.

2. The fact that Yiddish writers often found it uncomfortable to use Yiddish for personal purposes and especially for writing letters to their fellow writers should be noted. Abramovitsh wrote to his closest friend, Y. Binshtok, in Hebrew. Perets wrote to his family members in Polish. To Y. Dinezon, his lifelong intimate, himself a Yiddish writer, he wrote in Hebrew. Characteristically, in his letters to Dinezon, he would shift from Hebrew to Yiddish when his sentences would assume the form of verse, i.e., when they would to some extent be distanced from his nonliterary privacy. This may very well be a heritage of the ambiguous position Yiddish held as a language of "the people," not of the writer and his equals. Perets' adherence to this practice contradicts his professed attitude toward Yiddish, but this is not the first self-contradiction we have encountered in this matter. Perets would, for instance, exhort Byalik, the Hebrew poet, to shift to Yiddish ("awake and go to the people"), but he would take care to do it in Hebrew. See Perets' letter to Byalik (undated) in *Kol kitvey Perets*, Vol. X, second part, pp. 251–53.

3. See Perets' letter to Sholem Aleichem of June 17, 1888, ibid., pp. 211–13.

The quoted paragraph reads in the Hebrew original as follows: "Yesh hevdel gadol me'od beyn hanos'im ba'atsmam. Adoni malbish ra'ayonim arumim akherim me'olam akher, veyoter me'olam hama'ase, va'ani, kekhotev lahana'ato lefi matsav rukhɔ besha'a shehu tofes et ha'et, lakakhti mikol ha'olamot yakhad."

4. See, for example, Sh. Niger's *Dertseylers un romanistn*, Vol. I, pp. 162–89.

5. See *Kol kitvey Perets*, Vol. X, second part, p. 217.

6. See above, Chap. 2, note no. 67.

7. See *Kol kitvey Perets*, Vol. X, second part, pp. 221–22. The fact that he had in mind these two works, one (*The Nag*) a highly developed and complicated allegory on the fate of the Jewish people in exile, the second also containing allegorical elements, may explain his reference in his letter of June 17 (quoted on p. 71.) to the alleged combination of "naked" ideas and realistic description of society in Rabinovitsh's (actually Abramovitsh's) works.

8. See Sholem Aleichem's "A briv tsu a gutn fraynt," *Folks-biblyotek*, Vol. II, pp. 307–8.

9. *Ale verk fun Sholem-Aleichem*, Vol. XI, p. 125.

10. See the article "Far dem tararam" ("Before the Tumult Began") in M. Y. Berditshevski, *Yidishe ksovim*, Vol. II (New York, 1951), pp. 197–98.

11. See G. G. Sedgwick, *Of Irony—Especially in the Drama* (Toronto, 1935), p. 4.

12. See the article "Vider vegn Sholem-Aleichem" ("On Sholem Aleichem—Once Again"), in *Yidishe ksovim*, Vol. II, pp. 189–90.

13. The only important critic at the time who showed anything like real respect and understanding for Sholem Aleichem was Bal Makhshoves (I. Ely-

ashiv). See his essay on Sholem Aleichem in *Geklibene Shriftn*, Vol. I (Warsaw, 1929), pp. 91–109. Berditshevski's article on Sholem Aleichem preceded his by approximately five years. For a characteristically condescending and shallow evaluation, see D. Frishman's "Sholem-Aleichem," in *Kol kitvey David Frishman*, Vol. VII (Warsaw, 1931), pp. 80–82.

14. Linetski described his shift from Hebrew to Yiddish in analogies such as "I flung away the shabby-genteel violin and took to the modest, beggarly lyre." (See A. Litvak, *Y. Y. Linetski—kultur historishe shtrikhn fun der haskole epokhe* [Kiev, 1919], p. 33).

15. See Y. Reminik, "A kapitl forgeshikhte fun yidishn teater," *Shtern*, Vol. XVI (1940), No. 6, pp. 88–90. See also R. Granovski, *Y. Y. Linetski un zayn dor* (New York, 1941), p. 31.

16. See M. Graydenberg, *Fartseykhenungen vegn mayn foter, Tsaytshrift*, Vol. V (1931), p. 206. See also R. Granovski, *Linetski un zayn dor*, pp. 29–30.

17. Y. Reminik, "A kapitl forgeshikhte fun yidishn teater," p. 94.

18. See, for example, the opening *feuilleton* in the collection *Dos meshulakhes* (Zhitomir, 1875), pp. 3–10; and that of *Der pritshepe* (Odessa, 1876), pp. 3–22.

19. See, for example, A. Shteynman, *Betsel Mendele*, in *Midor el dor* (Tel Aviv, 1951), pp. 5–29.

20. See D. Eynhorn "Mendele bay der arbet," *Ale verk fun Mendele*, Vol. XX, p. 58.

21. For the autobiographical relation, see *Ale verk fun Sholem Aleichem*, Vol. XXVI, pp. 45–49. For the example from *Motl the Son of the Cantor Peyse*, see Vol. XVIII, pp. 261–63.

22. See the Soviet edition of Sholem Aleichem's works, Vol. II (Moscow, 1948), p. 284.

23. For the early variant of Sholem Aleichem's epitaph see ibid., p. 359. On Sholem Aleichem's liking for Leoncavallo's opera see Y. D. Berkovitsh, *Harishonim kivney adam*, part III, *Kol kitvey Y. D. Berkovitsh*, Vol. VIII (Tel Aviv, 1953) pp. 155–56.

24. Aristotle, *Poetics*, Chap. IV. Translated by S. H. Butcher (London, 1911), p. 15.

25. See Dinezon's article "Di yidishe shprakhe un ire shrayber," *Hoyzfraynt*, Vol. I (1888), p. 11.

26. *Ale verk fun Sholem-Aleichem*, Vol. XXVI, p. 17.

27. See Linetski's *Funem yarid*, pp. 2–3. This brochure appeared in 1909. The final version of Sholem Aleichem's autobiography was written between 1913 and 1916. The title *Funem yarid* is not Sholem Aleichem's only debt to Linetski. See Y. Reminik, "Linetski un Sholem-Aleichem, Shtern," Vol. XV (1939), No. 9, pp. 80–90.

28. The quoted *feuilleton* is titled "Di gas," and it was the first in a series called "Bilder fun der zhitomirer gas." It was published in the *Folksblat* in 1888 and collected for the first time in the Soviet edition of Sholem Aleichem's works, Vol. I, pp. 473–79.

29. My use of the psychopathological term "schizoid" here is conscious

and intentional. Of course, I do not intend to reflect on the mental stability of the writers under discussion. We have every reason to believe that Abramovitsh, Sholem Aleichem, et al. were stable people with a strong sense of identity. However, the cultural situation in which they found themselves forced on them its own logic, and this situation, as it has been described here, had many elements of the schizoid organization in it. The writers, we saw, behaved—in their artistic capacity (not as private citizens, sons, lovers, fathers, friends, etc.) according to the behavioral patterns emanating from a "divided self." No reader of R. D. Laing's famous treatise on the schizoid mentality, who has some knowledge of literature, can miss the direct and indirect bearings the author's argument has on the psychological theory of art in general and of literature in particular. Laing himself points them out, although he prefers not to elaborate on them (see his discussion of "The inner Self in the schizoid condition" in *The Divided Self* [New York, 1969], p. 89). If this applies to many writers in a personal-psychological way, it certainly applies to nineteenth-century Yiddish writers in a cultural or psycho-historical one. Those writers *did* divide their beings into the "unembodied," inner, personal selves and the "embodied" selves of their personae. Of course, they did it intentionally and creatively, rather than obsessively and pathologically. However, the behavior of some of the pathological "cases" which Laing discusses reminds one of their literary behavior in a very suggestive way (see, for instance, the analysis of the case of "David," ibid., pp. 69–77).

30. *Ale verk fun Mendele Moykher-Sforim*, Vol. III, pp. 161–62.

31. Ibid., p. 90.

32. See Abramovitsh's letter to Sholem Aleichem of March 27, 1888, *Shriftn*, Vol. I, p. 249.

33. See Abramovitsh's letter of April 15, 1888, ibid., p. 250.

34. See, for instance, the dispute of the "two Mendeles" in *Bymey ha-ra'ash* ("In Days of Tumult"), in *Kol kitvey Mendele Mokher-Sfarim*, pp. 413–14.

Chapter Four: On Native Ground

1. See Abramovitsh's letter to Sholem Aleichem of June 10, 1888, *Shriftn*, Vol. I, p. 251.

2. See Abramovitsh's letter of April 15, 1888, ibid., p. 250.

3. *Ale verk fun Sholem-Aleichem*, Vol. XI, p. 126.

4. The prologue was published in the *Folks-biblyotek*, Vol. I, pp. 1–9. It was republished twice in the piratical editions of Abramovitsh's works which appeared in New York in 1909 and 1910. After the publication of *Dos vintshfingerl* in its present form in the "Jubilee edition" (1911–1913) it has never been republished in Yiddish. In Hebrew it appeared once, when Abramovitsh began to serialize the novel (under the title *Be'emek habakha*, "In the Vale of Tears") in the monthly *Hashilo'akh* (see *Hashilo'akh*, Vol. I [1897], pp. 7–12).

5. See the excerpt from Abramovitsh's letter to Y. L. Binshtok of July 18,

1891, in Sh. Ginzburg's article "Mendele Moykher-Sforim in zayne briv," *Historishe verk*, Vol. I, p. 158.

6. See Abramovitsh's letter of June 10, 1888, *Shriftn*, Vol. I, p. 251.

7. The regime of Nicholas I (1825–1855) is considered the darkest time in the history of Russian Jewry in the nineteenth century. Bent on the Christianization of the Jews, by force if necessary, the Russian government drafted eight- and ten-year-old children into the army, where they were to remain for twenty-five years of service. Under this pressure the system of the autonomic Jewish congregation was reduced to moral bankruptcy (it was the responsibility of the congregation to supply the army with the Jewish draftees), and the tensions between rich and poor, *maskilim* and Orthodox Jews became dangerously high. See Louis Greenberg, *The Jews in Russia*, Vol. I (New Haven, 1944), pp. 29–55. See also Isaac Levitats, *The Jewish Community in Russia, 1772–1844* (New York, 1943), pp. 36–45.

8. Hershele's full name is not disclosed anywhere in the novel. Only in the epilogue does it appear in its Germanized form, Heinrich Cohen (see *Ale verk fun Mendele Moykher-Sforim*, Vol. XII, p. 422). As originally published in the *Folks-biblyotek*, the novel was attributed to an imaginary author who preferred to be known only by the pseudonym "Hamore Litsdaka" ("the teacher of righteousness," or "the guide to charity"). We have here, then, a most elaborate pseudonymic structure: a novel written by one "Hershele," signed by a rather equivocal pseudonym, and "published under the care of Mendele Moykher-Sforim"; a characteristically Abramovitsh-like intricacy.

9. *Folks-biblyotek*, Vol. I, p. 3.

10. Ibid.

11. *Ale verk fun Mendele*, Vol. XII, p. 416.

12. Ibid., p. 417.

13. See *Serkele*, Act V, scenes 1–3, in Etinger's *Ksovim*, ed. Max Weinreich, Vol. II, pp. 416–31.

14. *Folks-biblyotek*, Vol. I, p. 8.

15. *Ale verk fun Mendele*, Vol. XII, p. 426.

16. *Folks-biblyotek*, Vol. I, p. 5.

17. Ibid.

18. See M. L. Lilyenblum, "Bikoret lekhol shirey Gordon," in *Kol kitvey Lilyenblum*, Vol. III (Odessa, 1913), pp. 26–85.

19. The Soviet critics were usually prone to detect "reactionary nationalism" in those works of Abramovitsh written in the 1880s and 1890s. See, for instance, M. Viner, *Tsu der geshikhte fun der yidisher literatur in 19-tn yorhundert*, Vol. II, pp. 155–56. See also Sh. Niger's note 133 in his *Mendele Moykher-Sforim* (Chicago, 1936), pp. 307–8.

20. See Sh. Niger's *Mendele Moykher-Sforim*, pp. 200–17. See also Y. Klozner, *Historiya shel hasifrut ha'ivrit hakhadasha*, Vol. VI (Jerusalem, 1958), pp. 377–79.

21. See the excerpt from Abramovitsh's letter of March 12, 1881, to Y. L. Binshtok in Sh. Ginzburg, *Historishe verk*, Vol. I, p. 156.

22. See, for instance, Abramovitsh's introductory letter to Mendele which

opens the collection *Seyfer habeheymes* ("The Book of Cattle") in *Ale verk fun Mendele*, Vol. XV, pp. 3–18 (of the separately paginated section *Seyfer habeheymes*).

23. See, for instance, part VII, Chaps. 4–5. *Ale Verk*, Vol. XII, pp. 359–73.

24. See *Ha'avot vehabanim* (Odessa, 1868), Chap. 33, pp. 149–52.

25. See his article, "Kilkul-haminim" in his *Mishpat shalom* (Vilna, 1860), pp. 9–46.

26. Abramovitsh adapted into Yiddish L. Pinsker's famous brochure *Autoemancipation*, which eventually became the manifesto of the early Russian Zionists. This was wrongly interpreted as an indication of his own Zionist tendencies. See Sh. Niger's *Mendele Moykher-Sforim*, pp. 205–17.

27. See ibid.

28. For a description of the Zionists, see Abramovitsh's short story "Bymey hara'ash" ("In Days of Tumult") in *Kol kitvey Mendele Mokher-Sfarim*, pp. 408–9.

29. See Abramovitsh's parody on the new Lamentation-style poetry in his story "Beseter ra'am" ("In the Secret Place of Thunder"), *Kol kitvey*, p. 384.

30. What I have translated as "They would look completely different" reads literally, "They would have completely different faces."

31. See *The Art of Sinking in Poetry*, ed. by E. L. Steeves (New York, 1952), p. 46.

32. *Folks-biblyotek*, Vol. I, p. 4.

33. Ibid., pp. 5–6.

34. See the first verses of Horace's *Ars poetica*.

35. The noun *shnit* (from the verb *shnaydn*, "to cut") is rich in meaning. It means cut (physical), slit, harvest, manner, fashion. "A nayer shnit" is an idiomatic expression (deriving probably from agriculture) which does not necessarily retain direct physical associations. It may mean—in the abstract—a new manner, a new style, etc. Mendele, however, sets it here within a sartorial context, and thus he manages to revitalize the abstract expression and apply it to the well-tailored Hershele with extraordinary adroitness.

36. To sense the full thrust of Abramovitsh's presentation of the "sartorial motif" in the prologue to *Dos vintshfingerl* as well as in other works, one should know what place the problem of "proper" clothing occupied in the social consciousness of the maskilic intelligentsia in Eastern Europe. The animus the *maskilim* developed against the traditional Jewish attire (both male and female) was overwhelming. It was even stronger than their hatred for Yiddish. They considered it the visible and immediately effective barrier between the Jews and their neighbors and called for its immediate replacement by "proper" European clothes. Of course, they knew that European (i.e., Western European; what Orthodox Jews used to refer to as "Frenchified" or "Germanized") men's suits and women's dresses would form as effective a barrier between the Jews and their immediate non-Jewish neighbors as their traditional gabardines ever could be, for those neighbors were in most cases Slavic peasants, who still wore their traditional clothes (those clothes at the time were already idealized and even worn by Slavophile-nationalist intellectuals).

Nevertheless, the *maskilim* insisted on the Europeanization of the Jewish attire and in some cases even took action intended to ensure the implementation by law of their desired change. In 1843, for instance, a group of young people in Vilna, among them illustrious *maskilim* such as M. A. Gintsburg, M. Strashun, A. Ben Ya'akov, and even A. M. Dik addressed a special *proshenye* ("petition") to the minister of education in St. Petersburg, in which they encouraged the government to abolish by law the long *kapote* (gabardine) and the *shtrayml* (the fur-edged hat), the two most conspicuous items of traditional Jewish clothing. Their objections to these clothes concurred with those of the government, which had already taken the decision to tax the wearing of *kapotes*, *shtraymlekh*, etc. Although it is doubtful whether they had any influence in the matter, they took much pride in their contribution to this Europeanization of their brethren. Dik referred to the new clothing law in several of his novelettes (see Max Weinreich's *Bilder fun der yidisher literatur-geshikhte*, [Vilna, 1928], pp. 321–23) and even prepared an adaptation of a special pamphlet dedicated to it (by the Jewish-Russian author L. Levanda, *Di yidishe kleyder umvekslung vos iz geshen in dem yor 1844* [Vilna, 1870]). in which he explained why traditional Jewish clothing was harmful from a aesthetic, social, moral, and even hygienic points of view. In *Shloyme reb Khayims*, Abramovitsh's autobiographical novel (part I, Chap. 3), the reactions of the Jewish inhabitants of the small Lithuanian *shtetlekh* to the clothing law and their ways of circumventing it (of course, for them it was nothing but a *gzeyre*—an evil decree) were described with grace, humor, and retrospective compassion. The objection to the old Jewish clothing as well as to the old, traditional jewelry, by the way, supplied Y. Aksenfeld with the motif that governs the structure of the plot in his *Shterntikhl*. As the title of this first Yiddish novel suggests, it was the traditional female headband that symbolized for the author the medieval traditionalism and irrationalism of the old order in Jewish life.

37. *Kol-mevaser*, Vol. III (1865), No. 6.
38. See *Ha'avot vehabanim*, pp. 18–19.
39. Sh. Abramovitsh, *Dos vintshfingerl* (Warsaw, 1865), pp. 38–39.
40. For a detailed comparison of the two versions, see Y. Nusinov, "Di ershte oysgabe fun Vintshfingerl," *Shriftn*, Vol. I, pp. 199–218. For a general description of the first *Vintshfingerl*, see Max Weinreich, *Bilder fun der yidisher literaturgeshikhte* (Vilna, 1928), pp. 342–51.
41. *Folks-biblyotek*, Vol. I, p. 8. Incidentally, "setting a mirror" in front of the people for purposes of self-knowledge and self-correction was defined by young Abramovitsh in various instances as the most comprehensive and elevated function of literature. See, for instance, *Limdu hetev* (Warsaw, 1862), p. 29.
42. Ibid., p. 1.
43. Ibid., p. 8.
44. See *Dos vintshfingerl* (1865), p. 39.
45. *Folks-biblyotek*, Vol. I, p. 8.
46. Ibid., p. 7.
47. Ibid.

48. Ibid., p. 9.

49. See a survey of the "false opinions concerning the composition of Mendele's works" in M. Mezheritski, "Fishke der krumer—stil un kompozitsye," in *Di royte velt* (1927), No. 12, pp. 106–8.

50. *Folks-biblyotek*, Vol. I, pp. 4–5.

51. Ibid., p. 8.

52. Ibid., p. 3.

53. The protagonist of Abramovitsh's *Dos kleyne mentshele*, Yitskhok Avrom, appointed the *maskil* Gutman the executor of his will and left him large sums of money for educational and communal reforms. In the prologue to the 1865 *Vintshfingerl* Mendele relates how Gutman was prevented from executing the will. See p. 7.

54. *Kol shirey Y. L. Gordon*, Vol. IV, p. 90.

55. See the 1865 *Vintshfingerl*, p. 7. See also the reaction of the community of Glupsk to the cleaning of the river Gnilopyatke in *Masoes Binyomin hashlishi*, *Ale verk fun Mendele*, Vol. IX, p. 86.

56. *Folks-biblyotek*, Vol. I, p. 8.

57. See Abramovitsh's letter of June 10, 1888, *Shriftn*, Vol. I, p. 251.

58. See Abramovitsh's letter to Binshtok of June 11, 1891, in Sh. Ginzburg, *Historishe verk*, Vol. I, p. 158.

59. See *Ale verk fun Mendele*, Vol. XIX, p. 14.

60. See *Limdu hetev*, pp. 36–37.

Chapter Five: The Mendele Maze—1. The Pseudonym Fallacy

1. This, in fact, is what happened—for better or for worse—in large parts of the modernistic fiction written after the Mendele tradition had run its course, by writers who refused to employ the mediator persona of "classical," nineteenth-century Yiddish fiction. Here the consciousness of Hershele, the modern alienated Jew, is not an object of ironic scrutiny, as it was in the prologue to *Dos vintshfingerl*, but rather the point of view from which "the Jew" is observed; Hershele becomes the narrator instead of the comic-pathetic protagonist. To realize what a difference the presence or absence of a Mendele figure can make, one has only to cross the 1890–1900 line in the development of Yiddish fiction and venture into the works of Perets. There we find many instances in which the Hershele–Kabtsansk encounter is being repeated. However, the exclusion of the Mendele figure from these instances completely changes the nature of the encounter as well as the texture of its presentation. Not more than three years after the publication of Abramovitsh's prologue, Perets published a series of narrative sketches—half fictional, half reportorial—which elaborated on the Hershele versus Kabtsansk theme. Written as a result of the author's participation in a "statistical expedition" (in 1890 the economist and philanthropist Jan Bloch employed several Jewish intellectuals and writers in collecting economic data on life in the small Jewish *shtetlekh* of Poland—for political–apologetic purposes) and subsequently titled *Bilder fun a provints rayze* ("Sketches from a Tour of the Provinces," 1891), the series

looked, on its surface, to be a detailed repetition of the picture we have already seen. On the one hand, the small, ruined, half-empty *shtetl*, more dead than alive; on the other hand, the well-meaning and well-tailored stranger, born in the *shtetl*, but by now thoroughly transformed, coming back to "the people" to "study" them and, if possible, offer help. The inevitable misunderstandings occur, which even against the gloomiest and most disheartening background never exclude the comic. In a short time the whole town panics. The stranger, who is "writing them up," allegedly for beneficial purposes, may be a government spy on the scent of illegal business (and most of the inhabitants of the poor *shtetl* cannot afford to pay for licenses for whatever they manage to sell). The small crowd, which has followed him from house to house, evaporates, and the amateur statistician and would-be benefactor remains alone and frustrated, very much like Hershele in the synagogue courtyard of Tuneyadevke. A further ironic point is being scored here: this frustration has been brought about by the only local *maskil*, who in order to parade his knowledge of the world has picked a quarrel with the narrator and entered into a senseless argument with him in front of the suspicious crowd.

The situations in Abramovitsh's prologue and many chapters in Perets' *Bilder* are almost identical. This, however, only sharpens the differences between their descriptive renderings. What Perets presents us with is an avowedly partial and fleeting view of the situation. He structures his sketches and orchestrates his style in a manner that is meant to create precisely this impression of a personal, momentary, and tentative vision. Throughout the *Bilder* series he carefully sustains the form of reportage or of a diary kept by a reporter. He meticulously arranges his sentences in what seems to be haphazard, discontinued sequences, as if they were hurriedly jotted down. It is only when he quotes a story innocently related by one of the *shtetl* Jews that his rhythm relaxes and becomes more orderly and that the narrating assumes a folksy, "epic" tone (the tone that Perets was later to develop with great artistic dexterity in his hasidic monologues and pseudo-folktales). Otherwise, his writing purports to represent nothing more than a series of quick impressions followed by short musings, erratic, poetic comments. The whole series is structured not according to the reality described in it but rather around the moods of the narrator, as they gradually change from relative calm to bitter irony and finally to a frenzy bordering on insanity. This never happens in a story related by Mendele. Of course, Mendele too has his outbursts of pathos. He can be emotional, on rare occasions even sentimental, but that hardly affects the continuity and evenness of his descriptions. His narration, for all its satirical and rhetorical trickery, is never reduced to the status of a mere personal, impressionistic report. Rather it partakes of the nature of the fixed, objective reality that allegedly it represents. This reality is observed by a particular eye and registered through an individualized consciousness. Yet, this consciousness is not as individualistic as that of Perets' narrator; nor is the eye as humanly confined as his is. It is able to see more and differently, to offer the reader a less direct but rather broader perspective from which both Hershele and Kabtsansk can be observed and judged equally. It is a descriptive lens through which ironies can be sustained, not just allowed to twinkle and dissolve. Whatever distortion it causes to the reflected object, it always remains crystal clear. No poetic mist is ever allowed to cloud it.

2. *Folks-biblyotek*, Vol. I, p. 4.

3. *Kol-mevaser*, Vol. II (1864), No. 45, p. 685.

4. Ibid.

5. This is a central motif in Mendele's soliloquies. See, for instance, *Fishke der krumer* (final version), Chap. 5. *Ale verk fun Mendele*, Vol. III, pp. 35–37.

6. *Kol-mevaser*, Vol. II, No. 45, p. 684–85.

7. Ibid., Vol. III, 1865, No. 6, p. 95.

8. See Abramovitsh's unfinished story "Mayn [letste] nesie" ("My [Last] Trip") written probably in 1870 and published posthumously in *Shtern* (Minsk, 1939), Vol. XV, No. 7, pp. 1–4.

9. See Mendele's concluding remarks in the first version of *Dos vintshfingerl*, 1865, p. 42.

10. Abramovitsh, "Mayn [letste] nesie," p. 2.

11. See Mendele's introduction to the 1879 version of *Dos kleyne mentshele* in *Gezamlte verk* ("Collected Works"), Vol. III (Moscow, 1939), p. 202. See also below, pp. 165–68, 180–81.

12. See the second chapter of *Beseter ra'am* ("In the Secret Place of Thunder," 1886–1887), *Kol kitvey Mendele Mokher-Sfarim* (Tel Aviv, 1947), p. 385. Abramovitsh developed this theme of the "stranded" Mendele for the first time in an epistolary story (his only one) written in 1884 but left unfinished and untitled. It was published posthumously in *Mendele un zayn tsayt—materyaln tsu der geshikhte fun der yidisher literatur in 19-tn yorhundert* (Moscow, 1940), pp. 11–17. The Hebrew story, written two years later, picks up the theme where the Yiddish one left it.

13. See "Shem vayefet ba'agala" ("Shem and Japeth in the Train Compartment"), *Kol kitvey Mendele*, p. 399.

14. See the opening chapter of *Fishke der krumer*, *Ale verk fun Mendele*, Vol. III, pp. 9–10.

15. *Ale verk fun Mendele*, Vol. IV, p. 9.

16. *Folks-biblyotek*, Vol. I, p. 4.

17. *Ale verk fun Mendele*, Vol. XI, p. 19.

18. Ibid., p. 5.

19. Ibid., pp. 19–20.

20. Mendele's "bestial" metaphors and comparisons are, of course, only a part of the more comprehensive "biological analogy," which informs and conditions Abramovitsh's intellectual and pictorial imagination and decisively influences his representation of human existence in general and that of the Jewish existence in particular. Abramovitsh constantly compares human behavior and appearance to those of animals and he systematically explains psychological developments in terms of biological (especially botanical) processes of growth and decay. While this phenomenon certainly emphasizes his debt to the ancient literary traditions of the fable, the parable, and the satire on the one hand, and his intellectual commitment to the scientific-biological positiv-

ism of the time on the other hand, it was quite unsatisfactorily explained by most critics either as a manifestation of the author's "plastic" or painterly imagination (this by Abramovitsh's admirers) or as a symptom of his gross materialism, his lack of spiritual intuition and even his so-called anti-Semitism. One of the most influential of Abramovitsh's detractors in Hebrew criticism, the critic Sh. Tsemakh, went so far as to accuse him of "a zoological *Weltanschauung*." Abramovitsh, he said, "saw and described only the beast, the bestialized Jewish people. He did not see nor did he describe *man*, the *Jewish human being*." (See Tsemakh's seminal article "Ba'avotot hahavay," *Ma'asaf 'Erets'* [Odessa, 1919], p. 134.) For a more balanced discussion of the bestial analogy as a permanent feature in Abramovitsh's representation of humanity see G. Shaked, *Beyn skhok ledema* (Tel Aviv, 1965), pp. 46–56. The influence of the biological analogy (zoological and botanical) on the structural formation of Abramovitsh's early Hebrew novel *Ha'avot vehabanim*, and its bearing on its meaning were analyzed in my article "Arba he'arot lete'urey hateva beha'avot vehabanim le-Abramovitsh," *Moznayim*, new series, Vol. XXVIII (1969), pp. 255–65.

21. *Ale verk fun Mendele*, Vol. IV, p. 5.

22. *The Travels and Adventures of Benjamin the Third*, trans. Moshe Spiegel (New York, 1949), p. 9. For the Yiddish original see *Ale verk*, Vol. IX, pp. 3–4.

23. *Folks-biblyotek*, Vol. I, p. 2.

24. In order to make the reference to Isaiah meaningful, I have deviated somewhat from the Yiddish original. In Yiddish only a single word of Isaiah is evoked, but as this word, Hebrew and biblical, is very conspicuous, it suffices for its purpose. An exact English translation would not in this case have made sense.

25. *Folks-biblyotek*, Vol. I, pp. 2–3.

26. Ibid., p. 9.

27. *Hashakhar*, Vol. VI (1875), p. 585.

28. Linetski, *Der statek* (1876), p. 90.

29. Y. Dinezon, *Di yidishe shprakhe un ire shrayber, Hoyz-fraynt*, Vol. I (1888), p. 11.

30. See, for example, "Di gas," *Ale verk*, Soviet edition, Vol. I, pp. 473, 476. Sholem Aleichem asks here: "What has become of you, young *maskilim*, good boys, excellent youngsters, with your 'forbidden' books, which Mendele the Bookpeddler used to bring us four times a year and which we read almost not breathing lest we be heard, in secret places, in garrets, with trembling hands and pounding hearts?"

31. See above, Chap. 1, pp. 28–29.

32. Y. Dinezon, "Sh. Y. Abramovitsh un Mendele Moykher-Sforim," in *Ale verk fun Mendele*, Vol. XXII, pp. 79–80.

33. See Abramovitsh's letter to Sholem Aleichem of June 28, 1888. *Shriftn*, Vol. I, p. 255.

34. See the 1879 version of *Dos kleyne mentshele* in *Gezamlte verk* (Soviet edition), Vol. III, p. 363.

35. Y. L. Perets, "Mendele," *Ale verk fun Mendele*, Vol. XXII, p. 10.

36. Ibid., Vol. I, p. 50.

37. See N. Mayzl's summing up of some of the various differentiations in his article "Di grenetsn tsvishn Sh. Y. Abramovitsh un Mendele Moykher-Sforim," in *Dos Mendele bukh*, ed. N. Mayzl (New York, 1959), pp. 294–325. Mayzl's article, however, is vitiated by the author's bias toward the wholly untenable differentiation between Abramovitsh and Mendele as indicating the differences between the young, maskilic Abramovitsh and the old, "artistic" one.

38. For a characteristic instance see P. Shifman, "Mendele betor tipus vesemel," in *Hashilo'akh*, Vol. XXXIV (1918), pp. 84–91.

39. See M. Mezheritski, "Fishke der krumer—stil un kompozitsye," in *Di royte velt* (1927), No. 12, p. 104.

40. See the discussion of the characters in *Fishke the Lame* in Y. Goldberg, "Der veg-roman un der intimer stil—vegn 'Fishke dem krumen,'" in *Shriftn fun vaysrusishn melukhe-universitet*, Vol. I (1929), pp. 55–59.

41. For a discussion of Viner's and Erik's comments on the Mendele figure, see the following Chap. pp. 171–72, 184–85. For references to these comments see notes 5–7 in this chapter.

42. See Y. A. Klauzner, "Pirkey-Mendele," in *Metsuda*, Vol. VII (1954), pp. 347–56. Klauzner, perhaps more than any other critic, came close to what I consider the true understanding of Mendele. Some of his insights are further developed in the following chapters. However, he too marred his own distinctions by attributing to Mendele the alleged authorship of *all* Abramovitsh's stories (see below, Chap. 7), and he did not perceive either the development of the Mendele phenomenon or its wider literary–historical implications.

43. See G. Shaked, "Hamesaper vegiborav," in *Beyn skhok ledema*, pp. 63–71.

44. See *Kol kitvey David Frishman*, Vol. VI, pp. 70–111.

45. See A, Mukdoyni, "Tsvey mentshn," *Ale verk fun Mendele*, Vol. I, pp. 155–66.

46. Abramovitsh's exact date of birth is, incidentally, unknown. See Y. Klozner, *Historiya shel hasifrut ha'ivrit*, Vol. VI, pp. 321–23.

47. Justin Kaplan, *Mr. Clemens and Mark Twain* (New York, 1966), p. 9.

48. Harry Levin, *The Gate of Horn* (New York, 1963), p. 92. An interesting analysis of the Stendhal pseudonym can be found in Jean Starobinski's article "Stendhal pseudonyme," in *L'oeil vivant* (Paris, 1961), pp. 191–244.

49. In this as well as in many other respects the 1907–1913 "Jubilee" editions (Hebrew and Yiddish) differ from most of the earlier ones.

50. *Kol-mevaser*, Vol. II (1864), Nos. 45–51; Vol. III (1865), Nos. 1–4 and 6.

51. *Kol-mevaser*, Vol. II (1864), No. 45, pp. 684–85.

52. S. T. Coleridge, *Shakespearean Criticism*, ed. T. M. Raysor, new edition (London, 1960), Vol. II, p. 100.

53. See the English version of the *Dos kleyne mentshele* (*The Parasite*), trans. Gerald Stillman (New York, 1956), pp. 22–23. For the Yiddish original, see the *Gezamlte verk* (Soviet edition), Vol. III, p. 202.

54. See Tsederboym's note to Y. M. Lifshits' *Di fir klasn, Kol-mevaser*, Vol. I (1863), No. 24: "I have myself seen and also been told by others how both middle-class and common people who can read or even understand no language but Yiddish, old men and women sitting in the market places or on Friday night at home, coachmen, ditch-diggers, and artisans in tearooms, all read the *Kol-mevaser* with great hunger. Opening both mouths and ears, they enjoy everything they read; they are happy to hear news from the great world, but whatever they are told—let it be about ancient history or about science—is news for them. They discuss it and pass judgment on it."

55. *Kol-mevaser*, Vol. II, No. 46, p. 699. Here I have used Stillman's translation to the extent that it concurred with the 1864 version of *Dos kleyne mentshele* (cf. *The Parasite*, pp. 30–31).

56. See *Dos vintshfingerl* (1865), pp. 40–42. Also see below, pp. 234–36.

57. *Kol-mevaser*, Vol. IV, No. 6, p. 94.

58. See his commentary on Genesis 18:8.

59. See Abramovitsh's letter to his friend Y. L. Binshtok of December 15, 1864. *Tsaytshrift*, Vol. V, p. 15 (special pagination of Abramovitsh's letters).

60. It should not be overlooked that Abramovitsh published some minor works in Yiddish with which Mendele had nothing to do, such as *Der luft balon*, an adaptation done in collaboration with Y. L. Binshtok of Jules Verne's *Cinq semaines en ballons* (Zhitomir, 1869); the long and, I might add, quite mediocre allegorical poem *Yidl* ("The Little Jew," [Warsaw, 1875]); *Zmires yisroel*, free Yiddish adaptations of the traditional Hebrew hymns sung on the Sabbath (Zhitomir, 1875); *Peyrek shire*, a Yiddish verse elaboration on the mystical hymns added to the hasidic prayerbook (Zhitomir, 1875), and others.

61. The plan never materialized. In 1879, owing to several tragic occurrences in his family life, Abramovitsh began five years of utter paralysis in his activity as a writer.

62. See *Seyfer habeheymes* as originally published in *Der yid*, Vol. IV (1902), Nos. 26–29. In the Hebrew version the series was anonymously dedicated not to Mendele but to his old horse. The dedicator is definitely not Mendele himself. His fictional identity can be partly reconstructed by his dedicatory inscription. Mendele's horse, he says here, was the first horse he knew as a child. He confesses that he used to pluck hairs from the horse's scanty tail, and he is dedicating his work to "his honor and memory," as a gesture of repentance. See *Kol kitvey Mendele*, p. 353.

63. *The Parasite*, p. 19. For the Yiddish original see *Gezamlte verk* (Soviet edition), Vol. III, p. 199.

64. Ibid., pp. 21–22; *Gezamlte verk*, Vol. III, pp. 201–2.

65. In 1835 a rumor swept the Jewish towns and hamlets of Russia that the czarist government was about to issue a decree forbidding the marriage of Jewish girls younger than 16 and of Jewish boys younger than 18. The Jews regarded this as a cruel and dangerous threat. Not only were they used to marrying off their children at a very early age, but they also saw in early marriage a protection against the drafting of young Jewish men to the army (for twenty-five years!). In a few weeks many thousands of ten or even eight year-old chil-

dren were swiftly married. These crazy weeks were remembered for a long time as *di behole* ("the fright") or *di groyse behole* ("the great fright"). See A. M. Dik's story "Di shtot Heres" in Dik's *Geklibene verk*, ed. by Sh. Niger (New York, 1954), pp. 1–16.

66. This coincides with Abramovitsh's uncertainty over his own birthdate. See above, note 44.

67. *The Parasite*, p. 22; *Gezamlte verk*, Vol. III, p. 202.

68. See "Der Vorspruch des Mendele Moicher-Sfurim da Er mit eigenen, zum ersten mal gedruckten Schriften vor die Welt tritt," in Mendele Moicher-Sfurim, *Gesammelte Werke*, 1 Band (Berlin, 1924), pp. xi–xx.

69. Except for the inclusion of this introduction, Stillman followed the 1907 version of *Dos kleyne mentshele* in his translation.

70. To the best of my knowledge, this important self-introduction of Mendele as a fictional character was never discussed, perhaps even never mentioned, by any prominent Hebrew critic. This oversight is probably not unrelated to the fact that even the rudiments of a recognition of Mendele's character status had not emerged in Hebrew before the 1950s. Some Yiddish critics did mention the introduction, but they did it in a cursory manner and without pursuing its far-reaching implications. A critic who mentioned the introduction as indicating that at least in one particular work of Abramovitsh (*Fishke the Lame*) Mendele "was not a mere pseudonym, but also a participant in the story's action" was Y. Goldberg (see his article "Der veg-roman un der intimer stil—vegn 'Fishke der krumer'," in *Shriftn fun vaysrusishn melukhe-universitet*, Vol. I [1929], pp. 55–56). M. Mezheritski discussed the meaning of the introduction in his article "Fishke der krumer—stil un kompozitsye" (*Di royte velt*, 1927, No. 12, pp. 1101–14) and emphasized its importance as an indication of the social role of the Mendele figure, which is defined in economic terms. A more characteristic and less valuable comment can be found in Sh. Niger's monograph *Mendele Moykher-Sforim—zayn lebn, zayne gezelshaftlekhe un literarishe oyftuungen*. To Niger the introduction is "very valuable from the biographical point of view as well as highly characteristic from the artistic one" (2nd edition, New York, 1970, p. 127). Nevertheless, he says very little on it. From what he says it transpires that he grasps the artistic meaning of the introduction in terms of "evolution," i.e., it is the fact that the introduction "grew" and developed rather than that it said what it said on the rhetorical position of Mendele in Abramovitsh's works, that is considered so "highly characteristic." The reference to the great biographical value of the introduction (i.e., to the light it allegedly sheds on Abramovitsh's life) gives rise to the suspicion that the critic altogether missed the point the author had tried to make.

Chapter Six: The Mendele Maze—II. The Folkstip Fallacy

1. See E. M. Forster, *Aspects of the Novel* (New York, 1927), pp. 69–125.

2. Plato *The Republic* 10; Aristotle *The Poetics* 2.

3. See B. Rivkin, "Kmoy teritorye bimkoym religye," in *Literarishe bleter*

(1938), No. 27. In somewhat different form this was repeated in Rivkin's *Grunt tendentsn fun der yidisher literatur in Amerike* (New York, 1948), p. 153.

4. The reference to Mendele as *yehudi shebayehudim* ("the most Jewish of Jews," the essential Jew) was made popular by David Frishman. See *Kol kitvey David Frishman*, Vol. VI (Warsaw, 1930), p. 75. As for Mendele's being a mouthpiece for the "soul of the people," this was repeated many times. See, for example, R. Braynin, "Mendele in zayn redn," in *Ale verk fun Mendele*, Vol. XXI, p. 146.

5. M. Viner, *Tsu der geshikhte fun der yidisher literatur* (New York, 1946), Vol. II, pp. 51–52.

6. Maks Erik, "Vos shetsn mir in Mendele," in *Farmest* (Kiev, 1936), No. 1, p. 134.

7. M. Viner, *Tsu der geshikhte*, Vol. II, p. 52.

8. See the Hebrew short story "Beseter ra'am," *Kol kitvey Mendele*, pp. 37–38.

9. See the first version of Sholem Aleichem's "Dos groyse gevins," entitled "Tevye der milkhiker," in *Hoyz-fraynt*, Vol. IV (1895), p. 66.

10. Ibid., pp. 64–65.

11. See the opening paragraphs of "Byshiva shel ma'ala uvyshiva shel mata," *Kol kitvey Mendele*, p. 420; also, see the description of the Sabbath in the muddy streets of Ksalon—couched in the grandest messianic terms borrowed from Zechariah and Isaiah, "Beseter ra'am," ibid., p. 378–79.

12. See the argument between the "silly" Mendele and the "smart" one in "Bymey hara'ash," in *Kol kitvey Mendele*, pp. 413–14.

13. The name "Mendele" is actually an endearing diminutive twice removed. "Mendl" itself is diminutive of *man* ("man"), a traditional Yiddish equivalent for the Hebrew name Menakhem. Thus, formally, it always figures as a second name, the exclusive use of which is a sign of familiarity. Sheyne Sheyndl, Sholem Aleichem's famous heroine, addresses her husband as "Menakhem-Mendl" only in the stylized salutations of her letters; in the letters themselves she always addresses him as "Mendl." From this we can learn (a) the extent of the familiarity with which Mendele the Bookpeddler is treated (he is never formally addressed as "Menakhem-Mendl"), and (b) the commonness and generality of the name, which actually means nothing more specific than "little man," and which is so characteristically Jewish as to explain the epigram: *Oyb er heyst Mendl, meg ikh esn fun zayn fendl.* ("If he is called Mendl, I may eat from his pot.") The name Mendl is such an unequivocal indication of one's Jewishness, that in itself it guarantees the ritual lawfulness of one's *kosher* food.

14. *The Parasite*, p. 21, *Gezamlte verk*, Vol. III, p. 201.

15. Ibid., p. 22; *Gezamlte verk*, Vol. III, p. 202. I permitted myself to deviate here from G. Stillman's translation by retaining the Yiddish epigram with which the quoted passage is concluded in the original and retranslating it more or less literally. Stillman found an equivalent for the epigram ("You'll work all day for a wisp of hay") which retains the rhyme but not much of the sense of the original, and, of course, the epigram would have no bearing on my argument unless it deals with "many occupations" or with "many trades."

16. "Seyfer hagilgulim," in *Ale verk fun Mendele*, Vol. XV, p. 3 (special pagination).

17. *Ale verk fun Sholem-Aleichem*, Vol. X, p. ii.

18. Although Menakhem-Mendl wrote no less than five long letters to Sholem Aleichem and was answered personally at least once by him, the Menakhem-Mendl–Sholem Aleichem correspondence as well as other parts of the Menakhem-Mendl literature were not included in the collection of Menakhem-Mendl's letters when they appeared in book form. Written and published in different magazines and newspapers between 1900–1904, this correspondence was recently republished in *Sovetish heymland*, Vol. IX (1969), No. 2, pp. 73–94.

19. See Sholem Aleichem's preface to the 1910 edition of *Menakhem-Mendl* in *Ale verk*, Vol. X, p. ii.

20. See "Vos tut men," in *Der yid* (1900), No. 13, p. 2.

21. *Kol kitvey David Frishman*, Vol. VI, pp. 92–94.

22. M. Viner, *Tsu der geshikhte*, Vol. II, p. 51.

23. Cf. G. Shaked, *Beyn skhok ledema*, pp. 63–71.

24. Cf. Y. A. Klauzner's apt description of Mendele's function in this work in "Pirkey Mendele," *Metsuda*, Vol. VII, p. 350.

25. See above, Chap. 1, No. 38.

26. *Kol-mevaser*, Vol. III (1865), No. 6. p. 94.

27. *Ale verk fun Mendele*, Vol. IV, p. 6.

28. *The Nag*, trans. M. Spiegel (New York, 1955), p. 12. For the Yiddish, see *Ale verk fun Mendele*, Vol. V, p. 9.

29. See my article "Sifria-limtorafim—hareka lytsirat 'Susati'," *Hadoar*, Vol. LI (1972), No. 38.

30. *Kol kitvey Mendele*, p. 406.

31. Ibid., p. 419.

32. See *Di folks-biblyotek*, Vol. I, p. 5.

33. *Ale verk fun Mendele*, Vol. XVIII, pp. xxviii–xxix.

34. *Dos vintshfingerl*, 1865, pp. 2–5. Readers of Yiddish literature are well acquainted with this scene as it was incorporated by Abramovitsh in the mature versions of *Fishke der krumer* (from 1888 on).

35. *Fishke der krumer* (Zhitomir, 1869), p. 1.

36. *Ale verk fun Mendele*, Vol. II, p. 150.

37. Ibid., p. 153.

38. *Dos Vintshfingerl* (1865), pp. 38–39.

39. In an ironic remark, aimed at the pseudo-scholarly manner of writing fashionable at the time in Hebrew magazines, Mendele prompts the translator to add as many notes to the text as he can (see ibid., p. 9). As Tsederboym was notorious for adding his extensive notes to other writers' articles (in *Hamelits* and sometimes even in *Kol-mevaser*), this thrust was probably directed at him personally.

40. See above, pp. 99, 175 and also below, pp. 237, 239.

41. The major theme of the work as a whole being the callous dehumanization of sex and marriage in contemporary Jewish life, Abramovitsh saw fit to

divide it into two, almost equal, units. The first (Chaps. 1–5) emphasizes this theme by comparing two stories of "regular" matches conducted in conventional manners. The first story deals with the merchant class, where the financial arrangements preceding the wedding are considered so vital and all-absorbing as to exclude any attention to the people about to be married. This commercialization of marriage is pushed *ad absurdum* in the story of Alter, Mendele's fellow bookpeddler, concerning his farcical attempt at matchmaking which resulted in the matching of two boys. The second story is that of Fishke, the bathhouse employee, as an ersatz bridegroom. It is divided between Mendele himself and a fellow bath attendant, who together relate how Fishke, a disfigured cripple, was "pressed" into marriage with a blind beggar by a gang of wedding-guests who would not call off the wedding feast when it transpired that the original bridegroom had no intention of marrying the girl. This represents "regular" matchmaking in the milieu of the lower classes. These two stories are contrasted with Fishke's own pathetic story of misery and forbidden love in the hideous underworld of Jewish vagabonds and criminals into which he drifted with his shrewish and philandering wife, which occupies most of the second unit of the work (Chaps. 6–10). (Love and humanized relationships between the sexes exist among contemporary Jews, if at all, only outside the boundaries of socially acceptable frameworks). The super-plot makes this even clearer by the coincidental confrontation of Fishke with the unknowing father of his beloved beggar Beyle, whose indifference to his own family resulted in the loss of his daughter to criminal vagabonds.

42. See *Fishke der krumer* (1869), p. 24.

43. In the latter versions of *Fishke der krumer* it is specifically referred to. Mendele even interpolates a short illustration of Fishke's "original" narrative in phonetic rendering. See above, p. 93.

44. *Ale verk fun Mendele*, Vol. IV, p. 8.

45. Ibid., Vol. V, p. 9.

46. *The Travels and Adventures of Benjamin the Third*, trans. M. Spiegel, p. 11. For the Yiddish original, see *Ale verk fun Mendele*, Vol. IX, p. 5.

47. See *Di folks-biblyotek*, Vol. I, p. 9.

48. See I Kings 12:10.

49. *The Travels of Benjamin*, pp. 11–12; *Ale verk fun Mendele*, Vol. IX, pp. 5–6.

50. Judges 5:12.

51. Gen. 25:28–34.

52. Gen. 27:9.

53. *Kol kitvey Mendele*, pp. 377–82.

Chapter Seven: The Mendele Maze—iii. The Outlet

1. See, for example, his letters to Y. Aykhenvald and T. Leov written in 1858–1859 (published by Sh. Niger in *Reshumot*, first series, Vol. V [Tel Aviv, 1927], pp. 408–14).

2. See *Dos vintshfingerl* (1865), p. 4.

3. See the details of the "Faytelzon affair" in Y. Klozner, *Historiya shel hasifrut ha'ivrit*, Vol. VI, pp. 356–57. In 1911 the critic M. M. Faytelzon (1870–1912) contributed an article to the special Abramovitsh Jubilee issue of *Hashilo'akh*—in many respects one of the best articles on Abramovitsh written at the time. He dared, however, to mention in passing the possibility of a connection between Abramovitsh and nineteenth-century Russian fiction. That was enough to send the pampered and capricious author into a fit. He humiliated Faytelzon in public, and the critic never got over this humiliation. When in 1912 he committed suicide, he mentioned his clash with Abramovitsh in his last letter.

4. *Kol kitvey David Frishman*, Vol. VI, p. 74.

5. Ibid.

6. Ibid.

7. See Byalik's article "Mendele ushloshet hakrakhim," in *Kitvey Kh. N. Byalik* (Tel Aviv, 1938), pp. 338–39.

8. Ibid.

9. Even Y. A. Klauzner saw fit to repeat Byalik's beautifully phrased but hardly convincing admonition in his "Pirkey Mendele" (*Metsuda*, Vol. VII, p. 347). This bow to the poet's dictum is perhaps a symptom of one of the weaknesses inherent in his perspicacious study. Approving of Byalik's notion of Abramovitsh's total uniqueness, Klauzner nevertheless proceeded to examine the place of some of Abramovitsh's major works in the literature of the European novel, but he did it in a mechanical and subsequently unprofitable manner. He presented the question of Abramovitsh's "belonging" in the tradition of the novel as depending on the correspondence between his works and the abstract definitions of the novel and its subgenres, and rather unsurprisingly came up with the conclusion that Abramovitsh's works did not fit comfortably into the pigeonholes prescribed by the German "theory of the novel." An attempt at an examination of Abramovitsh's fiction against the concrete background of the historical development of the novel in various European literatures would have yielded different results.

10. See Sh. Tsemakh, "Ba'avotot hahavay," in *Ma'asef Erets* (Odessa, 1919), p. 129.

11. See, for example, Y. Goldberg, "Der veg-roman un der intimer stil," in *Shriftn fun vaysrusishn melukhe-universitet*, Vol. I, pp. 44–48. For other presentations of the problem, see M. Mezhritski's discussion of literary influences on *Fishke the Lame* in his "Fishke der krumer—stil un kompozitsye," in *Di royte velt* [1927], No. 12, pp. 111–17, and particularly M. Viner's article "Mendele Moykher-Sforim un di traditsyes fun der velt literatur," as well as Chap. 2 of his "Mendeles stil," in *Tsu der geshikhte fun der yidisher literatur*, Vol. II, pp. 5–14 and 32–46, respectively.

12. Cf. Goldberg's "Der veg-roman un der intimer stil," p. 47.

13. See Goldberg's comments on Abramovitsh's debt to the tradition of "the intimate style," ibid., pp. 52–55. See also M. Viner's *Tsu der geshikhte*, Vol. III, pp. 38–39.

14. See Daniel Defoe, *Moll Flanders*, in *Defoe's Novels and Miscellaneous Works*, Vol. III (London, 1912), p. ix.

15. See above, Chap. 3, p. 93, and Chap. 6, p. 194.

16. See Samuel Richardson, *Pamela*, Vol. II (New York, 1962), p. v.

17. See the first introduction to Rousseau's *Nouvelle Heloïse, nouvelle édition par Daniel Mornet*, Vol. II (Paris, 1925), p. 1.

18. Cf. "Preface du redacteur" with "Advertissement de l'éditeur" in *Les Liaisons Dangereuses*, Vol. I (Paris, 1932), pp. 9–15.

19. Ian Watt, *The Rise of the Novel* (London, 1963), p. 28.

20. See *Humphrey Clinker* (New York, 1950), pp. xxv–xxviii.

21. See Viktor Vinogradov's *Etyudi o stile Gogolya* (Leningrad, 1926), pp. 42–50. For this information I am thankful to my friend, Martin Horwitz.

22. See N. V. Gogol, *Evenings near the Village of Dikanka*, trans. O. Gorchakov, (New York, no date), p. 11.

23. See Sir Walter Scott's general dedication of and introduction to *Tales of My Landlord* preceding *Old Mortality* (in the Lovell, Coryell edition of the Waverly novels), pp. 7–11.

24. See *Ale verk fun Mendele*, Vol. IV, pp. 8–9.

25. *Aksenfelds verk*, ed. M. Viner, Vol. I, p. 240.

26. Aksenfeld, *Dos shterntikhl*, ed. M. Viner (Moscow, 1938), p. 49.

27. A. M. Dik, *Geklibene verk*, ed. Sh. Niger (New York, 1954), p. 63.

28. See *Yisrolik* (Lemberg, 1875–76), No. 9.

29. Linetski's entire speculation on the merits of autobiographies was plagiarized from M. L. Lileynblum's *Khatot ne'urim* (see Lileynblum's introduction to *Khatot ne'urim* [Vienna, 1876], p. 20).

30. For Abramovitsh's reference, see above, Chap. 4, p. 97; for Sholem Aleichem's references, see, for example, his novel *Kindershpil*, in *Ale verk fun Sholem-Aleichem*, Vol. XX, p. 71, or *Sender Blank*, in *Ale verk fun Sholem-Aleichem*, Vol. XI, p. 47; for earlier variants, see the Soviet edition of Sholem Aleichem's *Verk*, Vol. II, p. 317.

31. See above, Chap. 1, p. 23. Elye Bokher's romance, originally written in *ottava rima*, became popular in the nineteenth century in a prose adaptation titled *Bovo-mayse*.

32. See Dik's introduction to *Makhaze mul makhaze*.

33. See above, Chap. 1, p. 23.

34. *Dos vintshfingerl* (1865), p. 5.

35. Ibid.

36. For details on the Yiddish adaptations of Campe's *Entdeckung von Amerika* by Kh. Kh. Hurovits and by E. M. Gintsburg, see Y. Tsinberg, *Di geshikhte fun der literatur bay vidn*, Vol. VII, second part (New York, 1943), pp. 267–75, 324–27. See also Z. Reyzen, Campe's "Antdekung fun Amerike in yidish," in *YIVO-bleter*, Vol. V (1933), pp. 29–40.

37. See Y. Erter, *Hatsofe leveyt yisrael* (Tel Aviv, 1945), pp. 24–26.

38. Ibid., p. 19.

39. See above, Chap. 2, p. 55; see also Chap. 2, note 5.

40. See Abramovitsh's *Limdu hetev* (1862), pp. 28–29.

41. See, for example, "Adam hakohen" Lebenzon's *Be'urim khadashim o torat ha'adam* (Vilna, 1858), p. xvi. See also my article "Der onheyb fun aktueln hebreishn roman," in *Limdu hetev* (New York, 1969), pp. 7–15.

42. See E. Ts. Tsvayfel, *Minim ve'ugav* (Vilna, 1858), p. 52.

43. See Kalman Shulman's introduction to the fourth volume of *Misterey Paris*, his Hebrew adaptation of Sue's *Mystères de Paris* (Vilna, 1960). See also my article "Der onheyb fun aktueln hebreishn roman," p. 10.

44. See *Limdu hetev*, p. 29.

45. *Ale verk fun Mendele*, Vol. V, pp. 6–7.

46. See Abramovitsh's story concerning the conception and birth of his Mendele in Sholem Aleichem's *Fir zenen mir gezesn, Ale verk fun Sholem-Aleichem*, Vol. XV, pp. 155–56.

47. See above, pp. 150–51.

48. See above, p. 159.

49. *Dos vintshfingerl* (1865), p. 1.

50. *Ale verk*, Vol. IV, p. 6.

51. *Fishke der krumer* (1869), p. 1.

52. The story starts with indications of time and place: "Elul the 2nd, a year ago, 5629, I smuggled myself with my booth of books into the town of Kiev. . . ," *Shtern*, Vol. XV (Minsk, 1939), No. 7, p. 1.

53. Some of the major structural patterns of *The Travels of Benjamin the Third* have been recently analyzed in detail by M. Peri in his study, "Ha'analogiya umekoma bemivne haroman shel Mendele Mokher-Sfarim," *Hasifrut*, Vol. I (1968), No. 1. pp. 65–100.

54. *The Travels of Benjamin the Third*, trans. M. Spiegel (New York: Schocken Books, 1968), p. 15. The paragraphs have been rearranged according to the original (see *Ale verk fun Mendele*, Vol. IX, p. 7); the transliteration of *Zelde and Tuneyadevke*—corrected, and the English rendering of the latter as "Droneville"—eliminated from the text.

55. Abramovitsh himself in his superb translation of *The Travels of Benjamin* into Hebrew (1896) had to reduce to some extent the stylistic differences between the various "voices" in the work. However, he amply compensated himself and the readers by adding to the style new complexities. If he could not now, for instance, play the Hebrew against the Yiddish (as he did in the original), he could play one Hebrew allusion or quotation against the other.

56. *The Travels of Benjamin*, p. 80; *Ale verk*, Vol. IX, p. 70.

57. *The Travels of Benjamin*, pp. 100–1; *Ale verk*, Vol. IX, pp. 92–93.

58. *The Travels of Benjamin*, p. 49; *Ale verk*, Vol. IX, p. 37.

59. *The Travels of Benjamin*, p. 74; *Ale verk*, Vol. IX, p. 64.

60. *Ale verk*, Vol. IX, p. 73 (my translation). Spiegel chose not to translate this similie.

61. Ibid., p. 50 (my translation). The allusion to the Bible escaped Spiegel altogether.

62. *The Travels of Benjamin*, pp. 46–47, *Ale verk*, Vol. IX, pp. 34–35.

63. *Ale verk*, Vol. IX, p. 46 (my translation).

64. Ibid., p. 26 (my translation).

65. Ibid., p. 40 (my translation).

66. This argument was omitted from the English translation. See *Ale verk*, Vol. IX, p. 12.

67. Ibid., p. 68 (my translation).

68. See, for instance, the paragraph starting with "Consequently we shall omit numerous instances of the tricks that people played on Benjamin, instances that would stigmatize men through all history. . . ." *The Travels of Benjamin*, p. 79; *Ale verk*, Vol. IX, p. 69.

69. Ibid., p. 9.

70. *The Travels of Benjamin*, p. 17; *Ale verk*, Vol. IX, p. 9.

71. *The Travels of Benjamin*, p. 26; *Ale verk*, Vol. IX, p. 15. See the whole paragraph here; see also Mendele's comments on the nature of the "heavenly" calf, which found its way to the arms of the sleeping Benjamin in the concluding section of Chap. 5.

72. The great Hebrew fiction writer and critic Y. Kh. Brener did not hear in *The Travels of Benjamin* the jolly, wild capriccio music but rather the long, never-ceasing "gnashing of teeth" which accompanies it. See his article "Ha'arakhat atsmenu bishloshet hakrakhim," in *Kol kitvey Y. Kh. Brener*, Vol. III (Tel Aviv, 1967), pp. 66–67.

73. The playfulness and virtuosity of Abramovitsh in *The Travels of Benjamin* were emphasized in the above-mentioned study of the place of the analogy in Abramovitsh's structural techniques by M. Peri (see above, note 51).

74. See *Ale verk fun Mendele*, Vol. XI, pp. 19–20.

75. Ibid., p. 5.

76. Ibid., pp. 3–4.

77. Ibid., pp. 16–17.

78. Ibid., pp. 171–76.

79. Ibid., p. 187.

80. *Dos vintshfingerl* (1865), p. 40.

81. Ibid., pp. 41–42.

82. See below, pp. 93, 186, 187, 193–94, 200, 206. See also Chap. 5, note 41.

83. Compare the descriptions in *Fishke der krumer* (1869), pp. 1–3, with those in pp. 22–23.

84. See "Yidishe kinder—fun di ksovim fun Yisrolik dem meshugenem," in the short-lived weekly *Yisrolik* (1875–76), No. 8, pp. 1–4. Many fragments from Abramovitsh's diaries, which enable us to detect the development of this "mad" project, were collected and published by A. Vorobeytshik, the curator of the Mendele-Museum in Odessa, in *Mendele un zayn tsayt* (Moscow, 1940), pp. 5–22. Vorobeytshik also published posthumously another story written by Abramovitsh (probably in the 1880s) within the framework of this project and titled "Der baybak." See *Shtern*, Vol. XII (Minsk, 1936), No. 1, pp. 6–12. See also my article " 'Sifriya limtorafim'—hareka lytsirat 'Susati'," *Hadoar*, Vol. LI (1972), Nos. 38, 39.

85. See Sh. Niger's "Fishke der krumer—un vi mendele hot gearbet," in his *Mendele Moykher—zayn lebn, zayne gezelshaftlekhe un literarishe oyftuvnagen*, 2d ed. (New York, 1970), pp. 119–32.

86. *Kol-mevaser*, Vol. V (1867), No. 41, pp. 302–3.

87. There are, however, several interpolations in the stories that somewhat relieve the reader after the long verbal barrages of the Polish Boy. See, for in-

stance, the long story of the coachman, the grandfather of the Polish Boy's intended bride, ibid., No. 35.

88. See M. Viner's comments on Abramovitsh's debt to this satirical tradition in *Tsu der geshikhte*, Vol. II, pp. 114–16.

89. *Dos poylishe yingl* (Lemberg [1885, edition 3]), p. 132.

90. For a somewhat different comparison between Abramovitsh and Linetski, see the first chapter in M. Viner's essay "Mendeles stil," in *Tsu der geshikhte*, Vol. II, pp. 17–22.

Chapter Eight: The Disguised Traveler—Conclusion

1. See the text of this pamphlet (reprinted from the *Folks-biblyotek*) in Reyzen's *Fun Mendelson*, Vol. I, pp. 257–68.

2. See, for example, "Yudl khnyok un Yoylikl shrayber," in *Dos meshulakhes* (Zhitomir, 1875), pp. 14–17; "Itsikl briak un Benyomtshe der takhshet," ibid., pp. 31–43; "In Nivitse oyf der prizbe," in *Der kolboynik* (Odessa, 1876), pp. 30–37; "Poylishe yidn in an adeser tshayne," ibid., pp. 37–44.

3. See the text with introductions by E. Tsherikover and Kh. Borodyanski in *Historishe shriftn* of the YIVO, Vol. I (1929), pp. 628–94. This play, or rather dramatic symposium, is presented here as anonymous. However, Max Erik discovered the name of its author, Avraham Fishelzon, divulged in the form of an acrostic in the poem accompanying it. See his "Literarishe mistseln," in *Bibliologisher zamlbukh* (Moscow, Kharkov, Minsk, 1930), pp. 514–15.

4. See Linetski's *Der beyzer marshelek* (Warsaw; the first edition was published in 1869, another [second ?] edition in 1889), pp. 5–12.

5. See above, pp. 52, 217 (as well as Chap. 2, note 49), and below, p. 266.

6. See *Der pritshepe* (Odessa, 1876), pp. 46–56.

7. See Levinzon's *Hefker-velt*, ed. by B. Natanzon (Warsaw, 1902), pp. 41–61.

8. See the rhymed introduction to Aksenfeld's *Man un vayb, shvester un bruder* (Odessa, 1867).

9. See *Aksenfelds verk*, ed. by M. Viner (Kharkov and Kiev, 1931), Vol. I, p. 144.

10. See, for example, Dik's novelette *Di kremerkes oder Golde-Mine di broder agine* (Vilna, 1865). It is included in Dik's *Geklibene verk*, ed. by Sh. Niger (New York, 1954), pp. 113–63. Here the plot takes us from the Eastern Galician town of Brod to Baltimore, Maryland, to Johannesburg, and, by implication, even to India.

11. See Dik's *Yehudis di tsveyte* (Vilna, 1875); *Siyum hatoyre* (Vilna, 1868).

12. See, for example, G. Beloy's *Bashraybung fun mis Yuli Pastrani* (Warsaw, 1858). The subject of this "story" is a human freak carried by a circus from America throughout Europe.

13. See N. Oyslender, "Varshever mekhabrim in di 50-er–6o-er yorn," in *Bibliologisher zamlbukh*, pp. 164–97.

14. See A. Vevyorka's study of Shaykevitsh in his book *Revizye* (Kharkov and Kiev, 1931), pp. 7–96. See especially pp. 7–22.

15. Dan Miron, *Shalom-Aleichem* (Ramat-Gan, 1970), pp. 21–46.

16. See *Etingers ksovim*, ed. Maks Vaynraykh, Vol. II, p. 451.

17. Ibid., Vol. I, p. xxx.

18. See Reyzen's *Fun Mendelson*, p. 259.

19. See M. Viner, *Tsu der geshikhte*, Vol. I, pp. 202–3.

20. See *Dos shterntikhl*, ed. by M. Viner (Moscow, 1938), p. 96.

21. Ibid., p. 59.

22. See Sh. Niger's *Dertseylers un romanistn* (New York, 1946), Vol. I, pp. 54–55.

23. *Dos shterntikhl*, p. 102.

24. See Y. Perl, *Ma'asiyot ve'igrot*, ed. Kh. Shmeruk and S. Verses (Jerusalem, 1970). Perl had the ingenious idea of making three *Bratslaver hasidim* correspond across the border which separated the Russian Ukraine from Austro-Hungarian Galicia. The Ukrainian correspondents are preparing a full and authorized edition of their *tsadik*'s famous allegorical fables, and it happens that some important sequels to the well-known fables were left by Reb Nakhman in the hands of the Galician correspondent. Thus Perl was able to supply the first of Nakhman's stories, "Ma'ase me'avedat bat-melekh" ("A Story of a Lost Princess") not only with a new and striking conclusion, but also with a long "authentic" sequel, "Ma'ase me'avedat ben-melekh" ("A Story of a Lost Prince"), as colorful a fable and as haunting in its symbolism as the original, if not more so, and completely inimical to it in its meaning. It is, as a matter of fact, precisely the opposite in every detail. It seems that his intention was to apply this method of literary annihilation to every one of Reb Nakhman's fables.

25. See the editors' introduction, ibid., p. 23.

26. See the list of his works which Aksenfeld added to his letter to Gotlober written in 1862, in *Aksenfelds verk*, ed. by M. Viner, Vol. I, pp. 353–54.

27. See Reyzen's *Fun Mendelson*, pp. 360–62.

28. Our knowledge of this lost novel depends on the correspondence between Aksenfeld, the censor of Jewish books in Vilna, and the Russian ministry of education concerning the refusal of the Vilna printers to print the book. See some of the documents in *Tsaytshrift*, Vol. V (1931), pp. 176–80. See also Sh. Ginzburg's *Yisroel Aksenfeld*, in his *Historishe verk*, Vol. I, pp. 75–88.

29. For the influence of Perl, see *Kol-mevaser*, Vol. V (1867), No. 35; for that of Perl and Aksenfeld, see, for example, *Dos poylishe yingl* (Lemberg, 1885), pp. 74–84.

30. See N. Oyslender, "Mendeles mitgeyers in di 60-er–70-er yorn," in *Mendele un zayn tsayt* (Moscow, 1940), pp. 90–171. This is the only study of what might be called the "Abramovitsh school" prior to Sholem Aleichem. One possible and, of course, tentative candidate for the authorship of *Briv fun galitsyen* would be M. L. Rodkinson (1845–1904), the editor of *Kol-la'am* as well as the Hebrew magazine *Hakol*.

31. See Dik's *Geklibene verk*, p. 73.

32. See, for example, the opening of the *feuilleton* "Di simkhe," in the Soviet edition of Sholem Aleichem's *Verk*, Vol. I, p. 438, or the first letter in "An ibershraybung tsvishn tsvey alte khaveyrim," ibid., p. 165.

33. The outline of such an analysis may be found in my monograph, *Sholem-Aleichem—Person, Persona, Presence* (New York, 1972).

SELECTIVE BIBLIOGRAPHY

By no means exhaustive or even comprehensive, this bibliography is nevertheless intended both for the reader who has no Yiddish and who would like to be introduced to the historical, cultural, and literary background of the development discussed in this book, and for readers who possess a knowledge of Yiddish and Hebrew sufficient for further and more detailed study. Only writers who made their appearance in Yiddish literature before the 1880s are mentioned here. This excludes Sholem Aleichem and Y. L. Perets, who, although they figure prominently in some chapters of this study, define the chronological and historical limits of its subject matter rather than belong to it.

Items followed by (y) are written in Yiddish; (h) indicates Hebrew.

I. GENERAL BACKGROUND

A. Some General Historical Surveys

Baron, S. W. *The Russian Jew Under Tsars and Soviets*. New York and London, 1964.

Berenshteyn, M. V. "Di yidn in Ukrayine unter der tsarisher hershaft (1795–1917)," in *Yidn in Ukrayine*, edited by M. Osherovits, Y. Leshtshinski, F. Fridman, and A. Kihn, Vol. I, New York, 1961, pp. 69–117 (y).

Dubnow, S. M. *History of the Jews in Russia and Poland*. 3 vols. Philadelphia, 1916–1920.

Greenberg, L. *The Jews in Russia*. 2 vols. New Haven, 1944–1951.

Mahler, R. *A History of Modern Jewry, 1780–1815*. New York, 1971.

Margolis, A. *Geshikhte fun yidn in Rusland, 1772–1861*. Moscow, 1930 (y).

Weinryb, B. D. "East European Jewry (Since the Partitions of Poland, 1772–1795)," in *The Jews, Their History, Culture and Religion*, edited by L. Finkelstein, Vol. I, New York, 1949, pp. 343–98.

B. Social and Economic Background

Finkelstein, L., ed. *The Jews, Their History, Culture and Religion*. Vol. IV, "The Sociology and Demography of the Jews."

Friedmann, F. "Wirtschaftliche Umschichtungsprozesse und Industrialisierung der polnischen Judenschaft, 1800–1870," in *Jewish Studies in Memory of George A. Kohut*, edited by S. W. Baron and A. Marx, New York, 1935, pp. 178–247.

Leshtschinski, J. *Jewish Migration for the Past Hundred Years*. New York, 1944.

Leshtshinski, Y. *Di antviklung fun yidishn folk far di letste 100 yor*. Berlin, 1928 (y). "Di sotsyal-ekonomishe antviklung fun ukrayinishn yidntum," in *Yidn in Ukrayine*, Vol. I, pp. 163–227 (y).

Levitats, I. *The Jewish Community in Russia, 1782–1844*. New York, 1943.

Rombakh, Sh. "Di yidishe balmelokhes in Rusland in der ershter helft fun 19-tn yorhundert," in *Tsaytshrift*. Vol. I (1926), pp. 25–30 (y).

Rupin, A. *Die Soziologie der Juden*. 2 vols. Berlin, 1930–1931.

Weinryb, B. D. *Neueste Wirtschaftsgeschichte der Juden in Russland und Polen*. Breslau, 1934.

Yokhinson, Y. *Sotsyal-ekonomisher shteyger ba yidn in Rusland in 19-tn yorhundert*. Kharkov, 1929 (y).

Yuditski, A. *Yidishe burzhuazye un yidishn proletaryat in ershter helft 19-tn yorhundert*. Kiev, 1932 (y).

C. Shtetl Life

Ain, A. "Swislocz, Portrait of a Jewish Community in Eastern Europe," in *YIVO Annual of Social Jewish Science*, Vol. IV (1949), pp. 86–114.

Ausubel, N., ed. *A Treasury of Jewish Folklore*. New York, 1948.

Bastomski, Sh. *Baym kval: yidishe shprikhverter, vertlekh, glaykhvertlekh, rednsartn, fargleykhenishn, brokhes, vintshenishn, kloles, kharomes, simonim, sgules, zababones*. Vilna, 1920 (y).

Birnbaum, S. A. "The Cultural Structure of East Ashkenazic Jewry," in *Slavonic and East European Review*, Vol. XXV (1946) pp. 73–92.

Dawidowicz, L. S., ed. *The Golden Tradition—Jewish Life and Thought in Eastern Europe*. New York, 1967.

Heller, J. "Jewish Ways of Life," in *The Jewish People Past and Present*, Vol. II, New York, 1948, pp. 254–83.

Heschel, A. J. *The Earth Is the Lord's: The Inner World of the Jew in East Eu-*

rope. New York, 1950. "The Eastern European Era in Jewish History," in *YIVO Annual of Social Jewish Research*, Vol. I (1946), pp. 86–106.

Khayes, Kh. "Gloybungen un minhogim in farbinfung mitn toyt," in *Filologishe shriftn* of the YIVO, Vol. II (1928), pp. 281–328 (y).

Rubin, R. *Voices of a People—Yiddish Folk Song*. New York and London, 1963.

Schauss, H. *The Jewish Festivals*. Cincinnati, 1938. *The Lifetime of a Jew Throughout the Ages of Jewish History*. Cincinnati, 1950.

Schwarzbaum, H. *Studies in Jewish and World Folklore*. Berlin, 1968.

Shtern, Y. "A Kheyder in Tyszowce (Tishevits)," in *YIVO Annual of Social Jewish Science*, Vol. V (1950), pp. 152–71. *Kheyder un beys-medresh*. New York, 1950 (y).

Tsomber, L. "A bild fun yidishn kultur-lebn in a poylisher shtot in onheyb fun 19-tn yorhundert," in *Yunger historiker*, Vol. I (1926), pp. 56–65 (y).

Zborowski, M., and E. Herzog. *Life Is with People: The Jewish Little-Town of Eastern Europe*. New York, 1952.

Zelkovitch, J. "A Picture of Communal Life of a Jewish Town in Poland in the Second Half of the Nineteenth Century," in *YIVO Annual of Social Jewish Science*, Vol. VI (1951), pp. 253–66.

D. The Haskala Movement in Eastern Europe

Ben Adir. "Modern Currents in Jewish Social and National Life," in *The Jewish People, Past and Present*, Vol. II, pp. 285–329.

Erik, M. *Etyudn tsu der geshikhte fun der haskole*. Vol. I, Minsk, 1934 (y).

Ginzburg, Sh. *Historishe verk*. 3 vols. New York, 1937 (y).

Koyfman, Y. *Gola venekhar*. Parts III–IV. Tel Aviv, 1930 (h).

Mahler, R. "The Social and Political Aspects of the Haskalah in Galicia," in *YIVO Annual of Social Jewish Research*, Vol. I (1946), pp. 64–85.

Maler, R. *Der kamf tsvishn haskole un khsides in Galitsye*. New York, 1942 (y).

Margolis, M. *Dor hahaskala berusiya* (trans. Y—Sh). Vilna, 1910 (h).

Meisel, J. *Haskala, Geschichte der Aufklärungsbewegung unter der Juden in Russland*. Berlin, 1919.

Osherovits, M. "Di haskole in Ukrayine," in *Yidn in Ukrayine*, Vol. I, pp. 279–336 (y).

Raisin, J. S. *The Haskala Movement in Russia*. Philadelphia, 1913.

Rotenstreich, N. *Jewish Philosophy in Modern Times*. New York, Chicago, and San Francisco, 1968.

Sharfshteyn, Ts. *Toldot hakhinukh beyisra'el badorot ha'akhronim*. 2 vols. New York, 1945–1947 (h).

Shatski, Y. *Kultur-geshikhte fun der haskole in Lite*. Buenos Aires, 1950 (y).

Slutski, Y. *Ha'itonut hayehudit-rusit bame'a hayod-tet*. Jerusalem, 1971 (h).

Tsinberg, Y. "Di geshikhte fun der rusish-yidisher prese," in *Kultur-historishe shtudyes*, New York, 1949, pp. 87–158 (y).

II. NINETEENTH CENTURY YIDDISH LITERATURE

A. Lexicons and Bibliography

Liberberg, Y., ed. *Biblyologisher zamlbukh*. Vol. I. Moscow, Kharkov, and Minsk, 1930 (y).

Leksikon fun der nayer yidisher literatur. 7 vols. (incomplete). New York, 1956–1968 (y).

Reyzen, Z. *Leksikon fun der yidisher literatur, prese un filologye*. 4 vols. Vilna, 1928–1930 (y).

Shmeruk, Kh., ed. *Pirsumim yehudiyim bivrit hamo'etsot*. Jerusalem, 1961 (h).

"State of Research and Bibliography," a supplement to the article "Yiddish Literature," in *Encyclopedia Judaica*, Vol. XVI. Jerusalem, 1971, pp. 826–33.

Yeshurin, Y. *100 yor moderne yidishe literatur*. New York, 1965 (y).

YIVO biblyografye. Vol. I (covers the publications of the YIVO from 1925 to 1941), New York, 1943; Vol. II (1942–1950), New York, 1961 (y).

Zilbertsvayg, Z. *Leksikon fun yidishn teater*. 5 vols. Warsaw, New York and Mexico City, 1931–1967 (y).

B. General Historical Surveys

Erik, M. *Iberblik iber di geshikhte fun der yidisher literatur*. London, 1926 (y).

Erik, M., and A. Rozentsvayg. *Di yidishe literatur in 19-tn yorhundert*. Vol. I. Kiev and Kharkov, 1935 (y).

Gorin, B. *Di geshikhte fun yidishn teater*. 2 vols. New York, 1918 (y).

Lastik, Sh. *Di yidishe literatur biz di klasiker*. Warsaw, 1950 (y).

Liptzin, S. *A History of Yiddish Literature*. New York, 1972. *The Flowering of Yiddish Literature*. New York, 1963.

Madison, C. A. *Yiddish Literature—Its Scope and Major Writers*. New York, 1968.

Mark, Y. "Yiddish Literature," in *The Jews, Their History, Culture and Religion*. Vol. II, pp. 417–68.

Mayzl, N. *Doyres un tkufes in der yidisher literatur*. New York, 1942. *Tsurikblikn un perspektivn*, Tel Aviv, 1962, pp. 22–61 (y).

Niger, Sh. *Dertseylers un romanistn*. Vol. I. New York, 1946 (y). "Yiddish Literature in the Past Two Hundred Years," in *The Jewish People, Past and Present*, Vol. III, pp. 165–219.

Pinès, M. *Histoire de la littérature Judéo-Allemande*. Paris, 1910. (Also available in German, Russian, and Yiddish translations.)

Roback, A. A. *The Story of Yiddish Literature*. New York, 1940.

Shmeruk, Kh. "Yiddish Literature," in *Encyclopedia Judaica*, Vol. XVI, pp. 798–833.

Tsinberg, Y. *Di geshikhte fun der literatur bay yidn*. Vols. VII–IX. Vilna and New York, 1936–1966 (y).

Vaynraykh, M. *Bilder fun der yidisher literaturgeshikhte*. Vilna, 1928 (y).

Waxman, M. *A History of Jewish Literature*. Vols. IV–V. New York, 1941–1960.

Wiener, L. *The History of Yiddish Literature in the Nineteenth Century*. New York, 1899.

C. Historically Oriented Anthologies

Reyzen, Z. *Fun Mendelson biz Mendele*. Vol. I. Warsaw, 1923 (y).

Rozhanski, Sh. *Nusekh haskole*. Buenos Aires, 1968 (y).

Shtif, N. *Di eltere yidishe literatur*. Kiev, 1929 (y).

D. Historical and Critical Studies of Particular Aspects of Nineteenth-century Yiddish Literature

Bal-Dimyen [N. Shtif]. "Dr. Pineses geshikhte fun der yidisher literatur," in *Der pinkes*, edited by Sh. Niger, Vol. I, Vilna, 1913, pp. 313–48 (y). *Humanizm in der elterer yidisher literatur*. 2nd ed., Berlin, 1922 (y).

Bal-Makhshoves [I. Elyashev]. "Dos dorem-rusishe yidntum in der yidisher literatur in 19-tn yorhundert," in *Geklibene shriftn*, New York, 1953, pp. 77–111 (y). "Tsvey shprakhn—eyneyntsike literatur," ibid., pp. 112–23 (y).

Bernshteyn, Y. "Der tsaytikung-peryod in lebn fun udzere klasiker," in *YIVO-bleter*, Vol. III (1933), pp. 98–120 (y).

Erik, M. *Etyudn tsu der geshikhte fun der haskole*. Vol. I. Minsk, 1934 (y).

Leshtshinski, Y. *Dos yidishe ekonomishe lebn in der yidisher literatur*. Vol. I, Minsk, 1921 (y).

Niger, Sh. "Briv vegn der alter un nayer yidisher literatur," in *Bleter geshikhte fun der yidisher literatur*, New York, 1959, pp. 283–349 (y). *Di tsvey-shprakhikeyt fun undzer literatur*. Detroit, 1941 (y). "Di yidishe literatur un di lezerin," in *Bleter geshikhte*, pp. 37–107 (y). "Roman un romantizm," in *Shmusn vegn bikher*, Vol. I. New York, 1922, pp. 105–34. "Vegn der onheyb fun der nayer yidisher literatur," ibid., pp. 209–79 (y).

Oyslender, N. *Gruntshtrikhn fun yidishn realizm*. Kiev, 1920 (y). "Mendeles mitgeyers in di 60-er–70-er yorn," in *Mendele un zayn tsayt*, Moscow, 1940, pp. 90–171 (y). "Varshever mekhabrim in di 50-er–60-er yorn," in *Biblyologisher zamlbukh*, Vol. I, pp. 164–97 (y).

Reminik, Y. "Miteylungen tsu der geshikhte fun yidisher literatur un teater," in *Mendele un zayn tsayt*, pp. 221–38 (y).

Reyzen, Z. "Naye arbetn tsu der geshikhte fun der haskole literatur," in *YIVO-bleter*, Vol. I (1931), pp. 193–207; Vol. II (1931), pp. 367–89 (y).

Sadan, D. "Masat mavo," in *Avney bedek*, Tel Aviv, 1962, pp. 9–93 (h).

Tsinberg, Y. "Der 'Kol-mevaser' un zayn tsayt," in *Kultur-historishe shtudyes*, pp. 159–89 (y).

Vevyorke, A. *Revizye*. Kharkov, 1931 (y).

Viner, M. "Di rekrutshine un der sheyner literatur fun der haskole," in *Tsu der geshikhte fun der yidisher literatur in 19-tn yorhundert*, Vol. I, New York, 1945, pp. 150–92 (y). "Di rol fun shablonisher frarzeologye in der literatur fun der haskole," ibid., pp. 276–309 (y). "Di yidishe literatur baym onheyb funem 19-tn yorhundert," ibid., pp. 23–63 (y).

E. Some Memoirs

Abramovitsh, Sh. Y. "Reshimot letoldotay," in *Kol kitvey Mendele Mokher-Sfarim*, Tel Aviv, 1947, pp. 1–6 (h).

Berkovitsh, Y. D. *Harishonim kivney adam*. Vols. VI–X of *Kol kitvey Y. D. Berkovitsh*, Tel Aviv, 1951–1954 (h).

Braynin, R. *Fun mayn lebnsbukh*. New York, 1946 (y).

Dinezon, Y. *Zikhroynes un bilder*. Warsaw, 1927 (y).

Dubnov, Sh. *Fun zhargon tsu yidish*. Vilna, 1929 (y).

Gotlober, A. B. *Memuarn*. Vol. I of *Gotlober un zayn epokhe*, edited by A. Fridkin, Vilna, 1925 (y).

Granovski, R. Y. *Y. Linetski un zayn dor*. New York, 1941 (y).

Mayzl, N., ed. *Zikhroynes vegn Mendele*. Vol. XX of *Ale verk fun Mendele Moykher-Sforim*, Warsaw, 1928 (y).

Paperna, A. Y. *Zikhroynes*. Translated from the Russian by P. Ra-ski. Warsaw, 1923 (y).

Reyzen, A. *Epizodn fun mayn lebn*. Vols. I–II, Vilna, 1929 (y).

Sholem Aleichem. "Tsu mayn biyografye," in *Ale verk fun Sholem-Aleichem*, Vol. XXVII (*Funem yarid* II), New York, 1923, pp. 271–81 (y).

Spektor, M. *Mayn lebn*. 2 vols. Warsaw, 1927 (y).

Tsitron, Sh. L. *Dray literarishe doyres: zikhroynes vegn yidishe shriftshteler*. Warsaw, 1920–1922 (y).

III. SH. Y. ABRAMOVITSH (1836–1917)

A. Standard Editions

In Yiddish

Ale verk fun Mendele Moykher-Sforim. 17 vols. Farlag Mendele, Cracow, Warsaw, New York, and Vilna, 1911–1913. Vol. XVII is a collection of critical and biographical essays on Abramovitsh. This edition is usually referred to as the *Yubileum oysgabe*.

Ale verk fun Mendele Moykher-Sforim. 22 vols. Edited by N. Mayzl. Farlag
    Mendele, Warsaw, 1928. This is still the most extensive edition of
    Abramovitsh's Yiddish works. Vols. I, XX–XXII contain comprehensive
    selections of articles on the author—critical, biographical, and memoir-
    istic.
Gezamlte verk fun Mendele Moykher-Sforim. Vols. III–VI (incomplete). Edited
    by A. Gurshteyn, M. Viner, and Y. Nusinov. Farlag Emes, Moscow,
    1935–1940. This edition, although incomplete, is superior to the others
    in its textual accuracy and because of the historical-critical introduc-
    tions and explanatory notes added to the texts.

In Hebrew

Kol kitvey Mendele Mokher-Sfarim. 3 vols. Hotsa'at va'ad hayovel. Cracow
    and Odessa, 1909–1912. The so-called *Mahadurat hayovel.*
Kol kitvey Mendele Mokher-Sfarim. 7 vols. Hotsa'at Moriya. Jerusalem, Berlin,
    and Odessa, 1922. Vol. VII is a collection of critical and biographical
    articles on the author. Edited by Kh. N. Byalik and Y. Kh. Ravnitski.
Kol kitvey Mendele Mokher-Sfarim. 6 vols. Hotsa'at Dvir. Tel Aviv, 1936.
Kol kitvey Mendele Mokher-Sfarim, in one volume. Hotsa'at Dvir. Tel Aviv,
    1947. With a critical-biographical introduction by Y. Fikhman.
    (*A bilingual academic edition of Abramovitsh's works is in preparation
    by scholars of the Hebrew University of Jerusalem.*)

B. Some Translations

The main western language in which something like a competent translation of Abramovitsh's major works exists is German.

Mendele Moicher Sfurim. *Fischke der Krumme.* Translated by A. Eliasberg.
    Der Wunschring. Translated by S. Birnbaum. Olten and Freiburg in
    Breisgau, 1962. *Binjamin der Dritte.* Translated by E. Frisch. *Die
    Mähre* and *Schloimale.* Translated by S. Birnbaum. Olten und Freiburg
    im Bresigau, 1962.

In English

Mendele Mocher Seforim. "The Calf." Translated by J. Sloan, in *A Treasury of
    Yiddish Stories,* edited by I. Howe and E. Greenberg. New York, 1953,
    pp. 97–111. *Fishke the Lame.* Translated by G. Stillman. New York,
    1960. *The Nag.* Translated by M. Spiegel. New York, 1955. *The Para-
    site.* Translated by G. Stillman. New York, 1956. *The Travels and Ad-
    ventures of Benjamin The Third.* Translated by M. Spiegel. New York,
    1949.

C. A Chronological List of Abramovitsh's Important Publications

1857 "Mikhtav al dvar hakhinukh" ("A Letter Concerning Education"); Abramovitsh's first article, published in the first Hebrew weekly, *Hamagid* (h).

1860 *Mishpat shalom* ("The Judgment of Peace"; it can also mean "The Judgment of Shalom," i.e., of Shalom Ya'akov Abramovitsh); Abramovitsh's first book, a miscellany including the famous attack on Tsvayfel, which made the author the center of stormy polemics for years. It also includes some articles, juvenile poetry, and biblical commentary (h).

1862 *Limdu hetev* ("Learn to Do Good"); Abramovitsh's first work of fiction (h).
Toldot hateva ("Natural History"). Vol. I. The first part of Abramovitsh's comprehensive textbook of zoology. Adapted from a German book by H. O. Lenz (h).

1864 *Dos kleyne mentshele* ("The Little Man"); Abramovitsh's second work of fiction and his first Yiddish one; serialized in *Kol-mevaser* (y).

1865 *Dos vintshfingerl* ("The Magic Ring"); first version (y).

1866 *Eyn mishpat* ("The Fountain of Judgment"); a collection of articles (h).
Toldot hateva. Vol. II. Adapted from various authors (h).

1867 The enlarged and complete version of *Limdu hetev*, entitled *Ha'avot vehabanim* ("The Fathers and the Sons"), appears in Russian translation.

1868 *Ha'avot vehabanim* published in its Hebrew original.

1869 *Di takse, oder di bande shtot baley-toyves* ("The Tax, Or the Clique of the Benefactors of the Town"); Abramovitsh's first play (y).
Fishke der krumer ("Fishke the Lame"), first version (y).
Der luftbalon ("The Balloon"); adapted with Y. L. Binshtok from Jules Vernes's *Cinq semains en ballons* (y).

1871 "Et ledaber" ("A Time to Speak"); a polemic against M. L. Lilyenblum. Published in *Hamelits* (h).

1872 *Toldot hateva*. Vol. III (h).

1873 *Di klyatshe, oder tsar baley khayim* ("The Nag, Or Against Cruelty to Animals"); Abramovitsh's popular allegory on the persecution of the Jews in czarist Russia (y).

1875 *Dos yidl* ("The Little Jew"); another allegorical work on the situation and history of Jews as an exiled nation; in verse (y).
Zmires yisroel ("The Songs of Israel"); a Yiddish adaptation in verse of the traditional Sabbath songs, with a Hebrew commentary.
Peyrek shire ("A Sequence of Hymns"); a Yiddish adaptation and elaboration on *Perek shira*, added to the hasidic prayer book, in which the whole cosmos praises God in mystical terms. In verse (y).

"Ma anu" ("What Are We?"); an essay on the character and development of the Jewish nation. Serialized in *Hashakhar* (h).

"Yidishe kinder" ("Children of Israel"); a monologue of Yisrolik the Madman, the protagonist of *Di klyatshe*, published in the magazine *Yisrolik* (y).

1878   *Kitser masoes Binyomin hashlishi* ("The Abridged Travels of Benjamin The Third") (y).

"Ahava le'umit vetoldoteha" ("Patriotism and Its Consequences [or, its 'History']"); an essay examining the nature of patriotism and recommending a mild and well-controlled brand of it while warning against chauvinistic excesses; serialized in *Hamelits* (h).

1879   *Dos kleyne mentshele.* A much enlarged and improved version which appears as a first volume in a projected series of "Collected Works" (y). However, subsequent volumes do not appear.

1884   *Der priziv* ("The Draft"); Abramovitsh's second play, and his first publication after five years of silence (y).

Di Takse appears in Russian translation.

1885   *Masoes Binyomin hashlishi* appears in Polish translation.

1886   *Di klyatshe* appears in Polish translation.

"Beseter ra'am" ("In the Secret Place of Thunder"), first chapter; Abramovitsh's first Hebrew story since the publication of *Ha'avot vehabanim*, published in the first Hebrew daily, *Hayom* (h).

1887   "Beseter ra'am," the complete story, published in *Ben-ami* (h).

1888   *Fishke der krumer*, a much enlarged and improved version, published as the first volume of a new "Collected Works" project (y).

Dos vintshfingerl, enlarged version; prologue and Part I appear in the first volume of Sholem Aleichem's *Yidishe folks-biblyotek* (y).

1889   *Di klyatshe* published as a second volume of the "Collected works" (y). Subsequent volumes do not follow.

"Reshimot letoldotay" ("Sketches to My Biography"), published in *Sefer zikaron* (h).

Dos vintshfingerl, Part II; published in the 1889 volume of Sholem Aleichem's almanac (y).

1890   "Shem veyefet ba'agala" ("Shem and Japeth in the Train Compartment"), a short story published in *Kaveret* (h).

1892   "Lo nakhat beya'akov" ("There Is No Good in Jacob"), a short story, published in *Pardes*, Vol. I (h).

1894   "Bymey hara'ash" ("In Days of Tumult"), a short story, published in *Pardes*, Vol. II. With "Ptikhta demendele Mokher-Sfarim" ("Mendele Mokher-Sforim's Prologue"), an introduction to a projected autobiographical novel (h).

"Byshiva shel ma'ala uvyshiva shel mata" ("In the Heavenly Assembly and in the Earthly One"); first section of this discursive, polemic novelette, published in *Lu'akh akhi'asaf*, Vol. II (h).

1895 "Byshiva shel ma'ala uvyshiva shel mata," second section; published in *Lu'akh akhi'asaf*, Vol. III (h).

"Di alte mayse" ("The Old Story"), a Yiddish version of "Lo nakhat beya'akov" published in *Hoyz-fraynt*, Vol. IV (y).

1896 *Mas'ot Binyamin hashlishi*, the Hebrew version, published as a supplement to *Pardes*, Vol. III (h).

"Hanisrafim" ("Pauperized by Fire"), a short story, published ibid. (h).

1897 *Be'emek habakha* ("In the Vale of Tears"), the Hebrew version of *Dos vintshfingerl*, serialized in *Hashilo'akh* (h).

1899 *Shloyme reb Khayims* ("Shloyme the Son of Reb Khayim"), Abramovitsh's autobiographical novel, serialized in *Der yid* (y).

1900 *Sipurim* ("Short Stories"). This collection includes all the Hebrew short stories Abramovitsh had published since 1886 as well as the "Ptikhta levayamim hahem" ("Prologue to Those Old Days"). *Bayamim hahem* is one of the titles of the Hebrew version of *Shloyme reb Khayims* (h).

1901 *Sefer hakabtsanim* ("The Book of Paupers"), a large section of *Fishke der krumer*, serialized in *Hador*. The first draft of this translation was prepared by the poet Byalik. Abramovitsh contributed "the finishing touch" (h).

1902 *Seyfer habeheymes* ("The Book of Cattle"), serialized in *Der yid* (y).

"Yisrolik der meshugener" ("Yisrolik the Madman"), additional chapters to *Di klyatshe*, serialized in *Der yid* (y).

1903 "Di antdekung fun Volin" ("The Discovery of Volhynia"), a "historical" short story, published in *Hilf* (y).

Khayey Shlomo ("The Life of Shlome"), the Hebrew version of *Shloyme reb Khayims*, serialized in *Hazman*, Vols. III–IV (h).

1904 New chapters of *Dos vintshfingerl* published in *Der fraynt* (y).

1905 New chapters of *Dos vintshfingerl* published in *Dos lebn*, as is the short story "Seyfer hagilgulim" ("The Book of Metamorphosis") (y).

1907 Final versions of *Dos kleyne mentshele* and *Fishke der krumer* (y).

1909 The first volume of the "Jubilee edition" of Abramovitsh's collected Hebrew works. It includes the final versions of *Sefer hakabtsanim* and *Be'emek habakha*.

1911 Second volume of the Hebrew "Jubilee edition." Final versions of *Susati* ("The Nag"), *Mas'ot Binyamin hashlishi*, and *Bayamim hahem*.

The 17-volume Yiddish "Jubilee edition" begins to appear.

The series *Mibeyt gnazav shel yisra'el* ("Of the Jewish Treasure"), afterward entitled *Khagim uzmanim* ("Festivals"), begins to appear in *Hashilo'akh* (h).

1912 Third volume of the Hebrew "Jubilee edition." It includes an entirely new adaptation of the early novel *Ha'avot vehabanim* as well as the short stories and a Hebrew version of *Sefer habehemot* ("The Book of Cattle").

New chapters of *Shloyme reb Khayims* appear in *Der fraynt* (y).

1913   *Seyfer bereyshis*, a Yiddish translation of Genesis with Kh. N. Byalik and Y. Kh. Ravnitski.

"Fun mayn seyfer-hazikhroynes" ("From My Memoirs"), first chapter, published in *Di yidishe velt* (y).

The Yiddish "Jubilee edition" completed.

1915   "Fun mayn seyfer hazikhroynes," second chapter, published in *Di yidishe velt* (y). The Hebrew version of the first chapter of these memoirs is published in *Hatsfira*.

1916   "A farbenkenish" ("A Longing"), a further chapter of the memoirs, is published in *Undzer lebn* (y).

Posthumous Publications

1917   New chapters from *Sholyme reb Khayims* are published in *Untervegs* (y).

1918   *Misefer hazikhronot sheli* ("From My Memoirs"); the entire Hebrew version of the late memoiristic sketches is published in *Hatsfira* (h).

1937   "Der baybak" ("The Laggard"), a chapter from the "diary of Yisrolik the Madman" (probably written in the 1880s) is published in *Shtern* (y).

1939   "Mayn [letste] nesie" ("My [Last] Trip"), the opening chapter of a story (probably written in 1870–71), is published in *Shtern* (y).

1940   In the collection *Mendele un zayn tsayt* various formerly unknown fragments appear: "Aderabe, ver iz meshuge?" ("Well, Who Is the Madman?"), a variant of "Yidishe kinder" (1875); "Di milkhomes fun habose komande" ("The Battles of the Riffraff"), an epistolary story, written in 1882–84 and left untitled (the title was added by the editors of *Mendele un zayn tsayt*). Parts of it were incorporated in the Hebrew "Beseter ra'am" (1886–87); "Di oysgenarte bekhoyre" ("The Stolen Primogeniture"), a plan for a story, conceived in the late 1860s; "Rayoynes fun Hershel dem meshugenem" ("Reflections of Hershel the Madman"), prepared probably in 1870–72 for a story that was subsequently developed into *Di klyatshe* (1873). These were written in Hebrew but preserved only in Yiddish translation (y).

1947   *Keminheg yid* ("According to the Jewish Custom"), a scene from an unpublished variant of *Der priziv* (1884), appears in *Sovetish heymland*, Vol. II. Further excerpts from this variant are included in an article by R. Roskes-Vays. See section F in the present part (III) of the bibliography (y).

D. Bibliography

A full list of Abramovitsh's publications both in Hebrew and in Yiddish, prepared by Y. A. Klauzner and N. Ben Menakhem, as well as his published letters, prepared by Y. Sheyntukh, was published in *Mendele Mokher-Sfarim—reshimat ktavav ve'igrotav lehatkanat mahaduratam ha'akademit*, edited by Kh. Shmeruk and Sh. Verses, Jerusalem, 1965 (h).

A. R. Malakhi published a descriptive list of Abramovitsh's Hebrew publications between 1857 and 1886: "Habibliyografiya shel Mendele," in *Hatoren*. Vol. IV (1918), Nos. 40, 42, 44–47, 49–50 (h).

Thousands of books, pamphlets, articles, and reviews have been published on Abramovitsh, his life and works. They have never been fully listed. Fragmentary listings can be found in the various lexicons, histories, anthologies, etc. Somewhat fuller, but still quite rudimentary listings are Y. Yeshurin, "Sh. Y. Abramovitsh—Mendele Moykher-Sforim: biblyografye," published as a supplement to the edition of *Masoes Binyomin hashlishi* in the series *Musterverk fun der yidisher literatur*, Buenos Aires, 1958 (y); and Y. David, *Mendele Mokher-Sfarim babikoret ha'ivrit* (in stencil), Jerusalem, 1961–1962 (h). A fuller list of Yiddish articles, covering only the first decade after Abramovitsh's death (1917–27) was prepared by Y. Anilevitsh, "Naye Mendele-literatur," in *Bikher velt* (1928), No. 5, pp. 29–33; No. 7, pp. 38–41.

E. Documents, Biographies

Abramovitsh's letters were collected in *Dos Mendele bukh*, edited by N. Mayzl, New York, 1959, pp. 43–244. However, the many letters written originally in Hebrew (as well as the fewer Russian ones) have been rendered here in Yiddish translation only, and the translation is sometimes unreliable and often incompetent. The original letters can be found in different periodicals. Among others: *Reshumot*, old series, Vol. II (no date), pp. 427–31; Vol. V, edited by Sh. Niger (1927), pp. 408–19; Vol. VI (1930), pp. 513–19. *Shriftn*, Vol. I, edited by N. Shtif (1928), pp. 219–98. *Tsaytshrift*, Vol. V, edited by Sh. Ginzburg (1931), special pagination. *Kneset*, Vol. IV (1939), pp. 20–26. *Mendele un zayn tsayt* (1940), pp. 41–49. *YIVO-bleter*, Vol. XXXV (1951), pp. 215–21.

Excerpts and summaries of unpublished letters can be found in Y. L. Rozental, *Toldot khevrat marbey haskala beyisra'el*, Vol. II, Petersburg, 1890 (h); and in Sh. Ginzburg, "Mendele in zayne briv," in *Historishe verk*, Vol. I, New York, 1937, pp. 140–64 (y).

Biographical documents connected with Abramovitsh and his family were collected and partly published by M. Weinreich. See his articles: "Mendele dokumentn," and "Mendeles ershte 25 yor" (y), in *YIVO-bleter*, Vol. X (1936), pp. 167–80, 364–75; "Mendeles eltern un mitkinder" (y), in *YIVO-bleter*, Vol. XI (1937), pp. 270–86; "Pesye Abramovitsh khrakterizirt fun ir zun" (y), in *YIVO-bleter*, Vol. XIV (1939), pp. 335–38. See also Sh. Niger, "Vegn Mendeles zun Meyer" (y), in *Der tog morgn zhurnal*, March 20, 1954. Other documents were collected in *Mendele un zayn tsayt*, *Dos Mendele bukh*, and in the various biographical and memoiristic articles.

A detailed and reliable biography of Abramovitsh is still a desideratum. The first biography was written by the author himself in a letter to E. Daynard (1877). The original Hebrew letter is published in *Reshumot*, Vol. V, pp. 416–18. The second biography was written by Abramovitsh's close friend, Y. L. Binshtok, in Russian and published in *Voskhod* (1884), No. 12, pp. 1–32. It has been translated into Hebrew by Y. Klozner and published in *Hashilo'akh*, Vol. XXXIV (1918), pp. 14–29. In 1889 Abramovitsh contributed an autobiographical article to *Sefer zikaron*, a literary lexicon, edited by N. Sokolov. This article, entitled "Reshimot letoldotay" (in its Yiddish translation "Shtrikhn tsu mayn biyografye"), is incorporated in most of the editions of the collected works (see the Hebrew original in *Kol kitvey Mendele*, 1947, pp. 1–6; the Yiddish version in *Ale verk fun Mendele*, 1928, Vol. XIX, pp. 147–71). In 1911 Y. Kh. Ravnitski rewrote (with the author's help) and updated the biography (for the first volume of the Yiddish "Jubilee edition." See pp. vii–xli). A Hebrew version of this biography was included in Ravnitski's *Dor vesofrav*, Vol. I, Tel Aviv, 1927, pp. 34–61. In 1928 M. Weinreich included his study of Abramovitsh's literary beginnings, "Mendele's onheyb," in his *Bilder fun der yidisher literaturgeshikhte*, pp. 330–51 (y). In 1929 Z. Reyzen attempted in his *Leksikon*, Vol. I, pp. 7–37, a summing up of the biographical and bibliographical data then known (y). Sh. Niger published his extensive monograph *Mendele Moykher-Sforim—zayn lebn, zayne gezelshaftlekhe un literarishe oyftuungen*, Chicago, 1936. 2d. rev. ed., New York, 1970 (y). U. Finkel published his study of Abramovitsh's childhood and adolescence: *Mendele Moykher-Sforim—kindheyt un yugent*, Minsk, 1937 (y). A more recent and accurate reassembling of biographical data is to be found in the biographical chapters of the section dealing with Abramovitsh in Y. Klozner's *Historiya shel hasifrut ha'ivrit hakhadasha*, Vol. VI, Jerusalem, 1950, pp. 359–439 (h).

F. The Manuscripts, Variants, and Bilingualism of Abramovitsh's Works

Dubilet, M. "Viazoy hot gearbet Mendele Moykher-Sforim," in *Farmest*, No. 1 (1936), pp. 149–71 (y).

Gurshteyn, A. "Tsu der tekst-geshikhte fun 'Shloyme reb Khayims'," in *Gezamlte verk fun Mendele*, Vol. VI, Moscow, 1935, pp. 349–54 (y).

H(rushovski), B., ed. "Avodato shel Mendele al hanusakh ha'ivri: dapim min ha'arkhiyon," in *Hasifrut*, Vol. I, No. 1 (1968), pp. 63–65.

Makhlin, B. "Limdu hetev—Haoves vehabonim," in *Di goldene keyt*, No. 73 (1971), pp. 165–80 (y). "Varyantn fun Mendeles 'Di klyatshe'," in *Sovetish heymland*, Vol. VII (1967), No. 5, pp. 115–24 (y).

Miron, D. "Der khilek fun 'Limdu hetev' biz 'Haoves vehabonim'," in Sh. Y. Abramovitsh, *Limdu hetev*, New York, 1969, pp. 103–15 (y).

Niger, Sh. " 'Fishke der krumer'—un vi Mendele hot gearbet," in *Mendele Moykher-Sforim*, Chicago, 1936, pp. 139–53 (y).

Nusinov, Y. "Di ershte oysgabe fun 'Vintshfingerl'," in *Shriftn*, Vol. I (1928), pp. 199–218 (y). "Fun bukh tsu bukh," in *Tsaytshrift*, Vol. II–III (1928), pp. 425–82 (y).

Raskin, A. "Eynike bamerkungen vegn dem hebreishn tekst fun 'Shloyme reb Khayims' in farglaykh mitn yidishn tekst," in *Gezamlte verk fun Mendele*, Vol. VI, pp. 373–78 (y). "Mendele in yidish un hebreish," in *Sovetish heymland*, Vol. VII (1967), No. 12, pp. 13–21 (y).

Roskes-Vays, R. " 'Keminheg yid': an umbakanter ksav-yad fun Mendele Moykher-Sforim," in *For Max Weinreich, on His Seventieth Birthday*, The Hague, 1964, pp. 337–44 (y).

Sadan, D. "Beyn shtey leshonot," in *Avney miftan*, Vol. II, Tel Aviv, 1970, pp. 274–77 (h).

Sheyntukh, Y. "Sipurav haktsarim shel Mendele Mohker-Sfarim al nuskha'oteyhem," in *Hasifrut*, Vol. I, No. 2 (1968), pp. 391–409 (h).

Shmeruk, Kh. "Der tsveyter nusekh fun Mendele Moykher-Sforims poeme 'Yidl'," in *Shloyme Bikl yoyvel bukh*, New York, 1967, pp. 318–31 (y).

Vaynraykh, M. "Mendeles onheyb," in *Bilder fun der yidisher literaturgeshikhte*, pp. 334–51 (y).

Verses, Sh. "Haroman ha'ivri harishon shel Mendele vegilgulav," in *Sipur veshorsho*, Ramat-Gan, 1971, pp. 60–87 (h). "Forsh-problemn fun Mendeles ivris-tekst" (summary), in *Hakongres ha'olami harevi'i lemada'ey hayahadut*, the section *Leshon yidish vesifruta*, Jerusalem, 1965 (in stencil), pp. 35–37 (y).

Vorobeytshik, A. "Di manuskriptn fun 'Vintshfingerl'," in *Gezamlte verk fun Mendele*, Vol. V, Moscow, 1937, pp. xiii–lviii (y). "Hantshriftlekhe varyantn fun 'Shloyme reb Khayims' " in *Gezamlte verk fun Mendele*, Vol. VI, pp. 335–72 (y).

G. Critical Evaluations, Interpretations, Stylistic Analysis

In Yiddish

Altboyer, M. "Tsum slavizmen problem bay Mendele" (summary), in *Hakongres ha'olami harevi'i lemada'ey hayahadut, Leshon yidish vesifruta*, pp. 33–34.

Bal-Makhshoves. "An eynikl dem zeydn," in *Geklibene shriftn*, pp. 151–68.

"Reb Mendeles vegele," ibid., pp. 133–38. "Sh. Y. Abramovitsh," ibid., pp. 139–50.

Berditshevski, M. Y. "Mendele Moykher-Sforim," in *Yidishe ksovim*, Vol. II, New York, 1948, pp. 184–86.

Borokhov, B. "Undzer 'zeyde'—der Kolumbus fun mame-loshn," in Shprakhforshung un literatur-geshikhte, Tel Aviv, 1966, pp. 232–34.

Dobrushin, Y. "Der gotisher movoy," in *Ale verk fun Mendele*, Vol. XXII, 1928, pp. 215–24. Also in the author's *Gedanken-gang*, Kiev, 1922, pp. 37–47.

Entin, Y. "Mendele Moykher-Sforim," in *Di zeyln fun der nayer yidisher literatur*, New York, 1923, pp. 3–36.

Erik, M. "Vos shetsen mir in Mendelen," in *Farmest*, No. 1, (1936), pp. 131–47.

Finkel, U. "Mendele Moykher-Sforim," in *Sovetish heymland*, Vol. VII (1967), No. 5, pp. 115–24.

Frishman, D. "Fishke der krumer," in *Ale verk fun D. Frishman*, Vol. III, Warsaw, 1914, pp. 177–85. "Mendele Moykher-Sforim, zayn lebn un zayne verk," in *Ale verk fun Mendele*. Vol. I, 1928, pp. 7–63. Also in *Ale verk fun D. Frishman*, Vol. IV, Warsaw and New York, 1938, pp. 83–141.

Glatshteyn, Y. "Fishke der krumer," in *In tokh genumen*, New York, 1947, pp. 453–69. "Mendele Moykher-Sforim," in *In tokh genumen*, new series, New York, 1956, pp. 11–27. "Ven Mendele Moykher-Sforim hot geshvign," in *Oyf greyte temes*, Tel Aviv, 1967, pp. 11–15.

Goldberg, Y. "Der veg roman un der intimer stil," in *Shriftn, Vaysrusishe melukhe universitet*, Vol. I (1929), pp. 45–60.

Gurshteyn, A. "Vegn 'Shloyme reb Khayims,' " in *Gezamlte verk fun Mendele*, Vol. VI, Moscow, 1935, pp. 7–45. "Der yunger Mendele in kontekst fun di 60-er yorn," in *Shriftn*, Vol. I (1928), pp. 180–98. "Sakhaklen fun der Mendele forshung," in *Tsaytshrift*, Vols. II–III (1928), pp. 485–524.

Hrushovski, B. "Vegn di farbindungen fun stil elementn un kompozitsye in der proze fun Mendele Moykher-Sforim" (summary), in *Hakongres ha'olami harevi'i, Leshon yidish vesifruta*, pp. 39–40.

Mark, Y. "Mendeles loshn," in *Yidishe shprakh*, Vol. XXVII (1967), No. 1, pp. 1–17; No. 2, pp. 33–47; No. 3, pp. 65–79; Vol. XXVIII (1968), No. 2, pp. 33–51.

Mayzl, N. "Di grenetsn tsvishn Sh. Y. Abramovitsh un Mendele Moykher-Sforim," in *Dos Mendele bukh*, pp. 294–325. "Di shaykhusn tsvishn Mendele Moykher-Sforim, Sholem-Aleichem un Y. L. Perets," ibid., pp. 326–56. "Sh. Y. Abramovitsh," in *Forgeyer un mittsaytler*, New York, 1946, pp. 28–73.

Mezheritski, M. "Fishke der krumer—stil un kompozitsye," in *Di royte velt*, 1927, No. 12, pp. 104–28.

Miron, D. "Der onheyb fun aktueln hebreishn roman—historishe un kritishe bamerkungen tsu Sh. Y. Abramovitshes 'Limdu hetev'," in Sh. Y. Abramovitsh, *Limdu hetev*, New York, 1969, pp. 1–88.

Mukdoyni, A. [A. D. Kapel]. "Tsvey mentshn," in *Ale verk fun Mendele*, Vol. I, 1928, pp. 176–87.

Niger, Sh. "Der soyfer," in *Ale verk fun Mendele*, Vol. XXII, 1928, pp. 143–48. "Sh. Y. Abramovitsh," ibid., Vol. I, pp. 89–147. Also in the author's *Vegn yidishe shrayber*, Vol. I, Warsaw, 1912, pp. 7–67. *Mendele Moykher-Sforim—zayn, lebn, zayne gezelshaftlekhe un literarishe oyftuungen*. Chicago, 1936; New York, 1970.

Nusinov, Y. "Mendele Moykher-Sforim," in *Di royte velt*, Vol. V (1928), Nos. 2–3, pp. 167–74; No. 4, pp. 93–101. "Vegn Mendeles 'Vintshfingerl'," in *Gezamlte verk fun Mendele*. Vol. V, part I, Moscow, 1937, pp. vii–xxxii.

Oyslender, N. "Bamerkungen vegn Mendeles stil," in *Di yidishe shprakh* (1927), No. 7, pp. 3–16. "Der nusekh fun realizm" and "Mendele Moykher-Sforim," in *Gruntshtrikhn fun yidishn realizm*, Kiev, 1920, pp. 3–10, 49–98.

Perets, Y. L. "Mendele," in *Ale verk fun Y. L. Perets*, Vol. VII, New York, 1947, pp. 280–81.

Podryatshik, L. "Limdu hetev," in *Sovetish heymland*, Vol. X (1970), No. 8, pp. 145–48.

Prilutski, N. *Sh. Y. Abramovitsh*. Warsaw, 1920 (*Prilutskis ksovim*, Vol. II).

Rivkin, B. "Mendele Moykher-Sforim," in *Undzere prozaiker*, New York, 1951, pp. 11–43.

Rozentsvayg, A. "Mendele Moykher-Sforim," in *Geklibene verk fun Mendele Moykher-Sforim*, Kiev and Kharkov, 1936, pp. 7–35.

Serebryani, Y. "Dos vikhtikste in Mendeles shafn," in *Sovetish heymland*, Vol. VII (1967), No. 12, pp. 8–11.

Spivak, E. "Mendeles nusekh," ibid., No. 8, pp. 135–37.

Tshemerinski, Kh. "Yidishe gramatik bay Mendelen," in *Ale verk fun Mendele*, Vol. XXII, 1928, pp. 225–38.

Tsinberg, Y. "Abramovitsh—Mendele," in *Kultur-historishe shtudyes*, pp. 344–60.

Vayter, A. "Der onheyb," in *Ale verk fun Mendele*, Vol. XXII, 1928, pp. 123–27.

Verses, Sh. "Mendele Moykher-Sforim in shpigl fun der hebreisher literaturkritik," in *Di goldene keyt*, No. 51 (1965), pp. 188–209.

Veynger, A. "Lingvistishe kveles fun Mendeles shprakh," in *Shriftn, Vaysrusishe melukhe universitet*, Vol. I, pp. 68–76. "Vegn dem sotsyaln inhalt fun Mendeles shprakh," in *Di yidishe shprakh*, No. 7 (1927), pp. 15–20.

Viner, M. "Mendele in di 60-er un 70-er yorn," in *Tsu der geshikhte fun der yidisher literatur in 19-tn yorhundert*, Vol. II, New York, 1946, pp. 74–221. "Mendele Moykher-Sforim un di traditsyes fun der velt-literatur," ibid., pp. 5–14. "Mendeles stil—vegn 'Fishke der krumer'," ibid., pp. 15–73. "Onmerkung tsum suzhet fun Mendeles 'Masoes'," ibid., pp. 222–34. "Mendele Moykher-Sforim—tsum hundertstn yortog fun zayn geboyrn," in *Farmest*, No. 1 (1936), pp. 114–30.

Zaretski, A. "Tsu Mendeles verter-seyder," in *Di yidishe shprakh*, No. 7 (1927), pp. 19–26.

In Hebrew

Avrunin, A. "Limkorot signono shel Mendele," in *Leshonenu*, Vol. X (1940), pp. 159–72.

Ben Nakhum, D. "Mendele Mokher-Sfarim," in *Orlogin*, Vol. XIII (1957), pp. 13–30.

Ben Yeshurun, Y. "Hashpa'at haproza harusit al Mendele," ibid., Vol. VII (1953), pp. 216–19.

Braynin, R. "Sh. Y. Abramovitsh," in *Kol kitvey R. Braynin*, Vol. I, New York, 1922, pp. 172–98.

Brener, Y. Kh. "Ha'arakhat atsemenu bishloshet hakrakhim," in *Kol kitvey Y. Kh. Brener*, Vol. III, Tel Aviv, 1967, pp. 57–78. "Mendele," ibid., pp. 55–56.

Byalik, Kh. N. "Mendele ushloshet hakrakhim," in *Kol kitvey Kh. N. Byalik*, in one volume, Tel Aviv, 1938, pp. 236–39. "Yotser hanusakh," ibid., pp. 240–41.

Druyanov, A. "Sh. Y. Abramovitsh," in *Ktavim nivkharim*, Vol. II, Tel Aviv, 1945, pp. 690–730.

Epshteyn, Z. "Rekhov hayehudim vesofro," in *Kol kitvey Mendele*, Vol. VII, 1922, pp. 103–114.

Faytelzon, M. M. "Mi'mishpat shalom ad 'Bayamim hahem'," ibid., pp. 143–65. See also the author's *Bkhinot veha'arakhot*, Ramat-Gan, 1970, pp. 94–116. "Sh. Y. Abramovitsh ufe'ulato basifrut hazhargonit," in *Hatsifra*, Nos. 228, 229, 231, 240, 266, 269 (1890).

Fikhman, Y. "Mendele," in *Amat habinyan*, Jerusalem, 1951, pp. 11–121. "Hakitrug al Mendele," ibid., pp. 122–52.

Frenkel, Y. *Perush le'susati*,' Tel Aviv, 1945.

Fridman, D. A. "Mendele Mokher-Sfarim," in *Hatkufa*, Vol. II (1918), pp. 585–606. See also the author's *Iyuney proza*, Tel Aviv, 1966, pp. 7–34. "Mendele Mokher-Sfarim umigu'el Servantes," in *Hatkufa*, Vol. III (1918), pp. 676–700; *Iyuney proza*, pp. 35–67.

Frishman, D. "Mendele Mokher-Sfarim," in *Kol kitvey Mendele*, Vol. VII, 1922, pp. 41–75. See also *Kol kitvey D. Frishman*, Vol. VII, Warsaw and New York, 1931, pp. 70–111.

Goldberg, Ab. "Ahavat hateva umendele," in *Kitvey Ab. Goldberg*, Vol. II, New York, 1929, pp. 165–74.

Gurfayn, R. "Shloshet hagiborim shel hakomediya ha'enoshit shelanu," in *Orlogin*, Vol. III (1951), pp. 133–36.

Kariv, A. "Olam vetilo," in *Atara leyoshna*, Tel Aviv, 1956, pp. 30–71. "Klalot ufratot," ibid., pp. 72–115.

Katsenelson, Y. "Mendele im hakabtsanim," in *Musaf ledavar*, Vol. XI (1936), No. 18.

Kenig, L. "Khamato shel mi lakta?," in *Bkhinot*, No. 3 (1953), pp. 53–56.

Klauzner, Y. A. "Pirkey Mendele," in *Metsuda*, Vol. VII (1954), pp. 347–56.

Kleynman, M. "Ben shlosha dorot," in *Dmuyot vekomot*, Paris, 1928, pp. 111–40.

Klozner, Y. "Mendele Mohker-Sfarim," 5 articles, in *Yotsrim uvonim*, Vol. II, Jerusalem, 1929, pp. 62–124. "Hakholef vehanitskhi shebemendele," in *Yotsrey tkufa umamshikhey tkufa*, Tel Aviv, 1956, pp. 47–57. *Historiya shel hasifrut ha'ivrit hakhadasha*, Vol. VI, pp. 444–511.

Kurtsvayl, B. "Olamo ha'epi shel Mendele," in *Sifrutenu hakhadasha—hemshekh o mahapekha?*, Tel Aviv and Jerusalem, 1960, pp. 172–83.

Lakhover, F. "Sh. Y. Abramovitsh," in *Rishonim ve'akhronim*, Vol. I, Tel Aviv, 1934, pp. 69–87. *Toldot hasifrut ha'ivrit hakhadasha*, Vol. III(a), Tel Aviv, 1930, pp. 124–80.

Lubetski, Y. A. "Lidmuto harukhanit shel rav Mendele," in *Kol kitvey Mendele*, 1922, Vol. VII, pp. 136–42.

Meytus, E. "Mendele Mohker-Sfarim—meshorer hateva," in *Hashilo'akh*, Vol. XXXIV (1918), pp. 38–51.

Miron, D. "Arba he'arot lete'urey hateva be'ha'avot vehabanim'," in *Moznayim*, new series, Vol. XXVIII (1969), No. 4, pp. 255–65. "Pirkey mavo le'susati'," in *Hado'ar*, Vol. LI (1972), Nos. 35, 38, 39.

Peri, M. "Ha'analogiya umekoma bemivne haroman shel Mendele Mokher-Sfarim," in *Hasifrut*, Vol. I, No. I (1968), pp. 65–100. "Hamishva'a hameduma: nibuya shel situatsiya be'mas'ot Binyamin hashlishi'," ibid., No. 3–4 (1968–1969), pp. 719–21.

Pnu'eli, Sh. Y. "Mendele vetel olamo," in *Khuliyot basifrut ha'ivrit hakhadasha*, Tel Aviv, 1953, pp. 85–96.

Rabinovitsh, Ya'akov. "Me'at sfekot," in *Hatsfira*, 1911, Nos. 39, 40.

Rabinovitsh, Yesha'aya. "Hasiporet ha'omanutit shel Mendele," in *Hasiporet ha'ivrit mekhapeset gibor*, Ramat-Gan, 1967, pp. 11–17. "Mendele ufirtso ha'esteti," in *Yetser vytsira*, Jerusalem, 1952, pp. 171–80.

Ravnitski, Y. Kh. "Al hasignon ha'ivri shel Mendele Mokher-Sfarim," in *Dor vesofrav*, Vol. I, pp. 76–86.

Ribolov, M. "Mendele," in *Sefer hamasot*, New York, 1928, pp. 35–55. "Haluz shebemendele," in *Sofrim ve'ishim*, New York, 1936, pp. 44–53.

Sadan [Shtok], D. "Roshey prakim," in *Musaf ledavar*, Vol. XI (1936), No. 10.

Sha'anan, A. *Hasifrut ha'vrit hakhadasha lizrameha*, Vol. II, Tel Aviv, 1962, pp. 170–205.

Shaked, G. *Beyn skhok ledema* Ramat-Gan, 1965.

Shifman, P. "Mendele betor tipus vesemel," in *Hashilo'akh*, Vol. XXXIV (1918), pp. 84–91.

Shmeruk, Kh. "Tirgumey tehilim leyidish bydey Mendele Mokher-Sfarim," in *Hasifrut*, Vol. I, No. 2 (1968), pp. 337–42.

Shteynman, E. "Be'ad Mendele," in *Bema'agal hadorot*, Tel Aviv, 1944, pp. 113–41.

Tsemakh, Sh. "Ba'avotot hahavay," in *Me'asef erets*, Odessa, 1919, pp. 127–47. See also the author's *Masot urshimot*, Ramat-Gan, 1968, pp. 39–61.

Verses, Sh. "Haroman ha'ivri harishon shel Mendele vegilgulav," in *Sipur veshorsho*, pp. 60–87.

Vilna'i-Verses, Sh. "Dimyon va'agada be'olamo shel Mendele," in *Gilyonot*, Vol. XX (1947), pp. 179–83. "Hasifrut be'aspaklariya shel kitrug," in *Gilyonot*, Vol. XXV (1953), pp. 327–31.

Some Evaluations in English

Ba'al Makhshoves. "Mendele, Grandfather of Yiddish Literature," in *Voices from the Yiddish*, edited by I. Howe and E. Greenberg, Ann Arbor, Mich., 1972, pp. 32–40.

Liptzin, S. "Mendele," in *The Flowering of Yiddish Literature*, pp. 20–32.

Madison, C. "Mendele Mokher-Sforim—Foremost Yiddish Satirist," in *Yiddish Literature, Its Scope and Major Writers*, pp. 33–60.

Pinsker, S. "Mendele: Hasidic Tradition and the Individual Artist," in *Modern Language Quarterly*, Vol. XXX (1969), pp. 234–47.

Rabinovitsh, I. "The Fictional Writings of Mendele Mokher-Sefarim," in *Major Trends in Modern Hebrew Fiction*, Chicago, 1968, pp. 7–14.

Spiegel, S. *Hebrew Reborn*, New York, 1930, pp. 243–46.

We[rses], S. "Mendele Mokher-Seforim," in *Encyclopedia Judaica*, Vol. XI, pp. 1317–23.

Waxman, M. *A History of Jewish Literature*, Vol. IV, pp. 124–49.

H. MEMOIRS

In Yiddish

Abramovitsh, N. and A. Dobrin-Abramovitsh. *Der zeyde tsvishn eygene un fremde*. Warsaw, 1928.

Ben Ami, M. [Kh. M. Rabinovitsh]. "Reb Mendele shebal-pe," in *Ale verk fun Mendele*, Vol. XX, 1928, pp. 27–54.

Berkovitsh, Y. D. "Sholem-Aleichem un Mendele Moykher-Sforim," ibid., Vol. XXII, pp. 99–117.

Binshtok, A. "Derinerungen vegn Mendelen," in *Mendele un zayn tsayt*, pp. 62–91, 243–46.

Dinezon, Y. *Zikhroynes un bilder*, Warsaw, 1927, pp. 175–90.

Dubnov, Sh. *Fun zhargon tsu yidish*. Vilna, 1929. "Mendele—Abramovitsh," in *Ale verk fun Mendele*, Vol. XXX, 1928, pp. 49–78.

Dubnov-Erlikh, S. *Dos lebn un shafn fun Shimen Dubnov*, Mexico, 1952, pp. 77–86, 171–72.

Eynhorn, D. "Mendele bay der arbet," in *Ale verk fun Mendele*, Vol. XX, 1928, pp. 57–63.

Kats, M. "Tsu gast bay Mendelen," ibid., Vol. XXI, pp. 199–202.

Kitay, M. "Mendele in lebn," ibid., pp. 185–97.

Lerner, Kh. "Fun Mendeles sikhes khuln," in *Mendele un zayn tsayt*, pp. 246–47.

Lev, A. "Fun mayne derinerungen," ibid., pp. 247–50.

Shneur, Z. *Fun dem zeydns kval*, Berlin, 1922.

Sholem Aleichem. "Fir zenen mir gezesn," in *Ale verk fun Sholem-Aleichem* Vol. XV (*Yidishe shrayber*), New York, 1918, pp. 111–85. "Oyto-da-fe," ibid., pp. 31–40. "Vi sheyn iz der boym!," ibid., pp. 21–28.

Tsitron, Sh. "Sh. Y. Abramovitsh," in *Dray literarishe doyres*, Vol. I, Vilna, 1920, pp. 105–26.

Yong, B. "Bay Yoyel Linetski un baym zeydn Mendele," in *Mayn lebn in teater*, New York, 1950, pp. 253–60.

In Hebrew

Berkovitsh, Y. D. *Harishonim kivney adam*, part II, *Kol kitvey Y. D. Berkovitsh*, Vol. VII, Tel Aviv, 1953, pp. 98–124; part V, ibid., Vol. X, Tel Aviv, 1954, pp. 38–45.

Braynin, R. "Sikhat khulin shel sofrim," in *Hatoren*, Vols. II–III (1915–1916), No. 72.

Byalik, Kh. N. "Bigvurot," in *Kol kitvey Kh. N. Byalik*, in one volume, p. 242. "Umendele zaken," ibid., pp. 243–46.

Druyanov, A. "Ktanot," in *Ha'olam*, Vol. VII (1914), No. 50.

Eplboym, B. "Akharey mitato shel Mendele zal," in *Kol kitvey Mendele*, Vol. VII, 1922, pp. 226–30.

Fikhman, Y. "Pgishot im Mendele," in *Amat habinyan*, pp. 153–67.

Gintsburg, Sh. Mendele bama'abada," in *Bemasekhet hasifrut*, New York, 1944, pp. 64–68.

Klozner, Y. "Sikhot khulin shel rav Mendele," in *Hashilo'akh*, Vol. XXXIV (1918), pp. 119–28.

Lita'i, A. "Hagehenom sheba nidon Mendele bekhayav," ibid., pp. 107–11.

Rav Tsa'ir [Kh. Tshernovitsh]. "Mendele Mokher-Sfarim," in *Masekhet zikhronot*, New York, 1945, pp. 113–141.

Ravnitski, Y. Kh. "Mendele bekhek hateva," in *Dor vesofrav*, Vol. I, pp. 87–99. "Mendele Mokher-Sfarim va'akhad-Ha'am," ibid., pp. 100–6. "Mendele Mokher-Sfarim vekhibat-tsiyon," ibid., pp. 107–11. "Rav Mendele ba'avodato," ibid., pp. 69–75.

Shteynman, E. "Betsel Mendele," in *Midor el dor*, Tel Aviv, 1951, pp. 5–29.

Tshernikovski, Sh. "Mendele Mokher-Sfarim," in *Kitvey, Sh. Tshernikhovski*, Vol. VII, Jerusalem, 1932, pp. 211–15.

IV. FOUR OTHER WRITERS

Y. Perl (1773–1839)

A. Perl's two Hebrew belleteristic works published in his lifetime are *Megale-tmirin* (1819) and *Bokhen-tsadik* (1838). The Yiddish version of *Megale-tmirin*, which was discovered in the author's archives in Tarnopol, was published in *Perls yidishe ksovim*, Vilna, 1937, edited by Y. Vaynlez. Another major work, written both in Hebrew and in Yiddish, was recently discovered and published under the title *Ma'asiyot ve'igrot mitsadikim amitiyim ime'anshey shlomenu*, Jerusalem, 1970, edited by Kh. Shmeruk and Sh. Verses. For another discovery see Sh. Verses, "Khibur satiri lo noda shel Yosef Perl," in *Hasifrut*, Vol. I, No. 1 (1968), pp. 206–27.

B. For biographical studies see Y. Vaynlez, "Yoysef Perls lebn un shafn," in *Perls yidishe ksovim*, pp. vii–lxx (y); also Y. Klozner, *Historiya shel hasifrut ha'ivrit hakhadasha*, Vol. II, Jerusalem, 1937, pp. 278–314 (h).

C. For documentary material see Y. Vaynlez, "Fun Y. Perls arkhiv," in *Historishe shriftn* of the YIVO, Vol. I (1929), pp. 809–13 (y), and S. Kats, "Naye materyaln fun dem Perl-arkhiv," in *YIVO-bleter*, Vol. XIII (1938), pp. 557–76 (y). See also A. Rubinshteyn, "Ktav-hayad al mahut kat hakhasidim," in *Kiryat-sefer*, Vol. XXXVIII (1962–1963), pp. 263–72, 415–24, and Vol. XXXIX (1963–1964), pp. 117–36 (h).

D. For literary and historical commentary and evaluations see:

Davidson, I. *Parody in Jewish Literature.* New York, 1907, pp. 61–73.

Erik, M. *Etyudn tsu der geshikhte fun der haskole*, Vol. I, pp. 163–74 (y).

Kalmanovitsh, Z. "Yoysef Perls yidishe ksovim," in *Perls yidishe ksovim*, pp. lxxi–cvii (y).

Kurtsvayl, B. "Al hasatira shel Yosef Perl," in *Bema'avak al erkhey hayahadut*, Jerusalem and Tel Aviv, 1969, pp. 55–95 (h).

Lastik, Sh. *Di yidishe literatur biz di klasiker*, pp. 131–39 (y).

Maler, R. *Der kamf tsvishn khsides un haskole in Galitsye*, pp. 30–37, 42–57, 92–98, 164–202 (y).

Niger, Sh. *Dertseylers un romanistn.* Vol. I, pp. 36–46 (y).

328   Selective Bibliography

Sha'anan, A. *Hasifrut ha'ivrit hakhadasha lizrameha*, Vol. I, pp. 169–75 (h).
Shmeruk, Kh. "Dvarim kahavayatam udvarim shebadimyon in 'Megale-tmirin' shel Yosef Perl," in *Tsiyon*, Vol. XXI (1955–1956), pp. 92–99 (h).
Shmeruk, Kh. and Sh. Verses. "Mavo," in *Ma'asiyot ve'igrot*, pp. 11–88 (h).
Tsinberg, Y. *Di geshikhte fun der literatur bay yidn*, Vol. VII, pp. 283–88 (y).
Verses, Sh. "Iyunim bamivne shel 'Megale-tmirin' u'vokhen tsadik'," in *Tarbits*, Vol. XXXI (1961–1962), pp. 377–411. See also the author's *Sipur veshorsho*, pp. 9–45 (h).
Viner, M. *Tsu der geshikhte fun der yidisher literatur*, Vol. I, pp. 44–49 (y).

Y. Aksenfeld (1787–1866)

A. Publications: In the author's lifetime only *Dos shterntikhl* (1861) and *Der ershter yidisher rekrut* (1862) were published. *Man un vayb, bruder un shvester* (1867), *Di genarte velt* (1870), and *Kabtsn-oysher shpil* (1870) were published posthumously.

In *Aksenfelds verk*, Vol. I, edited by M. Viner, Kharkov and Kiev, 1931, *Der ershter yidisher rekrut* and *Di genarte velt* were included, as well as some letters and documents plus extensive introductions, appendices, etc., by the editor and A. Yuditski. In *Dos shterntikhl*, edited by M. Viner, Moscow, 1938, a story entitled "Nokh tsvey hozen" ("After Two Hares"), retranslated from a Russian translation (by L. Reznik), as well as two introductory articles, were added to the novel.

Dos shterntikhl un Der ershter yidisher rekrut, edited by Sh. Rozhanski, were included in the *Musterverk fun der yidisher literatur* series, Buenos Aires, 1971. Besides the novel and the play, the volume includes the editor's introduction as well as an article by Sh. Ginzburg (see below, section B).

B. For documentary and biographical material see *Aksenfelds verk*, Vol. I, pp. 345–56. See also references below.

Borovoy, Sh. "Aksenfeld-biyografisher etyud," in *Mendele un zayn tsayt*, pp. 172–96 (y). "Aksenfelds pruv tsu gindn a drukeray in Ades," in *Biblyologisher zamlbukh*, Vol. I, pp. 93–103 (y).
Ginzburg, Sh. "Nayes vegn Yisroel Aksenfeld," in *Filologishe shriftn* of the YIVO, Vol. II (1928), pp. 43–54 (y). This article was included in the Argentine edition of *Dos shterntikhl*. "Vider vegn Yisroel Aksenfeld," in *YIVO-bleter*, Vol. II (1931), pp. 9–12 (y). "Yisroel Aksenfeld," in *Historishe verk*, Vol. I, pp. 75–88 (y). "New Material Regarding Israel Aksenfeld," in *YIVO Annual of Social Jewish Science*, Vol. V (1950), pp. 172–83 (an English translation of the articles published originally in the *Filologishe shriftn* and *YIVO-bleter*).
Reminik, Y. "A kapitl Aksenfelds biyografye," followed by "Di serye dokumentn fun yor 1840–1842," in *Tsaytshrift*, Vol. V (1931), pp. 171–80 (y).

Reyzen, Z. *Fun Mendelson biz Mendele*. Vol. I, pp. 355–74 (y).

C. For literary and historical commentary and evaluations see:

Erik, M. "Vegn sotsyaln mehus fun Aksenfelds shafn," in *Tsaytshrift*, Vol. V (1931), pp. 125–69 (y).

Erik, M., and A. Rozentsvayg. *Di Yidishe literatur in 19-tn yorhundert*, pp. 50–85 (y).

Gorin, B. *Di geshikhte fun yidishn teater*, Vol. I, pp. 100–14 (y).

Lastik, Sh. *Di Yidishe literatur biz di klasiker*, pp. 160–75.

Leshtshinski, Y. *Dos yidishe ekonomishe lebn in der yidisher literatur*, Vol. I, pp. 33–42 (y).

Margulis A. "Tsayt un mentshn fun 'Dos shterntikhl'," in *Dos shterntikhl*, Moscow, 1938, pp. 32–45 (y).

Niger, Sh. *Dertseylers un romanistn*, Vol. I, pp. 52–60 (y).

Viner, M. "Vegn Y. Aksenfelds proze," in *Tsu der geshikhte fun der yidisher literatur*, Vol. I, pp. 193–207 (y). "Vegn Y. Aksenfelds pyeses," ibid., pp. 65–149 (y).

Wiener, L. *The History of Yiddish Literature in the Nineteenth Century*, pp. 140–45.

A. M. Dik (1814–1893)

A. A full listing of Dik's enormous belletristic output has never been attempted. Dik himself prepared several incomplete lists of his works, and they were published in Y. Rivkind, "A. M. Diks biblyografishe reshimes," in *YIVO-bleter*, Vol. XXXVI (1952), pp. 191–230 (y). See also Sh. Niger's "Heores un hoysofes" to Rivkind's study, ibid., pp. 230–40. See also Kh. Liberman, "Tsu der bibliyografye fun A. M. Dik," in *YIVO-bleter*, Vol. XIV (1939), pp. 171–74 (y).

B. Most of the nineteenth-century editions of Dik's novelettes are rather rare. The most convenient way to come by the better-known stories is through these two modern selections: A. M. Dik, *Geklibene verk*, 2 vols., edited by D. Kasel, Vilna (no date), and *Geklibene verk*, edited by Sh. Niger, New York, 1954.

However, the reader must be forewarned that in both selections Dik's highly Germanized Yiddish has been thoroughly "corrected" by the editors, according to modern norms of good Yiddish style. Sh. Niger also abridged some of the stories, rendering in "straight" prose passages written originally in rhyming prose, etc.

A selection of Dik's stories also appeared in Hebrew translation: A. M. Dik, *Rav Shma'aya mevarekh hamo'adot*, edited and translated by D. Sadan, Jerusalem, 1967.

C. Some biographical and literary studies are:

Berditshevski, M. Y. "Ayzik Meyer Dik," in *Yidishe ksovim*, New York, 1951, Vol. II, pp. 177–80 (y).

Glatshteyn, Y. "Ayzik Meyer Dik—dray mayses," in *In tokh genumen*, New York, 1947, pp. 437–53.

K[as]el, D. "A. M. Dik," in A. M. Dik, *Geklibene verk*, pp. i–xv (y).

Kon, P. "A. M. Dik, a lerer in der kroynisher shul far yidishe kinder in Vilna," in *YIVO-bleter*, Vol. III (1932), pp. 84–87 (y). "Diks umbakante khiburim in yidish un hebreish," in *YIVO-bleter*, Vol. I (1931), pp. 325–34 (y); Vol. II (1931), p. 188 (y). "Ven iz geboyrn gevorn Ayzik Meyer Dik?" in *Filologishe shriftn* of the YIVO, Vol. II (1928), pp. 329–44 (y); Vol. III (1929), pp. 616–17 (y).

Lastik, Sh. *Di yidishe literatur biz di klasiker*, pp. 206–16.

Manger, I. "Ayzik Meyer Dik," in *Noente geshtaltn*, Warsaw, 1938, pp. 63–72 (y).

Mayzl, N. "Ayzik Meyer Dik," in *Forgeyer un mittsaytler*, pp. 11–27 (y).

Niger, Sh. "A. M. Dik (1814–1893)—biyografish-kritishe notitsn," in A. M. Dik, *Geklibene verk*, New York, 1954, pp. vii–xxiii (y). "A maskils utopye" (with an untitled manuscript by Dik), in *YIVO-bleter*, Vol. XXXVI (1952), pp. 136–90 (y). "Amerike in dertseylungen fun A. M. Dik," in *YIVO-bleter*, Vol. XXXVIII (1954), pp. 106–15 (y). "Der ershter kultur-historiker in der yidisher literatur," in *Tsukunft*, Vol. XXXVIII (1933), No. 3, pp. 153–58. "Der ereshter yidisher humorist," in *Der tog*, New York, April 2, 1933 (y). *Dertseylers un romanistn*. Vol. I, pp. 63–73. "Di ershte verk fun A. M. Dik (fun 1856 biz 1860)," in *Pinkes*, Vol. II (1929), pp. 1–9 (y). "Tsu der frage vegn A. M. Diks geburtsyor," in *Pinkes*, Vol. I (1928), pp. 380–82 (y). "Ven hot A. M. Dik ongehoybn shraybn yidish?" ibid., pp. 289–93 (y).

Sadan, D. "Al hamekhaber ve'al khiburav," in A. M. Dik. *Rav Shma'aya mevarekh hamo'adot*, pp. 7–15. See also the author's *Avney miftan*, Vol. II, Tel Aviv, 1970, pp. 9–16 (h).

Sholem Aleichem. "Ayzik Meyer Dik: Der yantsitser orem-bokher," a chapter of "Der yidisher dales in di beste verke fun unzere folks-shriftshteler," in *Dos yidishe folksblat*, 1888, No. 40 (the literary supplement), pp. 1107–10 (y).

Vaynraykh, M. *Bilder fun der yidisher literaturgeshikhte*, pp. 292–329 (y). "Iyzik Meyer Dik un zayn redaktor" (a critique of Kasel's edition of Dik's Geklibene verk), in *Bikher-velt*, 1922, No. 4–5, pp. 344–50 (y).

Y. Y. Linetski (1839–1915)

A. Important publications (all unmarked items are in Yiddish):

1865   First Hebrew articles in *Hamelits* (h).

1867   *Dos poylishe yingl* ("The Polish Boy"), first part; serialized in *Kol-me-vaser*.

"Oysgebitn a shmate oyf a shmate" ("A Rag Traded for a Rag"), in *Kol-mevaser*, Nos. 19–20.

1868   "A geretenish fun erets-yisroel yidn" ("An Abundance of Palestinian Collectors"), in *Kol-mevaser*, Nos. 18–19.

1869   "A vibor oyf a ratman" ("An Election of a Councilman"), in *Kol-mevaser*, No. 2.

"In Nivitse oyf der prizbe" ("In Nivitse on the Porch"), ibid., No. 28.

Dos poylishe yingl, the complete work published by A. Tsederboym, the editor of *Hamelits* and *Kol-mevaser*. With an introduction by the publisher.

Hebrew dramatic *feuilletons* in *Hamelits* (h).

Der beyzer marshelik ("The Sharp-tongued Wedding-Jester"), a collection of satirical and lyrical verse published in two parts.

1872   *Der velt luekh fun yor eyn-kesef* ("The International Almanac for the Year 'Penniless' "),° a parody of Jewish almanacs, containing verse, weather predictions, riddles, jokes, etc.

1875   *Dos meshulakhes* ("The Visitation"), a collection of *feuilletons*, including the short satirical play "Di vibores" ("The Elections"), an enlarged version of "A vibor oyf a ratman."

Linetski begins to publish with Goldfaden the weekly *Yisrolik*, a considerable part of which is written by himself. He serializes here his first longer work of fiction after *Dos poylishe yingl*, *Der litvisher bokher* ("The Lithuanian Lad"), meant to form a sequel and counterpart to the former and, no doubt, ensure the success of the magazine by drawing on that work's enormous popularity.

1876   The continuation and termination of the publication of *Yisrolik*. *Der litvisher bokher* left unfinished.

Der kolboynik ("The Rascal"; the name can also mean a jack-of-all-trades), a collection of *feuilletons*.

Linetskis ksovim (i): Der pritshepe ("Linetski's Works [i]: The Bellicose"), a collection of *feuilletons*.

Linetskis ksovim (ii): Der statek ("The Well-Behaved Fellow"), a collection of *feuilletons*.

1882   Zionist pamphlets: *Amerike tsi erets-yisroel* ("America or Palestine"), *Aher oder ahin* ("One Way or the Other"), etc.

° Hebrew dates being stated in letters rather than numbers, they enabled letter-writers and authors to indulge in clever anagrams, *gimatries* (equations of words on the basis of the identical numerical values of their letters), etc., and replace the mere date by a word, a sentence, or even a biblical quotation. Linetski, of course, parodizes this "intellectual" pastime.

Linetski begins to publish *Mayn seyfer-hazikhroynes* ("My Diary"; the Hebrew *sefer-zikhronot* was used in this sense as well as in the sense of "memoirs"), a private monthly, humorous and Zionist in tendency.

1883   Continuation and termination of the publication of *Mayn seyfer hazikhroynes* (see "Mayse bereyshis" ["The Story of Creation"] in the January issue and "Lagoyle nisteroys badin" ["To the Revealer of Secrets in the Trial"] in the August issue).

        Geshikhte funem yidishn folk ("The History of the Jewish People"), adapted from Graetz. Publication in installments continues until 1886.

1888   A host of *feuilletons* in leaflet form: *Der fledervish* ("The Feather Duster"), *Der plapler* ("The Chatterbox"), *Der shnorer* ("The Beggar"), *Dos dreydl* ("The Dreydel"; the name can also mean "chicanery"), *Der afikoymen* ("The Afikomon," the piece of matzah hidden during the Passover feast for the children to discover, steal, and "sell" back to the head of the household for a gift). Obviously, some of these leaflets were meant to entertain the readers during the Jewish festivals.

        Der vorem in khreyn ("The Worm in the Horseradish"), first part, published in Sholem Aleichem's *Folks-biblyotek*, Vol. I. This is Linetski's first long work of fiction after *Der litvisher bokher*, and like it, meant to form a sequel to *Dos poylishe yingl*, as indicated by its subtitle: "Nokhveyenishn fun mayn poylish-yinglshn lebn" ("Aftereffects of My 'Polish-Boy' Life").

1889   *Der vorem in khreyn*, second part, in Vol. II of the *Folks-biblyotek*.

1890   *Khag hayoyvel* ("The Jubilee"), Linetski's public addresses on the occasion of his fiftieth anniversary, published as a pamphlet.

1897   *Dos khsidishe yingl* ("The Hasidic Boy"), an enlarged version of *Dos poylishe yingl*.

1898   *Nit toyt nit lebedik* ("Neither Dead nor Alive"), a somewhat enlarged version of *Der vorem in khreyn*.

1904   *Iber a pintele* ("Because of a Dot"), a verse translation of Y. L. Gordon's well-known Hebrew narrative poem *Kotso shel yod*.

1907   *Der nakhalne zhid* ("The Brash Kike"), a satire against anti-Semitism.

1909   *Funem yarid* ("Back from the Fair"), a bitter personal summing up.

     B. Linetski's works were never collected. His only longer work of fiction which was republished in full after his death was *Dos khsidishe yingl*, the enlarged and, according to most critics, coarsened version of *Dos poylishe yingl* (Vienna, 1921, with an introduction by M. Zilburg). The original *Poylish yingl* was republished in an abridged form (Kiev, 1939). The entire first part of *Dos khisidishe yingl* was included in Sh. Rozhanski's anthology *Nusekh haskole*, Buenos Aires, 1968, pp. 67–146.

     C. There is no detailed biography of Linetski, and it is doubtful whether

there will ever be one, because the indispensable documents were never collected and only few of them have been preserved. The nearest thing to a biography is M. Graydenberg's "Fartseykhenungen vegn mayn foter," in *Tsaytshrift*, Vol. V (1931), pp. 199–210 (y). For some remnants of documentary material see A. Vorobeytshik, "Tsushtayer tsu Y. Y. Linetskis biyografye," in
Shtern, Vol. XV (1939), No. 9, pp. 69–79 (y), and L. Dushman, "Y. Y. Linetski," ibid., pp. 91–95. See also some letters to Linetski in *Mendele un zayn
tsayt*, pp. 50–57, and in *Sholem-Aleichem—zamlung fun kritishe artiklen un
materyaln* (Kiev, 1940), pp. 233–42. Linetski's life story was sketched in a
short monograph by Sh. Ortenberg (see below, section D).

Some literary memoirs preserve a fairly lively image of the old Linetski in
his years of bitterness and grumbling. However, the descriptions they offer are
often biased. There are those written by the admirers of Abramovitsh, who regard Linetski's claim to an equal position as a "grandfather" of modern
Yiddish literature as pathetic and ridiculous. See, for instance, Y. D. Berkovitsh, "Yitskhak Yo'el Linetski," in *Harishonim kivney adam*, part V, *Kol kitvey Y. D. Berkovitsh*, Vol. X, pp. 46–55 (h); see also Chap. XIV in Berkovitsh's
"Mit der mishpokhe fun shriftshteler," in *Dos Sholem-Aleichem bukh*, pp.
179–83 (y). There are also those who basically identify with his protest against
the Yiddish "establishment." See, for instance, R. Granovski, *Y. Y. Linetski un
zayn dor*, New York, 1941. See also B. Yong, "Bay Yoyel Linetski un baym
zeydn Mendele," in *Mayn lebn in teater*, pp. 253–60 (y).

D. Some literary and historical comments on Linetski's work are:

Berditshevski, M. Y. "Y. Y. Linetski," in *Yidishe ksovim*, Vol. II, pp. 180–82
    (y).

Erik, M. "Aksenfelds kamf kegn khsides," in *Tsaytshrift*, Vol. V (1931), pp.
    128–30 (a comparison between Aksenfeld's and Linetski's antihasidism)
    (y).

Erik, M., and A. Rozentsvayg. *Di yidishe literatur in 19-tn yorhundert*, Vol. I,
    pp. 180–204 (y).

Finkelstein, Z. F. "J. J. Liniecki," in *Stürmer des Ghetto*, Vienna, 1924, pp.
    141–50.

Gurshteyn, A. "Y. Y. Linetski," in *Der emes*, October 9, 1929 (y).

Litvak, A. *Y. Y. Linetski—kultur-historishe shtrikhn fun der haskole epokhe*.
    Kiev, 1919. See also the author's *Literatur un Kamf*. New York, 1943,
    pp. 21–86 (y).

Mayzl, N. "Yitskhok Yoyel Linetski," in *Noente un vayte*, Vol. II, Vilna, 1926,
    pp. 25–31 (y).

Niger, Sh. *Dertseylers un romanistn*, Vol. I, pp. 77–78 (y). *Bleter geshikhte fun
    der yidisher literatur*, pp. 257–59 (y).

Notovitsh, M. "Linetski—der demokratisher oyfklerer," in *Sovetishe literatur*,
    1939, No. 10, pp. 110–24 (y). *Y. Y. Linetski, 1839–1939*. Moscow, 1939.

Ortenberg, Sh. Y. *Y. Linetski—zayn lebn un shafn.* Vinitse, 1931 (y).

Oyslender, N. "Linetski un Mendeles 'rikhtung,' " in *Mendele un zayn tsayt,* pp. 98–105 (y).

Reminik, Y. "Linetski un Sholem Aleichem," in *Shtern,* Vol. XV (1939), No. 9, pp. 80–90 (y). "Tsu der geshikhte funem 'Poylishn yingl,' " in *Tsaytshrift,* Vol. V (1931), pp. 181–98 (y).

Sholem Aleichem. "Linetski: Dos poylishe yingl," a chapter of "Der yidisher dales in di beste verke fun unzere folks-shriftshteler," in *Dos yidishe folksblat,* 1888, No. 42 (the literary supplement), pp. 1149–57 (y).

Shtif, N. *Di eltere yidishe literatur,* pp. 227–33 (y).

Viner, M. "Hel un tunkl," in *Tsu der geshikhte fun der yidisher literatur,* Vol. II, pp. 15–22 (a comparison between Abramovitsh's and Linetski's satire and style) (y).

INDEX

335